Gettysburg Heroes

GLENN W. LaFANTASIE

Gettysburg Heroes

Perfect Soldiers, Hallowed Ground

INDIANA UNIVERSITY PRESS

Bloomington and Indianapolis

This book is a publication of

Indiana University Press
601 North Morton Street
Bloomington, IN 47404-3797 USA

http://iupress.indiana.edu

Telephone orders   800-842-6796
Fax orders   812-855-7931
Orders by e-mail   iuporder@indiana.edu

The paper used in this publication meets the minimum requirements of American National Standard for Information Sciences—Permanence of Paper for Printed Library Materials, ANSI Z39.48-1984.

Manufactured in the United States of America

Library of Congress Cataloging-in-Publication Data

LaFantasie, Glenn W.
    Gettysburg heroes : perfect soldiers, hallowed ground / Glenn W. LaFantasie.
      p.   cm.
    Includes bibliographical references and index.
    ISBN 978-0-253-35071-8 (cloth : alk. paper) 1. Gettysburg, Battle of, Gettysburg, Pa., 1863—Influence.
2. Gettysburg, Battle of, Gettysburg, Pa., 1863—Biography. 3. United States—History—Civil War, 1861–1865—
Biography. 4. Generals—United States—Biography. 5. Soldiers—United States—Biography. 6. Gettysburg,
Battle of, Gettysburg, Pa., 1863—Social aspects. 7. United States—History—Civil War, 1861–1865—Social
aspects. I. Title.
    E475.53.L235 2008
    973.7′349—dc22

                                                                              2007032473

                        1 2 3 4 5   13 12 11 10 09 08

For Donna M. Hayes
and
Ryan T. Hayes

The Civil War is not ended;
I question whether any serious civil war ever does end.

T. S. ELIOT

Contents

Preface

In the wake of the Republican national convention that nominated him as the party's presidential candidate in 1860, Abraham Lincoln learned that a publishing house was planning to issue an unauthorized biography of him. Lincoln reassured a fellow prominent Republican that "wholly [on] my own, I would authorize no biography, without time, and opertunity to carefully examine and consider every word of it; and, in this case, in the nature of things, I can have no such time and opertunity." As a result, he refused to approve the book. Lincoln rightly feared the benefits that might befall his opponents if hundreds of pages of unauthorized text appeared about him in the public domain. Since 1860, hundreds of Lincoln biographies have been published, most of which have added steadily to his lustrous reputation, so in that light, and as far as the judgment of posterity is concerned, his worries seem to have been unfounded. Indeed, Civil War biographies in general are a popular genre, and this book, in its own way, adds to the long shelf of works devoted to the lives and careers of those Americans who participated in the nation's worst—and bloodiest—cataclysm. I even have something to say about Lincoln, and not all of it is necessarily complimentary, although my esteem for him—the greatest of all American presidents—remains unalterably high, as these pages make plain.

The essays collected here, most of which have been previously published in magazines and journals (although I have revised each of them and brought them all up to date), reflect my own interest in biography and how it enhances our understanding of the Civil War era. "The whole value of history, of biography," wrote Ralph Waldo Emerson in 1838, "is to increase my self-trust, by demonstrating what man can be and do." Emerson comes close to expressing my own view of the usefulness of biography, for I have learned a great deal from the individuals I have studied and written about. Many of those life lessons, in fact, have little to do necessarily with the Civil War or my focal point, the battle of Gettysburg. Instead, I have delighted in coming to know these figures from the past—some great, some obscure, but all of whom have revealed themselves to be very human in their responses to the worst crisis they would ever know as Americans and as individuals.

Seeing what men "can be and do," as Emerson put it, has impressed, astounded, and humbled me. Getting to know these historical figures over the past twenty years has given me endless insights into the nature of their world, the contours of their individual lives, and the vast dimensions of the Civil War and its many effects on American society. I have immensely enjoyed the company of these men, even when that has meant coping with the terrible things they witnessed and the awful experiences they endured. They have taught me much about fortitude, sacrifice, and courage. But they have also opened up new vistas for me about the modern world they brought into being and about my own place in it.

Like most other modern biographers, I am keenly aware that in the process of writing about people from the past I have forged my own relationship with them, if only by deciding what I want to say about them and which episodes in their lives have enthralled me enough to discuss them in print. As a biographer, I can claim, like the boy in M. Night Shyamalan's brilliant film *The Sixth Sense,* to see dead people, but they don't appear to me as apparitions, only in dusty records and faded manuscripts. And they don't talk to me. I have to pull their words out of texts that are often set down in nearly indecipherable handwriting or are buried in yellowing stacks of manuscripts and newspapers. Yet every biographer must be conscious of the unconscious, always aware, in other words, of what might lurk behind one's subject and behind one's deep fascination with him. In answering these questions about biography as an art and as an experience, I have learned something new about myself. These historical figures, then, have not simply taught me about their own lives. They have, in the end, illuminated my own. And they have revealed some provocative answers as to why I find the past so welcoming a place.

Biography is more than research, more than scholarship. It is more than lining up the facts of a subject's life and recounting them in their proper order. It is more than the interpretations one uses to give those facts meaning. Biography involves something of the heart, some intangible and almost irrational connection to the past that intimately links the historian to his subject and, as a result, makes him part of what he is studying. There is no escaping it. It happens to every biographer, although not every practitioner of the art is always entirely conscious of it or willing to admit its prevalence or force. Some biographers—the cave dwellers of the profession—even deny its existence. But it's no use. The emotional attachment is there, carrying you farther into the past and into the lives of the people you are examining than you might even care to go, like a drill into the earth's crust that will not stop its spiral, and it ultimately takes you down deeper and deeper until it—and not you alone—defines the scope and breadth of your exploration. James Atlas, the renowned editor and biographer, says a biographer must inhabit his subject's life. It sounds like good advice, but no biographer can actually become his subject—nor should he try. The best we can do, the most I have *tried* to do, is to walk in their shoes, see their world as they saw it, and realize, in the process, that a great gulf always separates our present from their past. The gulf can be bridged. But it can never carry us body and soul into the past. We must be content with inhabiting our own lives as we struggle to comprehend those who came before us.

* * *

The subtitle of this book is meant to be ironic. There were no perfect soldiers in the Civil War or at Gettysburg, although there were thousands who were certainly brave and true. Perfect heroes were conspicuously absent from the field at Gettysburg, as they are from every battlefield, every war. Every soldier, nevertheless, likes to think he is perfect. To be sure, James Longstreet, Frank A. Haskell, Joshua Lawrence Chamberlain, and William C. Oates all thought of themselves in terms of perfection, despite the fact that all of them admitted to making mistakes at Gettysburg. In their memory, though, they became increasingly perfect as time went on and as their errors faded or, in some cases, as they completely disappeared from view. Except for Haskell, who died in combat at Cold Harbor, this view of themselves grew with each passing year, as I suppose it always does in the mind of every soldier who survives a war. In their remembrances, they became more heroic, more audacious, more capable than they had actually been in the hellish midst of combat. Looking back, they marveled at their own accomplishments, suppressed their worst moments and fears, and defended their actions, whatever the actual outcome of those actions had been in the summer of 1863. Almost a century later, two other famous soldiers—Dwight D. Eisenhower and Bernard Law Montgomery—applied their own measure in deciding just how perfect the soldiers and generals at Gettysburg had been.

Like so many other veterans, the Civil War soldiers I have written about in this book found a certain attraction to the war and to soldiering. In that sense, too, they seem like perfect soldiers, since they relished the action made possible by the war and enjoyed the sense of danger it heightened in them whenever they participated in combat. There was something about the war, in fact, that they liked rather too much. General Robert E. Lee once felt the same emotion about the war. At the battle of Fredericksburg, he is believed to have said to Longstreet: "It is well that war is so terrible—we should grow too fond of it." Perfect soldiers discovered that war and battle ultimately defined their sense of self. Even when the war ended in April 1865, these perfect heroes could not leave it behind. The Civil War would shape the rest of their lives. It would never be strictly in the past for these men, no matter how many years they would live after Appomattox. The war would always live in their present. This book explores how the Civil War never went away for so many of the soldiers, North and South, who survived its terrible battles.

I am grateful to the original publishers of these essays for permission to reprint and use the material that first appeared in their pages. My wife, Donna LaFantasie, has helped me hone my thoughts and stay on course, no matter how muddle-headed or lost I tended to become. Sarah LaFantasie, my youngest daughter, figures prominently in the concluding chapter, but I hope she realizes that her good cheer and hearty enthusiasm actually may be found between the lines of every one of these essays. The book is dedicated to my eldest children, Donna Hayes and Ryan Hayes, whose love has never flagged, but who may not fully comprehend the fact that I am more proud of them than they are of me. I must offer profuse thanks to several benefactors and friends, all of whom gave generously to the cause: Oatsie Charles, Evelyn Furse, and Gladys Wyatt.

My deep appreciation goes to Robert Sloan, my editor at Indiana University Press, for making this book possible and, by thwarting my intolerable stubbornness, turning it into a better book than it otherwise would have been. My thanks go also to several editors—guiding lights, one and all—who published these essays in their magazines and journals, particularly Chris Anderson, Barbara Benton, Douglas Brinkley, Robert Cowley, Philip George, Richard Latour, Terry Johnston, Chris Lewis, Rod Paschall, Keith Poulter, Thomas F. Schwartz, Roger Vance, and Nicholas Wood. My friend Ira Meistrich heard many of these articles spoken out loud before they were ever put on paper. Shelley Roth offered sage advice at a time when it was badly needed. At Gettysburg College, Gabor Boritt let me try out my ideas at his famous summer Civil War Institute. D. Scott Hartwig, supervisory historian of the Gettysburg National Military Park, always helped with skill and a smile. As usual, Thomas A. Desjardin shared his great wealth of knowledge about the 20th Maine, Joshua Chamberlain, and the Gettysburg battlefield.

In so many ways, too many to count, Michael Vorenberg of Brown University has provided inspiration and guidance. Gordon S. Wood continues profoundly to influence my view of the past. As always, I must thank all my collegial colleagues at Western Kentucky University—including David Lee, Dean of the Potter College of Arts and Letters, Richard D. Weigel, former head of the Department of History, and Robert L. Dietle, present head of the department—for their ardent encouragement and steadfast support. I hope my students at Western know that I am grateful for all they have taught me.

Not all of these essays are biographies; nor do they all deal with a single figure or subject. But each one is, more or less, connected in some respect to Gettysburg. The essence of my approach in nearly all of them has been to train my biographical eye on the past in hopes of revealing, even in some small manner, how the Civil War (and particularly the battle of Gettysburg) became the central event in the lives of Longstreet, Haskell, Chamberlain, Oates, and other Union and Confederate soldiers who fought there. In these essays, which I have arranged in chronological order (more or less) not of publication but of subject, I have also pondered why Gettysburg continues to fire the imagination of Americans. I don't pretend to know all the reasons. Perhaps it is enough to acknowledge how right Lincoln was when he said that the world could never forget what the men who struggled at Gettysburg had accomplished there. Consider this book my own contribution in the effort to long remember.

Gettysburg Heroes

Introduction:
Gettysburg and Its Perfect Heroes

Gettysburg has many stories to tell. One of my favorite tales, although it must be apocryphal, is about a one-legged tramp who, some time after the Civil War, stopped at a farmhouse in Ohio to beg for dinner. The woman of the house asked him where he had lost his leg. "At Gettysburg," he replied. "Wait one minute," said the woman, "I'll get my husband."

The husband soon came in from the barn and asked the man where his regiment had seen action on the field at Gettysburg. "We were in the cemetery," said the one-legged man. "Oh, the cemetery," said the farmer thoughtfully. "My son Bill was in the cemetery, let me call him in." Within moments, Bill was before the one-legged man, asking him if he could remember the gravestone behind which he had taken cover. The one-legged man told him it was a granite monument with a Scotch-Irish name carved on it. Bill looked amazed and said: "My brother Bob hid behind just such a monument. I'll call him in." Brother Bob came into the kitchen and swore that the monument the one-legged man had described was the very one he had also taken cover behind. But, he insisted, he was the only one near that headstone. So, to clarify things, Brother Bob asked the one-legged man for his regiment and company. "Company B, 35th Ohio," explained the man with one leg. "Oh," said Brother Bob, "my brother Jim was in that outfit."

Jim was called into the kitchen and looked the one-legged man straight in the eye and said, "Stranger, the 35th Ohio wasn't within two hundred miles of Gettysburg." So the one-legged man quickly replied that the family had heard him incorrectly—he had actually said the 25th Ohio. "I'll get my brother Aaron," said Jim, "he was in the 25th Ohio." Aaron came in, called the stranger a wooden-legged liar, dragged him outside, and pitched him over the fence. The one-legged man, who later told his story to a friend, said with great dismay: "They've got this war business down so fine that you can't go around playing tricks in the country anymore. The best way is to own up that you got drunk, passed out on the tracks, and got in the way of a train."[1]

Ever since 1863, Americans—and not just one-legged hobos—have often tried to place themselves at Gettysburg. Tourists who visit the battlefield want to know not only what happened there but what the battle was like.[2] What must the soldiers who fought there have thought and felt? What did they see? How did the panorama of battle appear to the participants? What must it have been like to attack up the slopes of Little Round Top with the 15th Alabama? What did the men of the 20th Maine experience as they rolled down the hill's slopes into the ranks of their enemy? What was the sight that the Federal soldiers saw when Pickett's Virginians left the tree-studded crest of Seminary Ridge on the afternoon of July 3? What could those Virginians see, and what did they endure, as they approached the fences on the Emmitsburg Road? What did the scarred fields and hills of Gettysburg look like after the battle was over?

We can never precisely know the answers to these questions, for none of us was there, and the last veteran who actually did witness the battle of Gettysburg died long, long ago. Some veterans—like the perfect soldiers who belonged to the family in the old tramp's story—could remember exactly where they had fought at Gettysburg or even the kind of grave marker they had hidden behind on Cemetery Hill. They would remember those details for the rest of their lives. But their picture of the battle, their special memories of where they had stood and what they had done, died with them, leaving us bereft of the knowledge we crave to comprehend what Gettysburg must have been like for the soldiers who fought across its fields and hills.

Yet we actually know more about the battle and how it unfolded than any of the individual participants or witnesses ever knew, if only because the fog of war, faulty memories, and human incomprehension kept those who actually experienced Gettysburg from understanding the entire battle in all its complexity, all its nuance, all its terrible cost. Historians, by piecing evidence together, weighing the conflicting testimony of eyewitnesses, and analyzing events within the context of their larger meanings, have gained a perspective on the battle that its participants never had. While we may not be certain, in the end, as to the number of trees that stood in Ziegler's Grove on Cemetery Ridge or how the Union line looked without the Pennsylvania Memorial looming over it, we at least do know more about the battle than any one person who was there and saw its horror for himself could have possibly taken in. But when we add up the surviving accounts left by eyewitnesses, the total becomes something more than the sum of its parts. At the dedication of the 83rd Pennsylvania regimental monument at Gettysburg in 1889, Oliver W. Norton, a former member of the regiment and a Gettysburg veteran, declared that "none but the actors on the field can tell the story, and each one can tell of his own knowledge but an infinitesimal part." Every person, he said, "owed to the memory of those who died here, his best endeavor to tell truly the story of their deeds, that the historian of the future may have the material out of which to fashion a truer story of Gettysburg."[3]

*   *   *

Gettysburg is deeply and indelibly embedded in our national consciousness. Our attachment to it is emotional, even spiritual. Historians have called it the turning point of the Civil War and the "high-water mark of the Confederacy," but for tourists who visit the battlefield and for others, including Civil War buffs and reenactors who devour anything in print or online about the battle, there is something sacred and mystical about Gettysburg. As Robert Littell, the editor of *Reader's Digest,* wrote in 1938, the year of the seventy-fifth anniversary of the battle: "There is an aura of history over the quiet landscape; the air is heavy with heartbreak, and ghosts speak to you."[4]

In fact, the battle is no longer an ordinary historical occurrence. Unlike, say, the siege of Yorktown that ended the War for Independence, or the burning of the nation's capital by the British during the War of 1812, the events that transpired at Gettysburg have gently passed into the fuliginous realm of American mythology. What happened there, if the mythology is to be believed, was a cataclysm waged among gods (or, at the very least, by "killer angels"), a great and terrible battle that ultimately decided the fate of the nation.[5] Abraham Lincoln's Gettysburg Address, which called for a rebirth of freedom, has confirmed Gettysburg's pivotal place in history. It was there, on that hallowed ground, that a new America was born.

This epic version of Gettysburg is compelling. Like the ancient tales of Homer, the story has been repeated by numerous bards. Historians have pored over every conceivable aspect of the battle, have explored archival nooks and crannies to uncover fresh evidence, have analyzed Lincoln's Gettysburg Address from countless angles, and have written about Gettysburg—the place, the battle, the battlefield, the national symbol—in exhaustive (and exhausting) detail. There is a book that covers the battle hour by hour. There is a book about horses in the battle. There are now countless booklets about the ghosts of Gettysburg (apparently Gettysburg has more ghosts per capita than any other community in America). There are historical novels (good and bad), murder mysteries set in 1863, and studies of women and of Freemasons at Gettysburg. There are even books about what would have happened if Lee had won.[6] What's most striking about the serious works on the battle is that they all pretty much say the same thing, so much so that the repetition seems ritualistic, as if the tale were being recited by one village shaman after another.

The outpouring of Gettysburg books—like, I suppose, the one you are reading now—has never slackened, and probably never will. With so much attention focused on this one battle, it is possible to follow the events that took place during the three-day battle from beginning to end, from the very first shot to the very last, without any break in the action. In the formulaic retelling of the battle, every deed has meaning, every detail is important. It is almost as if every spent bullet and every lost button has been accounted for on the battlefield, but no one quite seems to know what to make of them; no one can quite grasp what all of this really means. We know and understand more about Gettysburg than we do any other battle in which Americans have ever fought, including the more recent battles of San Juan Hill, the Meuse-Argonne Offensive, and D-Day. But the narratives that rehash old stories or that result in the ghoulish parade of ghost booklets don't, in the end, tell us why Gettysburg is so important to Americans, why it seems to beckon us, why its very name still humbles us and inspires us, why it mystifies us, or why it touches us so deeply.

Perhaps the answers may be found in our own fascination with the nation's military heritage and the perfect heroes who, on so many different battlefields and in so many different wars, have given their all for their country. Americans are, after all, drawn to perfect soldiers and to all their shining swords and their spit and polish, their unbridled courage, their unfailing commitment, and their tremendous self-sacrifice—all of which together make up the American military tradition.[7] As a people, we have been proud of many perfect heroes in our past—George Washington and Nathanael Greene in the War for Independence; Oliver Hazard Perry and Andrew Jackson in the War of 1812; Zachary Taylor and Winfield Scott in the Mexican War; Thomas J. "Stonewall" Jackson, Robert E. Lee, William Tecumseh Sherman, and Ulysses S. Grant in the Civil War; Theodore Roosevelt in the Spanish-American War; John J. Pershing in World War I; George Marshall, Dwight D. Eisenhower, Douglas MacArthur, and George Patton in World War II; Colin Powell and Norman Schwarzkopf in the Persian Gulf War.

In that sense, in the way in which we glorify heroes and elevate victorious generals to high pedestals, there were perfect heroes at Gettysburg, too. No one who fought at Gettysburg was, of course, perfect, but those who did experience the battle—and who lived to tell about it—often thought of themselves or remembered themselves as possessing a kind of perfection. Since Gettysburg, we have also come to regard them as perfect (or almost perfect). James Longstreet, Frank A. Haskell, William C. Oates, and Joshua L. Chamberlain can be included among those who saw themselves heroically—and we pay tribute to them by agreeing that they were, indeed, heroes, although some Southerners might quibble about Longstreet's status as a hero or as anything close to perfect. Other veterans of the battle, especially those who spoke about their ordeal or wrote about it years after the fighting, also saw themselves as rather perfect heroes. In their lives and in their memories, few soldiers admitted to cowardice, fear of death, or the loathing of combat. Whenever they could confess their disgust with war, they became a different kind of hero—one who knew his true self and faced up to his own strengths and weaknesses.

Not every hero at Gettysburg led the charge with a hurrah or with the fluttering colors in his grasp. Some soldiers who showed true courage there might have skedaddled in other earlier battles or in later ones, too. Being courageous from one battle to the next was not necessarily a given. Men could break when they least expected it, even those soldiers who were considered the finest and the bravest in a regiment or a company or a mess. Cowardice could strike without warning, which is why many soldiers preferred not to condemn their comrades for running or shirking duty on the battlefield. It could easily be their own nerve that might break in the next battle. One Civil War veteran, William A. Ketchum of Indiana, believed that roughly 10 percent of his fellow soldiers were unconditionally brave, while another 10 percent were "arrant cowards." That left about 80 percent who operated fully within a broad range between cowardice and bravery. Ambrose Bierce, a Union soldier who later gained fame for his delightfully macabre Civil War stories, described how men generally went into battle: "The front was irregularly serrated, the strongest and bravest in the advance, the others following in fan-like formations, variable and inconstant, ever defining themselves anew."[8] Being a perfect hero was rather an impossible feat, given the challenges to one's courage every Civil War soldier faced from one battle to the next.

In hindsight, after the war was over and the reverberations of the cannons and the crackle of musket volleys had all faded away, the veterans, Union and Confederate, found it much easier to look back on their experiences as romantic, heroic, and stupendous. Even then, it took a while for the old soldiers to want to talk about what had happened to them. For nearly twenty years after Appomattox, the soldiers put their wartime memories into what historian Gerald F. Linderman calls a "hibernation." They rarely wrote or spoke about the war to anyone, even their closest relatives. Although they participated in Memorial Day services, marched in local parades, or delivered patriotic orations, most veterans did not share their memories in public or even with their own families. Many of the old soldiers (although most veterans, North and South, were only in their twenties or thirties when the war ended) did not want to talk about the horrors they had seen; just as many wanted to forget what they had been through.[9] But that all changed between 1875 and 1880, when the old soldiers began remembering the war all at once.

More than anything else, one national event—which bubbled over with militaristic, industrial, and patriotic fervor—aroused them out of their hibernation. The celebration of the American centennial in 1876 coincided very closely with the publication of Civil War veteran memoirs, including ones by Joseph E. Johnston (1874), Sherman (1875), Grant (1885), and McClellan (1887), the *Southern Historical Society Papers* (1876), the *Official Records of the Union and Confederate Armies* (1880–1901), the Century Company's multivolumed *Battles and Leaders of the Civil War* (1884–1889), and countless histories; John Bachelder's efforts to organize battlefield reunions at Gettysburg; and the advent of veteran organizations, such as the Grand Army of the Republic (which had been created in 1866, but which experienced a huge leap in membership during the decade between 1880 and 1890) and the United Confederate Veterans (founded in 1889).[10] In the decade after the centennial observance in 1876, veterans and civilians alike spoke and wrote of the war and what it had meant to them. The memories came in the form of a national awakening.

On May 10, 1876, President Ulysses S. Grant, perhaps the most famous Civil War veteran in the country, opened the Centennial Exposition in Philadelphia with a speech that made no mention of the war, sectional discord, or lost lives in battle. Instead, Grant praised the nation's hard work, innovation, and technological achievements—many of which were on display in various pavilions on the exposition grounds in Fairmount Park. On hand for the opening ceremonies were General William Tecumseh Sherman and General Philip Sheridan, two other notable Civil War veterans. One of the most popular exhibits in the exposition featured "Old Abe," a bald eagle that became the mascot of the 8th Wisconsin Infantry

("The Eagle Regiment") during the war.[11] In Philadelphia, where the nation had been founded a century before, it was finally acceptable to ponder the Civil War, its cost, and its outcome.

Indeed, the exposition itself—and the entire national centennial celebration—became an opportunity for the country to advance the cause of reconciliation between North and South. In every state, celebrations honored the Declaration of Independence and the creation of the United States. Parades, replete with flags, music, and patriotic exuberance, were a popular form of celebration and entertainment during the centennial events of 1876. Civil War veterans often marched conspicuously in these parades, which were held in countless American communities.[12] Speeches glorified the Declaration, the Founding Fathers, the revolutionary generation, and the steady rise of democracy since the nation's inception. Northern and Southern speakers also made explicit references to the Civil War. In Melrose, Massachusetts, Elbridge H. Goss commended "the 'Boys in Blue'" who had fought for the community and who had "lain down their lives for their country—for your homes and mine." Proudly he declared that Melrose's contribution to the war effort, including the sacrifice of its sons, was "a good one; one that each and all of us, citizen and soldier, may cherish and not be afraid to show." In the former Confederate states, Southerners also honored the patriotism of their brave sons in the war. At the same time, they applauded the reunion of the two sections, since by the summer of 1876 most of the eleven Confederate states had been readmitted to the Union and Reconstruction was drawing to a close. "Blood is thicker than water," an editorial writer in Macon, Georgia, reminded his readers. Now that "the delightful reunion of the North and South" had been accomplished, he believed "that a benign providence will yet interpose to the save the Great Republic of North America." Both sections, he wrote, had "suffered enough to induce the gravest reflection, and call for poignant regret at the hasty counsels that eventuated in such dire disasters to the entire nation." With relief, this editorial writer pointed to "the annealing hand of time" that was "steadily doing its work," and he hoped that "the several centennial celebrations all over the country have their effect also in composing differences, and restoring intercourse and good humor among the masses."[13] The hibernation was over.

The former soldiers started talking and could not stop. Those who lived into the new century continued to speak and write about the war, many of them remembering not only battles, but lost comrades, forged friendships, shared miseries, the pleasantries and hardships of camp life, the dusty marches, and all the sights and sounds of soldiering. In stark contrast to the fifteen years of relative silence after the end of the war, the veterans admitted that there were things they could not forget, even if they wanted to. During the war, one Virginian artillerist noted in his diary that the scene of devastation on the battlefield at Cedar Creek in October 1864 was "indescribable." "I will pass over the description," he wrote in his entry, "as it will be well remembered by me always." Many years after the battle of Gettysburg, when Ellis Spear, an officer in the 20th Maine, wrote his Civil War memoirs based on diaries and notebooks he had kept during the war, he remembered how his regiment had spent the Fourth of July on the battlefield, two days after the 20th's heroic charge down the slopes of Little Round Top. The regiment had been moved to the Emmitsburg Road, and there Spear recalled how "the ground was strewn with dead horses & dead men." In one spot, he counted nineteen dead horses in a pile. Both horses and men had become swollen; the men, he said, had turned black. Nearby was a barn around which the dead "lay thick" in heaps. The barn had burned down during the fighting and sat as charred ruins smoldering in the rain. Looking back on the scene, despite the haze of many years, Spear remembered seeing "the burned remains of men" and the "half-roasted remains of horses & men" within the barn's wreckage. The 20th Maine buried the men. In the early 1900s, J. M. Polk, a veteran of the 4th Texas, had Gettysburg on his mind when he thought about his comrades who had fallen there. "It has been forty years now," he reflected, "and I don't remember the names of my own company that were lost." He wanted to remember, but he couldn't. Those nameless ghosts would be with him for the rest of his life.[14]

One man kept memories alive of Gettysburg, even through the height of the hibernation that otherwise silenced veterans during the decade from Appomattox to the Centennial: John B. Bachelder. A struggling artist when the Civil War broke out, Bachelder accompanied the Army of the Potomac as a civilian hoping to witness an epic battle he could then render onto canvas. He missed the battle of Gettysburg, however, arriving on the battlefield a few days after the armies had moved south. It was then that he decided that the battle was the most crucial military encounter of the war, and he began almost immediately gathering eyewitness accounts of what had taken place. Thus began his obsession with the battle that lasted until his death in 1894. Although he maintained his home in Massachusetts, Bachelder spent much of his time in Gettysburg after the war. In 1869, he organized a reunion of veterans from the Army of the Potomac on the field at Gettysburg, where he led the former soldiers around the battleground, listened to their descriptions and reminiscences of the fighting, and pounded wooden stakes in the earth to mark the locations of regiments and batteries. In the 1870s, he continued to collect firsthand accounts of the battle from its survivors. He also commissioned a painting of Pickett's Charge by James Walker and wrote a guidebook to the battlefield.

In 1880, Bachelder was elected one of the directors of the Gettysburg Battlefield Memorial Association (GBMA), a group founded in 1864 by local citizens—who were later replaced by active members of the Grand Army of the Republic, a national Union veterans organization—that dedicated itself to the preservation and protection of the battlefield. Over the next decade and a half, Bachelder oversaw the erection of monuments commemorating the role that Union army units played in the battle. With the raising of these early memorials, which grew steadily in number after 1880, the veterans held dedication ceremonies that regularly featured speakers—generally men who had fought at Gettysburg—who recounted in lavish detail the exploits of their regiments and brigades and corps. Inscriptions and speeches offered a history of the battle from the unique perspective of the men (or at least some of the men) who had fought it. For the most part, southern veterans did not flock to Gettysburg to erect monuments, either because the GBMA had no interest in Confederate memorials or because southern veterans and the former Confederate states could not come up with the money or lacked the desire to put up stone reminders of a crushing defeat.

Besides his role in raising Union monuments that soon dotted the field, Bachelder worked to make sure that Gettysburg would not be forgotten in the public's memory. In 1880, the federal government appropriated fifty thousand dollars for Bachelder to write a history of the battle, and he began in earnest to collect the written testimony of every Gettysburg veteran—Union and Confederate—he could locate. The resulting history proved a disappointment, for rather than relying on the vast treasure trove of eyewitness accounts that he had assembled (and that remains one of the richest documentary sources for reconstructing the battle's details), Bachelder drew instead on the published official reports and other standard treatments of the battle. He played a major role in organizing the most important of the early veteran reunions on the field, the one that celebrated the battle's twenty-fifth anniversary in 1888, when both Union and Confederate veterans participated in the grand observance and famously shook hands with one another across the stone wall where Pickett's Charge had reached its climax on Cemetery Ridge. Bachelder also became the driving force behind the design and the erection of the High Water Mark Monument on Cemetery Ridge as a tribute to the Union and Confederate soldiers who had participated in what he believed to be the most crucial combat of the entire three days' battle. In 1893, Bachelder was appointed to a three-man commission to supervise the Gettysburg National Military Park (GNMP), which Congress had created to supersede the old GBMA. He died shortly after his appointment.[15]

While attending Bachelder's reunions, dedicating monuments, or writing up their own recollections of the battle, Gettysburg veterans offered their rather selective memories as vindications of their own actions or of the decisions made by their commanders on the field. Much of what they had to say was contentious, despite the romantic language they used to describe heroic deeds or to honor individual bravery. As a result, their remembrances often brimmed over in bitterness, denials, and accusations. Surprisingly, at least to students who come upon these veteran accounts for the first time, this remembrance literature is largely disputatious and frequently venomous. Although the veterans often praised the courage of their enemy, thus advancing the cause of reconciliation, they usually aimed their harshest words—and their worst criticisms—at rival units for unjustly hogging the battle's glory or at various commanders, including general and field officers, whom they deemed incompetent or reckless. Even as these veterans tried to assert the solidity of their Victorian manhood by emphasizing the equal courage of soldiers in combat, Union and Confederate, they also engaged in defending the overall mettle of their units and demonstrating how they—and only they—had been in the very worst fighting at Gettysburg. Small wonder, then, that veterans from different units often found themselves engaged in fiery disputes over who had done what in the battle and who had stood where at any given time. Old hatreds between North and South easily became forgotten amidst the jarring debates over who deserved the most credit for the Union victory or who earned the most blame for the Confederate defeat. So forgotten, too, were slavery (the cause of the war), African Americans (whom the war had freed), and black civil rights (which the war had failed to guarantee). Instead, the veterans concentrated on refighting the battle in words, discounting the exaggerated claims of gallantry made by their comrades in arms, and trying to recapture their lost youth. Steadily, with each new monument raised on the field, with each new speech dedicating their military memorials to posterity, the Gettysburg veterans told the nation how brave and determined they had been, and how—apart from their inept commanders or their boastful comrades in rival units—they had all been perfect heroes.[16]

At the dedication of the monument to the 83rd Pennsylvania on Little Round Top in September 1889, Oliver W. Norton, the regiment's former bugler, remarked to his fellow veterans that "each of us has in his heart the memory of some comrade who fell, dear to him but perhaps unknown to most of the . . . men who from first to last made up the Eighty-third." Like so many of his surviving comrades, Norton admitted that the memory of those fallen men still filled his thoughts and brought him sadness. But all was not grim when he looked back on the war. "Those were glorious days," he said, "when, with the blood of youth coursing through our veins, we consecrated ourselves to the Stars and Stripes, and devoted ourselves to the preservation of the government of the people, by the people, and for the people." The men of the 83rd Pennsylvania had established a war record of "glorious deeds." Among them was the regiment's defense of Little Round Top on July 2, a day, he said, that was "burned into my memory." Norton believed that all the men of the regiment were perfect heroes, but there was one officer who stood above all the rest—Colonel Strong Vincent, the regiment's commander and, later, brigade commander, who had been mortally wounded in the fight for Little Round Top. Vincent, in Norton's opinion, epitomized the perfect hero: "In the very flower of his young manhood, full of the highest promise, with the love of a young wife filling his thought of the future with the fairest visions, proud, gentle, tender, true, he laid his gift on his country's altar. It was done nobly, gladly. No knight of the days of chivalry was ever more knightly." The monument itself was a bronze statue of Vincent, and the memorial stood on what Norton considered to be "holy ground." His memories brought Vincent and all the regiment's fallen back to life: "May we not reverently say that those who have died for men are not dead, but are with us to-day, more living than when they stood to stem the tide of invasion?" Norton spent the rest of his life promoting Vincent as the savior of Little Round Top and trying to elevate the historical reputation of Vincent's brigade and the 83rd Pennsylvania and all their perfect heroes.[17]

Not only Gettysburg veterans such as Norton regarded themselves and their fallen comrades as perfect heroes. American society as a whole honored them, too. The New York Times account of the reunion held on the twenty-fifth anniversary of Gettysburg in July 1888 observed that the Civil

War had been the nation's "heroic age." All the soldiers of the Civil War, and not just the heroes of Gettysburg, deserved to be honored: "The lavish sacrifices of blood and treasure, the unyielding tenacity of the combatants, the constancy and firmness of the people on both sides . . . signalized the great conflict as the heroic age of the Republic." Gettysburg veterans were so highly regarded that they even received "premiums" after the war from the Union Army pension system in the form of enhanced access to pensions and increases in payments that did not go to their fellow Union veterans who had not served in the Pennsylvania campaign. For example, Gettysburg veterans were 2.65 times more likely to apply for a pension and 17 percent more likely to be granted an increase than former Union soldiers who had not fought in the battle. Apparently these advantages existed because the pension administrators assumed that Gettysburg veterans possessed "moral worth"—as did early enlistees who later applied for pensions—since they, unlike later conscripted soldiers and bounty recipients, were loyal volunteers who fought bravely for the Union cause, not for money and not because they had been drafted.[18]

Being a perfect Gettysburg hero may have improved the outcomes of a former soldier's pension application, but it could not stop the memories of those three fateful days in Pennsylvania. Many Gettysburg veterans, like Norton, could never forget what they had seen and experienced there. Others distrusted their memories and the details they tried to salvage from the past. "After twenty years," wrote one Union soldier to John Bachelder, "no man[']s memory unassisted can be safe." Even though details may have been forgotten over time by some of them, even by many of them, Civil War veterans nevertheless invariably praised the heroism and courage of their comrades, their enemies, and themselves. That courage could not be denied; nor could it ever be forgotten. "When we look back upon the exciting events of those four years of war," wrote one of William Oates's comrades in the 15th Alabama regiment in 1879, "the courage and endurance of the men" made him conclude that their valor had not been wasted. "No noble blood," he said, "was ever shed in vain." Yet remembering was often painful, raising not only memories of horrible gore and suffering, but old hatreds, hard bitterness, and powerful anger. One Union veteran wrote to his congressman in 1889 to tell him that he did not think Confederate monuments should be erected on the Gettysburg battlefield. The field, he believed, belonged to the Union veterans. "This is our one memorial battlefield," he explained. Some former Northern soldiers, however, felt differently and did not oppose Confederate monuments on the field. Praising and honoring their former enemies only added luster to the reputations of the soldiers who fought against them. "They gave us so much trouble," wrote Norman Camp, a veteran of the U.S. Signal Corps, to Bachelder in 1889, "that an honorable glorification of our prowess should perpetuate the glorious bravery of our misguided brothers, in memorial stones, roads, indicated lines of battle, etc. The more we honor the bravery of our adversary, the greater our glory in having conquered them."[19]

Yet the memories of these soldiers, Union and Confederate, stood starkly at odds with the reality of the war and all its hardships, all its fiery terror. Some soldiers spoke and wrote openly of the carnage they had witnessed at Gettysburg and on other battlefields. In the 1890s, when William Thomas Fluker Jr., who had served in the 15th Georgia Infantry at Gettysburg, recounted his experiences during the battle, he wrote mournfully of the carnage that had taken place where he and his comrades had seen action. "The slaughter in our front was simply beyond description," he declared. "The ground in front of us was covered in places with dead men. Where a line would stand for a few moments it was marked as distinctly by a line of dead as it ever was by the living. I saw them in one place as they fell, three deep piled on each other. I saw scores of them fall from thin ranks during the evening. I thought at the time, and think yet, that the death rate in our front would exceed five to one of us engaged." But other veterans could not bear such memories, and their view of the past became softened—romanticized, sanitized, and fairly bloodless in its depiction of combat. Oliver Norton, in his dedication speech, spoke of the terrible sight all soldiers beheld when they watched as "fallen heroes" were put to rest in the "long trench." But in his entire address he made no mention of combat, other than to allude to Strong Vincent's courage, to his "sword flashing in air," and to the colonel's own prophetic words during the march to Gettysburg: "What more glorious death can any man desire than to die on the soil of old Pennsylvania, fighting for that flag!" For Norton, and for so many other veterans who spoke of the war, their memories failed them, just as their words would do when they sought to communicate what Norton himself called "the correct story of Gettysburg."[20]

What so many veterans like Norton could not confront, even as they emerged from their hibernation and began publicly sharing their memories of the war, was the reality not only of the slaughter they and their comrades had endured, but of the excessive violence they had inflicted on their enemy. The worst horror of war for any soldier is not that he may be killed; it is that he must kill someone else. In such a Christian society as existed before and during the war in the United States, the commandment against killing was taken very seriously, North and South. Even though many Union and Confederate soldiers convinced themselves that God was on their side, it still was not easy to kill a man in anger. The soldiers felt plenty of rage toward their enemy—a burning hatred that sprang from years of sectional discord, the breakdown of politics and compromise in the decade before the war, and the emotional turmoil of secession and the surrender of Fort Sumter that had carried the nation to war. The hatred was tangible, and it lasted for some Americans through the war years and beyond. Edward Porter Alexander, an artillery commander in Lee's Army of Northern Virginia, once confessed that he always felt like kicking Union prisoners "all around." His greatest comfort, he once told a fellow officer, was "to know that I have killed some of them with my own hands, I have shot them with muskets and artillery and have seen them fall and afterwards went there and found them dead. [I]f they should kill me today and I had but time for one thought before I died it would be that my account with them was more than even." Many Union soldiers hated their Confederate enemies just as much. After Gettysburg, one soldier wrote home and described how the carnage had been so astronomical that "it seemed as if every man, on both sides, was actuated by the intensest hate, and determined to kill as many of the enemy as possible." One Union soldier received assurances from Confederate pickets that they would not fire while he helped a wounded comrade; no sooner had he raised the injured man's head to give him a drink of water then the Confederate pickets opened fire and killed the good Samaritan instantly. Hatred in the Civil War sometimes ran very deep.[21]

But hatred alone could not explain the severity of the violence and the extent of the destruction that Americans had committed against one another. Always mitigating against the brutality was an odd, yet persistent, sense that the enemy was more human than the soldiers' emotions— and particularly their animosity—seemed to suggest. William Fluker, the Georgian who had fought at Little Round Top, stopped long enough while describing how he and his regiment, or what remained of it, was "surrounded by death and suffering that no pen can picture" to mention that even while they hated the enemy with a vengeance "our deadly determination of a few minutes before to destroy life had changed to sympathy and sorrow for the suffering ones about us." Fluker and his fellow Confederates went to the relief of the men they had just struck down "as whole souled as we had gone to their destruction." Reconciliation sentiment after

1880, and especially in the early twentieth century, made Northern and Southern soldiers seem, in retrospect, more like friendly enemies than they had ever truly been throughout the war, but the plentiful stories of humanitarian and medical assistance given to enemies during the war, the fraternization of enemy pickets who regularly exchanged coffee for tobacco, and the tales of antebellum friendships (including those between men who had seen service in the Old Army together) that remained unbroken by the war attest to the persistence of an ambivalence that existed among Civil War soldiers on both sides. The fact that these enemies were both American, even given their political and cultural differences, went a long way toward making their foe seem more like a profligate brother than an alien bête noire. William Owen, who fought with the 20th Maine at Gettysburg, lamented that the sectional controversy had broken into warfare with "brother against brother" and "families divided against each other and enmity and jealousy between them." How long, he asked in May 1863, "can this last?" For all Americans, the war lasted longer than anyone had wished. But soldiers on both sides discovered that despite the fratricidal nature of their conflict, they shared a bond with their enemies as *soldiers*. As William C. Oates explained to his Gettysburg nemesis, Joshua L. Chamberlain, in 1897: "I have a great respect and kindly feeling for a good soldier without regard to the side on which he fought."[22]

Nevertheless, Civil War soldiers—at least after a year or so of war, and especially after the Emancipation Proclamation changed the nature of the conflict in January 1863—seemed to understand that the maelstrom they had been swept into engendered an excessive violence, a destructive brutality, that could only be described as revolutionary. As they fought from battle to battle, with each encounter raising the stakes and increasing the number of casualties, Union and Confederate soldiers came to know that they were fighting something more than a hard war—a modern war unlike any that mankind had ever fought, a total war of a kind for which, as yet, the world had no name. Even Oliver Norton—who in the postwar years would look back upon the war and see a heroic and knightly contest—had perceived a very different war, a war of great violence and destruction, while he was living through it. On July 5, 1863, he rode over the ground that the Army of the Potomac had defended on its left flank at Gettysburg and later wrote home about "the most horrible" carnage he had ever seen: "All over the field were scattered black and bloated corpses of men, and dead horses. . . . I saw the bodies of thirteen rebels lying in the mud with the pitiless rain beating on their ghastly faces. That would have been a horror at home; there it was only a glimpse of what might be seen." Edward Porter Alexander called the war "a contest to the death," which of course every war is in the end, but Alexander himself sensed that this war went beyond the bounds of earlier wars. Writing about the Confederate defeat at Franklin, Tennessee, in November 1864, Alexander observed that the battle was decided "with terrific slaughter" and that someone had written (and Alexander had taken it to heart) that "never before in the history of war did a command, of the approximate strength of [Colonel John S.] Casement's [brigade], in so short a period of time kill and wound as many men." Charles Francis Adams Jr. succinctly and graphically described the war as a "Carnival of Death."[23]

In time, the realization of the brutality that lay at the heart of the war shocked even the most hardened veterans. When peace finally came, when the bugles sounded no more, the former soldiers tried not to dwell on what they had witnessed. In the end, when they were aroused out of their hibernation, it is not surprising that so many of them should look back on this awful war by trying to emphasize its redeeming, rather than its repulsive, aspects. In doing so, the old veterans saw themselves and their comrades and even their enemies as perfect heroes, as grand in their memories as all the stories they had heard in their youth about the great heroes of the Revolution—their fathers, grandfathers, and great-grandfathers who had fought so valiantly to create the American nation. Standing in the shadow of their Revolutionary forefathers, the perfect heroes of the Civil War applauded themselves for having taken up their patriotic cause, having fought for liberty, and having defended American rights just like the Old Revolutionaries had done. So the perfect heroes of Gettysburg—like Longstreet, Oates, Chamberlain, and so many others—made their own contribution to the revolutionary tradition begun by the Founding Fathers. Subsequent generations of Americans have long remembered and honored them. "It is we few who have been entrusted with the memory of what happened here [in Gettysburg]," said a member of the Gettysburg Discussion Group, an Internet forum, in 1997. "To us has devolved the sacred memory of those men, their bravery, their accomplishments."[24]

Even one-legged tramps in the late nineteenth century who wanted only to sponge a meal could not avoid or forget Gettysburg's perfect heroes. Yet while our modern sensibilities do not allow us to appreciate the soldiers who fought at Gettysburg as quite the perfect heroes they wished to be, we can at least perceive through the mists of the past how those sturdy soldiers, their excessive violence against one another, their hatred of their enemies and their kindnesses to fellow soldiers, comrade and enemy alike, made the Civil War into America's first modern war. As such, they also forged a new and modern nation out of the old one they fought to preserve. But in a new America, the perfect heroes of the Civil War would feel increasingly out of place. No wonder they finally stopped battling with their memories and let themselves float downstream to a place in their minds where the war was filled with glory and where each of them could stand with pride as perfect heroes.

1   Lee's Old War Horse

One of the Confederacy's perfect heroes, James Longstreet, should have been honored by the South for all his great feats on the battlefields of the Civil War, but it was his fate to become an object of scorn and ridicule in the postwar era. What set his fellow Southerners off against him was the inconstancy that formed a pattern in his life. There was something about him that made people generally question his fealty, faithfulness, and dependability. In his autumnal years, Longstreet met one of his family's former slaves, his "old nurse" Daniel, on a visit to Mississippi. "Marse Jim," said Daniel, "do you belong to any church?" Longstreet replied matter-of-factly, "I try to be a good Christian." Old Daniel stopped laughing long enough to say: "Something must have scared you mighty bad to change you so from what you was when I had to care for you."[1] What old Daniel found so remarkable was not that Longstreet had embraced religion in his adulthood, for many a man turns to God as his years grow shorter, but that his master's convictions could have changed so radically over the years. Daniel was not alone. Others who knew Longstreet during his long life—as a soldier in the United States Army, as a general in the armies of the Confederacy, as a politician after the Civil War, or even as a friend—reacted to him in similar ways. In a famous quote, a subordinate once said of Longstreet: "I consider him a humbug."[2]

Generals are supposed to win their reputations on the battlefield, but in Longstreet's case his public image was mostly shaped by his actions after the Civil War, when he embraced the Republican Party and earned the enmity of a cadre of former Confederate officers who, while elevating the beloved Robert E. Lee to Southern sainthood, blamed Longstreet for losing the battle of Gettysburg, bringing about the defeat of the Confederacy as a whole, and betraying the "Lost Cause." After Longstreet's death, when the furor over his actions might have otherwise subsided, historians kept up the attacks on Longstreet and perpetuated the controversy surrounding him. Except for a handful of writers—including Michael Shaara in his famous novel, *The Killer Angels,* Glenn Tucker in two books written more than thirty years ago about Longstreet at Gettysburg, and two recent historians, Jeffry D. Wert and William Garrett Piston—Longstreet has had few defenders. Some Civil War historians, such as Robert K. Krick, mince no words about Longstreet and his faults. Says Krick rather saucily: "The record shows that Longstreet operated at times during the war with an unwholesome and unlovely attitude."[3]

There's good reason for such bristling criticism. Whether Longstreet was as "unlovely" as historian Krick claims is certainly debatable, but it is evident nevertheless that Longstreet's inconstancy—the apostasy his former slave found so manifestly amusing—hampered his effectiveness as a general officer during the Civil War and tarnished his good name in the years afterward. In fact, the issue of disloyalty runs like a dark river through Longstreet's life. His friends *and* his enemies never seemed quite certain about where he stood. For all the controversy surrounding him, when it comes to assessing Longstreet's merits and shortcomings as a military man the heart of the matter is to be found in trying to resolve his wavering loyalties—to his country's cause, to his superior officers, and to himself.

In an era when states' rights dominated the politics of the South, James Longstreet held no particular allegiance to any Southern state. Born on his grandparents' plantation on January 8, 1821, in Edgefield District, South Carolina, Longstreet spent his early years on his father's plantation in northeastern Georgia, not far from present-day Gainesville. His father was originally from New Jersey; his mother from Maryland. To prepare him for entry into West Point, Longstreet's father in 1830 sent him to attend an academy in Augusta and live with an uncle, Augustus Baldwin Longstreet, an accomplished attorney and judge who would later win attention for his collection of humorous frontier anecdotes, *Georgia Scenes,* and for his outspoken support of secession in 1860. When his father died in 1833, James Longstreet remained in Augusta and his mother moved to Alabama. It was from Alabama, in fact, that Longstreet received his appointment to the United States Military Academy in 1838.

At West Point, his fellow cadets called him "Old Pete," a variation of his family nickname, "Peter." Even as a young man, Longstreet offered an imposing presence. He stood two inches above six feet in height and carried more than two hundred pounds on his large frame. Later in life, he became barrel-chested and, to some extent, paunchy, but in his youth he was muscular and solid. Longstreet's deep-set blue eyes and his reserved manner (he was a man of few words) lent an air of coolness to his disposition. Yet he enjoyed practical jokes, had a fine sense of humor, and liked playing poker with his comrades. "As a cadet," Longstreet admitted, "I had more interest in the school of the soldier, horsemanship, sword exercise, and the outside game of foot-ball than in the academic courses."[4] Later, in the Civil War, one of his aides described him as "a soldier every inch."[5]

No one ever doubted his bravery in combat or his potential for leadership. During the Mexican War, he distinguished himself in one engagement after another. As a result of his courage and skill as an officer during the battle of Monterey in September 1845, Longstreet was promoted first to adjutant of the 8th Infantry and later to first lieutenant. A year later, at Churubusco, Longstreet and a fellow officer led a bold assault on the Mexican fortifications, with Longstreet carrying the colors and urging his men forward. Longstreet also carried the flag in an attack on Chapultepec a few days later. Hit in the thigh by a Mexican bullet, he gave the colors over to a fellow lieutenant, George E. Pickett, before falling in pain.

In the Civil War, Longstreet also gained a reputation for bravery and nerve. Edward Pollard, a Southern historian of the Civil War, said there was "a certain fierce aspect to the man."[6] His men adored him and admired the fact that he did not shrink from leading his troops into battle and putting himself in dangerous situations on the field of battle. They called him a "bulldog," and they seemed more than willing to follow him into the very fires of hell. One of his aides, Major Thomas J. Goree, admiringly observed Longstreet's "coolness and daring" under fire. He described how the general, during one battle, rode among his men "amid a perfect shower of balls . . . with a cigar in his mouth, rallying them, encouraging, and inspiring confidence among them."[7]

Yet Longstreet's enthusiasm for battle caused concern among many of his compatriots. While traveling with Robert E. Lee's Army of Northern Virginia during the summer of 1863, Lieutenant Arthur L. Fremantle of the British Coldstream Guards noted that Longstreet's fellow officers fully expected that he would expose himself on the battlefield in "a reckless manner." Reckless or not, Longstreet loved being in the middle of a fight. He sprang to life during combat. In the smoke and fire of battle, said Goree, Longstreet seemed to be "one of the happiest men in the world."[8]

Given his tendency to throw himself into the fray (Fremantle told how Longstreet, hat in hand, personally led a Georgia regiment in an assault against a Federal battery at Gettysburg), it is remarkable that Longstreet has earned such an undeserved reputation as a defensive fighter. Most of the claims for Longstreet's proficiency as a defensive tactician come from his adept handling of his troops at Fredericksburg in December 1862, when he positioned his men behind a sunken road on Marye's Heights and watched as wave upon wave of assaulting Union troops were mowed down under withering fire from the Confederate guns. Lee was fearful that Longstreet's line would break. Longstreet knew better. "General," he said, "if you put every man now on the other side of the Potomac on that field to approach me over the same line, and give me plenty of ammunition, I will kill them all before they reach my line."[9] The controversy over his actions at Gettysburg has also made historians believe that he favored defensive, rather than offensive, actions, for Longstreet very publicly criticized Lee after the war for not assuming a defensive posture at Gettysburg that would have allowed the Confederates to choose their own ground and wait for the Union Army of the Potomac to attack them.

While it is true that Longstreet would have preferred defensive maneuvers in Pennsylvania during the summer of 1863, he never consistently argued for defensive tactics, as some historians have implied. As a field general, Longstreet was a decided pragmatist, using offensive and defensive actions wherever they best suited the situation. His battle plans were, for the most part, aggressive and demonstrated, if anything, a tendency toward hard-hitting assaults, such as the ones he led during the Seven Days, at Second Manassas, and at Chickamauga. His soldiers never considered him to be simply a defensive fighter. "Longstreet is a bulldog soldier and cares nothing about flank movements," wrote one Texan under his command. "He takes a dead set at the center, and can whip any army on earth if he has men enough to fight until he is tired of it."[10] Although now mostly forgotten in the thick fog of controversy that has for so long shrouded him from view, Longstreet actually possessed an uncanny ability as a general to size up a situation and determine, coolly and objectively, whether to strike the enemy or hold his ground. For good reason, General Lee valued Longstreet and called him "the staff in my right hand" and "my old war horse."[11]

But off the battlefield, it was an entirely different story. Without the swirl of combat around him, Longstreet fumbled and faltered. Throughout his long career in the service of two armies, Longstreet revealed that he was a far better warrior than he was a steadfast soldier. Some writers have maintained that Longstreet was overly ambitious and that his hopes for advancement (or his despondency over failing to win promotion) frequently got him into trouble. The fact is that Longstreet never appeared to have clear goals in mind. Like most men, and like most good military officers, he wanted to get ahead in life, but unless he could direct his men to take a certain hill or break an enemy's line, he could not always define for himself where he wanted to go, what he wanted to be, or who he really was.

This indecisiveness was readily apparent during the years Longstreet spent as a young officer in the U.S. Army. Although he found military life appealing, he seemed unsure of where he wanted his army career to go. After the Mexican War, Longstreet married Louise Garland, the daughter of one of his post commanders, and took several brief assignments before settling down for a while in San Antonio, Texas, where he served as the adjutant of the 8th Infantry and later as chief commissary for the Department of Texas.

In June 1850, he asked to be transferred to the cavalry, but his request was denied. He longed for promotion, hoped that the cavalry might give him the advancement he wanted, and looked for other alternatives when that avenue became closed to him. Resigning his post as commissary, he returned to the 8th Infantry and began leading patrols into Comanche territory, leaving his wife and their two small children in San Antonio. The dusty forays into the desolate Texas countryside could not have encouraged him about his chances for promotion. He was personally ambitious, but he also wanted the extra pay that would come with higher rank so that he could better support his family and place his children in decent schools. Finally he received a promotion to captain in December 1852, and two years later, he moved to Fort Bliss, in New Mexico Territory, where he got a taste of Indian fighting against the Apaches and even assumed temporary command of the post on two separate occasions.

All in all, Longstreet spent four years at Fort Bliss—his longest assignment to date in the army. In 1858, he requested to be removed from frontier duty and to be assigned a staff job, probably with the hope that he could win a major's commission sooner behind a desk than in front of an Indian patrol. He was right. Longstreet was promoted to major in the paymaster department and ordered to Fort Leavenworth, Kansas, and later to Albuquerque, New Mexico.

As the sectional conflict between North and South heated up in the East, threatening the dissolution of the country, Longstreet and his comrades watched the events from afar with "intense anxiety" and in "painful suspense."[12] Although the evidence is sparse, and Longstreet himself left no explicit account of his actions during this period, it would appear that Longstreet interpreted Abraham Lincoln's election to the presidency in November 1860 as a dire threat to the welfare of the Southern states and took great interest in the course of secession as it spread its way through the states of the deep South after South Carolina withdrew from the Union on December 20, 1860. About this time, Longstreet wrote to Washington asking for an escort for himself and his family from Fort Bliss to San Antonio. The reason for the request is not known, but it was denied by the War Department. He also wrote a letter to a friend, Congressman J. L. M. Curry of Alabama, offering his services to the governor of that state, should Alabama decide to follow South Carolina out of the Union. Meanwhile, if one postwar source can be believed, his mother begged him to remain in service to the United States. But Longstreet had set his own course.

Why he offered himself to Alabama, and not Georgia, is a mystery, although he may have reckoned that his chances for gaining higher rank in the state militia were better in Alabama than they would have been in either Georgia or South Carolina. Whatever his purpose, his letter to Curry was, technically speaking, a treasonous act, for Longstreet was still wearing the uniform of a U.S. Army officer. But his oath to defend the U.S. Constitution and to protect the nation from its enemies did not weigh heavily on Longstreet's mind or conscience. During the secession crisis, his loyalties were at best ambivalent and at worst duplicitous.

Unlike other Southerners, who justified their Confederate allegiances because they claimed to feel a stronger loyalty to their native states rather than to the United States, Longstreet never declared that he possessed any special attachment to a state or even a particular affinity for the South. Some historians have strongly argued that he probably embraced firmly the tenets of states' rights so lovingly espoused by his famous uncle Augustus, but if so, there's little evidence to show that he knew much about the constitutional background to secession at all or that his actions in the winter of 1860–61 were the result of deep political convictions. What seems most likely is that he recognized a clear opportunity when it presented itself, and it was a fair bet that Alabama would follow in South Carolina's wake sooner or later.

But to take advantage of opportunity meant playing his cards close to his vest. After Alabama seceded, Longstreet wrote to Governor Andrew B. Moore in February 1861 and offered his services directly to the state, "should she need a soldier who has seen hard service." Moore forwarded Longstreet's letter to Confederate Secretary of War Leroy P. Walker. It would appear that Longstreet also arranged to have several prominent men endorse his suitability for high rank in the Confederate army by sending letters of support to President Jefferson Davis. Longstreet's brother

William also wrote to Davis and offered his younger brother's services "in any capacity that is within the scope of his profession."[13]

On March 16, 1861, Confederate officials in Montgomery appointed Longstreet to the rank of lieutenant colonel of infantry. Not knowing of the commission, but sure that some place would be found for him in the Confederate army, Longstreet planned to resign from the United States Army around the beginning of April. He delayed when two other paymasters resigned their federal commissions and his superior officer ordered him to take over their duties. To do so, however, meant waiting until mid-April when the payrolls would arrive. By the end of the month, he heard news of the firing on Fort Sumter and announced to his friends that he would leave the army. He also received word of his commission in the Confederate service. On May 1, he accepted the appointment.

The problem was he had not yet resigned his commission in the United States Army, so Longstreet essentially had entered the service of a foreign nation—or, at the very least, of states in rebellion—without ending his service to the United States. Eight days later he did resign from the United States Army, but at some point he actually accepted pay for concurrent service in the United States and Confederate armies. Unsurprisingly, Longstreet never mentioned this business in his memoirs. In fact, he intimates that he was called to service by Alabama, when in fact his call came from the Confederate States alone. As biographer Jeffry Wert concludes: "What motivated him or how he justified it to himself remains a mystery; what he did, however, was not the act of an honorable man and officer."[14]

During the war, Longstreet's inconstancy continued to plague him. Although his fellow officers and his own men invariably described him as brimming over with self-confidence, Longstreet never seemed to know what he really wanted. Probably he was happiest as a brigadier general serving under General P. G. T. Beauregard at the first battle of Manassas and as a major general under the command of General Joseph E. Johnston. He admired Johnston and considered him the most able general in the service of the Confederacy, but Johnston's severe wound at the battle of Seven Pines on May 31, 1862, removed him from command and elevated General Robert E. Lee to take his place.

Longstreet had mixed feelings about Lee. He served his new commander well and faithfully, but he stuck to his belief that Johnston was the better general. Although Lee praised Longstreet for his accomplishments and for his good advice, Longstreet himself never felt quite comfortable dealing with the godlike Lee. For one thing, he thought Lee was too aggressive.

"In defensive warfare," Longstreet said of Lee, "he was perfect. When the hunt was up, his combativeness was overruling." In the field, Longstreet said, Lee's "characteristic fault was headlong combativeness." Ultimately Lee simply took "too many chances."[15] For another thing, Longstreet kept trying to free himself from Lee's control over him.

Longstreet had never learned the lesson that one cannot be loyal and disloyal at the same time. After the battle of Sharpsburg in September 1862, Longstreet wrote Johnston to say that while the Army of Northern Virginia had won some great victories under Lee's command, "I feel that you have their hearts more decidedly than any other leader can ever have."[16] He offered to turn over to Johnston his command of the First Corps, if Johnston could arrange for Longstreet to win a command in the western theater. Nothing came of Longstreet's offer, but it revealed that his loyalty to Lee was tenuous at best.

Behind Longstreet's maneuvering for a western assignment was his burning ambition to obtain higher rank and an independent command. Although he never explicitly set forth his goals for higher rank or came right out and said that he wanted command of a particular Confederate army, Longstreet nevertheless ached with an ambition that occasionally rose to the surface of his dealings with Lee and with the War Department in Richmond. Just about the time that Longstreet was promoted to major general in October 1861, he had asked to be relieved from command of his brigade because he believed that he had been passed over for promotion and that one or two others who were his juniors in rank had been elevated to major general. General Beauregard had to assure Longstreet than no injustice had been committed against him and that his own promotion was on its way. Later, in October 1862, his promotion to lieutenant general—which flew through the Confederate Senate mostly on the weight of Lee's unqualified recommendation—occurred precisely at the time when Longstreet was privately offering the command of his First Corps to Joseph Johnston.

Although ambition moved the man, it did not dominate him. He once wrote of himself: "I am not prompted by any desire to do, or to attempt to do, great things. I only wish to do what I regard as my duty."[17] Nevertheless, Longstreet, who hoped for more glory than he was always accorded, tended to think more highly of himself than circumstances warranted. He was an outstanding field general, to be sure, one who became known for carefully sizing up a situation before committing his troops to battle, for knowing the lay of the land on the battlefield, and for hitting the enemy hard with overpowering force. Although his critics after the war accused him of slowness, based largely on an unlikely remark that Lee made during the postwar years, the fact is that Longstreet's reputation was as a fast hard-driver. Goree, in a letter home, told his mother that Longstreet was "exceedingly punctual and industrious." Whatever Longstreet set out to do, said Goree, he did "well and quickly."[18]

But what Goree failed to mention was that Longstreet frequently found it difficult to admit his mistakes, blamed others for errors that hid his own deficiencies, and, at least in later life, made incredible claims for achievements in which he actually played no part. A case in point was Longstreet's claim that he came up with the plan to have Jackson join forces with Lee for the series of battles on the Virginia Peninsula that later became known as the Seven Days. While Longstreet seems to have realized that Jackson's corps could be used to help keep Major General George B. McClellan's Army of the Potomac out of Richmond, it was Lee who came up with the actual plan and who issued the orders to Jackson. Longstreet did help Lee revise the battle plan and suggested the placement of Jackson's troops in the impending assault, but he could not honestly claim, as he did in a private letter, that the Confederate offensive "was planned by me."[19]

At the same time, Longstreet deftly blamed his own mistakes during the Peninsula campaign—namely, his failure to understand and follow precise orders at the battle of Seven Pines in May 1862—on the ineptitude of a fellow major general, Benjamin Huger. When he wasn't blowing his own horn, Longstreet spent a good deal of time pointing his finger at others.

Despite his own exaggerated sense of self-importance, Longstreet did not always perform up to his own grand expectations when he was given the opportunity to prove his talents and his value to the Confederate cause. When he finally did get a chance to exercise independent command, for example, Longstreet demonstrated rather conclusively that he lacked the necessary skills of an army commander. During the late winter and early spring of 1863, Lee sent Longstreet with two of his divisions to southside Virginia, in the vicinity of Suffolk, where Southern defenses needed strengthening and the surrounding farms offered a good opportunity for foraging. While his foraging parties collected meager supplies from the Virginia and neighboring Carolina countryside, Longstreet laid siege to Suffolk, which was held by a Union force under the command of Major General John J. Peck. When General Joseph Hooker's Army of the Potomac advanced on Lee's Confederate forces in the vicinity of Chancellorsville, Virginia, Lee ordered Longstreet to return with his divisions in haste. But Longstreet found that—because his supply wagons were still out foraging—he could not break off the siege fast enough to move his men north in time to help Lee defeat Hooker.

Some critics have accused Longstreet of tardiness in not responding to Lee's order with more alacrity, but the fact is that Longstreet moved as quickly as he could after receiving word of the crisis on the Rappahannock. Longstreet did not mishandle the Suffolk campaign or fail to obey Lee's order to rejoin the Army of Northern Virginia, but the overall execution of his mission seemed uninspired. The Suffolk siege got the Confederates nowhere, for Peck's Federal troops retained a firm grip on the town and the surrounding area, and the collection of supplies in southside Virginia did not come close to solving the problem of short rations that Lee's army had been living on for several months. Longstreet could show little for having spent eight weeks on the Suffolk campaign.

Later in the war, Longstreet got another taste of independent command. In the fall of 1863, Lee sent Longstreet and two of his divisions south to serve with General Braxton Bragg's western army in Georgia. Longstreet and his divisions arrived just in time to help bring on a Confederate victory at the battle of Chickamauga on September 20, 1863. Technically speaking, Longstreet and his men were on detached service, rather than under his individual command, for he was required to report to Bragg, whom he personally detested. In short order, after complaining endlessly about Bragg's shortcomings, Longstreet managed to win a new assignment for his divisions in East Tennessee, where they were told to dislodge Union General Ambrose B. Burnside's forces in and around Knoxville.

But things in East Tennessee did not go well for Longstreet. Disagreements with his subordinates were at the root of the problem. When he failed to prevent the Federals from reopening their supply line from Chattanooga to Alabama, Longstreet blamed three of his most reliable subordinates: Evander Law, Jerome Robertson, and Lafayette McLaws. Everyone seemed to have an axe to grind. Law believed he had been unfairly passed over for promotion, Robertson took Law's side and protested the unfair treatment, and McLaws, whom Longstreet accused of botching the capture of a Union fort on November 28, 1863, felt maligned and unjustly accused of mistakes that Longstreet himself had helped to put into motion. At a time when Longstreet should have been assuming responsibility for the failure of the East Tennessee campaign, he instead preferred charges against his three subordinates.

Feeling the burden of the fiasco at Knoxville, Longstreet realized that his experience as an independent commander had gone badly. Others also saw clearly that Longstreet did not measure up when he was left on his own. As Mary Boykin Chesnut, the famous Confederate diarist, recorded in her journal: "Detached from General Lee, what a horrible failure. What a slow old humbug is Longstreet."[20]

In his quest for independent command, Longstreet combined strategic thinking with his notion of gaining a command of his own in the West. He suggested to Lee, prior to his detachment to Suffolk in 1863, that he could lead the First Corps of the Army of Northern Virginia to reinforce Bragg in Tennessee, while Stonewall Jackson's corps stood its ground along the Rappahannock. Days later, Longstreet made it clear to Confederate Senator Louis Wigfall that he would be willing to accept a command in the West. By concentrating its force in Tennessee, reasoned Longstreet, the Confederacy could overwhelm Union General William Rosecrans's army there and regain its losses in that state. Lee, for his part, rejected Longstreet's suggestion by sending his two divisions to Suffolk and not to Tennessee.

Longstreet, however, was determined to push his plan further. On May 6, Longstreet met in Richmond with James A. Seddon, the Confederate secretary of war, to discuss the military situation in the West, the precarious state of affairs at Vicksburg, and Longstreet's own ideas about how these matters could be properly resolved. Already Lee had expressed disapproval of sending any of his divisions to reinforce Bragg and divert Grant's attention away from Vicksburg. Despite Lee's stand, Longstreet proposed his concentration plan to Seddon. As he saw it, once Rosecrans was whipped in Tennessee, a combined Confederate force could then invade Kentucky, forcing Grant to lift the siege at Vicksburg. In the end, President Davis sided with Lee and ordered Longstreet's divisions back to the Army of Northern Virginia. That decision, in turn, resulted in Longstreet's presence in the Army of Northern Virginia as Lee led it north into Pennsylvania in the summer of 1863.

The stage was thus set for the thunderous clash between Longstreet and Lee over the Gettysburg campaign. Here, then, is the controversy that, more than any other one involving Longstreet and his role in the Civil War, continues to mark the man and cast a gloomy pall over his actions on that famous battlefield—and over the defense of his actions that he so vociferously propounded until the day he died. Having failed to convince Lee or the Confederate high command that the western armies should be reinforced, Longstreet maintained that he extracted from Lee a promise to conduct a campaign during the Northern invasion of 1863 that would be "offensive in strategy but defensive in tactics, forcing the Federal army to give us battle when we were in strong position and ready to receive them."[21] If Lee did agree to such an approach in the coming campaign, he probably did not consider it a promise.

When the Army of Northern Virginia and the Army of the Potomac converged on Gettysburg during the first three days of July, Longstreet tried repeatedly to maneuver the army into a position either where the enemy would be forced to attack the Confederates or where Lee's forces could sweep around the flank of the Union army, but Lee would not hear of it. "The enemy is here," said Lee to Major General John Bell Hood, one of Longstreet's subordinates, "and if we do not whip him, he will whip us."[22] Lee's battle plan for the second day at Gettysburg particularly disturbed Longstreet, who argued strenuously with his commander to reconsider an attack that was meant to roll up the Union left flank. When Lee stood his ground, Longstreet knew he had no choice but to carry out his orders as faithfully as possible. The fighting on the second day resulted in some minimal Confederate gains along the Emmitsburg Road, but the lateness of Longstreet's attack made some of his fellow Confederates argue, long after the war had ended, that he had apathetically followed Lee's orders that day.

On the third day at Gettysburg, Lee decided to launch a bold frontal attack against the Union center, and once again Longstreet protested against such a risky assault. If Longstreet's own account can be believed, and there's no real reason to doubt its accuracy, he forcefully confronted Lee with objections to a massed attack through open ground, pointing out that "the conditions were different from those in the days of Napoleon, when field batteries had a range of six hundred yards and musketry about sixty yards." Finally, said Longstreet, Lee became "impatient of listening, and tired of talking, and nothing was left but to proceed."[23] Pickett's Charge, which the veterans often referred to as Longstreet's Assault, became the most famous charge in American history, and one of the worst disasters ever experienced by the soldiers of Lee's Army of Northern Virginia. The repulse of the Confederate onslaught on Cemetery Ridge ended the battle of Gettysburg and Lee's invasion of the North. "Never was I so depressed as upon that day," wrote Longstreet in a newspaper article published long after the battle.[24]

But it was Lee who assumed full responsibility for the defeat at Gettysburg; it was Lee who consoled his men as they limped back to the Confederate lines from Cemetery Ridge by telling them, "All of this has been my fault."[25] Nor did Southerners at the time blame Longstreet for the loss at Gettysburg. It might have remained that way, in fact, if Longstreet had not decided after the war to reveal the details of his debate with Lee over tactics during the Pennsylvania invasion and, more significantly, if he had not chosen to criticize Lee in the process.

In an interview with a Northern journalist, William Swinton, Longstreet made public his claim of Lee's promise to fight on the defensive during the Gettysburg campaign and his own disapproval of Lee's decision to attack the Union center on July 3. Swinton incorporated Longstreet's comments in a history of the Army of the Potomac, published in 1866, but while Lee remained alive no Southerners voiced any complaints about Longstreet's views on Gettysburg. Two years after Lee's death in 1870, however, former Confederates such as General Jubal Early, General William Pendleton, and Walter Taylor, one of Lee's staff officers during the war, began a broadside assault against Longstreet, his objections to Lee's conduct during the Gettysburg campaign, and the role he had played in bringing about the Confederate defeat in Pennsylvania. This Lee Cult, as it has now become known to historians, sought to silence any criticism of its revered general and to elevate him to an untouchable pedestal of fame and glory—an everlastingly noble symbol of the Lost Cause. To do so, the Lee defenders found that Longstreet was a convenient scapegoat for explaining the defeat at Gettysburg and for ensuring that Lee, despite the general's own admission to his men, would not be blamed for losing the battle that, in the estimation of many Southerners, had decided the outcome of the entire war.

Despite many attempts, Longstreet could never get across the idea that he and Lee had worked well together during the war, had enjoyed a close relationship, and did not regard one another as adversaries. Wrote Longstreet of his dealings with Lee: "The relations existing between us were affectionate, confidential, and even tender, from first to last. There was never a harsh word between us."[26] He proudly noted that throughout their campaigning together, Lee "usually had his headquarters near mine."[27] Lee's fondness for Longstreet was genuine. While Longstreet was on detached service in the West, Lee wrote him: "I missed you dreadfully and your brave corps. Your cheerful face and strong arm would have been invaluable. I hope you will return to me."[28] But few members of the Lee Cult believed that Longstreet held any sincere devotion to his commander.

Longstreet inadvertently played into the hands of his foes and gave them grist for their mill. His gruff ways and unpolished manners—hold-overs from his boyhood days in frontier Georgia—made him appear un-like the romantic image of a Southern cavalier. His ambition as an officer, particularly in the service of the Confederacy, made his desire for inde-pendent command look like an expression of disloyalty to his command-ing officer, Lee. His questioning of Lee's tactical decisions made Long-street look foolish and moronic, for Lee was regarded by Southerners as a military genius, which Longstreet clearly was not.

His lack of writing and rhetorical skills (he had been a poor student at West Point) revealed that he was not a strong contender when it came to a war of words. From time to time, Longstreet, realizing this shortcoming in himself, hired ghost writers and editors to help him put his arguments down on paper. As a result, numerous errors—the work of either care-less hired hands or Longstreet's fallible memory—found their way into his writings and hurt his effort to wrangle effectively with his assailants. His exaggerated claims for himself and his arrogant opinions convinced many of his readers that he was simply a prevaricator or a blowhard. Somehow Longstreet's opponents always seemed to have the upper hand and to speak the last word.

Not only did Longstreet dare to criticize the saintly Lee, but his political inconstancy convinced his fellow Southerners that he was a traitor to their cause. When asked in 1867 by a New Orleans newspaper to comment on Reconstruction policy in the South, Longstreet surprised everyone by re-minding his fellow Southerners that "we are a conquered people." Because the North had won the war "fairly and squarely," the South could follow only one course alone: accept the terms "that are now offered by the con-querors."[29] So committed was he to this policy that he decided to join ranks with the Republicans, and he said so in a public letter printed first in a New Orleans newspaper in June 1867 and then reprinted in papers and journals published around the country. Reactions in the South were im-mediate and damning. Longstreet was vilified as a traitor and a scalawag; he even received several death threats. In his naïveté, he could not under-stand what he had done to provoke such animosity. To Thomas Goree, he explained that he had only wanted to keep "the South out of the troubles that she has passed through since, and that was about the extent of my in-terest in affairs of state."[30]

Compounding his sin, Longstreet accepted a political appointment as surveyor of customs for the port of New Orleans from his close friend in the Old Army, Ulysses S. Grant, who had been elected president in the election of 1868. In 1873, the Republican governor of Louisiana placed Longstreet in command of the New Orleans militia, comprised mostly of blacks, and its Metropolitan Police Force. In a riot between the White League and the city's police and militia, Longstreet was wounded and taken prisoner by the rioters. Order was restored only when President Grant sent in federal troops.

In the late 1870s, after moving back to Georgia, Longstreet won appointments from the Hayes administration as a deputy collector of internal revenue and a postmaster. Longstreet's most important appointment came in 1880, when President Hayes named him minister to Turkey, a job the former Confederate did not enjoy; he spent most of his short sojourn abroad biding his time until he could return to Georgia. Back in the states, he accepted an appointment from President James Garfield as U.S. marshal for Georgia. In the late 1890s, when the Republicans regained the White House, Longstreet was named United States commissioner of railroads.

His string of Republican positions over the years did not endear him to white Southerners or, especially, to the Lee Cult of former Confederates. Although Longstreet remained a popular figure at Confederate reunions and other veterans' meetings, he found himself being cheered the loudest by Union veterans and the Northern authors of Civil War histories. As if his Republicanism and his heretical criticism of Lee were not enough, Longstreet also managed to alienate white Southern Protestants when, in 1877, he left the Episcopal Church and joined the Roman Catholic Church. His second wife, Helen Dortsch, whom he married in 1897, explained that Longstreet's conversion came about because many of his Episcopal associates refused to occupy the same pew with him after he had taken up the Republican cause. He remained a devout Catholic until his death in 1904.

In his later years, the Civil War continued to take its toll on him. He had been severely wounded in the Wilderness on May 6, 1864, mistakenly shot by a Virginia regiment; as a result, he lost nearly all use of his right arm and suffered from a throat wound that never fully healed. As an old man, he became deaf and lost some of his eyesight to cancer. In Gainesville, Georgia, he ran a small hotel. Occasionally he could be seen tending the vineyards near his modest home, dressed in a white linen coverall, hunched over as he pruned the vines, his white hair and ample white whiskers glistening bright in the southern sun.

It was a strikingly different picture than the one painted years before by Thomas Goree of the feisty general who, with lighted cigar in his mouth, went galloping into the heat of battle, swinging his sword above his head and beckoning his men onward. That image of Longstreet is the one that has been most readily forgotten since the days of the Civil War, lost in the mist of postwar controversy and under the shroud of Longstreet's own tergiversations. Even if Longstreet lacked direction as a young officer in the Old Army, even if he became carried away with ambitious thoughts of promotion and independent command in the service of the Confederacy, even if his postwar political activities defied the acceptable norms set forth by the white Southern establishment, even if he dared to criticize the military wisdom of Robert E. Lee, the fact remains that the thing Longstreet did best in life was to lead men into battle.

Some men are born to war. An aide, Moxley Sorrel, once observed that Longstreet was an "undismayed warrior." When in the blaze of battle, when the whole world seemed to be coming apart at its seams, Longstreet remained cool and calm. "He was like a rock in steadiness," said Sorrel. Longstreet came alive on the battlefield.[31] He was a true warrior, a beacon of courage and inspiration to his men. His record of heroism in the Mexican War, and his record of victories for the Confederacy in the Civil War, are testaments to his ability as a warrior.

All things considered, it was Longstreet's métier as a pure fighter, a warrior in the truest sense, that made him a great general. Every general makes mistakes. Longstreet certainly made his share of them. But in battle after battle, he proved how effective he could be as the staff in Lee's right hand. His gruff manners were not only a mark of his frontier upbringing; they revealed, perhaps too distinctly for some of his comrades, that he was unable to perfect a genteel mask for his warrior self.

But, sadly, he was a warrior who could wield only a sword; he had no ability with the pen. When it came time to do battle with the Lee cult, confronting fellow generals who had—to a man—proven themselves to be mediocre officers on the real battlefields of the war, Longstreet was outmaneuvered and outgunned. He was, quite frankly, out of his element. James Longstreet belonged on a battlefield. When there were no real wars to fight, when all the real battles were finished, Longstreet wandered about in life rather aimlessly, searching for himself and for his rightful place in the world.

There were some special places where he had shown his true warrior colors: Monterey, Churubusco, Chapultepec, First Manassas, the Peninsula, Second Manassas, Fredericksburg, Chickamauga, and the Wilderness. At Appomattox, it was Longstreet who asked Lee to delay, just even for a little while, before going over to see Grant. Small wonder. With the end of the Civil War, Longstreet the warrior disappeared almost entirely from view. Without war, Longstreet became someone other than the soldier he truly was. Today it is the man of inconstancy, the man of controversy, who stands now on the historical stage, waiting for scorn to be heaped on him repeatedly by those who see him as a Judas in the passion play of the South's Lost Cause. In forgetting that Longstreet was actually a rare breed, a man who was a natural warrior, a man who experienced his finest moments in the brutality of combat, a man whose instincts were so finely honed that he seemed in the swirl of battle to behave with the steadiness and dependability of an old war horse, we have forgotten who Longstreet truly was.

2   Frank A. Haskell:
Tragic Hero of the Union

If James Longstreet's inconstancy set a pattern in his life, just the opposite was true of Lieutenant Frank A. Haskell, a Union officer who watched
as Longstreet's butternut ranks streamed toward Cemetery Ridge on the
afternoon of July 3, 1863. Haskell, a studious lawyer from Vermont by way
of Wisconsin, who served as an aide to Union Brigadier General John Gibbon at Gettysburg, always walked the straight and narrow path toward
what he desired. There was no doubt in his mind, no misgiving in his
heart. As he stood at the center of the Union line on Cemetery Ridge, mar-
veling at the sight before him, he did not want to be any other place on
earth. He understood, as other perfect soldiers at Gettysburg also seemed
to realize, that this battle would go down in history as a milestone. The
war had reached its turning point, and Lieutenant Frank Haskell instinc-
tively knew it.

In a letter to his brother written after the battle, Haskell described the
scene in vivid detail: "More than half a mile their front extends, more than
a thousand yards the dull gray masses deploy, man touching man, rank
pressing rank, and line supporting line. Their red flags wave; their horsemen gallop up and down; the arms of eighteen thousand men, barrel and
bayonet, gleam in the sun, a sloping forest of flashing steel. Right on they
move as with one soul . . . magnificent, grim, irresistible."[1]

Haskell's long letter, which has been published in numerous book editions since its first appearance in print in 1881, is ranked today by historians as one of the best and most reliable accounts of the Union repulse
of Pickett's Charge, which many Civil War scholars often refer to as the
High Tide of the Confederacy, confirming Haskell's own suspicions that
this battle was like no other in the war. Haskell was there to see the high
tide swell and ebb before his eyes, and he could not put out of his mind
the horror and the majesty of the mighty storm that had swirled around
him. Luckily for posterity, he also had a way with words and the very good
sense to commit to paper all that he had seen and heard at Gettysburg. In

Bruce Catton's opinion, Haskell's account is "one of the great, almost unknown books to come out of the Civil War."[2]

Although Haskell is best known for his famous letter about Gettysburg, his career as an officer in the Union Army of the Potomac is less well remembered. His story is both heroic and ironic, for his tragic death on a battlefield in Virginia nearly a year after Gettysburg occurred in an attack that proved to be as futile and costly for the Federal army as Pickett's Charge had been for the Confederate Army of Northern Virginia in Pennsylvania. His death also took place just at the moment when Haskell was coming into his own as an officer and as a battle-hardened veteran. When the Army of the Potomac lost Haskell, it lost one of its best—a perfect hero who was, like all the young men who fell in this war, irreplaceable.

The road that led Franklin Aretas Haskell to war was a long one that wound from the viridescent mountains of Vermont to the flat midlands of Wisconsin and then on to the fields of battle in Virginia and Pennsylvania. He was born in 1828 in Tunbridge, Vermont, the son of a prosperous farmer. Haskell's bloodline was pure New England through and through, and he spent his childhood at East Hill, the family farm, learning to honor God, his parents, and his country. He attended a district school in winter and a "select" school in autumn until he was seventeen, when he took over as the local schoolmaster. His brother, Harrison Haskell, said that young Frank's desire to teach was fairly predictable—"the almost inevitable fate of all New England boys of any promise."[3]

Haskell's older brother became a strong influence over him. In 1848, Harrison persuaded Frank to leave Vermont and move to Columbus, Wisconsin, where Harrison had established a law practice and could keep a watchful eye over his brother. Under Harrison's tutelage, Frank began to prepare himself for college, an arduous task that involved hours of reading, studying, and recitation. He was a good student, particularly well read in history and literature.

Despite the long hours devoted to books and learning, Frank Haskell also spent time serving the community of Columbus, where the residents had come to know him as an industrious and ambitious young man. In October 1849, he was appointed town clerk; one month later he became superintendent of common schools. The following spring, he won election in his own right to the clerkship of the town. No doubt his brother, who was a prominent member of the community and a distinguished parishioner of the Congregational Church, helped Haskell to meet the right people and take advantage of opportunities as they came along. But Frank won his own laurels. As his brother described him, he was "better posted than most boys his age and station, for he always had had an eager thirst for knowledge and access to good books, which he read and remembered."[4] Haskell stood firmly on his own two feet.

The two years he spent in Columbus paid off for him. In 1850, he entered Dartmouth College as a freshman. Yet getting to college and staying there were two different matters. He quickly discovered that all his strenuous preparation did him little good in several of his courses. During his first year, his grades were as low as his spirits. To remedy the situation, he threw himself more completely into his studies, determined to get higher grades in all his subjects. According to Harrison Haskell, Frank's "indomitable will and industry" enabled him to improve his grades and achieve a ranking that gave him "a respectable position in his class." He worked hard and won the respect of his teachers and classmates, who admired him "for his excellent literary and poetic tastes, for his general intelligence, [and for his] good judgment and common sense."[5]

But not everyone saw Frank Haskell through the same lens. One teacher remarked that he was an excellent student, but that he was as "ambitious as Lucifer."[6] Haskell's New England ethic, which had been handed down through generations of Puritans and their descendants, called on each individual to work hard, make something of himself, and always strive to improve himself. At Dartmouth, Haskell broadened his understanding of himself and the world around him by joining a debating society, teaching district school again in the winters, serving on class committees, and discharging the duties of class president. But ambition was less of a problem for Haskell than was his general air of superiority. An imperious manner made him seem condescending to those around him. He obviously thought highly of himself and of his accomplishments, but he did not always win the respect and admiration that he felt should be his.

In July 1854, Haskell was graduated from Dartmouth with "distinguished honors."[7] He returned to Wisconsin, settling in Madison, the state capital, and studied law in the offices of a prominent firm. He was admitted to the bar in 1856, and quickly became a junior partner in a law practice established by a fellow Vermonter, Julius P. Atwood. Like most lawyers of the time, Haskell turned to politics, and he ran unsuccessfully for mayor of Madison on the Republican ticket. He was also a founder of the Governor Guards, a volunteer militia company. Without much effort, Haskell rose quickly through the ranks. In 1860, after having served for two years in the Guards, he was commissioned a first lieutenant.

As an officer, he followed the rules unquestioningly and without much flexibility. The men who served under him regarded him as a martinet. One soldier in the Guards later accused Haskell of having "little sympathy for a raw soldier, no matter how much he was suffering from heat, dust and thirst when on duty or on the march."[8] Around the streets of Madison, Haskell led his troops on marches to nowhere, always insisting on strict discipline and a spit-and-polish appearance among the men in the ranks. No doubt Haskell knew little about military regulations or the manual of arms. What he did know was that his men were obliged to obey his commands, and he seemed to thrive on the power that came with his authority as an officer.

Haskell, to be sure, cut a fine figure as an officer. Tall and trim, he looked like the beau ideal of a military man. He was not particularly handsome (he had a thin face, a weak chin, and a receding hairline that made him look older than his years), but he knew how to strike a military pose to great effect. His hazel eyes glowed with a look of fierce determination and ambitious intent. Here was a man who was going places. Success had come easily to Frank Haskell during most of his life, and even as a militia officer he expected to achieve more than most other men had desired for themselves.

His ambition—which burned as intensely for him as Longstreet's had done—meant that he must take careful steps to ensure high rank and advancement in the militia. When the Civil War broke out in 1861, it was Haskell's ambition that kept him from marching off to war with the Governor Guards. He waited for the right opportunity that would give him a position prominent enough to satisfy his ambition. Not that he lacked patriotic fervor. The firing on Fort Sumter in April 1861 angered him as much as it did practically everyone in the North, but he did not enlist in the war effort until the following June, when he was commissioned a first lieutenant and adjutant of the 6th Wisconsin Infantry.

At Camp Randall, outside Madison's city limits, Haskell instructed company officers and their men in the fundamentals of drill and discipline. Rufus S. Dawes, who later assumed command of the regiment, recalled Haskell and his efforts as drill master: "He took great interest and pride in the instruction of the regiment, and so elevated his office, that some men then thought the Adjutant must at least be next to the Colonel in authority and rank."[9] Dawes's remark, of course, revealed the resentment that other officers felt toward Haskell, who was perceived as haughty and too full of himself. Many men in the regiment also believed that Haskell's prim-and-proper adherence to rules bordered on the ridiculous. Haskell went so far as to require the troops to wear white cotton gloves while on duty. The gloves were to be kept "snow white" at all times, but naturally no one in camp could keep his gloves clean. As Dawes ruefully noted, "Fancy uniforms are useless sleeping in the mud."[10] It did not take long for Haskell to rescind the order about the gloves.

After the battle of Bull Run in late July 1861, the 6th Wisconsin received orders to join in the defense of Washington, D.C. The job of guarding the city put few demands on the regiment, and the men spent most of their time as they had in Wisconsin—drilling, drilling, and drilling some more. Haskell must have been in his glory. Boredom began to set in throughout the regiment until autumn arrived, when the 6th Wisconsin was assigned to a brigade that included the 2nd and 7th Wisconsin and the 19th Indiana regiments, the only brigade in the Army of the Potomac made up exclusively of regiments from the western states. In time, the brigade would earn a formidable reputation on the battlefield and would become known as the Iron Brigade.

While Haskell and everyone else in the Army of the Potomac waited during the final months of 1861 and the early months of 1862 for Major General George B. McClellan to move against the Confederates in Virginia, Haskell spent his time trying to gain higher rank. He used his influential friends in Madison to put pressure on the Republican governor of Wisconsin, Louis P. Harvey, but his hopes for advancement evaporated when Harvey died suddenly in the spring of 1862. Haskell did win a reassignment that spring, when he was appointed aide-de-camp to General Gibbon, commander of the western brigade, but he remained a lowly lieutenant despite the change in his duties.

Still hoping to win a field-grade commission in the 6th Wisconsin, or in any Wisconsin regiment, Haskell got his political friends to put his name before the new governor, Edward Saloman, a Milwaukee Democrat. Saloman, who detested the Republican power brokers in the state capital, complained that he had been openly harassed by Haskell's supporters. As a result, he gave the only available commission in the 6th Wisconsin to Rufus Dawes. Haskell was enraged over the outcome. "If I could win myself some great battle alone," he wrote home to his family, "and then could blow in the papers, and pay newspapers to blow for me, and then was besides a d—d politician, I suppose I could be promoted."[11]

Yet his situation was not completely dismal. As Gibbon's aide, he held a position of high visibility and weighty responsibility. The two men became close friends and worked exceptionally well together. Haskell learned a great deal from Gibbon, a regular army officer who had seen service in the Mexican War. "He is a most excellent officer," Haskell told his family, "and is beloved and respected by his whole command."[12]

By the end of the summer of 1862, Gibbon's brigade finally got a chance to prove itself on the battlefield. And Haskell got the opportunity to taste combat for the first time. At the battles of Gainesville and Second Bull Run in late August, the brigade passed its first tests under fire. Haskell learned his own hard lessons about the reality of war. What shocked and surprised him, beyond what he had expected to experience, was the despondency that came after a battle. It was difficult, he said, to "look upon our thinned ranks—so full the night before, now so shattered—without tears."[13]

There were more lessons to follow. At South Mountain on September 14, as McClellan's army positioned itself to stop Lee's invasion of Maryland, Gibbon's brigade slogged its way up to the heights of Turner's Gap, scrambling up the slopes in the face of flashing musket fire and searing artillery blasts, and dislodged the enemy from the crest. It was during this engagement that the brigade deservedly won its laurels and its celebrated name, the Iron Brigade. Three days later, in the bloodiest day of the entire war, Gibbon's ranks faced a maelstrom of fire and lead as they advanced toward the Confederate lines near Antietam Creek. While delivering a message to Major General Joseph Hooker, Haskell had his horse shot from under him. Over the green rolling hills and broad fields of Antietam, the day's slaughter was horrible. The Iron Brigade lost 47.5 percent of its men among the dead and wounded that day.

War changes every life it touches, and this war, this cataclysm of flames and tears, was changing Frank Haskell's life in ways no one could have anticipated. The world looked different to him now: gone were the pretensions of white gloves and orderly drills on the parade field. The soldiers who fought the war, who risked and lost their lives in battle after battle, took on a different appearance to him. Through the smoke of battle, the soldiers began to look like the Visigoths of old: "The dust and blackness of battle were upon their clothes, and in their hair, and on their skin, but you saw none of these; you saw only their eyes, and the shadows of the 'light of battle,' and the furrows plowed upon cheeks that were smooth the day before, and now not half filled up."[14]

And something else was happening to Haskell, something deep inside him, something that war does to those who engage in its brutality and witness its terrors. While he maintained his straight-laced military posture, he was becoming a warrior, a soldier who could unflinchingly look death in the eye, a fighter who could inflict death upon his foe without hesitating, a man who could call up violence from within himself and use it unsparingly against his enemy. At Antietam, during the peak of the fighting, Haskell rallied a New York regiment by seizing its battle flag and leading the troops himself into the fray. It was an uncommon act of valor for a staff officer who had always stayed a safe distance behind the front lines. He was lucky to have survived the holocaust of Antietam, but he apparently was unfazed by the danger around him. "I have not been afraid of anything in battle," he declared. "One does not mind the bullets and shells much," he added matter-of-factly, "but [one] only looks to the men and the enemy to see that all is right."[15]

He was growing fond of battle, an eerie affection that Robert E. Lee once acknowledged to be a soldier's peculiar—and disturbing—emotion.[16] During the lull between battles, Haskell became restless and yearned for another fight. The battles he had seen and survived were not enough for him. In one letter to his family, he confessed: "I want something more—a great, terrible, thundering battle, not for the fight but for victory, and victory not for fame but for peace."[17] The words he used masked the deeper feelings, which he claimed not to have. What he wanted most of all was to be in combat, for he had come to discover a new, exhilarating side of himself in the midst of singing bullets and whistling shells.

In December, another battle came when the Union Army of the Potomac at Fredericksburg nearly annihilated itself in endless blue waves that assaulted the fortified Confederate position along Marye's Heights. Gibbon fell wounded during the battle, and Haskell, who got through the engagement unharmed, won a furlough for the duration of Gibbon's recuperation. Home to Wisconsin went Haskell, and he spent the winter telling his tales of adventure to his family and friends. In the spring, after Gibbon recovered from his wound and took over the Second Division of the Second Corps, Haskell returned to the army and stayed on as Gibbon's aide.

On May 3, 1863, while the rest of the Army of the Potomac, now under the command of Hooker, staggered in a daze from the devastating blow that Lee and Jackson had brilliantly executed at Chancellorsville, Gibbon's division was part of a Union column that attacked Lee's right at Fredericksburg and, this time, successfully swept the Confederates off Marye's Heights overlooking the town. But the battle, which ended in a Union defeat, did not satisfy Haskell's longings for a decisive contest with the enemy. With the opposing armies occupying their lines along the Rappahannock and uneasily facing one another in their rifle pits, Haskell predicted that "we shall be up to something soon."[18] The armies could not sit looking at each other indefinitely. He was right. In June, Lee began to move his army into Maryland and Pennsylvania, and the Army of the Potomac, first under Hooker and then under Major General George Gordon Meade, took careful steps north to find the Confederates and stop them.

It was at Gettysburg, during the first three days of July, that Haskell's wish for a great and terrible battle was finally granted. When Lee's Army of Northern Virginia collided at last with Meade's Army of the Potomac, the gentle farmland of Pennsylvania was ripped apart, and the tiny town of Gettysburg would never be the same. All through the first two days of July, the Union and Confederate armies struggled for possession of local patches of earth that would later become battlefield landmarks—McPherson's Ridge, Cemetery Hill, Little Round Top, and Devil's Den. The losses on both sides were appalling. At the end of the three days, when Lee decided to lead his battered army back to Virginia, more than fifty-one thousand Union and Confederate soldiers were dead, wounded, or missing. Gettysburg was, by any measure, a devastating and decisive turning point in American history.

And Haskell was there to see it all and to witness its bloody climax. On the afternoon of July 3, he and a few fellow officers managed to rustle up some food and sat quietly under the hot sun eating their lunch on Cemetery Ridge, near a clump of trees at the center of the Union line. After finishing their lunch, the officers—including Meade and Gibbon and four other generals—relaxed in the warmth of the summer's day. "We dozed in the heat and lolled upon the ground, with half-opened eyes," Haskell reported.[19] After two days of horrific fighting at Gettysburg, the tranquility of the afternoon was a great relief.

The stillness was suddenly shattered at one o'clock. Just as Haskell was checking his watch, the silence was broken by the low boom of cannon and the high scream of shells. All at once, artillery along the Confederate line on Seminary Ridge, about a mile west of the Union line, roared and shook the ground. Almost immediately the Union guns replied in earnest, and the greatest artillery duel every to take place on the North American continent was exploding across the Pennsylvania countryside.

It was like nothing Haskell—or anyone else on that battlefield—had ever experienced before. "The guns," Haskell wrote in his famous letter to his brother, "are great infuriate demons, not of the earth, whose mouths blaze with smoky tongues of living fire, and whose murky breath, sulphur-laden, rolls around them and along the ground, the smoke of Hades." The noise of the cannonade was deafening and unnerving. "The projectiles," wrote Haskell, "shriek long and sharp: they hiss, they scream, they growl, they sputter—all sounds of life and rage; and each has its different note, and all are discordant."[20]

The cannonade lasted nearly two numbing hours. At about three o'clock in the afternoon, Haskell wrote, "the last shot hummed, and bounded, and fell." Silence returned to the fields of Gettysburg. Haskell interpreted it as an interval, like an intermission at the theater: "There was a pause between acts with the curtain down, soon to rise upon the great, final act and catastrophe of Gettysburg."[21]

Through the blue haze, when the Confederate infantry lines came into view, long gray lines of men marching under the azure banners of Virginia and the red battle flags of the Confederacy, the Union soldiers assembled along the crest of Cemetery Ridge could hardly believe their eyes. Few times during that war, or in any war before or since, was there ever such a spectacle as this. It was glory and majesty. It was shining elegance and martial splendor. It was the charge to end all charges. Some Union men held their breath; others unwittingly moaned.

For Haskell, and for many others that day, it seemed as if the Confederates were marching on dress parade. With admiration, Haskell the former adjutant watched the gray and butternut lines assemble in front of the trees on the opposite ridge. "Every eye," wrote Haskell, "could see his legions, an overwhelming, resistless tide of an ocean of army men sweeping upon us! Regiment after regiment, and brigade after brigade, move from the woods and rapidly take their places in the lines forming the assault."[22] But this was no parade or pageant. Through the lingering smoke that clung to the ground with cat's paws, the Confederates marched with grim determination across the golden fields of wheat and sorghum toward the ridge beyond.

As soon as the enemy came within range, the Union guns bellowed and tore gaping holes through the Confederate lines. "All our available guns are now active," Haskell reported, "and from the fire of shells, as the range grows shorter and shorter, they change to shrapnel, and from shrapnel to canister; but in spite of shells and shrapnel and canister, without wavering or halt, the hearty lines of the enemy continue to move on."[23]

It seemed like nothing could stop them. "And so across all that broad open ground they have come," he observed, "nearer and nearer, nearly half the way with our guns bellowing in their faces, until now a hundred yards, no more, divide our ready left from their advancing right. The eager men there are impatient to begin. Let them." All long the front, the Union infantry opened fire. The volleys blazed and rolled, said Haskell, "as thick the sound as when a summer hail storm pelts the city roofs, as thick the fire as when an incessant lightning fringes a summer cloud."[24]

Yet the Confederates moved ever forward, undeterred by the fury that greeted them, hunched over as if walking against a winter's wind. Finally, the big push came, and some of the Confederates poured over the stone wall at the angle and broke through the Union line. As the men crashed together, they produced not a bellow or a boom, but a mean, awful growl. Haskell could not forget the hideous sound: "The frequent dead and wounded lie where they stagger and fall; there is no humanity for them now, and none can be spared to care for them. The men do not cheer or shout—they growl; and over that uneasy sea, heard with the roar of musketry, sweeps the muttered thunder of a storm of growls."[25]

On horseback, with his sword drawn and his eyes fixed upon the enemy, Haskell watched in disbelief as the Confederate wave crashed against the stone wall and the makeshift breastworks along the crucial stretch of ridge in front of a copse of trees. Just as the Confederate surge took place, the line of the Union's Philadelphia Brigade, a crack unit that had been thrown off balance by the mighty gray thrust, wavered and fell back. Ever the good officer, the perfect hero, Haskell knew what to do, and he helped shore up the brigade's line and prevent a rout. "On some unpatriotic backs, of those not quick of comprehension," he said disparagingly of the Philadelphia Brigade, "the flat of my saber fell, not lightly; and at its touch their love of country returned; and with a look at me as if I were the destroying angel, as I might have become theirs, they again faced the enemy."[26] Rallied and reformed by the quick actions of Brigadier General Alexander S. Webb, who commanded the Philadelphia Brigade and won a Congressional Medal of Honor for the defense of Cemetery Ridge against Pickett's Charge that day, the Union regiments behind the stone wall at the Angle held their line and repulsed the mangled Confederates.

But it was amazing how close the gray legions had come to defeating their foes, how the outcome had hung for a few bloody moments on, in Haskell's words, "a single spider's thread."[27] Truth be told, Haskell exaggerated—as perfect heroes tend to do—his own role in plugging up the Union line at the Angle, and he rather overstated the hysterical rout of the Philadelphia Brigade. While it is certain the brigade faltered, offering the Confederates a rather frightening, but only momentary, advantage, it must be said that Webb's command performed admirably that afternoon and never broke in the kind of pell-mell rush for the rear that Haskell had described. Long after the war, his words would arouse a firestorm of controversy and a spirited defense from the surviving members of the Philadelphia Brigade, all of whom felt unfairly treated by Haskell, the self-proclaimed hero of the day. Webb himself took offense at Haskell's account and claimed that it was written in ignorance.[28] Long after the fact, it does appear that Haskell unjustifiably painted a glamorous picture of himself on the battlefield while blackening the reputation of one of the army's best brigades. Nevertheless, he did behave heroically on Cemetery Ridge, there is no doubt to that, and Major General Winfield Scott Hancock, commander of the army's Second Corps, singled him out for praise.

Yet the Confederates did nearly succeed in their assault. Without Haskell and Webb and thousands of other heroes whose stories have been told over and over again, or whose unsung feats of bravery can only be imagined, the result on the afternoon of the third of July might have been different. If it seems today that Pickett's Charge was foolhardy, a mistake that was doomed to fail, one might easily draw a different conclusion from Haskell's own experience defending Cemetery Ridge. The Confederates came so close to winning the day, he said, that the Union defenders were stunned by their own victory. "The judgment," Haskell remembered, "almost refused to credit the senses."[29]

The great and terrible battle he had so desperately desired now left him speechless. "Many things cannot be described by pen or pencil—such a fight is one," he wrote. As with all battles and the sorrow they have wrought, the horror of Gettysburg escaped description and defied belief. "He who never saw," Haskell asserted, "can have no adequate idea of what such a battle is."[30] What's more, he said, no one will ever write a complete history of the battle of Gettysburg. Even the eyewitnesses, those lucky souls who somehow survived this tempest of death and destruction, would have a tough time grasping what this monstrous battle was all about. It was, he argued, impossible for the participants to see beyond the tiny portion of the battlefield they had personally occupied. No matter how hard anyone tried, Gettysburg could never be captured in words.

He could not have been more wrong, of course. Haskell's own words did not fail him. With facility of language and the poetry of words, his account of Gettysburg tells us what America's most famous and bloodiest battle was like. We will never know the true horrors he and his fellow soldiers witnessed, but it is just as well. The sight of all those dead and dying men, all the mutilated and all the maimed, would be more than we could humanly bear. Far better to let Haskell and his contemporaries speak to us from their distant places and with voiceless words, reassuring us that we will never comprehend the terrors and the hardships they had to endure.

During the fight on Cemetery Ridge, Gibbon was seriously wounded and taken from the field. Over the next few months, Haskell stayed with the Second Division as an aide to Brigadier General William Hays, who temporarily took over division command during Gibbon's absence. He later served briefly as an aide to Brigadier General Gouverneur K. Warren. In November, Haskell linked up with Gibbon again, who was now back on his feet, and they both reported to Cleveland, Ohio, where Gibbon had been ordered to take charge of conscripts.

Actually there was little for Gibbon and Haskell to do in Cleveland, so they journeyed together to see the battlefield at Gettysburg and to attend the dedication ceremonies of the Soldiers' National Cemetery there on November 19, 1863. Haskell thought the cemetery was an abomination, "a badly arranged graveyard" located where no real fighting had occurred. He thought it was preferable to bury soldiers where they had fallen on the field, and he did not understand why the Union dead could not have remained on the Gettysburg battlefield where their comrades had buried them last July. The idea of a landscaped cemetery, with rows of graves and markers, struck him as an unworthy memorial to the men who had died in this great battle. He regretted that everybody else seemed to think the cemetery was "splendid." Writing home the next day, Haskell made no mention of Lincoln's Gettysburg Address, although he and Gibbon most certainly heard the president deliver it.[31]

Gibbon was reassigned to Philadelphia, and Haskell went with him; Haskell stayed there until February 1864. During that winter, Haskell's thoughts turned once again to the prospect of promotion. "I desire promotion—am ambitious," he confessed to his brother Harrison, but he chose not to return to Wisconsin to work for his own advancement.[32] Still holding the rank of lieutenant, he swore that he would accept no promotion lower than that of full colonel. Harrison Haskell diligently bombarded the new administration with petitions and appeals in his brother's behalf, and a new governor pushed the commission through. In February, Frank finally got what he wanted when he was commissioned a colonel in the newly created 36th Wisconsin Infantry. By the end of February, Colonel

Haskell was in Wisconsin raising troops for the new regiment and training the men to be soldiers.

In May, the 36th Wisconsin was ordered to Virginia and joined the Army of the Potomac in its spring campaign against the Confederates. The campaign, which was being directed by Ulysses S. Grant, was already underway, and the army had already lost its first battle at the Wilderness. Despite the defeat, Grant pushed the Union army forward. Haskell and the 36th Wisconsin arrived in Virginia just in time to be placed in reserve during the next battle at Spotsylvania Court House, but the fresh regiment did not experience its first real combat until two weeks later, on May 31, at Bethesda Church.

Haskell was where he wanted to be, commanding his own troops in a war that was both terrible and great. But fate, as it turned out, proved to be ruthlessly unkind to him. On June 3, 1864, less than four months after Haskell's regiment was mustered into service, the 36th Wisconsin was chosen for extremely hazardous duty. It was assigned to be among the forward ranks that would strike Lee's defenses in a direct frontal attack at Cold Harbor. Early in the morning, Haskell moved his men forward in a grand assault that became a senseless slaughter, a pointless sacrifice of lives. It was like Pickett's Charge, only this time Haskell was with the long wavering lines that marched toward the enemy through open ground. This time Haskell and his men were learning what it was like to advance against a steady hail of shot and shell. This time Haskell was experiencing what it was like to be mowed down, rank after rank, brigade after brigade, regiment after regiment.

When his brigadier went down, Haskell assumed command, but the fire from the Confederate guns was ripping the ranks of the 36th Wisconsin to shreds. He ordered his men to lie down, and, under the circumstances, they quickly obeyed. But to set a good example for his men, Haskell remained standing, leaning on his sword, oblivious to the danger all around him, the very picture of the model officer—the perfect soldier—under fire. He did not stand there long. An instant later he was hit in the temple by a minié ball, and his body slumped to the ground. Mortally wounded, he was carried from the field by his orderly, who himself was wounded twice. Three hours later, Frank A. Haskell was dead. He was thirty-five years old.

His body was transported home to Portage, Wisconsin, where he was buried on June 12. Haskell's family, friends, and fellow soldiers could not hold back their grief. General Gibbon, hearing the news of Haskell's death, exclaimed: "My God! I have lost my best friend, and one of the best soldiers in the Army of the Potomac has fallen!" Hancock mournfully declared in a field order: "At Cold Harbor the Colonel of the Thirty-sixth Wisconsin, as gallant a soldier as ever lived, fell dead on the field." Haskell's eulogist, the Reverend A. J. M. Hudson, spoke of the young officer's bravery in battle and of the heroism he had particularly displayed in rallying troops to the defense of Cemetery Ridge at Gettysburg. "That one act," the Reverend Hudson proclaimed, "is fame enough for any man."[33]

Fame is always fleeting, however, and Haskell's name has never become widely known, except to the relatively small number of people who had heard about his deeds at Gettysburg or who have, in fact, read his own words describing the battle and the climatic repulse of Pickett's Charge. Of the millions of tourists who have visited the battlefield and have stood at the stone wall where Pickett's men crashed into the Union line, few have ever heard of Haskell or of what he did there. No marker at Gettysburg tells Haskell's story, no monument bears his name. His only memorial is the eloquent account of Gettysburg, his graphic picture in words of a great and terrible battle, that he bequeathed to posterity. For that one act of composition, rather than for any other individual deed in life, Frank Haskell is well remembered.

3 Becoming Joshua Lawrence Chamberlain

When it comes to Gettysburg heroes, Joshua Lawrence Chamberlain outshines all the rest. Although he was hardly the perfect soldier, modern Americans have come to see him as one. In the minds of many, he stands as the ultimate model of what a military hero should be. Yet Chamberlain's reputation was made over time; it did not spring forth fully formed, complete in all its glory and honor, from the head of Zeus or on the field of battle. Indeed, Joshua Chamberlain was actually an unlikely hero. But once he accepted the mantle of a perfect hero, he wore it proudly and for the rest of his life.

Soldiers are made, not born. Nothing in Joshua Lawrence Chamberlain's life prior to the Civil War suggested that he would one day become known as "the Hero of Little Round Top," that he would earn a Medal of Honor, and that he would gain great fame and even celebrity with a following of devoted admirers in his own lifetime and in our own modern age. Nothing that he achieved prior to the outbreak of the war seemed to prepare him for his moment of truth on the hillside at Little Round Top during the battle of Gettysburg on July 2, 1863, when his quick thinking and iron determination enabled his regiment, the 20th Maine Infantry, to hold the left flank of the Army of the Potomac and throw back a fierce enemy assault. In fact, Chamberlain's life during the antebellum years took him about as far afield of military matters and battlefield heroism as a man could get.

He was born, the eldest of five children, in Brewer, Maine, on the bright morning of September 8, 1828.[1] His father, Joshua, was a farmer who worked a spare one hundred acres of land that he had acquired from his own father, also named Joshua. Chamberlain's mother, Sarah Dupee Brastow of Massachusetts, was a descendant of Huguenots who had escaped persecution in France by fleeing to Boston in 1685. The Chamberlains named their first son Lawrence for the American navy hero of the War of 1812, Captain James Lawrence, the man who had told his men, "Don't give up the ship," as he lay dying on the decks of the warship *Chesapeake* during a desperate battle with the British on Lake Erie in 1813.[2]

Lawrence Chamberlain's given name broke with the family custom of naming the eldest son Joshua, after the Old Testament warrior who had knocked down the walls of Jericho. It was, apparently, his father's idea to name him after the naval hero, but the decision to sever the family tradition seems to have made Chamberlain's mother nervous. As a result, she changed his name to Joshua Lawrence several years after his birth when, in an act of loyalty "to her husband's house," she set the boy's name down in the Brewster record books as the third Chamberlain named for the ancient ruler of Israel. Despite the change, the family—including his mother—continued to call him Lawrence.[3]

Chamberlain's father tried to make a go of it as a farmer, but his tiny farm yielded small rewards. The elder Joshua was a good and honest man, a leading member of the community, and a devoted family man. In his later years, Joshua Lawrence fondly described his father as "a stalwart, earnest, thoughtful, inward-looking man," who seemed capable of accomplishing any task and doing so with "a deep vein of poetic imagination."[4]

Yet there was another side to his father that proved to be more difficult to reckon with. The elder Joshua often assumed a sober, strict, and even demanding mien. When it came to his children, and particularly to his sons (Joshua Lawrence had three younger brothers: Horace, John Calhoun, and Thomas), the father believed his place was not to instruct or guide, but to order them to fulfill their obligations, no matter how difficult those duties might be. The stories told about him hardly seem complimentary.

Joshua Lawrence experienced his father's gruff tendency to command rather than instruct when, during one haying season in his youth, the boy inadvertently drove a wagon through a stream bed and got a wheel caught between two stumps so that he could not move forward or backward. "Clear that wheel!" came his father's shout from behind. "How am I going to do it?" replied the boy. "Do it; that's how!" was the father's only answer. Joshua Lawrence eventually freed the wheel on his own. He had come to know the meaning of orders and how to obey them.[5]

In his childhood, Joshua Lawrence did those things that most boys living on a working farm must do: he cleared woods, plowed grasslands into crop fields, sowed and hoed the furrowed land, and harvested the crops. Looking back on his childhood through eyes that tended to sentimentalize his past and all of his agrarian experiences, Chamberlain sang lilting prose songs of his days on the family farm and remembered the "glory of that summer's work": "One would gladly be alone in such a service, when a field that had been associated with many works of youthful years was to be sealed down under a sod for the long, eventful years to come. To a thoughtful spirit, sowing is a solemn, caring, trustful service. It is a communion with all forces of the Universe."[6]

In later life, while writing his memoirs, he mentioned incidents of family fun, such as witty anecdotes about his youngest brother ("mother's pet") and "pretended jealousies" and allusions to merry occasions with the family assembled before the fire in the kitchen where games would be played, songs sung, pantomimes acted out, and popcorn popped, but the overwhelming impression Chamberlain left of his childhood was of the long hours he spent by himself.[7] In his own words, he lacked "self-assurance" and "self-assertion." He preferred to be by himself because he suffered from a speech impediment that made him appear, in his own estimation, stupid and uninformed. The effect of his stammer caused a "sleepless anxiety" that wore down his self esteem. He became almost incurably bashful.

His father, who was not at all bashful, decided to do something about his son's retiring ways. When Joshua Lawrence was fourteen years old, his father enrolled him in a military academy in Ellsworth, about twenty-five miles from the Brewer farm.[8] He stayed at Ellsworth's school for only a short time before his family called him home. His father, who had been speculating in timber lands, lost nearly everything he owned. Both of Chamberlain's parents reacted to the financial disaster by falling apart—his mother became bed-ridden with a spinal disorder; his father soon suffered a similar paralysis. According to Chamberlain, his father "appeared at first to be utterly broken in courage and at a loss [as to] which way to turn."[9]

The son came to the rescue. At once, Joshua Lawrence found work to bring in some money. For a while, he did some land surveying and cleared a wood lot for a neighbor. At a rope walk in Brewer, he hatcheled hemp and laid the mighty ropes and cables. He assisted a traveling medicine show by handing out liniment to buyers in the audience. He spent time working in a brickyard, where he arranged bricks in orderly rows or covered them up to protect them from threatening rain showers. Then he turned his attention to the farm itself, and took on all the "planting, ploughing, sowing, hoeing, haying, harvesting, threshing, husking, shelling, housing the fodder, and cellaring the vegetables."[10]

Chamberlain also took on less physical labor, although the work was demanding nevertheless. In 1844, he began teaching school in a remote rural area. He did so despite the fact that with all his success in the military academy, all his effort to elevate his family out of the pits of financial disaster and despair, all his courage and strength that enabled him to take on strenuous jobs of various kinds, he still was not, as he recalled in his later years, "very self-assured [in] any way."[11]

In the spring of 1846, at the age of eighteen, he returned home from his teaching assignments to the farm in Brewer. His mood was buoyant and optimistic. Most of all, he reveled in the opportunity to get back to nature, to shake off the cobwebs of the classroom and the dust of mill towns, and to smell and feel "the renovated earth." Nevertheless, his parents—who had by now recovered from their maladies—wanted to know what he would make of himself and how he planned to support himself.

His father, on the one hand, favored the army and saw his son attending West Point. Chamberlain thought his father's hopes for his future came from being impressed "by the examples and traditions cherished in his youth" (the same traditions that had led him to name his son after a hero of the War of 1812 in the first place) and from possessing "a chivalrous strain of blood in his composition." His mother, on the other hand, could not accept the army as a "profession" and wished for her son to enter the ministry instead. She argued that the military seemed "narrowing and enervating." In times of peace, the nobility of military service was lost; in wartime, it carried with it the obvious "unpleasant suggestions" of battle and death.

No one talked of his taking over the farm, or a portion of it, as his own. For all that Chamberlain had done to save his family's farm, there was no living there for him. Doubtless he did not see himself as a farmer anyway, no matter how eloquently he waxed about nature and its virtues. He would have to choose a profession for himself. The trouble was that he had no particular interest in either the military or the ministry. He was not, as he explained in his later years, "much inclined to either course," for they both offered "but little scope and freedom." He felt that the lives of military officers and clergymen "bound a man by rule and precedents and petty despotisms, and swamped his personality."[12]

He chose to postpone having to decide between the military or the ministry by declaring that he would attend Bowdoin College around the time of his nineteenth birthday, just slightly more than a year away. In the meantime, he worked diligently to prepare himself for entry into the college. He managed his time carefully by following a strict schedule that he kept pinned to his bookcase door. In the garret, he fixed up a study, where he found "perfect seclusion and self-command," two things that he valued very highly. He shut himself off in his room for long hours and practiced Greek from dawn until midnight. Occasionally his father would come up to the garret and the two of them would practice broadsword fencing.

Finally, in February 1848, his sponsor, William L. Hyde (Bowdoin, class of 1842), drove him south in a sleigh through miles of endless snow to Brunswick, a small lumbering and mill town near the northern reaches of Casco Bay, for his entrance examinations into Bowdoin. Chamberlain impressed the examining board and passed with something called "advanced standing" that would allow him to matriculate with the current freshman class. He was told to begin his formal studies at six o'clock on the following morning. His career at Bowdoin had begun.[13]

Chamberlain spent his first day at college, like most freshmen, in utter confusion, but things soon settled down for him. He endured some minor hazing and ardently applied himself to his studies. Though surrounded by the communities of the college and the town, Chamberlain described himself once more as being on his own "to face those fields where one must sow in tears that he may reap in joy; where ashes to ashes, dust to dust, and life for life must be given, so that life may be unto life." It was both a stern and a lofty metaphor for his isolated life at Bowdoin.

Not only studying consumed him. For his first two years at Bowdoin, he kept a Sunday school at a church two miles down the Bath road, where he walked in good weather and bad. He also taught school during winter vacations to "mostly grown-up sailor boys and mill men behind in studies but forward in manners." He did little socializing, kept mostly to himself, and worked hard at overcoming his speech impediment, which he finally conquered by using the technique of pretending he was about to sing instead of speak when a word beginning with a hard consonant threatened to trip him up. By his own measure, he led a spartan existence, occasionally working in the library as an assistant, attending dinners at the homes of professors, or going to church.[14]

In his second year, Chamberlain made some friends, who called him "Jack," but he refused to drink even a glass of cider, and he seems to have been something of a prude, a straitlaced fellow who got on his friends' nerves more than once. He continued to distance himself from his college chums, and they, in turn, kept secrets from him or refrained from telling certain stories in his presence. No doubt he was less popular than he thought. Chamberlain did, however, win the respect of his friends when he was called to the president's office and ordered to reveal the names of some boys who had raised hell during an arbor celebration. He decided to refuse on principle, informed the president that what was being asked of him was dishonorable, and walked out of the office fully prepared to take whatever punishment might come. In the end, his friends voluntarily turned themselves in so that Chamberlain would not be unduly disciplined.[15]

When his first two years were finished, he gratefully went home to Brewer for a three-week vacation. Just when everything seemed to be going so well, tragedy struck Chamberlain and sabotaged his studies. Sometime after his twenty-first birthday, he fell ill with fever and spent the next nine months laid up at home. (There was a disturbing pattern to illnesses in the Chamberlain family, which laid parents and children low in times of extreme stress.) His mother and sister Sarah (called Sae) cared for him and got him back on his feet. When he was ready to return to Bowdoin, however, he had totally missed his junior year, so he was forced to take his third year of studies with an entirely different class, the class of 1852.

He quickly got back into the grind of studying, however, and his junior year was spent mostly with his head in his books. During his senior year, however, he enjoyed a number of "distractions," as he called them, that took his mind off studying and gave him something to do besides school work. At the First Parish Church, he became "conductor" of the church choir and an occasional organist. At the college, he joined a literary society called the Round Table that met every fortnight to read and discuss original papers on various topics.[16]

His fondest distraction of all was the "Saturday Evenings" club he attended at the home of Harriet Beecher Stowe, the daughter of the prominent minister Lyman Beecher and the wife of Calvin Stowe, a portly professor of theology at the college. During the long winter nights of howling winds and drifting snows in Brunswick, Hattie Stowe, who had a flair for words, worked on her literary pieces. In response to the Fugitive Slave Law of 1850, which empowered the federal government to assist in the return of runaway slaves to their rightful owners, she began writing a novel that she hoped would reveal once and for all the evils of slavery. By April 1851, she had finished the first chapter of a serialized novel called *Uncle Tom's Cabin.*

On Saturday evenings at the Stowe house, Chamberlain and the assembled multitudes—students, faculty, friends of the family—heard Mrs.

Stowe read aloud chapters from her novel, which she completed in the spring of 1852. The book seems not to have impressed Chamberlain very much. Hattie Stowe wanted her work to make every American feel a personal guilt for slavery's inhumanity. What struck Chamberlain instead—and what stayed with him for years to come—was Mrs. Stowe's "sweetness of . . . spirit, and her charming hospitalities."[17]

Spending those Saturday evenings at the Stowe house at least seems to have released Chamberlain from his self-imprisonment. For the rest of his senior year, his social engagements increased and he found himself more fully involved in the life of the college and its intellectual community. There was another reason for coming out of his shell: he was falling in love with Frances Caroline Adams, the minister's daughter.

On Sundays, as he conducted the choir or played the organ, Chamberlain could look out and see the plain face of Frances Adams, the adopted daughter of the Reverend Dr. George E. Adams. For reasons that are not quite evident, her biological parents gave her up to the Reverend Adams, a relative, and his wife, who were themselves childless. Frances's new parents adored her and she came to think of them as a father and mother, although she did stay in touch with her biological parents and even visited them occasionally.[18]

Little is known about how Chamberlain and Fanny began their relationship. But what is clear from the mountain of letters that they wrote back and forth to one another is that this was no romance made in heaven. From a modern perspective, which cannot do justice to their private thoughts and the pattering of their hearts, it's difficult to know what they were feeling and what they were really trying to say to one another. What they wrote, back and forth, sometimes over and over, reveals all too painfully that no matter how hard they tried, no matter how earnestly and honestly they sought to express themselves, they succeeded only in communicating at cross purposes.

At first, Fanny Adams seemed to cling to Chamberlain as if he were a life raft. In February 1850, her adopted mother, Sarah Folsom Adams, died, and the household that lived in the First Parish parsonage on Maine Street discovered that its anchor was gone. Fanny had barely adjusted to the loss when the Reverend Adams, after attending a conference in Chicago, announced that he was engaged to marry Helen M. Root, the sister of the noted musician George F. Root (who a decade later would compose such songs as "The Battle Cry of Freedom" and "Just Before the Battle, Mother"). Miss Root was only six months older than Fanny. On December 30, 1851, the devout Reverend Adams and the young Miss Root were married in a ceremony that Fanny attended as a witness.[19]

Two days later, Fanny professed her undying love for Chamberlain in a letter that ran thick with syrupy effusions intended to assuage her lover's doubts about her feelings: "How could you think that I would shrink from you ever! you who seem so holy, so pure and noble to me. . . . I would be everything to you; I would nestle closely in your arms forever, and love you and cling to you and be your 'bird': dear, precious heart!" Despite such professions of love, which were very real and sincere, Fanny also had her doubts about Chamberlain and her feelings for him. It seemed like she wanted to love him, wanted even to throw herself at him, hoping that he could be someone who would take care of her and would not abandon her; yet her own fear of making a commitment, of risking the chance of such an abandonment, held her back.[20] Her ambivalence toward him was something that would define their relationship for the rest of their lives.

For his part, Chamberlain had fallen in love with love more than he had with Fanny. A strong romantic streak, and a Byronic tendency to blurt out his passions as words spoken on a stage or a deathbed, gave an overblown quality to his private expressions of desire. What he loved was the idea of having someone he could be devoted to, not the woman who Fanny actually was. "Fanny, dear Fanny," he would plead with her, "only tell me that you do love me as I *do* love you."[21] In letter after letter, his pleas for eternal expressions of her devotion to him, coupled with an overbearing neediness, made it appear as if he never received—or read—any of Fanny's replies, for nearly every new letter sounded the same note and asked for all the same reassurances. Fanny professed her love over and over again, but he could not overcome his own fear that she cared less for him than he did for her. "This anxiety and imagining," she told him bluntly, "*wears me out.*"[22]

In the winter of 1852, Fanny went off to New York for an extended stay to study music with her new uncle by marriage, Professor Root, and her absence from Brunswick made Chamberlain pine for her from morning till night. He sent her flowers and wrote letter after letter in which he poured out his misery to her. "How sad you have been for me," she remarked in one reply, "and I not near to soothe and comfort you when you were ill!" His neediness and insecurity, however, became readily apparent to her, and she found it difficult to see his ardor in a positive light. Even from a distance, he was smothering her with his love.[23]

Meanwhile, Fanny's father disapproved of her relationship with Chamberlain, and he let both of them know it. Even after the couple announced in late spring that they were engaged to be married, the Reverend Adams opposed their romance and union, saying that he did not think much would come of it or that it would really last very long. Chamberlain tried to brush the pastor's opposition aside, but it remained as one more obstacle in the couple's path. He hoped that such storms would strengthen their affection for one another and "bind us closer." They didn't. Fanny became increasingly aware that her relationship with Chamberlain was influenced by the tangled knot of feelings she had for her father.[24]

Despite all the distractions (love and otherwise) that Chamberlain experienced in his senior year at Bowdoin, he—like Frank Haskell, that other studious Gettysburg hero—did not let his academic standing slide. When the school term drew to an end, Chamberlain took satisfaction in knowing that he had earned honors in every department at Bowdoin, including mathematics, his weakest subject. As a reward for his outstanding scholarly achievement, he was asked to deliver the First Class oration at commencement. At the graduation exercises, which were celebrating the college's fiftieth anniversary, he started out in good form but faltered when he noticed several dignitaries in the crowd (the Bowdoin luminaries—Henry Wadsworth Longfellow, Nathaniel Hawthorne, and Franklin Pierce—were all there). His speech turned into a disaster. He uttered practically meaningless phrases and an extemporaneous conclusion, exiting the platform as rapidly as he could.[25]

After recovering from the embarrassment of his performance, Chamberlain faced the necessity of deciding between the inescapable choices that had been earlier presented to him by his parents: on one hand, West Point; on the other, the ministry. After weighing the issue, he chose the ministry and made plans to attend the Bangor Theological Seminary.[26] But his choice was determined not only by his desire to please his mother. There were deeper, spiritual reasons that lay behind his decision. He had always taken Christianity and his own faith seriously. Raised in a household where the doctrines of Puritan and Huguenot Calvinism flowed together, he had a religious upbringing that stressed that "integrity and honor [were] the law; good work, good will, good cheer, the rule." Before entering college, he had been accepted into the Brewer First Congregational Church, although he had not gone through a "conversion experience" like others in the church had done during the religious revival known as the Second Great Awakening.

As the years passed, and he put more thought into his piety, Chamberlain veered more and more toward a kind of Christian transcendentalism, not unlike the beliefs that sustained Ralph Waldo Emerson, William Ellery Channing, and Theodore Parker. He did not go so far as to challenge the divinity of Christ, as some Unitarians did, but he did embrace the transcendentalist notion that the individual was the spiritual center of the universe and that happiness depended on self-realization. In this sense, Chamberlain was not only a romantic, as he demonstrated in his love letters to Fanny, but a Romantic, who had come to accept the principles of European Romanticism, a movement centered in Germany that glorified nature and individualism and heroism.

Chamberlain's own commentary on how he came to choose the roads he would follow in life affirmed the transcendental character of his beliefs:

> He must [he wrote about himself in the third person] look away from the confusions and beguilements of beginnings to the consummate while unto whose needs and masteries these things were preconfigured; he must rise to the heights of life,—which means, in truth, to withdraw within the consciousness of nature's true nobility, the supremacy of the spiritual over the material, and hence the transmutation of the material into the spiritual, which is the mystery and glory of life, the redemption of flesh through spirit,—of body through soul.

In this way, he said, one can then "set his compass and fix his resolve."[27]

So Chamberlain went off to seminary in October 1852. He and Fanny agreed to put off their marriage for the three years it would take him to complete his studies in Bangor. Once enrolled, he immediately immersed himself in his work and tried not to think too much about her. He was appointed one of the speakers at an exhibition of the seminary's Rhetorical Society, and to fulfill the honor, he gave a lecture on "The Melancholy of Genius."

Melancholy was a word much on his mind as he pored over his theological readings. He tried to be positive about his separation from Fanny, telling her that the three years would go by "like a flash" and that after the time had elapsed "we shall come *home* forever." But Fanny was having doubts again. It would be a mistake, however, to assume that her mood swings were unusual or purposely designed to keep Chamberlain off-balance. Actually their courtship, with all its ups and downs, certainties and doubts, and prolonged delays before marriage, followed the typical course of prenuptial conventions of the time. Courtship was a game played between males and females, and the game commonly consisted of one party or the other being coy or flirtatious, using double entendre to mask sexual desires, and playing hard to get.[28]

Before the end of 1852, Fanny—who seemed unable to shake off her ambivalence toward Chamberlain—accepted a teaching position at a girls' school in Milledgeville, Georgia. She found Georgia dismal and cold, but she did become extremely fond of the South, its people, and its way of life. More than anything, she liked her newfound independence. Like other American women of her time, Fanny was trying to break free of the bounds dictated by the cult of true womanhood and the ideal of domesticity that limited the sphere of women during the mid-nineteenth century. Although she was by no means a radical feminist, working politically and socially as other women were doing for equal rights and suffrage, she clearly defined herself in ways that differed greatly from the roles played in the home by her own mothers—natural and adoptive—and by most of the women she knew in Brunswick.[29]

When it came to thinking about marriage from her vantage point deep in the heartland of the South, where the notion of female purity defined the ideal of Southern womanhood and men held white women on a pedestal, Fanny began to worry about the sexual obligations and the burdens of childbearing that were expected of every married woman. She informed Chamberlain that she wanted only a platonic marriage, given the fact that "children are the result of a tyrannical cruel abuse and prostitution of women." Chamberlain could not believe her words and begged her to reconsider her position. "I do not like to contemplate you as a fossil remain," he wrote. A year later she relented, but obviously she would have preferred to set forth a marriage contract that differed from the one Chamberlain had in mind.

After Chamberlain rejected Fanny's suggestion that he move South and find work there, and after she rejected his suggestion that she move back north, his despair over his relationship with her worsened, and he became depressed. "The sky is all overcast," he wrote Fanny, "and the rain is rushing down, and the wind is sighing and moaning, and my heart is overspread with loneliness and gloom." Throughout his life (except during the war years), these bouts with depression would recur, and each time would make the world into a very dark place. In his relationship with Fanny, his depression only tended to make their courtship even more complicated than it already was.

There were also vague hints in his letters that his despondency had caused him to be unkind to Fanny in some way—perhaps by berating her or denigrating what he considered to be her nasty habits—and though he promised repeatedly to change his ways, he seems to have persisted in following the same injurious patterns of behavior. In one letter, he fiercely scolded her for failing to write to him for a period of three weeks, and he did not hold back any of his anger. She, in turn, questioned why he did not write her more regularly and complained that even when she did receive his letters they seemed to take forever to reach her in Milledgeville.

Chamberlain's angry streak troubled her and kept her feeling uneasy about him. She once told him she was constantly fearful that she might "wound" him in some way without meaning to. It didn't help matters much when an acquaintance told her that Chamberlain's temperament "would be a great source of distress to me through life" and that it would be impossible to avoid arousing his ire inadvertently. But she did not put all the blame on him for the rough ride their relationship had turned out to be. Occasionally suffering from bouts of depression herself, she wondered if their troubles might actually be her fault. For all the pure affection they felt for one another, they utterly failed to communicate their feelings in a straightforward manner. Love, which is never easy, had run into the rocky shoals of misunderstanding, poor communication, crossed purposes, and each partner's protracted—and unsuccessful—search for self.[30]

In his final year at the seminary, he wrote four required sermons, which he preached in different parishes. As a result, he received three or four invitations to serve as a pastor in churches, but he turned down the offers. He graduated from the seminary in the late summer of 1855, and a week later he accepted a master's degree from Bowdoin (on the basis of his course work at the seminary) by delivering an oration on "Law and Liberty" at the Bowdoin commencement. This time, unlike his undergraduate speech, his delivery was polished and professional; the oration was very well received by the audience and in the local press. In the crowd, listening to his every word, was Fanny, who had finally agreed to end her Southern sojourn (her "exile," as she called it) and return to his arms.

Even though he made a favorable impression with his speech, and Bowdoin—a day after his Master's oration—offered him a teaching position at the college, his employment prospects were severely limited, and he had to negotiate strenuously to get the Bowdoin offer in the first place. Displeased with his salary, Chamberlain put off the wedding, an ironic twist that showed his male concern for being unable to support a wife more than it did any change of heart about Fanny. She stormed at him for delaying the marriage, and finally he agreed to marry her as soon as the first term at Bowdoin ended. The Reverend Adams, who had a keen eye, noted how miserable Fanny and Chamberlain both appeared. On December 7, 1855, at 4:30 in the afternoon, they were married in the First Parish Church. No one seemed particularly ecstatic. "I feel sadly about poor Fanny," wrote Adams. He feared "she will not make herself happy."[31]

The couple, from all appearances, were happy enough at first, but not carefree. Living in rented rooms, Chamberlain worried about money and his career. When Fanny went away to visit family or friends in other places, his insecurities and loneliness would surface again, and he would write her aching letters longing for her return home, fearful ones propounding her desertion of him, or jealous ones accusing her of infidelities. Meanwhile, he taught long and hard at Bowdoin. If he had regrets about choosing a scholar's life, he did not say so openly. In August 1856, he was appointed professor of rhetoric and oratory. The promotion came just in time. In the golden days of Indian summer in 1856, Fanny gave birth to a baby girl, whom they named Grace Dupee but called Daisy. Chamberlain hoped that the baby would help usher in a new life "for all in that house."[32]

Becoming parents did not solve the problems in the Chamberlains' relationship. Within a few short years after their marriage, they experienced some terrible losses, all of which kept their emotional lives on edge and in turmoil. A year after Daisy was born, Fanny was pregnant again and gave birth prematurely to a boy, but the infant lived only a few hours. A healthy son, whom they named Harold Wyllys, arrived about a year later, which brought joy to their hearts. But their emotional ups and downs continued when a baby girl, Emily Stelle, died in September 1860, leaving, as Chamberlain said, "but a summer smile and aching hearts, as she departed with the flowers." That same year, Fanny's natural father, Ashur Adams, and a brother, George Wyllys Adams, both died. In 1861, Chamberlain's brother, Horace, died of lung disease at the age of twenty-seven on the couple's wedding anniversary.[33]

If coming events cast their shadows before them, as poets and prophets think they do, then the shadows of secession and impending civil war seem not to have enshrouded Joshua L. Chamberlain much at all. He cared little about politics—or at least he didn't talk about political matters in his surviving correspondence—and took even less note of such pressing national issues as slavery, abolitionism, sectional discord, or constitutional acrimony. In this regard, Chamberlain was a strange transcendentalist. Unlike so many of his brethren, who looked to the glorification of consciousness and will, he rejected the idea of social reform—as Hawthorne had—and felt no burning compulsion to change the world around him. Fanny expressed no great concern over the impending crisis. In fact, she failed to see why slavery, which she considered a benign institution, was dividing the nation.[34] The Chamberlain household conspicuously lacked any overt display of social conscience.

In his autobiography, Chamberlain wrote that the mighty events leading up to the Civil War "took possession of every heart" and pushed everything else in his own life aside, including his personal woes. Yet, for all his apparent patriotic fervor, he did not go rushing to the flag when Lincoln was elected or when the first shots were fired on Fort Sumter. He declared that the "flag of the Nation had been insulted" and that the "honor and authority of the Union had been defied" by the secessionists who had aimed their guns at Sumter. "The country," he said, "was roused to the peril and duty of the hour." But he was not similarly "roused"—not personally, anyway. Even though he felt "an irresistible impulse . . . to have a hand in this business," he did not dash off to enlist in the spring of 1861.[35]

One reason for his hesitation may have been the fact that his father had come out against the war. How vigorously the father presented his views to his son cannot be known. Some later accounts called Chamberlain's father a Democrat, which probably was the case, but whatever political party he belonged to, he believed, at the very least, that the conflict was "not *our war*," as he phrased it in a letter to Joshua Lawrence. Nor did Fanny, understandably, want her husband to go to war. His employment at Bowdoin earned them a comfortable living, the children needed him, and, like most wives in wartime, she had no desire to risk becoming a widow if the worst should happen on the battlefield.[36]

Despite these hindrances, Chamberlain eventually decided to join the war, and he seems to have planned fairly carefully how to achieve his ends—most likely without consulting Fanny. His biggest obstacle was his position at Bowdoin, where he knew he could not obtain a release from his teaching duties to saunter off with the army. At the college, President Woods expressed an opposition to the war as fiercely as Chamberlain's father had done, and the faculty pretty much resented losing students to the army, not to mention fellow professors. So Chamberlain began arranging things in such a way that he could use deception to get what he wanted— not, by any means, the most honorable course to follow, but it did prove to be an effective way to extricate himself from his trap in Brunswick.

The college unwittingly played into his plan. The previous year he had been given a new assignment and a lifetime professorial chair in the department of modern languages. With the appointment came the promise of a two-year leave of absence that Chamberlain had contemplated using to travel abroad in Europe, with all of his expenses to be paid by the college. By the summer of 1862, however, he had changed his mind. The reversals of the Union army on one battlefield after another convinced him, as he said many years later, that he belonged among the Union's fighting forces.

Chamberlain saw the war as an opportunity to test and prove himself. War was mostly honor and chivalry, in his estimation. As he wrote years later: "Fighting and destruction are terrible; but are sometimes agencies of heavenly rather than hellish powers. In the privations and sufferings endured as well as in the strenuous action of battle, some of the highest qualities of manhood are called forth,—courage, self-command, sacrifice of self for the sake of something held higher,—wherein we take it chivalry finds its value." All war, he said, "is for the participants a test of character; it makes bad men worse and good men better." Chamberlain perceived himself to be a knight errant about to embark on a glorious crusade.[37]

He put things in motion by offering his services to Governor Israel Washburn Jr. of Maine. In mid-July 1862, Chamberlain followed up with a formal letter asking for a field officer's commission, promising he could fill a regiment with an overflowing tide of students, and indicating that he could free himself from Bowdoin in August. Everything did not go smoothly. The press learned of Chamberlain's negotiations with the governor and announced that the professor had been offered a colonelcy. Embarrassed by the leak and the inaccuracy, Chamberlain apologized to the governor. But now the story was out. Everyone, including his colleagues at Bowdoin, knew what Chamberlain was up to.[38]

Opposition to Chamberlain's enlistment in the army began to surface almost immediately. The attorney general of Maine wrote privately to the governor that Chamberlain was not good officer material. More damning was the howl sounded by members of the Bowdoin faculty, who, somewhat justifiably under the circumstances, felt that their colleague had been duplicitous. The professors remonstrated with the governor, portrayed Chamberlain as nothing more than a mild-mannered professor, and argued that their fellow faculty member "had no military stuff in him."

Chamberlain wanted to believe that bitter infighting among faculty members—each side wanting to get its grip on his endowed chair—was behind the college's extreme response to his military plans, but it seems more likely that his colleagues quite simply felt betrayed and angry. For one of the first times in his life, Chamberlain had not acted according to Hoyle, and while it would be unfair to imply that his scheming was dishonorable, one must at least accept the truth that his tactics could hardly be considered above board, either.

After the unexpected public reaction to his negotiations with the governor, Chamberlain withdrew his request for a regiment all his own and told Washburn that he would settle for "a subordinate position." On August 8, 1862, Governor Washburn named Adelbert Ames, a regular Army officer, as colonel and Joshua Chamberlain as lieutenant colonel of the 20th Maine Regiment, the last of five regiments being raised that summer for three-year enlistments. Chamberlain accepted the commission enthusiastically, although he did point out to the governor that he was still under fire from his fellow Bowdoin professors. In time, though, his academic colleagues gave up their effort to block his commission. They had little choice, of course, for Chamberlain had won his first military victory by having outflanked his enemy.[39]

Suddenly he was full of energy. He seemed, in fact, like an entirely new man. Three days after receiving his commission, he went back to Augusta, perhaps to confer in person once more with the governor, perhaps to make sure his opponents would not block his path at the State House. Then he lunged into recruiting men for the 20th, a job made less difficult by the fact that volunteers had poured forth in response to Lincoln's call for three hundred thousand troops that summer. The governor designated Camp Mason in Portland on the sparkling Casco Bay as the 20th's rendezvous point.

Being a soldier agreed with Chamberlain. He found not only a new energy in his life, but a new purpose. On August 18, Chamberlain arrived at Camp Mason and assumed responsibility for keeping the recruits together and out of trouble until Colonel Ames, who was detained in Virginia, could take over.[40] It was a motley assemblage of men and boys. They came from all walks of life, but mostly they were laborers who knew how to put in a good day's work—farmers, lumbermen, fishermen, sailors, with a small assortment of merchants and clerks (and at least ten Bowdoin graduates). There was no discipline, and Chamberlain was at a loss as to how to get some and enforce it.[41]

The disorder melted away when Adelbert Ames showed up one evening, probably on August 24 or 25, to take up his command. A regular Army officer who had graduated fifth in his class from West Point in May 1861, Ames had already distinguished himself on the field of battle at Bull Run, where he had been badly wounded. Within days of arriving at Camp Mason, he had worked wonders, putting the men in uniform, distributing company books, obtaining the officers' commissions from Augusta, and circulating manuals on tactics and army regulations around the camp.

Chamberlain and Ames hit it off right from the very beginning. Practically nothing is known about their interaction during those arduous days after Ames's arrival at the camp, but the two men must have gotten right down to working together; in a short time, it became clear that they genuinely liked one another. Chamberlain, who was a good judge of character, saw that Ames could teach him what he needed to know. At Camp Mason, Chamberlain appropriately occupied the background as Ames asserted his command and organized the men.[42]

On August 30, the regiment of 939 officers and men was ordered to move out, but when night fell, the 20th was still at Camp Mason, and everyone—including Fanny and the Reverend Adams, who had come to see Chamberlain off—found themselves trying to keep dry under soggy canvas tents that snapped and fluttered in a cold wind-and-rain storm. Throughout the night, thunder boomed and lightning bolts flashed through the sky over the muddy grounds of Camp Mason, a portent of sights and sounds to come. The inclement weather kept the 20th Maine in Portland for several more days.

Early on the morning of September 2, the 20th Maine finally struck its tents, loaded its gear, and marched off to the train depot. Down streets lined with tall elm trees, the Reverend Adams walked with the soldiers; Fanny rode in a carriage. At the station, goodbyes were said, tears were shed, and the men were loaded into the cars. Chamberlain's father could not be there to wish him well, so he sent an odd letter pointing out—with a bit of antiwar pomposity—that the war might not be as noble a cause as Joshua Lawrence considered it to be, but urging him, nevertheless, to take care of his younger brother Tom (who had also enlisted in the regiment) and to "come home with honor."

By three o'clock that afternoon, the 20th Maine regiment had arrived in Boston and marched past waving and cheering pedestrians down to the old wharves, where the men were directed on board the steamer *Merri-*

mac, bound for the seat of war. At 5:00 AM, under the brightening sky, the steamer slipped across the silken harbor and steered its course for Washington, D.C.[43]

Chamberlain felt the momentousness of the occasion. In an earnest letter home that he wrote to Fanny while sailing south on the *Merrimac*, he thanked her for "the force of your noble self-sacrifice, your heroism greater than mine, [and for] inspiring my soul." Like many other soldiers, he transformed his quest for adventure into a sacrifice made for wife and family. "I shall be calm and brave *for you*," he told Fanny, and he insisted that his actions sprang from duty and honor.

In later years, he marveled at how well he had done in becoming a soldier so quickly. He had to call on all his "inborn aptitudes"—including self-discipline and a "habit of sustained attention"—to become an army officer as rapidly as events had necessitated.[44] Behind him, far beyond the smooth ocean waters, over the now invisible landmarks of Boston's Old North End, and down the many winding roads that would one day carry him back to Maine, he left his wife, his children, and his Bowdoin colleagues to find their own transcendental happiness in whatever fashion might suit them. He was off to find his own.

War changes men. In Chamberlain's case, his transformation into a soldier—and, less than a year later on the fields of Gettysburg, into a warrior—appeared to take place almost instantaneously. Army life, as his letters and remarkable accomplishments in uniform reveal, not only appealed to him, he seemed in fact to thrive on it. But he was not really a "killer angel," as Michael Shaara portrayed him in his Pulitzer Prize-winning novel.[45] Chamberlain never really seemed to have the killer instinct in him. Instead, he was a golden knight, a gentleman soldier, a genteel and humane commander. The changes he had experienced in the short time between his decision to join the army and the 20th Maine's orders to leave Portland demonstrated that he had found in the soldier's life a new persona, one that suited him far more comfortably than the roles of troubled husband, reluctant scholar, and unhappy professor.

Soldiering seemed to be good for him, changing him for the better, bringing out his best qualities, making him feel more alive than he had ever felt before. Like James Longstreet, Chamberlain was more himself in war than out of it. When the war was over and he tried to return to his life with Fanny (and their relationship continued to disintegrate), when he turned to a political career in hopes of finding a new source of satisfaction (and learned that politics was not his forte), when he attempted to lead Bowdoin as its president (with mixed results), when he sought to become an entrepreneur and a speculator (and failed miserably)—in all of these postwar endeavors he discovered, sadly and tragically, that nothing quite gave him the satisfaction he had found leading men into battle and fighting for the Union.

4   Joshua Lawrence Chamberlain and the American Dream

An air of expectation filled the Boston Music Hall as the audience waited for Joshua Lawrence Chamberlain, the incumbent governor of Maine and "the Hero of Little Round Top," to be introduced. Chamberlain was going to speak on one of his favorite subjects, "The Left at Gettysburg," and his skill as a public orator had already brought him considerable fame in his home state and throughout New England. It was "the celebrity of Gen. Chamberlain," said one newspaper, that had drawn the sizable crowd to the music hall that November evening in 1868. The people of Boston wanted to see for themselves this great hero of the war and hear him tell his tale.

He did not disappoint them. Chamberlain described in vivid detail the bloody afternoon of July 2, 1863, when he had saved the Union army by ordering his regiment—the 20th Maine Infantry—to make a desperate bayonet charge down the slopes of Little Round Top in the face of a superior Confederate force. For more than an hour, the audience was entranced by his "glowing eloquence" and "graphic power." The lecture, said one reporter, was "a masterly production."[1] No one who saw his performance that night could have ever doubted that Joshua Lawrence Chamberlain was a true American hero.

Today Chamberlain enjoys an even loftier status as a hero than he did in his own lifetime. Over the past three decades, he has become a household name, a role model, and the subject of a popular novel, a television documentary, and a theatrical movie. The story of his courageous defense of Little Round Top has been told over and over, and with each telling his reputation seems to grow by leaps and bounds. His bravery on that hillside and his stouthearted service throughout the war have earned him a permanent place in America's gallery of honored heroes.

What appeals to us most about Joshua Lawrence Chamberlain is his simplicity and purity. Unlike heroes of our own time, whose greatest achievements invariably become tainted by disappointing character flaws and inconsistent actions, by secret vices and unsavory motives, Chamberlain is an unsullied champion who seems never to have let himself or his contemporaries down. When events called for him to be intrepid and steadfast, as they did that summer afternoon on the jagged slopes of Little Round Top, he neither faltered nor failed. Later in life he did not damage his hard-earned reputation by becoming morally or politically corrupt. He stayed the course; he remained true to himself. He was, quite frankly, what we'd like to think we all are or could be: a hero for all seasons.

Yet there is more to Chamberlain that meets the eye. He is remembered today precisely as he wanted to be remembered during his own lifetime. If Chamberlain could return from Valhalla, where he no doubt resides with all the other great heroes of the Civil War, he would surely be quite pleased with his celebrity. Although there is no denying that he was brave and daring, and that his deeds at Gettysburg were truly remarkable, the fact is that our image of him as a hero is derived from his own image of himself. The Chamberlain we know is the Chamberlain he wanted us to see, and while there is nothing particularly wrong with that, it does tend to give us pause if we happen to scratch the veneer and encounter something odd or unexpected about him that doesn't quite fit the image. Beneath the surface of the polished past, the hero and his deeds take on a different luster—not unimpressive, by any means, but not exactly shiny either.

After receiving a commission in the summer of 1862 from the governor of Maine to be the lieutenant colonel of the 20th Maine regiment, Chamberlain left his post as a professor of rhetoric and oratory at Bowdoin College and marched proudly off to war. He soon began to act very much like a soldier. After the battle of Antietam, Chamberlain wrote home to his wife, Fanny, complaining about the monotony of camp life and the desolation of the countryside. Yet he took to soldiering quickly, without real effort, and he suddenly discovered that there was something about army life that greatly appealed to him. He wrote to Fanny: "A dashing rain & furious gale in the night makes me put on a skull-cap (given me by the major) & pull the talma over me—head & all—curl up so as to bring myself into a bunch, & enjoy it hugely."

Chamberlain found out, too, that there was something about war itself that was oddly to his liking. At the battle of Fredericksburg in December 1862, when the 20th Maine was one of the endless line of Union regiments raked by the merciless enemy fire that swept across the broad fields below Marye's Heights, Chamberlain came face to face with the horrors of combat. The ground, he remembered years later, was slippery with blood.

Pinned down by the Confederate guns, he spent a long, macabre night huddled between the bodies of two dead soldiers, resting his head on the corpse of a third and using the flap from the dead man's coat to protect his face from the chilling wind. All night he listened to the dreadful moans of the wounded on the field. "It was heart-rending," he said. "It could not be borne."[2] Yet he lived through the Fredericksburg ordeal and saw for himself the worst that war could bring.

He did not let the brutality of war torment him, however. As some men can do, he was able to shut out the ghastly realities of battle and put its frightening horrors out of reach. It was not that the human misery of war failed to touch him. He saw all its bloody consequences plainly, and he lamented the suffering and loss that each battle brought with it. It was rather that he began to regard war from his own perspective, one that enabled him to see it as not precisely the war it was, but as he thought it really should be.

Claiming that he never felt afraid in battle, he scoffed at those who admitted their fear. "A soldier has something else to think about," he said. Most men might flinch a little at the thought of their "present peril," but as a rule, "men stand up from one motive or another—simple manhood, force of discipline, pride, love, or bond of comradeship"—to face the blazing guns without trepidation. Officers, said Chamberlain, are far too busy to think about their personal welfare on the battlefield. "The instinct to seek safety," he maintained, "is overcome by the instinct of honor." For Chamberlain, war was mostly chivalry and honor. Like the knights of old, he saw the two contending armies as representing good and evil, white knights battling black knights in epic duels that would determine the fate of the United States. In his eyes, officers displayed knightly countenances as they rode by on noble steeds. He named his favorite horse Charlemagne and marveled that his mount suffered almost as many wounds as he did before war's end. The effects of warfare on its participants, he strongly believed, were salutary, not hellish.[3]

No episode captured for Chamberlain all the chivalry and honor of the entire wartime experience more than did the surrender of General Robert E. Lee's Army of Northern Virginia to the Army of the Potomac at Appomattox Court House in April 1865. Having been given the honor of officially receiving the Confederate surrender on April 12, Chamberlain took the opportunity to pay homage to his former enemies. As Major General John B. Gordon, the Confederate officer in charge, approached the stretch of line where Chamberlain and his staff waited, a Federal bugle sounded, the first Union regiment stiffened to attention, and each regiment down the line did the same. Gordon, recognizing the salute, immediately swung his horse around to face Chamberlain and, giving a slight kick of his spurs, managed in picture-book style to have his horse bow in front of his victor as the southern general lowered the tip of his sword to his toe. "Honor answering honor" was what Chamberlain called it. For the rest of his life, he was praised in the South for his gallantry.[4]

A vibrant Victorian sense of self-sacrifice and self-discipline enabled him to see the war in these rosy shades, through the romantic lenses of chivalry and honor. "War," he said, "is for the participants a test of character."[5] Judging his own war record, Chamberlain concluded that he had passed the test of war with flying colors. He believed that the real test for every person came from a clash from within one's self, from the conflict of warring spirits. "There is," he explained in his later years, "a two-fold nature in us, or perhaps two natures, I should rather say two souls." One soul acts exclusively in the interest of the individual self. The other soul looks to a "life associated with others." This latter soul, he thought, was truly the "better soul," which found its ultimate source in love. When a person was sorely tested, as Chamberlain had been in battle after battle during the Civil War, "this better soul of man sinks self and sense and moves and acts in the communion of a larger life." His own experience had shown him that "great crises in human affairs call out the great in men." They rise up to reach their better souls.[6] In this notion, Chamberlain's transcendentalist view of the world became perfectly expressed.

As an army officer, Chamberlain sought to grab hold of his better soul by using all his self-control and self-determination to put his men first, assert his leadership through personal heroism, and demonstrate his willingness to suffer great privations for the cause of the Union and the sake of his command. According to one contemporary account, Chamberlain made sure that on forced marches or in bivouacs "he never took rest for himself until he had seen his men made as comfortable as possible." He was wounded six times during the war, twice almost fatally, and in every instance he showed great courage in moving his men forward or fighting on despite his injuries. At Petersburg, where he was shot through both hips and was believed to be dying, General Ulysses S. Grant promoted him on the field to the rank of brigadier general.[7]

Chamberlain survived, of course, and his victory over death only added to his illustrious reputation. Brigadier General Charles Griffin, commander of the Army of the Potomac's Fifth Corps, once remarked that "it is magnificent to see Chamberlain in battle," and Chamberlain's men whole-heartedly agreed with the general's assessment. One private in the 20th Maine wrote to the state's adjutant general after the war to say, rather grandly, that Chamberlain was "one of those rare individuals thrown conspicuously out to our admiring view by the revolution and evolution of the stupendous enigma of War."

His men loved him. His superior officers loved him. Even his enemies loved him. He was, said General Gordon after the Appomattox surrender, "one of the knightliest soldiers of the Federal army." There seemed to be no doubt among nearly everyone who knew him that he had succeeded in embracing his better soul. Wrote Theodore Gerrish, a 20th Maine veteran: "There were but few officers who displayed greater bravery, faced more dangers, and shed their blood on more battle-fields than did Gen. Joshua L. Chamberlain."[8] He was the perfect hero in everyone's eyes.

So he was in his own eyes, too. As he explained in a Memorial Day address delivered in Springfield, Massachusetts, in 1897, he believed that "everyone has in him, slumbering somewhere, the potencies of noble action, and on due occasion these are likely to make themselves manifest and effective." The secret to unlocking those potencies could be found in the two souls residing in each person, for by striving for one's better soul, the soul of love and community, one could thus find the path toward greater glory, the road toward true heroism. "Every man has in him the elements of a hero," he said. His own heroism sprang from an assertion of will, a conscious effort to put others before himself and to achieve, as he put it, a "largeness of action." In all of this, there was something lofty and spiritual, the fulfillment of divine destiny.[9]

In fact, he based his conception of a true hero not on a knightly archetype out of Sir Walter Scott but on a divine model—Joshua, the Old Testament warrior and his own namesake. In a long article published in 1883, Chamberlain delineated, with a fair amount of discursive argumentation, ten qualities "of nature and character" that made Joshua an outstanding military commander. Each of the ten traits—inspiration, resolution, straight-forwardness, severity of discipline, justice, prudence, sagacity, promptness of action, thoroughness of execution, and balance of character—allowed Joshua to meet the many challenges involved in moving his people to the Promised Land, conquering their enemies, and establishing a nation.

But these traits did not belong to the hero of Jericho alone. Most of them were qualities that Chamberlain prized in himself. When he spoke of Joshua as "a man tried and true," he could just as easily have been speaking about himself. "Here stands the man," wrote Chamberlain of the biblical commander, "clear in the light of his mission,—his traits almost suggested by the situation, correlated to the demand."[10] That was precisely how Chamberlain thought his own virtues had surfaced through his character—tested by the necessity of the moment, forged by the emergency at hand. In Joshua the commander, Chamberlain saw a clear reflection of himself.

The battle of Gettysburg gave Chamberlain a perfect opportunity to prove to himself and the whole world that he was, like his Old Testament exemplar, a hero of extraordinary merit who could—and did—defeat the Canaanites swiftly and decisively. At Gettysburg, he was able to call on all the virtues—the ten traits of Joshua—that made a military commander great. As a result of what he and the 20th Maine accomplished on the slopes of Little Round Top, Chamberlain received the praise and thanks of his superior officers, and his reputation for bravery and skill began to grow. The fame that came to Chamberlain from his actions at Gettysburg did not emerge overnight; it spread slowly over time, like the plodding movement of clouds across the sky.

Chamberlain got to tell the story of his regiment's defense of Little Round Top for the first time in the official report he wrote after the battle for his superior officers. Writing the story out helped him organize his thoughts, put events in their proper order, and figure out how much—and how little—he wanted to share with his superiors. Not surprisingly, Chamberlain cast himself in a role that fit his picture of himself—his conception of what a heroic field officer should be. He seems not to have worried about appearing boastful or vain, for he freely portrayed himself as the hero of the day. More to the point, the story of Little Round Top that he told in these reports was the story he would tell over and over for the rest of his life.

It was the bayonet charge, that great lunge into uncertainty, that stirred everyone's emotions, including Chamberlain's. His official report to Colonel James C. Rice, the brigade commander, dramatically narrates the story of the charge and the events leading up to it, replete with flourishes and crescendos. Having been placed on the extreme left of the Union line along the southern slope of Little Round Top, Chamberlain's men held off a powerful Confederate force for over an hour until their ammunition was nearly exhausted. "It was imperative," he wrote, "to strike before we were struck by this overwhelming force in a hand-to-hand fight, which we could not probably have withstood or survived." He ordered the bayonet, and the word "ran like fire along the line, from man to man, and rose into a shout." The left wing moved down the hill, swinging in a great right wheel, and swept the surprised Confederates before it. His men, who wanted to press on all the way to Richmond, took 400 Confederates prisoners. One hundred fifty of the enemy had been killed or wounded on the hillside. Out of his regiment of 386 men, Chamberlain lost 136, including 30 dead and many seriously wounded.[11]

He knew that he had accomplished a wondrous thing. The day after the battle, he wrote to Fanny: "The 20th has immortalized itself." With an understandable delight in himself and his marvelous deeds, the kind of glee and swagger that is allowable between husband and wife, he wrote to Fanny again a few weeks later and repeated most of the information he had already told her about Little Round Top. To the governor of Maine, he wrote a lengthy letter telling how the regiment had "won distinguished honor" at a place on the battlefield "where the fiercest attack was made." And he pointed out to both wife and governor that his little regiment had defeated a whole Confederate brigade.[12]

When word of what he and his men had done reached the high command of his corps, the top brass could not restrain themselves from heaping praise on him, and certainly he deserved every word of it. After the 20th Maine was relieved on July 3, Chamberlain reported that his corps's brigade commanders greeted him by shaking his hand and telling him, "Your gallantry was magnificent, & your coolness & skill saved us." Both Colonel Rice and Brigadier General James Barnes, the brigade's division commander, singled Chamberlain out for favorable mention in their official dispatches. Barnes even included a long, rather melodramatic description of the 20th's defense of Little Round Top. Chamberlain wrote Fanny: "I am receiving all sorts of praise but bear it nicely."[13]

It was an honest thing to say. One of the reasons people liked Chamberlain so much and enjoyed praising him for his accomplishments was because he never went fishing for the compliments or asking for advancement or any special consideration. To Fanny, he once said: "I hate to see a man always on the spring to get the best of everything for himself. I prefer to take things as they come." People could see that he was not a self-seeker. "Never was," said one newspaper of him thirty-five years after Gettysburg, "and never will be."

Yet in the weeks following Gettysburg, his ambition did begin to get the better of him, and his hopes were raised about the possibility of promotion. Like James Longstreet and Frank Haskell, Chamberlain could not avoid dreaming of advancement and the glories that might come from a higher rank. In August, after assuming temporary command of the Third Brigade of the Fifth Corps, he was given permanent command of the brigade by General Griffin. With his new responsibilities, Chamberlain worked to gain some prominent support for winning a promotion. After receiving a letter of commendation from General Barnes for his "gallant charge upon the enemy" at Gettysburg, Chamberlain sent the general an unofficial "memoranda" that told, in terms similar to the ones he had used in his official report, his version of the events that had transpired on Little Round Top. A few days later, Colonel Rice wrote an unsolicited letter to Senator William Pitt Fessenden of Maine and recommended Chamberlain for promotion to brigadier general, attributing the victory on the army's left at Gettysburg to Chamberlain's "moral power" and "personal heroism."[14]

The wheels were in motion. By the end of October, Chamberlain had received support for his promotion from Major General O. O. Howard (a fellow Mainer), Brigadier General Adelbert Ames (the former commander of the 20th Maine), Congressman John H. Rice of Maine (who wrote his letter of recommendation directly to President Lincoln), Israel Washburn (the Republican former governor of Maine), General Griffin (Chamberlain's Fifth Corps division commander after Gettysburg), Colonel Charles Gilmore (who assumed command of the 20th Maine after Chamberlain's elevation to brigade command), and Hannibal Hamlin, the vice president (who also wrote to Lincoln). The not-so-luminary also endorsed Chamberlain's promotion. E. B. French, an obscure auditor in the Treasury Department, sent papers to Secretary of War Edwin M. Stanton commending Chamberlain as "highly cultivated" and "patriotic." Most of the letters, especially the ones from military men, mentioned his bravery at Gettysburg.[15]

Although it was all made to look like spontaneous combustion, Chamberlain was the heat behind this firestorm of endorsements. To his regret, however, the campaign for his promotion failed. He attributed his lack of success to a prejudice in Washington against the Fifth Corps, a bias that kept many colonels commanding brigades throughout the corps, but it was also apparent that politics had also worked against him. He had marshaled plenty of support, and much of it from all the right places, but it was simply not enough to push the promotion through. "I was without political influence in Washington," Chamberlain explained in his later years, "without which, in those days, no military merit in the field could claim attention among the many nearer interests that pressed upon the Government." Although he had been elevated to command of a brigade, without promotion he didn't much appreciate the honor. Without extra pay or allowance, he complained, the elevation to command without rank was an "injustice" that "quite cancelled the compliment" of having been given the responsibility for the brigade.[16] Nevertheless, his bid for higher rank did win some rewards. It affixed in the minds of many people his heroic action on Little Round Top, and his name became more widely known in military and political circles.

During the remainder of the war, his heroics helped spread his name and build his reputation even more. He distinguished himself at Petersburg in June 1864, where he was critically wounded (and received, at last, the brigadier general's commission he so ardently sought). In several battles in March and April 1865, as the war rushed to its dramatic finale, Chamberlain performed brilliantly at Quaker Road (where he was wounded again and received a brevet rank of major general), at White Oak Road, and at Five Forks. He was a hero, plain and simple. Years later, in his home state of Maine, crowds would welcome him to their town halls and auditoriums by having the band strike up "See the Conquering Hero Comes."

The public knew him best, however, for what he had done at Gettysburg. After the war, when he served three terms as governor of Maine and twelve years as president of Bowdoin College, he labored hard and deliberately to forge that association more solidly in people's minds. On the campaign trail in Maine or the lecture circuit around New England, Chamberlain told his story over and over about the desperate fight and the bold bayonet charge on Little Round Top. By 1868, he was widely known in Maine as "the Hero of Little Round Top."[17]

He told his story often, and he told it very well. Occasionally he spoke about the surrender of Lee and the chivalrous moment when he and General Gordon exchanged salutes, but mostly he told the people of his state about Gettysburg and the brave deeds of the 20th Maine. He often spoke without notes to packed halls, and his Gettysburg lecture could sometimes last as long as an hour and a half—sometimes longer. When he gave his Gettysburg talk in Boston in the fall of 1868, a reporter commented on Chamberlain's effective delivery: "The Governor's voice is full, rich and sonorous; his manner bright and interesting, and his gesture free, graceful and impressive.... He writes with a considerable degree of elegance, and what is more important, with an uncommon amount of vividness and graphic power." In the 1880s, one newspaper account described Chamberlain's ability to bring the Little Round Top engagement to life: "The interest was positively painful at times, so real did the lecturer make it by his eloquent speech." His audiences loved every minute of it.[18]

Chamberlain's thoughts never seemed to be very far away from Gettysburg. He returned to the battlefield several times after 1863. While serving on court-martial duty in Washington during the spring of 1864, he took Fanny to Gettysburg to show her the places he had defended, and he visited the field again in the autumn of 1865. Four years after Appomattox, he went to Gettysburg for a reunion of officers who had served in the Army of the Potomac. Organized by the Gettysburg Battlefield Memorial Association and John B. Bachelder, a former civilian observer with the Army of the Potomac whose interest in the battle was becoming his life's work, the reunion was intended to help locate and mark where each unit had been positioned on the battlefield. Chamberlain walked the ground, pointed out where his line had been formed, told the story of the 20th Maine's daring counterattack, and watched as wooden stakes were driven into the soil to show where his men had stood.[19]

In October 1889, Chamberlain was back in Gettysburg—this time to participate in the dedication of the two monuments to the 20th Maine that had been erected on the battlefield by the survivors of the old regiment. He was the man of the hour. At the dedication ceremonies, held on October 3, he delivered two of the many speeches made that day—the first, in the afternoon on Little Round Top, went into the details of the fight and the gallant charge that had occurred twenty-six years before; and the second, in the evening at the Adams County Court House, explored the meaning and importance of the Union cause in the context of his transcendentalist theory about each individual's two souls—an idea not unlike Ralph Waldo Emerson's conception of the "over-soul." For the evening program, Chamberlain closed by saying: "In great deeds something abides. On great fields something stays. Forms change and pass; bodies disappear; but spirits linger, to consecrate the ground for the vision-place of souls."[20]

But even as Chamberlain spoke at Gettysburg it was becoming less certain if his own great deeds, his heroic actions on Little Round Top, would endure precisely as he wanted them to. Since the end of the war, other veterans of the fight for that rocky hill had given their own versions of the story in speeches, books, newspapers, and other publications, and while these authors did not necessarily set out to challenge Chamberlain's account or his credibility, their reminiscences sometimes presented a differ-ent picture of what had occurred on that hillside.[21]

Sounding uncharacteristically defensive, and more than a little peevish, Chamberlain took note of the fact in his afternoon address, which was de-livered at the site of the 20th Maine monument on Little Round Top, that the remembrances of some veterans did not comport with the story he had been telling for years. He tried, however, to dismiss the inconsistencies and their importance. Several of the regiment's former officers, he said, had claimed the distinction of being the one who notified Chamberlain, as the fighting began to heat up on Little Round Top, that a Confederate column was moving around the 20th's left flank. Without setting the rec-ord straight, one way or another, as to the identity of the officer who *did* bring him the news that day, Chamberlain attempted to reconcile the con-tradictory claims by declaring that "they are all right; no one of them is wrong." He took issue, though, with those who had maintained that at the moment of the charge, the men of the 20th Maine had hesitated, ever so briefly, before moving forward down the hill. "No man hesitated," he in-sisted, although he did admit—for the first time, publicly—that his order to charge "was never given, or but imperfectly," and that the men had be-gun to move even before he had finished uttering, "Bayonet! Forward to the right!" These conflicting accounts, he said, were "all of them true in their time and place, and so far as each actor is concerned." Truth, in other words, was in the eye of the beholder.

But the discrepancies could not be so easily cast aside. The facts about Little Round Top seemed suddenly slippery, and Chamberlain could no longer hold on to them as if they were his exclusive property. Nonetheless, he did what he could to sustain his own version of the Little Round Top story. For the most part, he simply did so by ignoring the inconsistencies and continuing to tell his own tale, just as he had always done. In one in-stance, when he learned that an author of "a graphic account of the Little Round Top incident in brief," which was intended to be published to raise funds for a Grand Army of the Republic post, had entirely omitted any reference to the 20th Maine's moment of glory at Gettysburg, Chamber-lain hounded the poor man until he received an apology and assurances that the missing episode would be included in the author's larger work in progress.[22]

When several friends and supporters decided in 1893 to ask the War Department to award Chamberlain a Medal of Honor for his bravery on Little Round Top, the formal application included a description of his courageous acts that adhered in all its particulars to Chamberlain's account of the battle, drawn largely from the official reports that he and his superior officers had written. A few important persons—including former Army of the Potomac generals Alexander S. Webb and Fitz John Porter, and Governor Henry B. Cleaves of Maine—wrote letters recommending Chamberlain for the medal. There were, however, no letters from anyone in his command, a surprising fact given the active role that the Twentieth Maine Regimental Association otherwise played in sustaining the good name of the regiment and the high standing of its veterans. The man who submitted the application, brevet Brigadier General Thomas Hubbard, a friend and former student, pointed out that Chamberlain, who was suffering badly from his old wounds, "has still many friends and admirers; but in his sickness and advancing years he is less in the public eye."[23]

The War Department awarded Chamberlain the Medal of Honor on August 11, 1893, "for distinguished gallantry at the battle of Gettysburg, Penna., July 2, 1863." He cherished the medal for the rest of his life and made sure that he received new issues and ribbons whenever the government changed the design slightly. He considered the medal itself a "sacred" honor, something "not to be bought or sold, or recklessly conferred."[24] He had every right to feel proud, and every reason to believe the medal would elevate his fame higher.

As it turned out, the Medal of Honor did not make a national hero, although he did win some acclaim from the fact that his name was mentioned repeatedly during the postwar years in a fair number of books that described, either briefly or sometimes at surprising length, the charge of the 20th Maine down the slopes of Little Round Top.[25] Mostly Chamberlain himself kept his version of the story going—less so by lecturing than he used to do, for his wounds bothered him more and more as the years went on, but more by keeping his name before the public and making sure that no one, at least in Maine, forgot what the 20th Maine had done or who "the Hero of Little Round Top" was. He was quite pleased when the War Department constructed a new road on Little Round Top and named it "Chamberlain Avenue."[26]

He happily complied when the state commission established to erect the Maine monuments on the Gettysburg battlefield asked him to rewrite a "historical sketch" of the 20th Maine that had been drafted by Ellis Spear for its final report. Besides writing the short history of the regiment, Chamberlain also supplied the report's editors with his field notes for a detailed description of the fight at Little Round Top, and though the evidence is awfully sketchy, he may have actually drafted the Little Round Top account himself. At the very least, the editor relied heavily on his knowledge of Little Round Top and his memory of the events surrounding the battle. In return, Chamberlain worried about the completeness and the accuracy of the regimental rosters that the commission intended to publish, and he worked hard to reduce the possibility of error in those lists.[27]

He was worried about some other matters, too—so much, in fact, that he decided to get in touch with William C. Oates, his former adversary, because, as Chamberlain put it, he was "having some controversy with some of the 'Gettysburg Commission' of this State in regard to points of our respective movements on the Round Tops." Taking exception to an article Oates had published nearly twenty years earlier in the *Southern Historical Society Papers,* Chamberlain argued that it was not possible, as Oates had claimed, for the Confederate troops to have passed over the summit of Big Round Top before attacking the 20th Maine on Little Round Top. He also tried to convince Oates that, contrary to what the former Confederate colonel had written, the Rebel force could not have hit Chamberlain's men as soon as it had emerged from the woods at the foot of Big Round Top, for it was Chamberlain's contention that his regiment was already heavily engaged in the fighting before Oates's troops arrived on his left flank.

Oates answered Chamberlain with a friendly fourteen-page letter that confirmed in detail that the Confederates under his command had indeed scaled Big Round Top's peak and that they did not engage the Federals until coming out of the woods in the valley between the two Round Tops. No doubt Oates's reply did not help Chamberlain in his dispute with the Maine commissioners. How Chamberlain resolved that controversy with them is uncertain, but it was not the last time he would become entangled in disagreements over what actually had taken place on Little Round Top. Although he professed a few years later to be uninterested in the sordid little squabbles that many Civil War veterans took so seriously, Chamberlain found himself nevertheless in the center of two very heated quarrels that called into question his own version of the Little Round Top story.[28]

The first of these disagreements, as anyone might have predicted, was with William Oates. Their exchange of letters in 1897 appears to have simply set the stage for a more vigorous disagreement that heated up in 1902, when Oates sought to erect a monument to the 15th Alabama, the regiment he commanded at Gettysburg, in proximity to the existing memorial to the 20th Maine on the southern slope of Little Round Top. The battlefield was then under the administration of three park commissioners who reported directly to Elihu Root, the secretary of war. For a variety of reasons—including a rule that required monuments to be placed on the battlefield at the "brigade line" where units deployed to go into battle rather than the spot where a unit engaged its enemy (which meant that Confederate monuments could be erected only on Seminary Ridge) and a suspicion that Oates's account of his assault on Little Round Top was factually unreliable—the commissioners initially approved Oates's request, then later changed their minds. When Oates filed a formal application to Secretary Root for approval of his monument in 1903, the Gettysburg commissioners turned to Chamberlain for help and asked him to comment on the extent to which Oates's description of the fight for Little Round Top was "at variance with the records."

Chamberlain told the battlefield commissioners he did not object to a monument for the 15th Alabama, "but I expect it to be placed on ground where it [i.e., the Confederate regiment] stood at some time during the battle." And that was the rub, for Oates argued that he had turned the 20th Maine's right flank and had pushed its left wing so far up the hill that he was justified in placing the Alabama monument on a prominent boulder *behind* the 20th Maine lines that Chamberlain had so carefully marked for Bachelder in 1869. Chamberlain declared that Oates's description of the battle differed "widely from the well established record of facts in the case." John P. Nicholson, chairman of the battlefield commission, agreed with him and sent Chamberlain's assessment off to Secretary Root. "Chamberlain is not accurate in his statements," Oates complained to William M. Robbins, the Southern member of the three-man commission, "[and] his memory is at fault in some respects." Worse, said Oates, was Chamberlain's egotism about the battle: "He is like many others on both sides at this late date who are disposed to make themselves the whole push."[29]

As the dispute dragged on, wearing everyone down, the battlefield commissioners tried to persuade Oates to revise his statements about the battle and submit them to review to Chamberlain—all in an effort, they told Oates, "to avoid any controversy in the matter." Oates refused to do so, but he did visit the battlefield in the summer of 1904 and showed Commissioner Robbins how deeply the Alabamians had penetrated the wings of the 20th Maine. Angry and frustrated, Oates finally wrote directly to Chamberlain and said that the commissioners had claimed that the former commander of the 20th Maine was opposed to the monument. He asked Chamberlain to reconsider the events and acknowledge that some aspects of the battle might have unfolded as Oates believed they did. "No man can see all that occurs in a fight," he said, "even between two regiments." Chamberlain answered with a stern letter, one might even call it grumpy, saying he was sorry that his earlier correspondence had impressed Oates so little and denying that he had played any part in the commissioners' decision. "It is really my desire to have your monument set up," he wrote, "only let us make sure of our ground for the sake of historical fact." When Chamberlain sent copies of the correspondence to Nicholson, the Gettysburg commissioner was elated. Oates, declared Nicholson, "has not the slightest idea of admitting the views of any one in the controversy except himself."[30]

The irony, of course, was that just the opposite was true. Chamberlain's unwillingness to consider even the possibility of Oates's differing views had sounded the death knell for the Alabama monument, which was never erected. In another disagreement over Little Round Top (a deeper, more personal conflict than the one he had had with Oates), Chamberlain chose to handle it in pretty much the same way. When Ellis Spear, a good friend who had served as an acting major at Gettysburg and had commanded the left wing on Little Round Top, painted a different picture of what had transpired on July 2, Chamberlain stood his ground and refused to take Spear's perspective into account.

During the years after Appomattox, Spear's various writings about Gettysburg seemed to support Chamberlain's description of the action, and the two men remained close friends and sometimes exchanged new information they had acquired about the battle and the old regiment. But in a Memorial Day speech, given in May 1888, Spear said he had never received an order on Little Round Top to fix bayonets or charge; instead, he maintained, there was suddenly "a shout of forward on the center from the company or companies next [to] the colors[,] and through the smoke they seemed to be moving forward[,] and the colors lifted up [and] began to advance."

A few years later, Spear told John Bachelder that on July 2 he had informed Chamberlain of the threat to the 20th Maine's left flank and had asked permission to pull back two companies on the left wing, which Chamberlain allowed him to do. He repeated that he never received an order to charge from Chamberlain, but that he had heard the men tell a story after the battle about how Company K, near the center of the regiment, had wanted to retrieve some wounded men in front of their lines, called to other companies to cover them, and moved forward; when they did, said Spear, the whole line advanced and the regiment swept down the hill. Concerned that his recollections differed from those of Chamberlain, Spear wrote to his former commanding officer in 1895 and conspicuously repeated the same points he had earlier made to Bachelder—except the story of Company K, which he had told Bachelder he could not vouch for.[31]

Chamberlain dealt with the different details about Little Round Top, the ones he had heard from Oates and Spear or had read in the accounts written by Holman Melcher and Theodore Gerrish, by dismissing them. Spear, who seems genuinely to have liked and respected his former commanding officer, was unwilling to push Chamberlain about the Gettysburg inconsistencies; so "the Hero of Little Round Top" continued to have his day in the sun. But finally Chamberlain stepped over the line, at least so far as Spear was concerned, when he wrote an account of Little Round Top for a book on Medal of Honor winners that presented the victory on that hillside as practically a single-handed act. In telling his story this time, Chamberlain had disregarded all the little details that Spear knew to be true, particularly that Spear had recommended refusing the regiment's line and that Chamberlain had never "sent word" to him "to make a right wheel of the charge." Worse still, Chamberlain had painted himself as the solitary hero of the regiment.[32]

While Spear tried to keep up the pretenses of friendship, sending Chamberlain a warm Christmas greeting in 1910, his ire reached its apex two years later when Chamberlain published "My Story of Fredericksburg" in *Cosmopolitan Magazine*. Less than a year after that, another article by Chamberlain—"Through Blood and Fire at Gettysburg"—appeared in *Hearst's Magazine,* a popular periodical. Upset that Chamberlain was perpetuating untruths, Spear publicly challenged Chamberlain's recollections not only of Fredericksburg, but of Lee's surrender and Little Round Top as well.[33]

What bothered Spear the most—and in later life became something of a strange obsession—was Chamberlain's "egotism," as he called it. He was not alone. Oliver Norton, who, as we have seen, also served in the Fifth Corps at Gettysburg as Colonel Strong Vincent's bugler, wrote Spear in 1916, two years after Chamberlain's death, complaining that Chamberlain's attitude was "about the same as that of the Texas man who said he was 'a bigger man than old Grant.'" Spear replied that Chamberlain's egotism was indeed "colossal," and he noted that his fellow Mainers called him "the Hero of Little Round Top," implying that Chamberlain had welcomed such public recognition. Norton believed that the only true savior of that hill was Strong Vincent, who had been mortally wounded there. Although Norton's book, *The Attack and Defense of Little Round Top,* published in 1913, even-handedly related the details of the 20th Maine's charge on Little Round Top, he focused most of his attention on demonstrating Vincent's timely arrival and personal heroism at the summit of the hill. In their old age, both Spear and Norton came to consider Chamberlain a skilled prevaricator and self-promoter.[34]

Yet nothing could really stop "The Hero of Little Round Top." Chamberlain's heroic reputation, particularly in Maine, did not diminish over time; if anything, it grew stronger. Even when Chamberlain himself was not doing the talking or the writing, his name and great deeds were being frequently praised by others. Books and articles on Gettysburg, which poured forth in abundance in the years leading up to the fiftieth anniversary of the battle in 1913, repeatedly mentioned Chamberlain and the valiant charge of the 20th Maine.[35]

In the public's mind, he was closely connected with Gettysburg and its legacy. He visited the battlefield again in 1909 and 1911. The governor of Maine appointed him to serve as the state's representative on the national committee formed to plan the fiftieth anniversary commemorations at Gettysburg. Chamberlain returned to Gettysburg one last time in May 1913 to attend a meeting of the planning committee; poor health kept him away from the big celebration the following July. In his final years, he planned to write a book on Gettysburg, but he spent most of his time, painfully, laboring on his long memoir about the battles leading up to the end of the war and Lee's surrender, a work that was not published until after his death. When he died on February 24, 1914, his last words should have been "Fix bayonets" or "Forward to the right"; there's no record, however, that he said anything at all in his final moments. Throughout Maine, people mourned the passing of "the Hero of Little Round Top."[36]

His sun began to set after his death, but not for very long. With the fading away of the Civil War generation, Chamberlain's name was no longer known to a very large public, even in Maine. For a few decades, from the time of his death through the years of the Great Depression, he seems to have slipped from view, unheralded and unknown, except perhaps by only a few. Then, suddenly, he was remembered again in a small book by a very famous author. In 1938 Kenneth Roberts, the Maine author of several popular historical novels, including *Arundel* (1930), *Rabble in Arms* (1933), and *Northwest Passage* (1937), published a book called *Trending into Maine,* which contained a retelling of Chamberlain's exploits on Little Round Top in a chapter entitled "Maine Stories I'd Like to Write." Roberts approvingly quoted a newspaper reporter who had once remarked about Chamberlain: "The brush of the artist never had a grander theme. It should be put on canvas or sculptured in marble and placed in the rotunda of the capitol at Washington to show to the world the stuff of which American patriots are made. As an example to inspire patriotism it would rank with Leonidas and his three hundred Spartans. America is secure against the world as long as she has such sons to spring to her defense in the hour of darkness and danger."

Chamberlain also gained favorable notice from some prominent Civil War historians after World War II, namely Earl Schenk Miers and Bruce Catton. But it was a wonderfully written history of the 20th Maine Regiment by John J. Pullen, who told the story of the unit and its famous commander with lively style and great gusto, that must be given the credit for reintroducing Chamberlain to a modern audience. Pullen's book, published in 1957, presented Chamberlain just as he always wanted to be seen. Wrote Pullen: "He was destined to become one of the most remarkable officers in the history of the United States—a veritable knight with plumes and shining armor."

Although Chamberlain was sometimes missing from popular books about Gettysburg, he became more and more a mainstay in the literature about the battle after Pullen's book came out. In 1960, the first full-scale biography of Chamberlain, written by Willard M. Wallace, was published. Relying on a good selection of manuscript sources from Maine and elsewhere, Wallace reconstructed Chamberlain's multifaceted life as a mosaic of experiences, public and private. The Chamberlain story was regaining visibility, not unlike in the days when Chamberlain himself would repeat his own tale to audiences around his state and region.[37]

It was, however, a novel that finally thrust Chamberlain onto a national stage—and, later, an international one—by portraying his heroism in a grittily realistic manner. When Michael Shaara's *The Killer Angels* was published in 1974 few people had heard of Joshua Lawrence Chamberlain. Shaara's novel, which told the story of the battle of Gettysburg through the eyes of a handful of main characters, changed that forever. Shaara portrayed Chamberlain as a thinking man gone to war, but mostly as an everyman, someone not unlike all of us, caught up in a deadly situation in which he must, out of necessity, rely on his keen wits to get himself— and the men he commands—through the terrible ordeal of Little Round

Top. Chamberlain succeeds, of course, and feels very good about his accomplishment—"an incredible joy," as Shaara described it: "He looked at himself, wonderingly, at the beloved men around him, and he said to himself: Lawrence, old son, treasure this moment. Because you feel as good as a man can feel."[38]

Although Shaara brought Chamberlain to life as no writer had been able to do before, there was still something oddly familiar about his characterization. To be sure, Shaara drew heavily and rather shamelessly on Pullen's history of the 20th Maine for his information. But mostly Shaara made use of Chamberlain's own story, Chamberlain's own words. The character in the novel seems so recognizable because he is, quite simply, Chamberlain talking again about Little Round Top, just as he had done for most of his life. Shaara fleshed him out, but it is really Chamberlain come back again, Chamberlain the Old Testament warrior—the student of Joshua—talking about "Man, the Killer Angel," worrying about departing the earth "in a chariot of fire," seeing a vision of the battlefield before him "like a Biblical dream."[39]

Over the past thirty years, Shaara's novel has gained a large and loyal readership. It might have been an obscure work, passed over by all except a few devoted fans, but it won the Pulitzer Prize in 1975 and has gone through scores of printings in cloth and paper editions since then. The book has become a popular assignment as a supplemental reading in high school and college history courses—and even in military-training classes. In 1983, the popularity of the novel led curriculum designers at the U.S. Army Command and General Staff College at Fort Leavenworth back to Pullen's book and convinced them to devote long sections of a field manual on military leadership to Chamberlain and the fight for Little Round Top.[40]

Shaara's novel drove the Chamberlain legend in the years after winning the Pulitzer. Books and articles on Gettysburg featured Chamberlain and the 20th Maine more prominently than many earlier works had done.[41] But in September 1990, unlike the results of any earlier telling of the Chamberlain story, his notoriety suddenly soared when Ken Burns, a documentary filmmaker, decided to include Chamberlain as a key historical figure in his epic television documentary *The Civil War*, which was broadcast on PBS. Watched by fourteen million viewers in its initial showing, the documentary became the most popular program ever offered on public television. Burns later explained that his inspiration for the film came from reading Shaara's *The Killer Angels*. An accompanying book, *The Civil War:*

An Illustrated History, hit the best-seller lists and stayed there through the following Christmas.[42] Chamberlain had become an American hero of the 1990s. He was a television star.

Like other celebrities, Chamberlain successfully made the transition from small screen to big by appearing in 1993 as a prominent character in the motion picture *Gettysburg,* produced by Turner Pictures and directed by Ronald F. Maxwell. The movie is an adaptation of Shaara's novel, so the Chamberlain we see on the screen is, for the most part, Shaara's characterization of him from *The Killer Angels,* although the scenes depicting the Little Round Top fight seem to be based more on Chamberlain's heroic legend than on the novel per se. Chamberlain (and the actor Jeff Daniels, who portrays him) attracted the attention of several film reviewers, whether or not they cared for the movie as a whole. One reviewer wrote: "Mr. Daniels's luminous performance as the heroic colonel dominates the first half of the film. And when the actor all but disappears in Part 2, he is sorely missed." The reviewer praised Chamberlain as an extraordinary leader, with "sad blue eyes," who wins the loyalty of his men and prevents the Confederate army from gaining "a clear path to Washington."[43]

Americans tend to venerate their heroes, and while Joshua Chamberlain stands on a lower tier than some national legends, he has become duly venerated nonetheless. Chamberlain is "irresistible," says one historian, but the simple fact is that he has become too good to be true. The portrait of the man painted by one of his most recent biographers, the late Alice Rains Trulock, is so thoroughly admiring, so laden with excessive homage, so quick to defend and explain away, that the reader yearns for even a tiny flaw in the man, a peccadillo to smile at—anything that would demonstrate conclusively that he was as human as the rest of us. Sad to say, Trulock gives us only the public man, the paladin, the only man Chamberlain wanted his contemporaries or posterity to see.[44] Likewise, numerous military artists have recently depicted Chamberlain in a romantic vein. Illustrators such as Dale Gallon, Mort Künstler, Don Troiani, Keith Rocco, and several others, have created portraits and prints of Chamberlain and his fighting men on Little Round Top. One cannot walk past the many book shops and galleries in Gettysburg without seeing Chamberlain's likeness in the window. Not only is Chamberlain irresistible, he is also quite profitable.

Books, articles, and prints continue to spread Chamberlain's legend far and wide, often without much literary grace or artistic creativity. Only two books in the spate of works that have appeared recently manage to present a realistic picture of Chamberlain, the soldier and the man: Michael Golay's lively portrait of Chamberlain (contained in a dual biography that also sketches the life of E. P. Alexander, the Confederate artillerist), and Thomas A. Desjardin's carefully researched and balanced account of the 20th Maine's role in the battle of Gettysburg.[45] But mostly the hero-worshiping goes on and on, for Chamberlain has become the man Civil War buffs love to love.

There is a high price for such veneration. Not only do we lose sight of the man, but we also end up misconstruing his real accomplishments. This has certainly been the case with Chamberlain's charge on Little Round Top. Chamberlain and his superior officers at Gettysburg believed that the counterattack against the Confederates saved the left flank of the Army of the Potomac and perhaps even kept the entire army from destruction, but many others realized that Chamberlain and his 20th Maine played only one small part in winning the day. On the western side of the hill, between the crags and crevices of its rocky face, the other regiments of Vincent's brigade (and, later, Brigadier General Stephen H. Weed's brigade and Lieutenant Charles E. Hazlett's battery) fought a desperate battle—a very near thing—and successfully repulsed the formidable Confederate onslaught there.

So the Chamberlain we have come to know is, in a sense, the same man Chamberlain saw in the mirror every morning. That man knew what the stakes at Gettysburg were, and it was just no use trying to tell him otherwise. He was, as he liked to be called, "the Hero of Little Round Top." Once, at a Bowdoin commencement exercise, he passed a student who remarked to a friend, "There goes the man who took Little Round Top." Without stopping or turning his head, Chamberlain replied in a loud voice: "Yes, I took it and I held it."[46]

There is, after all, no getting around the fact that the charge of the 20th Maine was remarkable—brave, effective, and deadly. Somehow it doesn't seem to matter much whether it truly saved the Union left or not, whether Chamberlain gave the order or not, or whether his men began flying down the hill before Chamberlain could say anything at all. What's important, in the end, is that the charge did happen, and on that gray summer's evening, when hope seemed to be in especially short supply, the men of the 20th Maine put their courage behind the muzzle of a .58-caliber musket and the point of an eighteen-inch bayonet.

Like nothing else in his life, the charge at Gettysburg defined who Joshua Chamberlain was and who he would always be. But his greatest achievement—greater than any assault he led, any wound he survived, any medal he earned, any obstacle he overcame—was how he had lived his dreams and made them come true. He wanted to be a chivalrous knight and an Old Testament warrior, and so in his own eyes and those of his contemporaries he became those things. The Civil War gave him the opportunity to turn his deepest aspirations into reality. But it is our need for heroes, our admiration for those who are able to rise above their own limitations to turn their dreams into reality, that has enabled Chamberlain to achieve the glory he longed for through the war and most of his life. All in all, he accomplished what few men, either in his own time or in our own, can every honestly claim: he lived his dreams to the fullest.

5   Finding William C. Oates

Little Round Top was a place where heroes could be found in abundance on July 2, 1863, although in recent times it seems almost as if Joshua Lawrence Chamberlain fought on that hill by himself and against an amorphous foe. Yet, as I've shown, there were men engaged in that fight who did not agree with Chamberlain's account of the battle, including men in the ranks of the 20th Maine as well as his adversary that day, William C. Oates, the colonel who commanded the 15th Alabama regiment at Gettysburg. Indeed, as a historian I was not attracted to the Little Round Top story by having first encountered Joshua Chamberlain and his exploits, but rather by having stumbled upon William Oates by accident. Sometimes historians and biographers find themselves traveling down roads they never intend to follow and discovering views of the past they never expect to behold. When I started to research and write about Oates some fifteen years ago, I did not know how enthralled I would become with his life, his times, and his family.

My discovery of Oates came truly out of nowhere. In the early 1990s, I was asked by Bantam books to edit a new edition of Frank Haskell's classic account of Gettysburg, which, as we've seen, is one of the most vivid surviving recollections of the battle. After I submitted the completed manuscript to Bantam, my editor thought the book would be too short, so he suggested adding a comparable Confederate description of the battle.[1] My thoughts immediately turned to Oates, whose Gettysburg chapters from his Civil War memoirs, *The War between the Union and the Confederacy,* published in 1905, offered an exciting eyewitness recitation of his regiment's exploits in the Pennsylvania campaign, particularly of the Alabamians' failed attempt to dislodge Chamberlain and the 20th Maine from Little Round Top.[2] I had read Oates's book, but I knew little about him beyond what he and his regiment had done at Gettysburg. Bantam wanted me to write a detailed biographical introduction, so I began to search for sources on Oates and his life.

Secondary accounts of Oates were not terribly hard to find, for Shelby Foote had much to say about him in the second volume of his massive narrative history of the Civil War, and the standard books on Gettysburg, including Glenn Tucker's *High Tide at Gettysburg* (1958) and Edwin B. Coddington's *The Gettysburg Campaign* (1968), contained plenty of useful information on the man and his Civil War experiences. Elsewhere, I discovered that Robert K. Krick, a National Park Service historian and perhaps the foremost living expert on Lee's Army of Northern Virginia, had published a fine short biography of Oates as an introduction to a reprinted edition of Oates's memoirs.[3] Krick cited several primary sources in his preface, but the one I found most intriguing was a surviving fragment of Oates's unpublished autobiography, which belonged to the Alabamian's granddaughter, Marion Oates Leiter Charles, who lived in Washington, D.C. I called Krick—an enormously helpful man who will practically give the shirt off his back to fellow Civil War writers and researchers— and he told me that he had consulted the Oates autobiography sometime in the 1970s, but that he thought Mrs. Charles had died since then. I determined that he was wrong, and I subsequently succeeded in getting to know Mrs. Charles over the next several months, when she finally agreed to let me see and use not only Oates's unpublished autobiography but an entire collection of family papers in her possession.

For the next few months, I consulted the Oates manuscripts as often as I could, making some attempts to organize the documents into a comprehensive family archive while also learning about Oates's life and taking notes as I went along. My fascination with William C. Oates drew me deeper and deeper into the record of his life and the history of his family. But the family papers did not tell me everything I wanted—or needed— to know about William Oates. In fact, the papers in Mrs. Charles's possession documented Oates's antebellum and postwar life in fairly good detail, but his Civil War experiences were hardly touched on at all, and his seven terms as a U.S. congressman and one term as Alabama governor were barely covered. Little seemed to have survived concerning Oates's military service, first as a Confederate officer and later as a brigadier general in the U. S. Army during the Spanish-American War. Those gaps were easily remedied by filing requests for copies of Oates's service records in both wars from the National Archives.

But there were other questions that neither the family papers nor any amount of digging in other sources ever answered. Not surprisingly, Oates's tales of his adventures in Texas as a teenager could not be corroborated in other sources, but there is also little to go on concerning his early experiences as a lawyer and a rising star in Abbeville, the Henry County seat.

What had caused his illness and absence from his regiment during the battle of Sharpsburg in 1862 remains a mystery. More perplexing, however, were the reasons behind the failure of the Confederate Congress to confirm his commission as a full colonel in Lee's Army of Northern Virginia. After the war, Oates returned to Abbeville and resumed his ambitious pursuit of the law and politics. He took up with a woman whose name, as Oates rendered it in a document written thirty years later, was Sarah (Sallie) Vandalia Knight Allen, an African American woman. In 1865, she gave birth to one of Oates's two illegitimate sons, Claudius Oates. Practically nothing is known about this woman, except the color of her skin (black), the year of her birth (1834), and her occupations (maid and milliner). Only slightly more is known about Oates's son Claudius, whom he called Claude. The mother of his other illegitimate son, Joshua Oates, was a young white woman, fifteen years old, named Lou (or Lucy) Hickman. As a young man, Joshua Oates became a physician, but then he turned to fire fighting as a profession in Mobile. Hardly anything else is known about him, and precious little is known about his mother, who remained a single mother throughout her adulthood until she disappeared from the census rolls after 1900.

Intrigued more than ever with Oates's life story, I decided to visit Montgomery, Alabama, to see what I could find there about these missing pieces and anything else that might come to light about him and his world. The National Endowment for the Humanities supplied me with a travel grant, and Mrs. Charles gave me some names to look up while I was there in the place of her birth. The flight was long. In those days, you couldn't get from Washington to Montgomery on a direct flight, so you had to change in Charlotte to a prop plane that carried you from the Upper South to the Lower South in about the same amount of time it takes to read a Faulkner short story.

My first stop in Montgomery was the Alabama Department of Archives and History (ADAH), a huge white-columned government building south of the dome-topped state capitol, where I spent most of my time going through the voluminous records of Oates's one term (two years) as governor (it's quite possible that every building in Montgomery is white-pillared, though I'm not sure about this). After a few days worth of research, I decided to explore Mrs. Charles's vacant house in Montgomery—Belvoir, the mansion her father had built in the 1920s for his young wife and family. The house looked remarkably like Tara in the movie version of *Gone with the Wind*—red faded brick, white-columned portico, and evidence of once-lavish gardens separating the house from the road. But upon closer inspection, the house was badly in need of repair.

Inside, toward the rear of the house, I found a magnificent library still filled with volumes, a bright room lit by huge French doors and windows. In front of one set of windows stood a magnificent oak desk, a double desk, that once belonged to William C. Oates Sr. and formerly occupied his own library in his house on North Ripley Street in Montgomery. On the walls were displayed Oates's two ceremonial swords, one from the Civil War, the other from the Spanish-American War. His military commissions from the Confederate and the United States armies also occupied prominent places on the walls. I spent a long afternoon looking through the books in the library. Several of them—especially books about the Civil War—contained Oates's annotations on the blank flyleaves and in the margins. I browsed through nearly every volume in the library, stopping to transcribe any of Oates's notations that I found. On the flyleaf of the first volume of Sherman's *Memoirs,* published in 1875, Oates had written: "They [i.e., the memoirs] are interesting but satisfied me that although an able General[,] Sherman is a very heartless or hard-hearted man. There was none of the milk of human kindness within him."[4]

I seemed to be getting closer and closer to Oates with practically every step I took in Montgomery, but I knew I would have to travel outside the city to find any more of him. Gassing up my rented car, I headed out one gray morning on an excursion through the Alabama countryside, driving south from Montgomery toward William Oates country, over almost deserted roads into the southeastern corner of the state, down to what Alabamians have long called the wiregrass region. It took me less time than I expected to reach Troy, and from there I drove east to a little hamlet called Monticello.

Just north of Monticello, out in the middle of nowhere, I found what I was looking for—Oates's Crossroads, now called Ebenezer Crossroads after the white clapboarded Baptist church, a church that Oates's father had helped to build, that stands guard over the intersection of three roads. There wasn't much to see. A few modern houses stood along the roadside. Off to the northeast a line of blue hills ran across the horizon, and it was evident that the settlement of Oates's Crossroads sat on a broad and high plateau some forty-five miles west of the Chattahoochee River valley. I walked into a farm field to get a better look at the hills beyond, and the view from that vantage point was magnificent. The clouds had broken apart, and it was difficult to tell where blue hills and blue sky met in the distance. Oates's father was to be congratulated for having a good eye when it came to picking a homestead.

From the crossroads, I followed country roads—some dangerously narrow, it seemed to me—to Abbeville, where Oates had raised the Henry Pioneers militia company in the summer of 1861 and where he had practiced law. Taking care not to miss anything important as I came into town, I pulled the car to the center square and parked it so I could look around. Abbeville was, in many respects, a major disappointment. I expected to see an old courthouse in the town center, the place where Oates would have argued so many of his cases, but that structure had been gone for decades, replaced around the turn of the century by a more modern building that in turn had been torn down and replaced by the nondescript edifice in front of me. I later found out that a gas station now occupies the site of Oates's house and law office. At the cemetery behind the Baptist Church, I paid my respects at the grave of Oates's mother.

With help, I located the Abbeville Public Library, which proved to be a fortunate stop on my day trip. There, in the local history room, I unearthed some good local historical sources on Abbeville and its favorite son, William Oates. The librarian was helpful and sweet. She couldn't seem to get over the fact that someone had come all the way from Virginia just to find out more about William C. Oates. I failed to get her name, and I'm sorry for that, because she let me photocopy to my heart's content without charging me a dime.

From Abbeville, I drove north twenty miles to Eufaula, a prosperous town sitting on a high bluff overlooking the Chattahoochee and the shores of a wide and sparkling lake created by a dam on the river. Eufaula, the Barbour County seat, has lost none of its Southern beauty and charm since the time when Oates studied law there in the late 1850s. Several antebellum mansion houses are still standing in the heart of the town, and I drove past a rather out-of-place statue of a Confederate soldier holding his ground where the town center used to be. A few miles north of town, I found the old Roseland plantation house of the Toney family, Oates's in-laws. It has been much altered over the years and looked little like the photographs I had seen of it. I did come upon a groundskeeper, though, who knew where the old slave quarters had once stood and pointed out where the cotton fields had once come up close to the rear of the house. "There's no way to keep the place up," he said, explaining that the present owner was thinking of selling. More modern houses already surrounded the plantation house, some of them clearly in view from the front yard, so it seemed likely that the house might be sold if only to be razed for suburban development—something that I hoped would not come to pass. After letting the groundsman get back to work on his rider mower, I walked around the spacious yard as the evening fell swiftly. As everything became shade and shadows, I drove back to the state capital, listening to the whine of country music on the radio and feeling satisfied that I had come very close to finding a slice of William Oates's life in the rugged terrain of the Wiregrass Country.

My last day in Montgomery began in the rain and with a chill in the air. Before driving to the airport, I had one final stop to make in the city. I headed north out of downtown Montgomery to Oakwood Cemetery, Oates's resting place and the location, interestingly enough, of Hank Williams's grave. I found the country singer's memorial without difficulty, and in fact without wanting to, but spotting Oates's plot took me nearly an hour, despite the fact that his burial site is marked rather ostentatiously by a tall marble obelisk upon which stands a life-sized statue of Oates himself. In the pouring rain, I finally discovered the monument, which Oates had designed himself and for creation and placement of which he had left instructions in his will.

Half-lit in the grayness of the morning, the statue looked eerily lifelike—quick, not dead—and unnervingly realistic, particularly with its missing right arm and pinned sleeve. Inscriptions, also composed by Oates before his death, covered two sides of the memorial. Below the statue, the inscription reads:

WILLIAM C. OATES
BORN NOVEMBER 30, 1833
DIED SEPTEMBER 9, 1910

BORN IN POVERTY,
REARED IN ADVERSITY,
WITHOUT EDUCATIONAL ADVANTAGES,
YET BY HONEST INDIVIDUAL
EFFORT HE OBTAINED
A COMPETENCY AND THE
CONFIDENCE OF HIS FELLOW MEN,
WHILE FAIRLY LIBERAL TO
RELATIVES AND TO THE WORTHY POOR.
A DEVOTED CONFEDERATE SOLDIER,
HE GAVE HIS RIGHT ARM FOR THE CAUSE.

HE ACCEPTED THE RESULT OF
THE WAR WITHOUT A MURMUR;
AND IN 1898-9, HE WAS
A BRIGADIER GENERAL OF
UNITED STATES VOLUNTEERS
IN THE WAR WITH SPAIN.

And, on the rear of the memorial, the inscription simply says:

A SOLDIER IN TWO WARS,
CAPTAIN, COLONEL,
AND GENERAL;
LEGISLATOR, MEMBER OF
CONGRESS, AND GOVERNOR.

Buried beside Oates are his wife, his son, and his son's wife. While I stood beneath Oates's monument, the rain slackened, and the cemetery—despite a cold wind sent to remind Alabamians that winter had not entirely retreated—looked surprisingly green and lush. My eye caught no one else—no living soul—in Oakwood Cemetery. The old graveyard was serene and hushed. The sky above was a solid blanket of flannel gray. A lonely songbird called out a brief, but hopeful, trill. Oates would have been pleased with the way his statue and memorial came out—a fitting and impressive monument to a man who was always quite aware of his own place in the world. I think he would have especially enjoyed the fact that forevermore he stands looking down on that world, eternally perched above the fray.

*   *   *

Near the High Water Mark on Cemetery Ridge at Gettysburg, a massive white building shaped like a drum straddles the eastern slope of the ridge along the center of where the Union lines stood in the summer of 1863. The ultra-modern building, designed by the famous architect Richard Neutra, is called the Cyclorama Center, and it was completed in 1961 as the Gettysburg National Military Park's visitor center just in time to be open for the commemoration of the Civil War Centennial. I first saw the Cyclorama Center, which still houses the epic 1883 painting of Pickett's Charge by Paul Philippoteaux, soon after it opened, and I remember standing on an observation deck atop a low extension of the building in the spring twilight. Hardly any tourists were around, and the battlefield—once a scene of blood, horror, and death—was tranquil and silent. The only sounds one could hear were the soft cadences of songbirds settling down for the evening and the gentle rustle of the wind.

All at once, the stillness was broken by muffled chimes coming from the very top of the drum-shaped building, and it became almost immediately evident that the bells were ringing out the melodies of Civil War songs, the tunes that had been sung over and over by the boys who fought at Gettysburg one hundred years before. A chill ran up my spine, and it was a stirring moment for me, for I had not expected my emotions to be tugged as I stood looking over the battlefield in the fading light. As day turned slowly to night, and while the monuments on Cemetery Ridge became silhouettes on the landscape, I felt for those few minutes that I was in touch with something beyond myself, beyond perhaps even my soul, there in the advancing dusk at Gettysburg. It was an evening I would long remember.

When, several years later, I returned to Gettysburg to do research on the battle—research that has been used to write this book—I went to the Cyclorama Center late in the day to hear those chimes again, but I was disappointed to learn, by standing on the observation deck until darkness descended around me, that the bells no longer ring over the battlefield and the experience I had had in my youth can never be repeated again. In fact, it's now become almost a certainty that the Neutra structure will be razed in the near future, the Cyclorama canvas will be moved to a new venue, and the landscape along that portion of Cemetery Ridge will be "rehabilitated" to its 1863 appearance (according to National Park Service plans that intend to accomplish the impossible). Unlike others who have protested the destruction of the building because of its architectural significance, I lament its intended demise because I associate the place with a very sentimental experience I had on the battlefield, and for that reason, I'd like the building to remain standing, even if the soft bells no longer chime out their moving Civil War airs.

Beneath the observation deck of the Cyclorama Center is where I did a great deal of my research for this book, for it is there in the "office wing" that the Park Service maintained for a while its archives and library, and now the library alone. I first visited the park's research facility looking for sources on Frank Haskell and other materials on Pickett's Charge, the famous climactic encounter between the Army of Northern Virginia and the Army of the Potomac on July 3, 1863, for that Bantam book I mentioned earlier. What I stumbled upon—and I don't quite remember how it occurred—was a fairly thick bound volume of letters and other documents pertaining to William C. Oates. Almost all of the correspondence in the volume concerned Oates's unsuccessful attempt to raise a monument to the 15th Alabama and to his younger brother John, an officer in the regiment who had fallen in the battle—an attempt, as I've mentioned, that was thwarted in part by his old adversary, Joshua Lawrence Chamberlain. Probably what excited me most, besides the voluminous letters between Oates and the park officials that documented his monument campaign in extraordinary detail, were a few other letters in the bound book demonstrating conclusively that he and Chamberlain had directly corresponded with one another more than forty years after the battle of Gettysburg had been fought.

It required many future trips to Gettysburg to get the photocopies I needed of the Oates documents there and to research other aspects of the battle—primarily events that took place on the southern portion of the battlefield—with which I was less familiar than I already was with Pickett's Charge, an assault in which Oates and his men did not participate. The Park Service research files of primary source material are rich and rewarding.

My research was not limited to poring over manuscripts, old files, newspaper clippings, and dusty books. I took to the field as well. On a drizzly day in May, I kept my youngest daughter, Sarah, who was fourteen at the time, out of school and took her with me to Gettysburg for a dad-and-daughter outing. I announced to her that we would follow the route William Oates and the 15th Alabama took in their approach to Little Round Top on July 2. Doing so, she soon discovered, involved walking across sodden fields, jumping fences and stone walls, crossing a rickety bridge over a chilly stream, and climbing over rocks and fallen trees up the very steep slopes of Big Round Top, just as Oates and his Alabamians had done. We made the journey without mishap. And Sarah, in good cheer as always, hiked every step with me without once complaining or revealing any sign of being uninterested.

But that really doesn't tell the story of our day. Together we explored the past, found it in the cool mist at Gettysburg, and to this day remember that time as something special—not because it helped me write a biography of Oates, which I have since done, or even this book that you hold in your hands, but because it made me realize how closely the present is linked to the past, how much a part of it Sarah and I were, and how—in our own relationship as father and daughter—we discovered something we had not expected to find that day.

* * *

"Biography," writes Paul Murray Kendall, "deals in the peculiarities of one life."[5] Based on my experience writing about William Oates, I'm afraid I must demur. Somehow, without my fully understanding from the outset that it would, my desire to write several articles, some of which are collected in this volume, and a biography of him brought about a collision of my present with the past and made me comprehend, as I had never done before, Faulkner's injunction that the past is never really dead.

Yet, to be sure, Oates is a voice from the distant past. In coming to know him, in reconstructing his life as thoroughly as the sources have allowed me to do, I've perceived that he possessed many admirable qualities and many despicable ones, which is hardly surprising. He strived all his life to be an honest man, but he often confused outspokenness with honesty, personal opinion with truth. Too often he justified his own dishonesty and hypocrisy as a means to fulfilling his own ambitions, for he was able, like many politicians then and now, to rationalize that the ends he personally wanted were the same ends the public should desire, whether they really did or not.

He firmly believed in Southern institutions and ideas, such as slavery and the white supremacy that perpetuated it, and he supported secession, states' rights, and the Confederacy, arguing to his last days that the South was not wrong in taking its stand against the Union, against its American brethren, against four million black slaves. Like many other white southerners, he seemed untroubled about keeping African Americans in subservient roles while exploiting them for personal gain and even sexual pleasure. Deep inside, he was a violent man who could not always control his reflex to strike out first and ask questions later. His heart was constricted by his hard attitudes toward blacks, immigrants, Northerners, Republicans, Populists, and practically anyone who was unlike him. He was, as one Alabama historian describes him, "a conservative among conservatives."[6] In many respects, that's putting it mildly.

But he had many admirable qualities, too. He was, in his own way, a caring man—he cared deeply for his family, especially for his younger brother who died at Gettysburg, for his mother and his other siblings, and for his wife and son. In the Civil War, he cared about and for his men, and while many of his comrades saw him as ambitious and dangerously impetuous, it is quite evident that his men respected him and considered him an able and honest leader. He was a generous man, sometimes taking family members under his own roof and supporting them financially for long periods of time. Oates was always a hard worker, and after the war he reaped monetary rewards for his labors that far exceeded anything he had ever imagined for himself. Always frugal with a dollar, he spent his money prudently but not miserly. He swore off liquor at a young age, avoided dairy products because he was allergic to them, and enjoyed nothing better than a long cool glass of water.

He was also courageous without being overbearing about it. He carried his bravery well as an inner trait and never flaunted it or tried to make it into more than it was (except, perhaps, when he was on the political stump). He loved war, hated battle, and admitted often that he had been deeply frightened by the horrors of combat on more than one occasion. Oates called himself a colonel until he achieved higher rank—a brigadier generalship—in the war with Spain, but he technically never rose above the rank of lieutenant colonel in the Confederate service, and his claim that he was about to be commissioned a brigadier general when Appomattox ended the Confederacy forever appears, on its face, to have been more pipe dream than reality. But no one ever questioned William Oates's mettle as a soldier or an officer. He was a born warrior, even though he came to know—and fear the fact—that all war is hell.

What I also learned about Oates was that he could not put the Civil War—and especially Gettysburg—behind him. After Appomattox, the war shaped and conditioned his politics, his public persona, his personal feelings—in short, his worldview. As with Longstreet and Chamberlain, everything Oates did for the rest of his life seemed to be related to the war and its legacy. The war never really ended for any of them. Even in his final years, when Oates fought very hard to erect the monument on Little Round Top, he could not shake off old animosities of the war years and embrace the spirit of reconciliation between North and South with any great fervor. For William Oates, the Civil War remained an event that had no conclusion; it kept playing itself out, over and over again. Peace came for him only when he died in 1910, but even then he bequeathed to his family and his heirs a strong link to the war and its meaning.

In my quest to know William Oates and to reconstruct his life within the context of his times, I have not found all the answers I was looking for; no historian is ever that fortunate. There are still many things about Oates that are not known or that aren't knowable, but his life story has given me greater insight into the Civil War generation, how it survived its greatest upheaval, and how it remembered and interpreted what it had experienced. I have also gained a clearer perspective on what the Civil War generation left as a legacy to the nation, for it is through the eyes of those who experienced the war—and mostly those who survived it—that we have come to understand it, to frame a picture of it in our mind's eye, to behold it through their words and through our imaginations. My delving into Oates's life, and my getting to know Oatsie Charles, his granddaughter, who is a living link to the past, revealed to me that we cannot, as Lincoln so aptly put it, escape history.

It is fitting, I suppose, that Gettysburg is still a hub where more than a dozen modern roads, like the spokes of a wheel, converge on the town. Following those roads, I have come to know a fascinating Confederate colonel, his charming granddaughter, and—although this facet should not have been as surprising as it turned out to be—a portion of myself.

6 An Alabamian's Civil War

For William Calvin Oates, as we have already seen, the Civil War lasted a very long time. It began for him, as it did for all Americans, with the fall of Fort Sumter in Charleston harbor in April 1861. It reached its zenith on the afternoon of July 2, 1863, when Oates and his brave regiment failed to dislodge the 20th Maine from the slopes of Little Round Top at Gettysburg. His Confederate service ended in 1864 outside of Petersburg when he lost his right arm in a fierce fire fight. But Oates's war did not terminate with his wound or with Lee's surrender at Appomattox. Instead, as I have shown, it lived on for him in his thoughts, in his actions, and in his memory until the day he died. It remained part of his daily consciousness. William C. Oates never put the war behind him.

Today Oates is not widely known, although Civil War scholars and buffs readily recognize his name. Mostly he is remembered for having lost the fight for Little Round Top. This ignominious distinction was not the kind of fame Oates aspired to during his lifetime. But he never quite achieved the renown that he thought he deserved, not during his lifetime or after his death. Despite his own best efforts—which bear a striking similarity to Chamberlain's—to elevate himself and his fame, Oates remains a Civil War figure who occupies a fairly low tier beneath the likes of Robert E. Lee, Thomas J. "Stonewall" Jackson, J. E. B. Stuart, and Jefferson Davis.

In his own lifetime, though, he was better known than he is to us today. When he died in 1910, obituaries sang his praises and mourned his passing. "Alabama loses, in the death of William C. Oates, one its ablest and most patriotic citizens," declared the *Montgomery Advertiser*. In the pages of the *New York Tribune*, he was remembered "as a man of independence and character, who lived up to the traditions of the old South, and was always ready to sacrifice himself to those traditions."[1]

But he quickly faded from view and from memory after his death. And his obscurity presented me with a problem as his potential biographer. Even when one considers the fairly prominent role he played at Gettysburg, or even considering other aspects of his career as a Confederate officer or as a politician in postwar Alabama, Oates did not seem to have led an important life—a *major* life as biographers would put it. Instead, his life was clearly a minor one, a life not well or widely remembered, despite all his own yearnings for fame and distinction.Some people do lead minor lives, I suppose. Not everyone is famous. Most people are ordinary. Yet some people who are ordinary can also be, at the very same time, extraordinary. Individuals who have lived a minor life—as the pretentious and dismissive term is used by biographers to describe someone who is not famous—still may give us a valuable perspective on the past, or a glimpse of their age and how they fit into it, or a insight into ourselves and how our own lives and times differ from theirs. A minor life is not necessarily an uninteresting or an insignificant life.

Yet, in the end, to proclaim that a life is major or minor is just a little more than presumptuous. How is a major life defined differently—or lived differently, for that matter—from a minor life? Does Jefferson Davis loom in greater importance as a life than William Oates, simply because one was president of the Confederacy and the other was a mere colonel in its army? Certainly we cannot say with certainty that one man's life was any more important than the other's, although we might acknowledge that Davis clearly played a more important role in the history of the Confederacy than Oates did. Oates was not—and still is not—as famous as Jefferson Davis. But his life was not necessarily minor, either.

What came to me gradually, over the course of many years of research, and not in any eureka moment punctuated by a thunderclap, was that William C. Oates offered me an opportunity to explore a fascinating—and sometimes unsettling—life of a man who wrestled with the Southern demons of slavery, race, violence, and bigotry. He also struggled with the issues of truth and honesty, occasionally compromising his principles more than he should have or settling for prevarications when he really knew better. Indeed, William Oates led a phenomenal life—just as Geoffrey Wolff, the novelist and biographer, has said that a life, even a minor life, can be like a lightning strike.[2] Oates, as I came to learn, was a lightning strike in Southern and Civil War history.

*   *   *

The lightning struck first on November 30, 1833, when William C. Oates was born in Pike County, Alabama. His humble beginnings marked him as a man who would never amount to much. He was the son of William and Sarah Oates, poor farmers who struggled to survive in the Wiregrass Country, where nothing grew quickly except one's debts. His formal edu-

cation was paltry, and he attended school off and on throughout his childhood, but most of what he learned came from teaching himself. As a child,
he liked practical jokes and rigorous play, although he and his younger
brother John occasionally would pretend to be stump preachers delivering
fire-and-brimstone sermons under the trees near their father's cabin.

Life in frontier Alabama was precarious and violent, and Oates was a
pure product of his environment. His father, who drank too much, often
took out his frustrations on his children. "When he became angry," Oates
remembered, "it was a word and a blow[,] and sometimes the latter came
first."[3] Oates learned how to take care of himself and soon became a
brawler of renown. At seventeen, he attended a séance and exposed the
spiritualist as a fraud. The medium's father, a man named Post, came after
Oates threateningly, but the young man grabbed a mattock and brought
Post down with a single whack to the head. Convinced Post was dead,
Oates fled to Florida, where he joined the crew of a merchant schooner
plying the waters of the Gulf of Mexico. Although Post did not die and recovered from his cracked skull, Oates believed he had killed the man, and
he wandered through Florida and Louisiana eluding the Alabama authorities who had issued a warrant for his arrest.

After dallying with women and getting himself into trouble and as-
sorted fistfights, he eventually made his way to Texas, where he got into
one brawl after another and became, as he later explained, "much addicted
to gaming at cards." His quick temper and violent tendencies got him repeatedly into tight fixes, although he always managed to outfight his opponents or get out of town before they had a chance to best him. On one
occasion, a decision to "pocket" an insult kept him from facing down a
known gunman on the streets of Waco.[4]

Always he stayed one step ahead of the law; miraculously he avoided
killing anyone or getting himself killed at the hands of his enemies.
William Oates was a tough customer who seemed unable to control his
outbursts of anger or his swinging fists. As a trademark of his fighting
style, he liked to press his thumbs into his opponents' eyes. The technique
worked without fail to disable his adversary and give Oates the victory.

Oates remained in Texas only for a year or two. In another one of the
momentous lightning strikes that occurred throughout William Oates's
lifetime, his younger brother John, who had been dispatched by the family
to find William and bring him home, ran into him by chance in the town
of Henderson, Texas, and persuaded him to return to Alabama, despite

the arrest warrant that was still pending in Pike County. The two brothers traveled back to the Chattahoochee Valley together, where William Oates settled down by enrolling in an academy, teaching school, and studying law. He stayed out of Pike County, though, for obvious reasons, and managed to avoid the local authorities there. For a while, he even attended church in Eufaula, a prosperous trading town on the Chattahoochee River, but for the most part Oates and organized religion could never quite see things eye to eye.

By the late 1850s, Oates had successfully turned his life around, completely leaving behind his lawless ways and embracing a professional career as an attorney (he passed the Alabama and Georgia bars in 1858) and the owner of a weekly newspaper in Abbeville. He had experienced a personal awakening that owed little to any religious conversation and a great deal to his own determination to pull himself up by the bootstraps. Oates was now a changed man, a pillar of the community. His metamorphosis may have been influenced by his mother, a pious woman who seems to have been something of a clairvoyant. But it was Oates himself who turned his life around and who realized that in following his former ways, he was never going to amount to anything at all. Together, he and his brother John opened a law practice in Abbeville and became well respected.

When the Southern states began to secede in 1860, Oates—who bitterly opposed Lincoln's election—wanted his state to move cautiously and avoid following the fire-eaters into rash action. When Alabama joined the Confederacy, however, he threw his full support to his state and his new country. He claimed later in life to have owned slaves, but there is no evidence to confirm that fact. For the rest of his life, he fervently believed that the outbreak of war between the North and South had nothing to do with slavery, but he admitted that the peculiar institution did seem to be the cornerstone of the disagreements between the two sections.

Even after Sumter fell and Lincoln called for troops to restore the Union, Oates did not rush off and join the army without giving the whole matter due consideration. He told a friend that he was worried about his law practice, for his brother had gone off to war and left him alone to handle their business affairs. Nevertheless, Oates soon decided that the South's great cause was more important than his law practice, and in July 1861, he raised a company of volunteers, the Henry Pioneers, and became captain by an acclamation of the men in the ranks. Almost at once, the small company marched north to rendezvous with other militia units gathering at Fort Mitchell on the Chattahoochee River. As the Henry Pioneers left Abbeville, the father of one of his recruits said to him: "Captain Oates, take care of my boy."[5]

He could be entrusted to maintain good order and keep his men out of harm's way, if he could help it. In physical appearance, he looked like a leader of men and behaved with a confidence that belied his own youth. Tall in stature and robust in build, Oates was a huge man—he stood six feet, two inches tall—who commanded attention wherever he went. He had a wide, handsome face, with jet black hair and gleaming dark eyes. Later, as the war went on, he grew a scraggly beard that actually made his face look younger rather than more mature. Still possessing a violent streak, Oates was known as a man of action who did not suffer fools gladly and who could easily trounce a man with his words and fists before most men could blink an eye.

At Fort Mitchell, a crumbling stockade left over from the Creek Indian wars, the Henry Pioneers were mustered into Confederate service as Company G of the 15th Alabama regiment, under the command of Colonel James Cantey. In less than a week, the new regiment received orders to move north and join General Joseph E. Johnston's army that was occupying the defenses near Manassas and Centreville in Virginia. On the long train ride from Georgia to Virginia, Oates and his men thrilled at the well-wishers who waved handkerchiefs and cheered enthusiastically at trackside as the troops were sped north.

With Johnston's army, the 15th Alabama spent a long and cold winter wondering if they would ever fight its enemy in battle. War, nonetheless, was already taking its toll on the regiment, and disease decimated the ranks as the winter of 1861 melted into the spring of 1862. More than two hundred men of the 15th Alabama lost their lives to measles while encamped in northern Virginia. Oates and his comrades began to see that war, whether fought on the battlefield or endured in the camps, was a hard road for every soldier who shouldered a musket.

After months of inactivity, the 15th Alabama was placed in Major General Richard S. Ewell's division and sent to the Shenandoah Valley to reinforce Major General Thomas J. "Stonewall" Jackson's small army there. Oates and his men soon learned what it was like to be in Stonewall's "foot cavalry," and they marched up and down the valley following the intrepid Jackson from one battle to the next. That spring the 15th Alabama mostly stood on the sidelines as Stonewall Jackson's army fought its splendid "Valley Campaign," which earned Jackson a high reputation among the Confederate public and kept the Union forces at bay between the Appalachians and the Alleghenies. The soldiers of the 15th Alabama had so far spent the war as observers, not as fighting men.

Until they came to Cross Keys. The 15th Alabama fired the opening rounds of that battle when it erupted on Sunday morning, June 8, in the tiny village of Cross Keys, Virginia. After being pushed back from its picket lines by a vanguard of Major General John C. Fremont's advancing Union army, Oates and the other officers of the 15th Alabama regrouped the men, who hankered to dash for the safety of the rear. With their lines reformed, the Alabamians got back into the battle. During a crucial moment, Brigadier General Isaac R. Trimble, the 15th Alabama's brigade commander, took personal charge of the regiment, his white hair gleaming in the sunlight and the fire glowing in his eyes, and led the men forward, steadily pushing back the bewildered and outmaneuvered Federals to the outskirts of the village. It was the 15th Alabama's baptism by fire, and despite the regiment's skittish behavior at the start, it did pretty well for itself in the end.

About a week later, after Jackson had won yet another victory at the battle of Port Republic, Stonewall's army was called east to reinforce General Robert E. Lee's Army of Northern Virginia, which was holding back the advance of Major General George B. McClellan's Army of the Potomac across the Virginia Peninsula. At Gaines Mill, on June 27, 1862, the 15th Alabama saw action again when it attacked the Union lines and kept up a heated exchange of fire for more than an hour. A last-minute assault again saved the day and swept the Union forces from the field. Oates was proud of his regiment and his men in Company G. But the fighting had cost the Alabamians severely. The regiment, Oates later said, "made a glorious record [at Gaines Mill], but at a frightful cost."[6]

Events were moving swiftly. After Lee succeeded in making McClellan pull his forces back to the James River, the Confederate commander looked to shift the fighting back to northern Virginia and away from the valuable prize of Richmond. Jackson began to move north toward the Potomac, but at Cedar Mountain his troops squared off with a Federal force under the command of Major General John Pope on August 9. Once again, Oates and the 15th Alabama remained unengaged that day, except toward the battle's conclusion when it came under fire and Oates had the unnerving experience of having a shell explode in his face without it injuring him at all.

As Pope retreated north, Jackson's divisions swung around the Federals and surprised them along an unfinished railroad embankment on the edge of the old Manassas battlefield. On August 28, as the Confederates poured volleys down on the Union columns, Oates watched as everything became "enveloped in smoke and a sheet of fire seemed to go out from each side to the other along the whole length of the lines." The battle continued on the following day, but as Jackson's men defended their position along the embankment against wave upon wave of Federal soldiers, Oates confessed that the "blood and suffering" were so great that he became nauseous.[7] On the third day of the battle, August 30, the Union assaults caved in when they were hit on the flank by an overwhelming Confederate force—Longstreet's entire First Corps. "What a slaughter! What a slaughter of men that was," recalled one of Oates's soldiers in Company G. In a sequel to Second Manassas, the 15th Alabama fought hard in the rain on September 1 at Chantilly Farm, where the regiment broke in panic and Oates bemoaned "the disgraceful conduct of our men."[8]

At Antietam, later that month, the 15th Alabama redeemed itself by remaining in the thick of the fighting, but Oates was absent from the army on the bloodiest single day of the Civil War; he was recuperating in a farmhouse south of Sharpsburg from a nasty attack of dysentery. He rejoined the regiment to discover, however, that he was suddenly in command not only of his company but of the entire 15th Alabama. Losses from casualties and sickness had been so great ever since Gaines Mill that he was the only senior officer left on his feet. Several months later, in December, the regiment suffered even further loss at Fredericksburg when it defended the right flank of Lee's line against a crushing Federal attack near Harrison's Crossing. It was the first time that Oates commanded the 15th Alabama in battle, and while he worried about making a mistake on the battlefield, he actually showed great poise and level-headedness under fire.

During the winter of 1862–63, Oates and his regiment were camped south of Fredericksburg and waited, with the rest of the army, for the spring to bring new battles and new campaigns. A reorganization in Lee's Army of Northern Virginia placed the 15th Alabama with other Alabama regiments in a brigade commanded by Brigadier General Evander M. Law, an officer whom Oates admired and respected. The Alabama brigade was in Major General John Bell Hood's division, which, in turn, was one of the divisions in Lieutenant General James Longstreet's First Corps. Oates regarded Hood highly among Lee's fighting generals, but he was mixed in his opinion of Longstreet, whom he considered to be erratic in his performance on the battlefield.

In the spring of 1863, the regiment was ordered with the rest of Longstreet's corps to southside Virginia, where the Confederates successfully foraged for food and supplies for Lee's army, but failed to break the Federal occupation of Suffolk. As a result of this detached duty, Oates and his regiment—and, indeed, Longstreet's entire corps—missed the battle of Chancellorsville in late April and early May 1863, when Lee managed to defeat Major General Joseph Hooker's superior numbers despite Longstreet's absence. When news of Stonewall Jackson's death reached Oates and his men, they could not believe that their beloved former commander was gone.

By May 1863, Oates had risen in rank from captain to colonel. He was a solid officer—a stern disciplinarian, but fair to the men. What he lacked in military knowledge and bearing, he made up for in sheer courage. In battle, Oates was out in front of his men, urging them on, although he admitted in his later years at being scared to death going into a fight. As he confessed in his later years: "We were not all of us as brave as Caesar, nor were men with few exceptions, at all times alike brave. Much depends on the nervous system at the time."[9]

His men liked him and respected him, though some thought him too audacious. He was, said one man in the ranks, "too aggressive and too ambitious but he usually was well to the front and did not require his men to charge where he was unwilling to share the common danger."[10] All in all, the men were grateful for his leadership and for his good judgment, both on the field and off. Said one of his soldiers to his parents: "[I] have a good captain to attend to me."[11]

In the spring of 1863, Oates retained command of the regiment, but his promotion to full colonel became entangled in red tape and mired in controversy. His commission was delivered to Lee, but for reasons that are not known, the Confederate Congress failed to confirm the promotion, which technically meant that Oates never reached a rank higher than lieutenant colonel in the Confederate army. Nevertheless, he claimed for himself the rank of colonel for the remainder of his service (and—whether he had been confirmed or not—for the rest of his life).

It was to the 15th Alabama that he gave his primary loyalty and fondness, because, as he declared years later, "there was no better regiment in the Confederate army."[12] At Gettysburg in July 1863, on the rocky slopes of Little Round Top, Oates again led his boys into battle. Here was another crucial moment in his life—another lightning strike. Along the extreme left of the Union line, the 15th Alabama crashed into the solid defenses of the 20th Maine regiment, and with iron nerve attacked up the slopes of the formidable hill. Five times or more Oates and his Alabamians surged forward trying to dislodge Colonel Joshua L. Chamberlain and his men from their line along the ledges. After an hour of desperate fighting, some of it in hand-to-hand combat, Chamberlain's troops rolled down the hill in a bold bayonet charge that wiped Oates's Confederates from the hillside at the very moment that Oates had given his men the order to retreat. The result was chaos. "We ran," Oates confessed, "like a herd of wild cattle."[13] In the rush of retreat, he had to leave behind his younger brother John—his childhood companion, his adult law partner, his best friend—who had been mortally wounded in the fighting. Oates never gave up mourning his personal loss—or the larger loss the Confederacy suffered—at Gettysburg.

Although Oates's men praised him as "a handsome and brave leader," some believed he was far too impetuous on the battlefield for his own good or for theirs.[14] He displayed those traits at the battle of Chickamauga in Georgia on September 20, 1863, when, after becoming separated from his brigade, he tried without proper authority to order South Carolina troops into the battle. The 15th Alabama was also accused of accidentally firing on other Confederate troops—a charge Oates claimed was untrue, although some historians think he and his men might very well have cut down their comrades in a volley of friendly fire.

Whatever did happen at Chickamauga, it was plain that Oates was not at his best on that battlefield. He seemed almost dazed and confused as he tried to make sense of tangled terrain and the broken battle lines, and his snap decisions in the heat and smoke of battle put his men in jeopardy during several crucial moments on September 20 and September 21. For the rest of his life, he defended his actions at Chickamauga, but his arguments appeared strained and, in the end, remained unconvincing.

After Chickamauga, the Confederates attempted to seal off the Union army's line of communications around Chattanooga, and Oates and the 15th Alabama were assigned to defend a stretch of ground at Brown's Ferry along a bend in the Tennessee River. On the morning of October 27, in a dense fog, Union forces attempted to break through at Brown's Ferry. Oates threw in company after company, trying to hold the Federal advance back, but his effort was futile. The bluecoats steadily gained ground, and as they did Oates was struck in the thigh and hip by an enemy minié ball. To Oates, it felt like "a brick had been hurled against me."[15] He was carried to safety by his men, but his wound was severe, and the military doctors sent him home to Alabama to recuperate for four months.

In March 1864, Oates—walking with a cane—limped back into service as commander of the 15th Alabama in Lee's Army of Northern Virginia. Two months later, at the battle of the Wilderness, Oates distinguished himself, and removed whatever tarnish had stained his military reputation, when he and the 15th Alabama performed a flanking maneuver that enabled the Alabama Brigade to overwhelm Federal troops along the Plank Road on May 6. Oates's superior officer, Colonel William F. Perry, called the assault "one of the most brilliant movements I have ever seen on a battle-field." Later that afternoon, however, both of the Alabama Brigade's flanks were enveloped by a Union assault, and the whole brigade broke and ran—the only occasion during the entire war when the brigade as a whole was driven from the field. Oates was philosophical about the rout, given the superior Federal forces that the Alabamians faced. As he recalled years later, "we had a lively run for three or four hundred yards."[16]

From the Wilderness, Lee moved his army toward Spotsylvania Court House, and as he did, Oates and the 15th Alabama were drawn into a defensive action near Laurel Hill on May 8. Overwhelmed by the enemy, Oates and his regiments retired, surviving friendly fire from their rear, and went into battle line behind some hastily constructed log breastworks. Two days later, as part of a grand assault by Grant against Lee's fortified lines near Spotsylvania, the Federals tried to take the Confederate breastworks along the Alabamians' front in two separate attacks, but the Alabama Brigade—feeling particularly secure behind its defenses—easily repelled the charges.

When Grant attempted another breakthrough along the Confederate right on May 12, at the salient known as the "mule shoe," he shattered the Confederate lines in a maelstrom of bullets and bayonets, only to find that he could not hold the ground his men had taken at such a high cost. Meanwhile, Oates and his regiment remained behind their sturdy defenses on the Confederate left while death and destruction reached a horrible crescendo at the Bloody Angle that day.

The fighting would not stop. Throughout the remainder of May and into June, the armies under Grant and Lee fought almost incessantly, day after day. All the while, Grant kept moving his army to the left, toward the North Anna River, where he hoped to catch Lee away from his entrenchments. The 15th Alabama had a pretty easy time of it, avoiding any major confrontation with the enemy, until the last day of May. Ordered to hold an abandoned trench, Oates and his men drove off an annoying party of Union sharpshooters, but later in the day they faced a large enemy force bearing down on them. In the nick of time, Major General John B. Gordon—the same man who would later salute Chamberlain at Appomattox—arrived with his Georgia brigade to reinforce the Alabamians.

On June 3, the 15th Alabama occupied a section on the left of Lee's defensive line near Cold Harbor, between the Pamunkey and Chickahominy rivers, not far from the Gaines Mill battlefield, where the regiment had fought in June 1862. Frustrated in his efforts to force Lee out of his trenches for a fight in the open, Grant decided to launch a frontal attack on the Army of Northern Virginia and use the overwhelming might of the Union army to crush Lee once and for all. Although the most concerted Federal assaults were made against Lee's right, Oates and the 15th Alabama—holding defenses on the Confederate left—were hard hit by Union troops in a bloody assault that caught the Alabamians somewhat off guard. After Oates regained his composure and his men hastily loaded their muskets, the 15th Alabama opened fire when the enemy was only about thirty steps away. The Union troops could stand it only for a few minutes. They retreated in haste, leaving their dead and moaning wounded behind. When they reformed and hit the Confederate lines again, they were struck by frontal and flank fire, and the blue ranks fell in heaps. Oates remembered years later that he could see "the dust fog out of a man's clothing in two or three places at once where as many balls would strike him at the same moment." In two minutes, said Oates, "not a man of them was standing."[17]

In the wake of Cold Harbor, Oates's rival for command of the regiment—Alexander Lowther—renewed his efforts to gain the 15th Alabama as his own. When Lowther appealed directly to President Jefferson Davis, Oates found himself politically outflanked and outgunned. Command of the 15th Alabama was handed to Lowther. To appease Oates, the Confederate leadership offered him command of the 48th Alabama instead. He took it, but he did not serve long at its head. At Fussell's Mills (near Petersburg, Virginia), while commanding the 48th Alabama, Oates lost his right arm to the "hard blow" of a Yankee minié ball on August 16, 1864.[18] The wound was slow to heal. He returned to Alabama, hoping all the while to rejoin the 48th Alabama as soon as gained his strength back. That moment never came. With his arm gone, and the Confederacy facing its final months, William Oates was out of the war. In April 1865, the remnants of the 15th Alabama stacked their arms when Lee surrendered at Appomattox, but Oates was not there to witness this final chapter in the Confederacy's tragic history.

Back in Alabama, Oates recuperated slowly and resumed his law practice in Abbeville. He worked extremely hard, and, unlike other Southerners who suffered great privation after the war, he began to make a small fortune by taking any law case that came his way and by speculating successfully in land and cotton. With this success, he turned his attention to local and national politics. Outraged by the Reconstruction policies of the Republican Party, he renewed his affiliation with the Democratic Party in earnest and quickly rose as a leader among the Alabama "Bourbons"— white Democrats who sought to regain political control of their state and region. Running as "the One-armed Hero of Henry County," and blatantly using his war record and his personal sacrifices for the Confederate cause as a political trump card, he served in 1868 as a delegate to the Democratic National Convention, and from 1870 to 1872 he won election to the Alabama House of Representatives.

Postwar politics for Oates were simply an extension of the war itself. He fought at the grassroots level against the imposition of Federal policies on state affairs, championed states' rights as though the war had never happened, campaigned vigorously against black suffrage and civil rights as if the Thirteenth, Fourteenth, and Fifteenth Amendments had never been ratified, and argued strenuously that secession was a constitutionally sound principle, despite the outcome of the war. As a delegate to the Alabama constitutional convention in 1875, Oates found himself in a position to put some of these beliefs into practice as he helped to shape fundamental law for the state at the same moment as congressional Reconstruction was waning in the South.

His hard work in local and state politics paid off. In 1880, he was elected from Alabama's Third District to the U. S. House of Representatives, where he served seven consecutive terms. In Washington, he made a name for himself, rubbing elbows with Democratic party leaders and with President Grover Cleveland. Oates's wife, Sarah Toney Oates, a beautiful young woman whom he had married in 1882, became known for her social graces and her splendid parties. On their wedding day, he was forty-eight and she was nineteen.

In Congress, Oates labored tirelessly for states' rights and for legislation that would benefit Alabama and his constituents. But he also carried the legacy of the war with him through the halls of Congress. Whenever legislation granting pensions to Union generals or their widows came up on the floor, Oates consistently cast his vote against such proposals. He was, however, willing to concede that the most capable Union generals, including Grant and Sherman, deserved postwar rewards and acknowledgment of their service to the nation, and he even supported the case of Fitz John Porter, the Union general cashiered by John Pope after the battle of Second Manassas, when legislation was introduced in Congress to restore Porter's good name.

But for the most part, Oates spent his seven terms in Congress trying to regain the ground that the Confederacy—and the Democratic Party—had lost during the Civil War. In many respects, he was successful, if only by adding his voice to those of other vocal Southern Democrats who believed that they had fought for a just cause in the war and that they had no reason to apologize for their actions. Oates also fully embraced the rhetoric and ideology of the "Lost Cause," a mindset that romanticized the Confederacy's purpose, the South's noble ideals, and the tragedy of the defeat suffered by the Southern people. But for Oates, the Lost Cause actually became a blueprint for the future, an optimistic political program by which the South might accomplish what it had originally set out to achieve by leaving the Union.

As Oates wrote to E. P. Alexander, Longstreet's former artillery chief, in 1868: "I am one of those who do not believe that the cause is wholly lost. I believe that it is only stifled by force & rests in obeyance & will again lie revived & ultimately triumph, but perhaps in a different form. It may be clad in new habitments, but the principles—which were truth & can never perish—will be triumphant in the end." The "principles" to which he referred were states' rights and white supremacy. "And now that I am fighting for the Democracy [i.e., the Democratic Party]," Oates continued, "it is but a continuation of the great conflict with this difference: the other was for constitutional liberty as bequeathed to the American people by Washington & his compeers, outside of the Union—the present issue is for the same principle within it."[19]

In 1894, seeing a political opportunity present itself back home, he resigned from Congress and ran for governor of Alabama in a contest that became infamous for its double-dealing, dirty politics, and corrupt bargains. He won the election, but he kept a campaign promise to serve only a single two-year term as governor. In politics, he was known as a die-hard conservative and "a party regular par excellence."[20] Oates was a fierce opponent of immigration, organized labor, and Free Silver. Like other

Southern Democrats, he detested the Populists and approved the use of fraudulent tactics to defeat them at the polls.

His racial views were typical of the patrician class in the South, despite his own humble origins, and he fully believed that African Americans were racially inferior to whites. Nevertheless, he asserted that "there are some white men who have no more right and no more business to vote than a Negro and not as much as some of them."[21] He thought that conservative black leaders, such as Booker T. Washington, should provide a model for African American self-improvement and personal advancement.

After leaving the governor's office, Oates hoped to run for the U.S. Senate, but he failed to win his party's nomination. Instead, the Spanish-American war gave him an opportunity to serve his country. In 1898, he received a brigadier general's commission from President William McKinley, and he commanded three different brigades during the short war. "I am now a Yankee General, formerly a Rebel Colonel, and right each time!" he declared with delight.[22] He served diligently and patiently in Georgia and Pennsylvania, all the while hoping to command Alabama troops and be placed in combat, but the war ended before any such transfer to the theaters of war could be effected.

By 1900, a wave of reconciliation had succeeded in bringing North and South closer together in a spirit of brotherhood. Across the nation, Union and Confederate veterans attended battlefield reunions and expressed joy that old animosities had faded away and that they had helped to forge a stronger nation out of the discord that had once driven America apart. Reconciliation did help the nation to heal its old wounds, but it did so by relegating the causes of the war—particularly slavery and the issue of black civil rights—to the dustbin. Both sides could honor each other's courage and commitment only by agreeing that race had played no significant part in the war or its outcome. Oates readily accepted this premise and, for the rest of his life, steadfastly maintained that the sectional debate over slavery had not caused the war.

But with the advent of the twentieth century, some of Oates's cherished racial opinions—beliefs that were legacies of the antebellum period or of the war itself—began to change. At the Alabama constitutional convention of 1901, where he served as an at-large delegate, Oates spoke out strongly against "grandfather clauses" and other measures that were aimed at disfranchising black voters. He had come to see over the years that African Americans were sometimes better informed as voters than whites. And while his arguments in favor of black suffrage were not entirely motivated by humanitarian concerns, for he wanted to cultivate African American votes for the Democratic Party rather than to deprive them of their suffrage rights under the assumption that blacks would vote only for Republicans in any given election, he nevertheless articulated a change of heart in how he viewed African Americans and their humanity.

He had not given up his commitment to white supremacy or his belief that whites should control the government, whether local, state, or national. However, his expression of support for African American suffrage carried with it an unavoidable corollary: if enough blacks voted in elections, it might be conceivable that they would one day vote members of their own race into office.

Apart from the suffrage question, though, Oates also spoke out at the convention against the epidemic of violence—particularly vigilante lynchings—being committed against black people. Even more than his remarks against the "grandfather clause" and prohibitions against black suffrage, his words pleading for the cessation of violence against African Americans struck a dramatic humanitarian chord. "When the negro is doing no harm," Oates said to the convention in bewilderment, "why [do] people want to kill him and wipe him from the face of the earth?"[23] His words were like a bolt of lightning striking the conventional hall. But they went totally unheeded. White terrorism against blacks continued unabated in Alabama and throughout the South. And when the state constitutional convention finally adjourned, it recommended a document that effectively abolished the African American right to vote. Although Oates disliked the proposed constitution, he decided in the end not to oppose its ratification.

The Civil War not only lived on for Oates in politics and the legacy of racial issues, it remained a focal point in his life for deep personal reasons. Ever since the battle of Gettysburg, when he had left his mortally wounded brother on the slopes of Little Round Top, the war and its losses had plagued him. Two anniversaries especially haunted him: December 24, his brother John's birthday, and July 2, the day when his beloved brother had been struck down. After the war, he was able to track down the Union doctor who had treated John Oates's wounds in a field hospital outside Gettysburg. The physician sent a kind response to Oates's queries about his brother's last days, and he informed the surviving Oates that the young man had said on his death bed: "Tell my folks at home that I died in the arms of friends."[24]

When Oates was assigned to Camp Meade, south of Harrisburg, during the war with Spain, he took advantage of his proximity to Gettysburg to visit the battlefield with his wife and son, William Jr. It was during that visit that Oates first decided to erect a monument at Little Round Top to the memory of his deceased brother and the other soldiers of the 15th Alabama who had died at Gettysburg. After some preliminary inquiries, it was not until 1902 that Oates was able to petition the Gettysburg Battlefield Commission, which served as an arm of the War Department, for permission to place a monument on Little Round Top. For two years, Oates attempted to work through the bureaucratic web spun by the commissioners and to overcome resistance to the monument expressed, as we have seen, in ambiguous language by his old battlefield nemesis, Joshua Lawrence Chamberlain. The commissioners never approved Oates's application for a monument, Oates uncharacteristically ran out of steam, and the hillside at Gettysburg remained barren of Confederate memorials, as it does to this day.

But the memories of the war brought not only sadness to his heart. He took great pride in the deeds of the 15th Alabama during the war, and, after 1880 or so, he began to compile a history of the regiment by corresponding with its surviving members and by researching its accomplishments in the *Official Records* and other published documentary sources. Ultimately the massive book that took shape from this effort was a combined history of the regiment and personal memoir, which finally was published in 1905 as his magnum opus, *The War between the Union and the Confederacy and Its Lost Opportunities*. Today his book is highly regarded by historians, who value its accuracy and candor. Some have even proclaimed it one of the best Civil War reminiscences ever written. Throughout the book, Oates did not mince words in criticizing the Confederate high command and the mistakes that had led to defeat. His favorite targets were Jefferson Davis and James Longstreet, but he generally had uncomplimentary things to say about most of his superior officers and several others in the Confederate army who seemed, in his own humble estimation, to toss away the hopes of the Confederacy by failing to take advantage of countless opportunities that could have brought success to the cause. Oates even dared to criticize Lee's strategy at Gettysburg, which in the opinion of most former Confederates was tantamount to heresy. "Lee, with all his robust daring and adventurous spirit, should not have ordered the impossible, as was apparent to the skilled observer," Oates said of Pickett's Charge.[25]

During the final years of his life, he practiced law and concentrated on his real estate ventures, amassing a small fortune in the process. Because of the racial views he had expressed during the state constitutional convention, he was ostracized from Alabama politics. He traveled in Europe with his wife and son, and Oates's letters about their grand tour provide an entertaining glimpse of the Continent through his very Southern eyes. At home, he was not forgotten, and Oates remained for many years a household name that Alabamians equated with the heroism of the Civil War and the politics of the postwar Democratic Party.

When he died in Montgomery on September 9, 1910, he was remembered for his military and public service. At his graveside in the Oakwood Cemetery, various artillery, cavalry, and infantry companies, dressed in khaki uniforms of the day, bowed their heads in quiet tribute to this soldier of two nations, the Confederate and the United States of America. "A great figure in our history has passed," reported the *Birmingham Ledger,* "for he made his record on the battlefield, in the capitol at Washington[,] and in the historic state capitol in Montgomery."[26] The Civil War for Oates had finally ended.

*   *   *

Oates's life is a Southern story—as much a part of the South, in its own way, as the hard destruction of the Confederacy, the sentimental poems of Paul Hamilton Hayne, the horrid injustices of Jim Crow, the white supremacist bombasts of Theodore Gilmore Bilbo, the agonizing childhood of Richard Wright, the decay and anguish that pervade Faulkner's novels, the stars falling on Alabama, and the tidewater mornings of William Styron. It is the story of how one white Southern man from the humblest of backgrounds rose to great heights but failed to achieve lasting glory or immortality. It is the story of a very ordinary man who possessed some extraordinary talents and who, despite all his best efforts, could not escape his past.

"The great man, with his free force direct out of God's own hand," wrote Thomas Carlyle, that somber Scottish worshiper of heroes, "is the lightning."[27] Yet Oates—who was not necessarily a great man, but was most assuredly an enthralling and an intriguing man—was his own lightning strike. Perhaps great men—great figures in history, men and women—are precisely as Carlyle described them: like lightning out of heaven. William Oates struck the earth with his own fire, which came streaking forth not so much from heaven, but out of the captivating and ever-so-mysterious blackness of the Southern night sky.

7   Hell in Haymarket

Perhaps one reason the Civil War would not end for William C. Oates was because its human cost was so high. As we have seen, the loss of his brother at Gettysburg haunted him for the rest of his life. There were other human losses, too, particularly early in the war, long before the 15th Alabama fired any shot in anger at an enemy or participated in any combat on a battlefield.

Disease and primitive medical knowledge were actually the Civil War soldier's worst enemies. For every soldier killed in battle, two died of disease. During their first summer of service in the Confederate army, Oates and his comrades of the 15th Alabama Infantry watched as the first casualties dropped from their ranks, not from wounds inflicted by their Federal foes, but from the deadlier onslaught of microbes and viruses in their camp. The Alabamians learned before they ever fired a single shot in anger that war often brought suffering and death where they were least expected and that this particular war would seldom show mercy to anyone caught in the swath of its deadly scythe.

After Oates formed the Henry Pioneers in July 1861, he marched his men north to become Company G of the newly established 15th Alabama Infantry, under the command of Colonel James Cantey, a Mexican War veteran. Oates, as I've pointed out, was named captain of Company G by the endorsement of the men—something that Oates claimed was not an election but an expression of support meant to acknowledge the role he had played in recruiting the company.[1] From Fort Mitchell on the Chattahoochee River, Cantey moved the 15th Alabama—about one thousand men strong—north by train to Richmond, where the regiment spent a few weeks drilling and training. Then, on August 21, the Alabamians received orders to the front. When they heard the news, the men cheered and sang all through the night.

The next morning, Cantey led the regiment through the streets of Richmond to the railroad depot, where President Jefferson Davis reviewed the troops and complimented Cantey on their fine appearance. The newly elected governor of Alabama, John Gill Shorter, a prominent Democrat from Eufaula with whom Oates was politically allied, was also there to see the 15th off, and he delivered a short address before the men boarded the cars. According to one Alabama soldier, Gill's speech "did our hearts good," for apparently the governor stirringly invoked the memory of Patrick Henry who, eighty years before, had denounced King George III by declaring, "Give me liberty, or give me death!" The connections between the American Revolution and the Civil War generation, as we have seen, were very tangible and inspiring. Once on the train, the men gave a rousing "rebel yell," the whistle blew, and the wooden stock cars lurched forward toward Manassas Junction.[2]

All around Centreville and Manassas, where the Confederates had won their first major victory in a battle fought on July 21 against a Union invasion force under the command of Brigadier General Irvin McDowell, the Southern lines had been extended by General Joseph E. Johnston, who expected that Union forces would cross the Potomac again in another attempt to march on Richmond. Reinforcements from all over the South were rushed to the Manassas defenses as war fever spread throughout the Confederacy and recruits poured into the army in the wake of the fighting along Bull Run creek. By August, Johnston's army numbered less than forty thousand soldiers, but the general felt he needed more men to keep the Federal army from contemplating—and perhaps succeeding in—another push south.

As the train carrying the 15th Alabama passed through little hamlets—places no bigger or even smaller than Abbeville—on its ambling journey north, loyal Virginians stood by the tracks cheering the soldiers and waving their hats and handkerchiefs. At each stop, where the train took on fuel or water, Gus McClendon, one of Oates's privates in Company G, remembered that "the patriotic ladies and beautiful Virginia girls would be gathered . . . to welcome us, distributing their fruits and flowers and cheering us on with expressions of delight when informed we were from Alabama."

It took all day for the train to reach Manassas Junction, where the men of the 15th Alabama got off the cars, formed ranks, and marched about five miles from the station to an old field called Pageland, a flat open plain just north of the Warrenton Turnpike where the Page family had intended to build a mansion and develop a plantation, although they never got around to it. On the march, Captain Benjamin Gardner of Company I led his men behind him while he strolled forward holding a great umbrella over his head. "It had a most unmilitary appearance," Oates remembered years later, "but the captain was large and corpulent, a lawyer by profession, unused to the sun, fifty-two years old, and therefore excusable."[3]

Oates and his company—and the rest of the 15th Alabama—went into camp beside the 21st North Carolina, the 16th Mississippi, and the 21st Georgia regiments. Across the broad expanse of field, row upon row of tents could be seen and practically nothing else. The noise of camp—officers shouting, feet plodding on dry sod, bugles blowing, drums tapping—echoed over Pageland in one vast discord of sound. The water was bad in the camp, the weather was hot, and many a thirsty soldier decided to drink the tainted water rather than suffer from dehydration. Colonel Cantey saw to it that his companies drilled hard every day, and from miles around one could see the dust rising from Pageland like the billowing smoke of a forest fire.

"Drilling and performing the routine of camp duty was the regular order," recalled Oates many years later. Despite the arduous regularity of going through the order of drill every day for at least four hours, the men did have some respite and moments of gaiety and laughter. Oates fondly remembered "the fife of old Hildebrand, and Jimmie Newberry's and Pat Brannon's drums, as they were heard at reveille and tattoo." Colonel Cantey's teamster also brought a smile to the men's faces: he "was the only man connected with the regiment," Oates said, "who could surpass the Colonel in profanity." But camp life involved mostly endless marching and backbreaking work. As Gus McClendon remembered: "The fatigue duty consisted of policing the camp, looking after its sanitary condition, cutting and hauling wood, and going with the forage and commissary wagons to the depot at Manassas Junction, to assist in loading them with the supplies for man and beast."[4]

With the camp less than two miles from the fields where the battle of Manassas had been fought, Oates decided to take Company G and some other men from the regiment on a tour of the ground. It had been just a month since the Confederate victory had been won, and the Alabamians were all curious to see what a battlefield really looked like. At first, the terrain matched their own romantic conceptions of the battle and the heroes who had fallen fighting for their righteous cause. Oates recalled that white posts "had been set up to mark each of the places where fell General [Bernard] Bee, of South Carolina, Colonels [Francis] Bartow, of Georgia; [C. F.] Fisher, of North Carolina, and [J. B.] Jones, of Alabama."

The men walked over the ground with expressions of awe and wonder on their faces. Caspar W. Boyd, a private in Company I, wrote home to his parents that he "found a sight ther that I never saw befor." Some of the dead from the battle had been hastily buried and their arms and hands protruded from beneath thin mounds of dirt. Boyd and his comrades even discovered severed hands and feet on the ground. The carcasses of dead horses still littered the field. He remarked that they strolled by the Widow Henry house, where the widow herself had been "kiled on her bed" during the battle.[5]

Oates distinctly remembered, almost forty-five years later, the pungent smell of fennel and pennyroyal—weeds that had been mashed down during the battle and that still gave off their recognizable aromas—as he and his men visited the battlefield that warm August day. Some of the men thought the smell came from "dead Yankees," concluding that Northerners must have a different smell in death than Southerners did. A few of the Alabamians reacted to the battlefield with less solemnity than did Oates or Caspar Boyd. Gus McClendon reported that some of the men treated the outing like a picnic, and they felt "like birds turned out of a cage." Nevertheless, he and his companions could not avoid being amazed at the sight of a stand of pine, where the 7th Georgia had been known during the battle to have held its ground, that had been chopped to pieces by musket volleys. "It was a wonder to us," wrote McClendon, "how a man could live in such a place."[6]

If nothing else, the excursion to the Manassas battlefield gave the Alabama boys reason to ponder war and its grim realities. Besides the remains of soldiers in shallow graves, Oates and his men roamed fields where the grass was still stained red with dried blood, where unexploded shells lay exposed to view, and where minié balls covered patches of ground in a thick lead carpet. To McClendon, the "horrible" battlefield offered "sad scenes" that "furnished food for reflection." Although some tried to treat the tour as a frolic, no one who visited the battlefield that day would ever regard war in quite the same fashion as he had done before.

"At the time," wrote McClendon, "I was full of malice and hatred for the 'Boys in Blue' and was just as anxious to kill him as he was to kill me, yet when I would stop and take a second thought, and gaze upon those little mounds I could truthfully say of the dead 'Boy in Blue' that sometime, and somewhere, he had been 'somebody's darling.'" When the men walked solemnly back to Pageland and reached their camp, they thought their short journey had showed them the worst of war. They had no idea of the far worse horrors yet to come.[7]

Those horrors began at Pageland. It was in the Confederate camps there that, in the words of one private in the 15th Alabama, "the reaper commenced the harvest of death" that would continue for the regiment until its surrender at Appomattox. When the 15th Alabama had first arrived at Pageland, its closest neighbor in the camp, the 21st North Carolina, was already struggling with an epidemic of measles and serious outbreaks of mumps and typhoid. All of these diseases were—and still are—highly contagious, although in our modern times we have grown accustomed to dealing with them during childhood or having vaccines and other medicines that quickly wipe them out. In the Civil War, measles was by far, as Oates himself declared, "the worst enemy of our army," for it spread rapidly among the adult soldiers who had developed no immunity to the disease and who could do nothing to fight it.[8]

Measles cut through the ranks of the 15th Alabama encampment like a biblical plague or the medieval Black Death. No one, including the small number of surgeons assigned to the army, knew that the disease was carried on droplets through the air and that proximity to the virus meant almost certain infection. In this respect, it is somewhat miraculous that the entire Confederate camp at Pageland was not stricken down with the disease. Infected soldiers experienced high fever, rash, runny noses, watery eyes, and coughing. Having no vaccine or effective treatment, few men who were infected survived the illness. After the initial symptoms, their condition generally grew worse—some soldiers came down with pneumonia and encephalitis (brain inflammation); others suffered middle-ear infections, severe diarrhea, and convulsions. The worst cases—and there were hundreds of them among the troops of the 15th Alabama—resulted in death.[9]

The first man to die in the regiment was Andrew J. Folmar, eighteen, a private in Company I. Then many others took sick rapidly and had no strength or immunity to fight off the overwhelming disease. About one hundred men died in the regiment over the span of six weeks. A military funeral and burial were performed for each death, and the obsequies soon became part of the camp's daily routine. Overcome with emotion from this profusion of sickness and death, one private wrote in despair: "Beneath the soil of Prince William [County], now slumber in quiet repose, secure from summer's heat and winter's cold, from the cares of life and shock of strife, the noblest and best of the regiment." Those who fell to sickness were stricken by the fear—and the almost certainty—of approaching death. Sick and well alike yearned to feel the comforts of home and to be magically transported from this strange land where so many men were dying. For those on death's doorstep, the longing for home was even more pronounced. "The thought of home is ever uppermost in the mind," admitted one Alabamian, "and a wish exists to be buried with their fathers and the companies of their youth."[10] Their wish would not be granted.

At Pageland, the "Dead March" was so frequently heard that men became inured to it and soon did not even inquire as to who had died this time or who was being buried. The endless deaths produced a "crude shock" among the men of the 15th Alabama and, as anyone might expect, "threw a gloom" over the camp that could not be shaken off. So many men were sick that the routine camp duty for those who remained healthy became more strenuous than ever, for now there were fewer hands to do the work. Throughout the desolation of this epidemic, the 15th Alabama—just like all the other regiments—was ordered to keep up its drill four hours a day, although those who had no sickness began to lose their strength under the physical burdens they had to bear.[11]

Oates became outraged at the desperate situation. He faulted the army for keeping the sick in the same camp with the healthy men, which ensured that those who were not yet sick soon would be. Years later he wrote in anger: "I do not know who was responsible for it, but it was a great mistake. There was not that care taken of the men of any regiment, so far as my observation extended, which foresight, prudence and economy of war material—leaving humanity out of the question—imperatively demanded. . . . Had the Confederate authorities made more persistent efforts than they did, hospitals could have been established in sufficient numbers to have saved the lives of hundreds and thousands of good men, which were for the want of them unnecessarily sacrificed." Oates also believed that the surgeons could be blamed as well. They were "criminally negligent," he said, "for not earnestly protesting against such sacrifices of human life." He reached a bitter, but obvious, conclusion: "This folly lost to the service more men than were put out of it by the enemy's bullets."[12]

Someone in the high command eventually decided that the Alabamians had stayed at Pageland long enough, and around the middle of September the 15th Alabama—along with several other regiments—received orders to transfer its camp closer to Centreville. Oates and the other men of the 15th struck their tents under a sweltering sun, leaving many of the regiment's sick behind (about three hundred men), and marched up and down the swales along the Warrenton Turnpike toward Bull Run creek. Surely the sights and sounds of death had been more than enough for them at Pageland, but the Alabamians once more had to march through the Manassas battlefield, where those dour reminders of war and combat remained exposed in their shallow graves. One of Oates's men later wrote that the decomposing carcasses of humans and beasts spoke "in dumb eloquence" of man's inhumanity.

From the battlefield, Oates led his men—now beaten down by the heat, their own fatigue, and somber thoughts of death—along the Alexandria Pike until they reached a vast open field, not altogether unlike Pageland, about five miles east of the little village of Centreville. There they established Camp Toombs, named in honor of Robert Augustus Toombs of Georgia, who had resigned his appointment as Confederate secretary of state to become a brigadier general (Oates called him "Georgia's most erratic and greatest talker"). Not far from the camp were "bold springs" of water, the kind Virginia was noted for, Oates said happily.

The measles, predictably so, followed the column from Pageland to Camp Toombs, even though the sickest men had been quarantined at Pageland. The men of the 15th Alabama, and of a good number of other regiments as well, kept dying. Barnett "Bud" Cody—a private in the 15th Alabama who was the son of a clergyman and Oates's playmate in their younger days—got sick, and he began to fear for his own life. The doctor told him to stay in his tent, which soldiers were not allowed to do, especially when it came time for drill and dress parade. Oates, however, released Cody for duty for several days and allowed him to get stronger. Other men were not as fortunate. The army had an epidemic on its hands, and no one seemed to know quite what to do about it.

The men turned to religion, as people—and particularly soldiers—do everywhere in times of doubt or utter despair. They were desperate, these young Confederate boys who cherished their Bibles and wrote home to their families to inform them that they kept up with their Scripture readings, despite the taxing demands that the army placed on them every day. While he was on guard duty one day, a little girl gave Gus McClendon a Bible as a present, all carefully inscribed with the girl's name. He carried the book through several battles, treasuring the gift and honoring the girl who had given it to him. In camp, an itinerant preacher arrived to do some Bible beating and held a prayer meeting that attracted large numbers of soldiers. The preacher handed out Bibles to the men, but only if they would promise to carry the Good Book with them, which many of them did.[13]

As the Confederates who assembled around Fairfax Court House and Centreville waited for the war to erupt into battle again—which it did not do during these long weeks in the early autumn of 1861—someone at head-quarters finally decided to establish separate hospitals for each regiment's roster of sick men. The 15th Alabama's was established at Haymarket, a little village with a handful of houses and shops along a thoroughfare that went west to Winchester and east to Manassas. Ill and dying soldiers from the 15th Alabama, including the ones who had been left behind at Pageland and those who had more recently succumbed to disease in the new camp near Centreville, were transported in uncomfortable springless wagons to the field hospital in Haymarket.[14]

The village, located about six miles southwest of the Manassas battlefield, was not a perfect place to set up a hospital. South and west of the town, a marshy stretch of woods produced more than a sufficient quantity of the "bad air" and "bad water" that Civil War doctors incorrectly believed were the causes of contagious diseases. Haymarket, once the seat of the county district court, was laid out along a broad tree-lined main street of dirt with a few bisecting narrow lanes. The town had begun in the eighteenth century as a tavern called Red House, which served travelers who journeyed on the Carolina and Dumfries roads, two of the busiest trade routes in eastern Virginia.

In 1799, the General Assembly had enacted a charter of incorporation for Haymarket, and the district court convened there shortly after. A commission was appointed in 1800 to find the land and necessary buildings that could be used as a courthouse. The commissioners eventually purchased land and buildings south of the village center from William Shinker, one of Haymarket's founders, and converted them for use as a courthouse, clerk's office, and jail. The local Masonic chapter used the new courthouse for its lodge meetings.[15]

Court days in Haymarket were raucous ones, with everyone gathering in the little village from miles around—crowding the place beyond its capacity—to plead their cases or to defend themselves in the impressive brick edifice that held the district court. The court's first session was held in the spring of 1803. A racetrack near the courthouse provided local sportsmen with a chance to run their steeds. But these days of court edicts, market prosperity, and courtyard frivolity were short-lived.

In 1807, district courts were abolished by the state General Assembly, and Haymarket no longer enjoyed the hustle and bustle of court days or the distinction of serving the community as a judicial center. Worse, the town, while located at a crossroads, was not a hub of either roads or commerce. After the court was abolished, the General Assembly ordered the buildings in Haymarket to be sold. By 1814, during the War of 1812, the court buildings were occupied by the Hygeia Academy, but the school thrived only a brief time before its doors closed in 1816. Later the fields around the vacant buildings got good use by local children, who played their games there, and by horse breeders, who still took advantage of the racecourse to test the speed and agility of their horses.[16]

During the early 1820s, an Episcopalian minister tried without success for eight years to form a new parish in the old courthouse. Finally, in 1830, the Episcopal Church purchased the old court building—the imposing brick one that had served as the district court—and established a substantial flock of worshippers. A small wooden steeple was added to the gable roof above an octagonal cupola. The parish was named St. Paul's. Twenty years before the Civil War, Bishop William Meade wrote: "The old courthouse at Hay-Market has been purchased and converted into a handsome and convenient temple of religion. A race-course once adjoined the courthouse, and in preaching there in former days I have, on a Sabbath, seen from the court-house bench, on which I stood, the horses in training for the sport that was at hand. Those times have, I trust, passed away forever."[17]

By the 1850s, the village's struggling economy was boosted by the arrival of the Manassas Gap Railroad, which laid its tracks practically through the center of Haymarket. But sectional tensions could be felt in the village, just as they could in every town throughout the nation. In November 1859, John Brown's raid on Harper's Ferry threw Haymarket into a frenzy, and a militia company—the Prince William Rifles—was organized to put down any slave rebellion fomented by outside agitators like Brown. The company could often be seen drilling on the front lawn of St. Paul's Church, the young men marching proudly with their Springfield muskets resting on their shoulders. When the Commonwealth of Virginia later put the political issue of secession to a vote, only one Haymarket man voted against leaving the Union.

When the war broke out, the young men of Haymarket—like the boys in Oates's Company G—volunteered for service in the Prince William Rifles, drilled some more in the fields beside the church, and later became Company F of the 17th Virginia Infantry. Young men and boys were conspicuously missing from the population of Haymarket in the summer of 1861, for they, with their Southern brethren, were serving dutifully in the Confederate army. During the first battle of Manassas, when the roar of battle could be distinctly heard in Haymarket and the thunder of cannon interrupted the church service that Sunday morning, the village became a field station for Confederate wounded, and the townspeople did what they could to tend the maimed and shattered boys who were carried into their hamlet with the sorrowful look of war in their eyes.[18]

Now, only a few months later, Haymarket would serve as a hospital again. The men of the 15th Alabama were brought to St. Paul's, and as many of them as would fit were laid out on the pews in this house of God. For some, those who held to their faith, knowing they were housed in a church gave them succor and hope. For others, they must have been pleased, at the very least, to have a sturdy and dry roof over their heads. Many of the sick, however, were quartered in tents raised in the fields around the church, the fields that already held those soldiers who had not recovered from their wounds after Manassas. Others were given beds of straw and hay under the only protection available—the tall trees that shaded the yard around the church.

The sick were attended to by Dr. Francis A. Stanford, a native of Georgia, who had enlisted in the 15th Alabama at Fort Mitchell on the Chattahoochee, and by a Dr. Shepherd of Eufaula, a surgeon who was nearly seventy-five years old. Stanford had carefully selected Haymarket as the site of the regimental hospital. One soldier said of Stanford that he neglected "no opportunity to provide for the well-being of the invalids." This Alabamian had nothing but praise for the good doctor: "All of his time and talent is devoted to his profession and the amelioration of the suffering. Day by day we see him on his rounds of mercy from the rising of the sun until 'the going down thereof,' and from dark until midnight, in fair weather and foul, and oh! ungrateful humanity; we hear him abuse the remaining six [hours of the day]."

Convalescents provided the nursing care to their comrades at the hospital. Oates visited St. Paul's and described what he saw there with a critical eye: "At this improvised hospital there was neither accommodations nor comfort; no bedding but the soldier's blanket, with his knapsack for a pillow, and no nourishment but army rations; a scant supply of medicine and no medical attention worth having, except such as old Dr. Shepherd . . . could give. . . . The nights in October were cold, and early in the month there was frost, and the suffering of the sick men was intolerable. . . . It was no uncommon sight at that hospital to see six or seven corpses of Fifteenth Alabama men laid out at once."

There were, probably, worse places to die than under those high trees ("heavenly trees," the locals called them and still do) or in the peaceful fields surrounding the church or in the quiet chancel of St. Paul's in Haymarket. But the men did die, and whether the place was good or bad, serene or bedlam, the only thing that mattered was that poor boys who could not do anything to save themselves, young men a very long way from their homes in Alabama, were slipping away.[19] In time, the epidemic abated and the deaths finally ceased, but the Confederate forces in northern Virginia had already paid a very stiff price by losing good men—young men who had not yet even experienced the horror of combat but who had come to know the face of hell by confronting an invisible enemy against whom they had no defense.

At Camp Toombs, where the remainder of the 15th Alabama spent that autumn, camp life fell into the same old routines. Company and battalion drilling, said Oates, was the daily occupation. Years afterward, he remembered: "Occasionally we were aroused by a rumor, incident to such a life, concerning the advance or other movements of the enemy; but, having no foundation, the excitement soon subsided. Later in the war the soldiers denominated such rumors as 'grapevine telegrams' and paid no attention to them." In the loneliness of an army camp, with thousands of fellow soldiers all around, some of the men, Oates claimed, died of homesickness.[20]

As for the sick and dying at Haymarket, Oates could not take his mind off them. Their suffering, as he had said, was unbearable—to them and to their comrades who survived. The numbers have never been ascertained about precisely how many men the 15th Alabama buried in the fields around St. Paul's Church, where their remains still lie after all this time. A stone marker near the entrance to the church states flatly, without mention of the dead of the 15th Alabama: "In this area are buried eighty unknown Confederate soldiers who died of wounds after the battle of Manassas, July 21, 1861."

Oates thought that at least 150 men died there and were buried in the churchyard, but in old age, as he wrote his memoirs and strained to remember the details of the Haymarket hospital, he caught himself and confessed that the number must have been much greater. The adjutant's report for the month of November 1861 alone listed 60 dead. With sadness in his heart, Oates said he thought the estimates were all low. And he was probably right. It seems likely that no less than 200 men from the 15th Alabama—and perhaps considerably more than that—fell from disease at Haymarket and are buried in the fields to the north and west of the church building.[21]

Eventually the hospital at St. Paul's was abandoned, and soldiers—for the time being—left Haymarket and its villagers to themselves. But the war kept intruding on the little town. During the Second Manassas campaign in August and September 1862, the village was occupied by both Union and Confederate troops. Major General J. E. B. Stuart's cavalry skirmished with Union cavalry on the outskirts of town on August 28, and later that afternoon Federal infantry left their gear in the village before marching off to face Longstreet's Confederate phalanx as it tried to break through Thoroughfare Gap, a few miles to the west. For the next two days, Haymarket remained behind the Confederate lines.

Tragically, the town was burned by Federal troops under Brigadier General Adolph Wilhelm von Steinwehr on the night of November 4 and 5, 1862. All the buildings in Haymarket except four perished in the flames. Townspeople were forced out of their homes in the dead of night. St. Paul's Church was spared the torch, but the pews and pulpit were used by Union troops to stoke their evening campfires. The rest of the town lay in ashes.

For the remainder of the war, Haymarket became nearly a ghost town. After the battle of Gettysburg, the village became the scene of a cavalry engagement between J. E. B. Stuart's Confederate mounted troopers and a division of George Armstrong Custer's Federal horsemen. Fierce fighting took place just west of Haymarket, but the Federals managed to hold their position and retain their possession of the town.[22]

Today the village is peaceful (except around a truck stop open twenty-four hours a day, where attendants announce over a loudspeaker system which pump is ready for use). But dramatic changes are taking place in Haymarket and altering the character of the village. Preservationists thought they had won a major battle in the early 1990s when they defeated the attempts of the Disney Company to build an American history theme park on the village's outskirts. The battle over that particular development scheme was won by those who wished to preserve the local rural character of the landscape. But that war is inexorably being lost. In the past few years, suburban development has reached all the way from Washington, D.C., thirty-six miles to the east, and has turned the town into a bedroom community of commuters, townhouses, strip shopping centers, self-service gas stations, a McDonald's, and numerous subdivisions. Across the street from St. Paul's Church, where a piece of woods and fields stood at the time of the Civil War and remained undisturbed until the late 1990s, sit row upon row of oversized houses on postage-stamp lots. Headstones in the church graveyard are located only a few feet from the driveways of the houses in the front row.

Much of Haymarket's quiet charm and rural setting is vanishing rapidly. Probably few who live in the town know anything about what happened there during the Civil War, and certainly fewer still know about the soldiers of the 15th Alabama who suffered horribly at St. Paul's, who died in the church and under its trees, and who remain in their unmarked graves somewhere in the churchyard.[23]

Haymarket was not unique in the autumn of 1861, for there were hospital sites just like the one at St. Paul's near practically every army camp, Union and Confederate, from Virginia to Texas. The hell faced by the men of the 15th Alabama in Haymarket was experienced by thousands of soldiers on both sides. Few of the men who got sick in their camps recovered from their illnesses; most who contracted the measles or the mumps or whooping cough or typhoid—or any of the other highly contagious and highly lethal diseases that sliced through Civil War armies—died without every really understanding what had happened to them or why they had to die. Over the next four years, disease continued to take its toll in the Confederate and Union ranks, and the terrible scenes that had taken place at Haymarket would repeat themselves across the American countryside until the war, and all its hard suffering, finally ended.

What William C. Oates and the boys of the 15th Alabama learned at Haymarket in the autumn chill of 1861 was a lesson learned by every soldier in every war. It is a lesson as old as time. War is all misery, cruelty, and hell. And, all too often, young soldiers—brave and true boys (and nowadays, brave and true girls, too)—give their lives for no good reason at all.

8   William C. Oates and the Death of General Farnsworth

If nothing else, William C. Oates was a superb lawyer. Having served his law apprenticeship with the famous firm of Pugh, Bullock, and Buford in Eufaula, Alabama, during the late 1850s, he had acquired great skills in researching, filing, and presenting his cases. He earned a tidy sum of money working at his profession before the Civil War, and in the postwar years he accumulated a small fortune in fees from his clients. He even managed to win an acquittal in a murder charge brought against his brother, J. Wyatt Oates (although Counselor Oates admitted to bribing the jury to get the favorable verdict). He knew his way in and out of the courtroom, his talents as an attorney became widely known in the Wiregrass Country of southeastern Alabama, and he was paid handsomely for winning numerous cases, especially if they involved property law and disputes over fee simple ownership of real estate.

On the Civil War battlefield, though, Oates was both brilliantly capable and shockingly incompetent. Even at Gettysburg, where he won fame— if not military victory and honors—in his fight against Joshua Chamberlain's famous 20th, he ignored direct orders by scaling Big Round Top before descending and attacking Little Round Top, and his actions, although consistently brave and diligent, suggest an officer who worked by instinct alone rather than by the rigors of duty, discipline, and obedience.

At Chickamauga, where he and the 15th Alabama became dangerously separated from their brigade, Oates led his men blindly through terrain he did not know, got the regiment involved in firefights it could not possibly win, attempted to order a South Carolina unit into battle (by overruling the South Carolinians' officers and breaking the chain of command), and opened fire on troops who turned out to be Confederate soldiers. Later, at the battles of the Wilderness and Spotsylvania, he redeemed himself by displaying exceptional courage and by using his head when it came to issuing commands to his regiment. Nevertheless, it must be said that Oates was a good soldier, a born fighter, an intrepid commander, but a less than capable field officer who, on several occasions, revealed his weaknesses on the battlefield during the heat of combat and under the pressure of flying lead. Put plainly: Oates was a far better lawyer than he was army officer.

So it comes as something of a surprise to learn that Oates the lawyer failed to discern how he had been fed unreliable information when a fellow Alabama officer informed him that Elon J. Farnsworth, a brave Union cavalry officer, had committed suicide during a hot engagement that occurred between Brigadier General Evander M. Law's Alabama brigade and Union horse soldiers on the afternoon of July 3 at Gettysburg. But that is precisely what Oates did, letting down his guard as an officer and his skepticism as an attorney.

What had led Oates to believe mistakenly that Farnsworth had killed himself was the testimony of a comrade-in-arms, an Alabama officer who swore that he had seen the Union general put a pistol to his head and pull the trigger to avoid being captured. The report was not what it seemed, as it turned out, but Oates did not question the Alabamian's testimony—either during the battle or for the rest of his life. He took it for gospel. As a result, Oates became a controversial figure after the war when he publicly retold his version of Farnsworth's death and received harsh criticism from some—mostly former Union cavalrymen who had ridden with Farnsworth—who vigorously challenged the veracity of his account.

*　*　*

Oates and the remnants of the 15th Alabama regiment awoke on the morning of July 3 to find themselves enveloped in a thick veil of fog and smoke. They had spent a nightmarish night on Big Round Top—barely sleeping, if at all—as the wounded groaned through the pitch blackness and unidentifiable sounds caught their rapt attention as they listened for anything that might resemble Union soldiers creeping up on them.[1]

The men were almost totally worn out, having marched the day before more than twenty-five miles from Chambersburg, Pennsylvania, to fight a desperate and bloody struggle for possession of a small hill on the southern edge of the Gettysburg battlefield. When the enemy holding the hill—the 20th Maine Infantry—rallied in a counterassault and came lunging headlong down Little Round Top like a runaway freight train, the Alabamians had been in the process of retreating (or at least some of them had). The Federal soldiers hit them with a force they had never experienced before, and their retreat-in-progress turned into a rout.

Colonel Chamberlain—whom, as we've seen, would win fame and laurels (including a later Medal of Honor) for his heroism that day—and his hearty men drove the 15th Alabama off the small hill and chased them over the steep crest of a larger wooded hill to the south, Big Round Top, an eminence rising 585 feet above the farm fields of Gettysburg. Oates and his Alabamians felt blessed, despite all the casualties they had suffered on that hazy afternoon of July 2, not to have been annihilated by the fierce and determined soldiers of the 20th Maine.[2]

With the spreading daylight on the morning of July 3, Oates and his men of the 15th Alabama knew that Union soldiers occupied the summit of Big Round Top and had been there through the dark night. What they didn't know was that the Federals holding the crest above them included the 20th Maine, which had been ordered to the hilltop after defeating the Alabamians the evening before. Oates positioned his men facing up the hill and behind a stone wall erected by the soldiers. No one relished the thought that the Federals might at any moment sweep down upon them in a repeat performance of the furious bayonet assault that had broken the 15th Alabama on Little Round Top.[3]

Oates extended his picket line beyond the stone wall so that it nearly touched the left of a skirmish line established in the early morning hours by the 1st Texas, almost forming a salient where Plum Run, a small farm stream, wound along the base of Big Round Top. The Texas skirmishers, facing south, were active that morning, and Oates and his Alabamians, who faced to the east, could hear the unsettling popping of irregular musket fire to their rear. To their left and north, skirmishers from the 4th Alabama and 47th Alabama exchanged deadly fire with Union picket lines up on the slopes of Big Round Top. Oates and his regiment kept their heads down while the occasional bursts of musket fire sounded around them. Heavy sharpshooting continued until about 10:00 AM, when the gunfire slackened and the woods became uncomfortably quiet.[4]

About an hour later, Federal cavalry under the command of Brigadier General H. Judson Kilpatrick, an officer who had already earned a reputation as "flamboyant, reckless, tempestuous, and even licentious," deployed south of Big Round Top in the vicinity of Bushman's Hill. Kilpatrick's orders were to attack the Confederate right flank, and to do so an elaborate plan was devised by which an entirely separate regular brigade of cavalry commanded by Brigadier General Wesley Merritt would be moved up from Emmitsburg, Maryland, and would attempt to roll up Confederate forces posted across the Emmitsburg Road, about three miles south of Gettysburg; at the same time, Kilpatrick would strike the enemy infantry lines, stretched across the valley to the southwest of Big Round Top, with his remaining brigade, led by Brigadier General Elon J. Farnsworth. Like the more famous George Armstrong Custer, who commanded one of Kilpatrick's brigades but who had been detached for duty to the east of Gettysburg on the morning of July 3, the other cavalry brigadiers held commissions less than a month old, and in the case of Merritt and Farnsworth, only a few days old. All were men in their middle to late twenties. All were brave and stalwart soldiers. But today their skills as field officers would be sorely tested.[5]

Despite clear signs of enemy activity to his front, Kilpatrick, who would later earn the epithet "Kill-cavalry," refrained from ordering an assault while he waited for Merritt's men to come up the Emmitsburg Road. Around 1:00 PM, Federals and Confederates alike shuddered in shock and surprise as a tremendous cannonade exploded across the flat fields between Seminary Ridge and Cemetery Ridge to the north—the deafening thunder of what was to become the greatest artillery duel ever waged on the North American continent. The bombardment was a preliminary to a grand Confederate infantry assault, later known as Pickett's Charge, that Lee had ordered to strike the center of the Army of the Potomac on Cemetery Ridge. "It was the most powerful cannonade that ever occurred in the world's history of warfare," wrote Oates with great exaggeration long after the war. He remembered that the "ground fairly trembled, [and] the air was sulphurous and full of smoke."[6]

As the cannons boomed and the earth shook, General Law, who had assumed command of Major General John Bell Hood's division after Hood went down with a serious wound the day before, detected movement on his flanks and determined that the Federal cavalry was amassing for a possible attack on the Confederate right. Taking no chances, Law directed the batteries of Captain James Reilly and Captain William K. Bachman, positioned on high ground along Warfield Ridge, to shell the Federal cavalry at the edge of the woods on Bushman's Hill. The shells, unfortunately, fell short of their mark, giving the 1st Texas skirmishers some uncomfortable moments as they scrambled for cover to protect themselves from their own guns. Although the artillery fire did not inflict any enemy casualties, the Federal horsemen withdrew from open sight and took refuge under the heavy foliage of the trees on Bushman's Hill.[7]

Even as Reilly's and Bachman's guns fell silent, the cannonade up the Emmitsburg Pike continued to roar in earnest. Law now realized that the Federals—Merritt's regulars—were coming dismounted up the road in an attempt to turn the Confederate right flank and get in the rear of Lee's Army of Northern Virginia. In response, Law extended the lines of the 7th Georgia and 8th Georgia toward the right to stop the Federal advance. He personally took command at one point and helped to prevent a breakthrough by Merritt's troopers. Heavy skirmishing broke out along this front, and the two sides exchanged musket fire until 3:00 PM.[8]

The battlefield below Big Round Top grew silent once more. To the north, just a mile or so up the fence-lined Emmitsburg Road, the artillery duel was over, and Longstreet was about to give a nod of his head to order fifteen thousand Confederates across the broad expanse of wheat and rye between Seminary and Cemetery Ridge in what would become one of the last great Napoleonic charges of the Civil War. In the shadow of Big Round Top, Oates and his Alabamians could not know what was about to take place to their north; they surely had no understanding that the High Water Mark of the Confederacy was soon to be reached under a copse of trees on Cemetery Ridge by a mere handful of their comrades, and they could not foretell that the tide of Confederate victories, which had brought everlasting fame to Robert E. Lee and his remarkable army, would recede slowly and steadily into a sea of defeat.

Instead, there was only stillness. The light breeze caught the soft sounds of horses neighing and the murmur of Union troopers talking in the woods, and along the 15th Alabama's stone wall under the tall shade trees of Big Round Top there was an uneasiness among the men that so often came with the certainty of impending battle. Oates and his Alabamians felt the strain of fatigue, yet they remained alert—almost unnaturally so. They listened with cocked ears for the telltale noises of clicking metal bits, rattling sabers, clanging canteens, pounding hoofs. It was getting warmer, even under the cool shade of the spreading white oaks, and either the afternoon temperature was rising or the heat of anticipation was making the men perspire. They listened some more to muffled sounds. The quiet was almost as unbearable as the shattering din of artillery.

Along the forward skirmish lines of the Alabamians, the men suddenly heard something they did not expect to hear. It sounded like two Union generals arguing, as indeed it was. Kilpatrick wanted Farnsworth to order a cavalry charge against the Confederate infantry lines below Big Round Top. Both generals sat their horses beneath the shade of towering oaks. Farnsworth, as courageous and as impetuous as Kilpatrick, looked over the ground before them and turned to his commander with disbelief.

"General, do you mean it?" asked Farnsworth. "Shall I throw my handful of men over rough ground, through timber, against a brigade of infantry? The 1st Vermont has already been fought half to pieces; these are too good men to kill."

Kilpatrick, who had just received word from the Union right that Pickett's charge had been repulsed, wanted to have his order obeyed and to turn the Confederate flank if he could. He exploded in rage at Farnsworth. "Do you refuse to obey my orders?" Kilpatrick roared. "If you are afraid to lead this charge, I will lead it."

Farnsworth could not believe his ears. "Take that back!" he demanded, rising in his stirrups.

Red hot with anger, but realizing that he had spoken too forcefully to his subordinate, Kilpatrick—without giving up a look of defiance in his eyes—repented by saying, "I did not mean it; forget it."

The two generals remained for a moment in uncomfortable silence beneath the trees. Then Farnsworth spoke quietly: "General, if you order the charge, I will lead it, but you must take the responsibility."

Apparently Kilpatrick said he would, to which Farnsworth replied, "I will obey your order."[9]

It was a fatal mistake—the kind of error young officers make under the strain of pressure or when cool-headed logic gives way to heated emotions. Born in Michigan and raised in Illinois, Farnsworth was expelled from the University of Michigan for involvement in "a drinking frolic" that resulted in the death of a fellow student. When the Civil War broke out, he was commissioned a first lieutenant in the 8th Illinois Cavalry, a regiment raised and outfitted by Illinois Congressman John F. Farnsworth, his uncle. He was straight and tall, pale in complexion, with a drooping mustache that gave him the look of a desperado. The men of the regiment liked him for his shrewdness and wit.

In 1862, he had a Southern minister arrested for refusing to offer up the standard prayer for the president of the United States, an impulsive act that was more bold than politic. After a long illness that year, Farnsworth returned to duty and served on Brigadier General Alfred Pleasonton's staff. At the battle of Brandy Station, in June 1863, Farnsworth distinguished himself on the field and took over command of the 11th Illinois when its other officers were all struck down. On June 28, he was promoted from captain to brigadier general and assumed command of a brigade under Kilpatrick. In cavalry engagements during the early phases of the Gettysburg campaign, Farnsworth demonstrated his mettle at Hanover on June 30 and Hunterstown on July 2. He knew how to lead a cavalry charge and get the most out of his men, but now, on the field at Gettysburg, the cards were stacked against his formidable abilities.[10]

Realizing that he had no choice but to lead his men in an assault against the Confederate infantry huddled behind good defenses below Big Round Top, Farnsworth gritted his teeth and took action to obey Kilpatrick's orders. He instructed the 1st West Virginia to strike the Confederate infantry lines, and all along the plain beneath Big Round Top could be heard the screams of charging horsemen and the thunder of galloping hooves. The Union cavalry bolted from the woods and dashed toward the lines of the 1st Texas Infantry, which had taken up a strong defensive line behind a rail fence and a stone wall not far from the Bushman house. The cavalry broke through the 1st Texas skirmish line and drove toward the wall. It looked like a great blue wave rolling across the horizon as it prepared to crash along the shore. The Texans waited, muskets tight against their shoulders, for the right moment. Finally it came, and the 1st Texas opened fire with a blinding flash as the devastating volley exploded over the stone wall. The West Virginians went down in the smoke and chaos of blood and yelping horses. Hand-to-hand fighting erupted near the wall, the Texans using their muskets as clubs against the enemy.

Somehow the Union horsemen got over the wall and behind the Texans, but the force of the attack was broken, and eventually the West Virginians retired in battered clumps of men and horses back to the safety of the woods. Next came the 18th Pennsylvania and 5th New York cavalry, which, shielded by the woods, suffered fewer casualties as they charged the Texas line, but were decisively repulsed nonetheless. The Union horsemen plunged toward the stone wall, getting almost up to the muzzles of the Texan muskets; the Confederate volley fire and the canister from Reilly's battery ripping through the blue ranks meant, however, that the second charge had failed as well.[11]

At about the same time, Farnsworth went to the front ranks of the 1st Vermont and, true to his word, personally led his regiment against the left flank of Law's brigade, the position along the southwestern slope of Big Round Top where Oates's 15th Alabama and the other Alabama regiments occupied the line. Farnsworth had divided the 1st Vermont into three battalions—one commanded by Captain Henry C. Parsons, another by Lieutenant Colonel Addison W. Preston, and the third by Major William Wells. Farnsworth and Wells rode together at the head of Wells's battalion.[12]

The attack caught Oates—and the other Alabama regiments in Law's brigade—by surprise. Although skirmish fire had kept the 15th Alabama snugly behind its stone wall on the slope of Big Round Top, some of the more adventurous men in the regiment had wandered away from the wall and down the hillside to fetch water from Plum Run, the putrid stream that ran through the fields of the Slyder farm. Around 5:00 PM, when the 1st West Virginia broke through the Texas picket line, Oates must have realized that there was more to threaten him from behind than in his front. Then, as Farnsworth and the 1st Vermont came slashing through the woods, it was clear that Oates and his Alabamians were on the wrong side of their wall.[13]

Warned of the attack by the Texans who had overheard the argument between Kilpatrick and Farnsworth, General Law strengthened his lines and shifted men around to buttress the Confederate defenses. Just as a courier arrived from Law to tell Oates to close up on the 1st Texas skirmish line, Farnsworth's horsemen galloped into the 15th Alabama and rode past the regiment, leaving Oates and his men befuddled and disorganized. But the Alabama regiments farther down the stone wall had their wits about them and were ready when the blue-coated troopers pounded across their front. The volleys from the Alabamians ripped through the Union ranks, and horses and men went down together in the smoke and dust that floated like a suspended cloud inches above the ground.

Diverted by the flaming guns of Reilly's battery, Farnsworth and the 3rd Battalion drove straight into the 4th Alabama, which was waiting patiently for the Union cavalry to arrive. The Alabamians poured tearing musket fire into the horsemen, and Farnsworth turned the battalion toward the Slyder house. But as he and the brave Vermonters cleared the farmyard, they were hit by combined blasts from Bachman's battery and the muskets of the 9th Georgia. As if to emphasize some terrible symbolism, the route of Farnsworth's charge now resembled a huge question mark, the dot at the bottom indicating the Union cavalry's jumping-off place and the curve at the top revealing how Confederate fire had forced the assault practically to turn on itself.[14]

Before Farnsworth reached the stretch of small undulating hills that lay between the Bushman and Slyder farms, his horse was shot from under him and he fell to the hard ground, shaken but not seriously hurt. A corporal gave him his horse, and Farnsworth swung himself up into the saddle. Shattered by the direct fire from Bachman's guns, Farnsworth tried to direct the assault once more toward Reilly's battery, but he discovered that the agile 4th Alabama was dogging his troopers, and it seemed as if shells and minié balls were coming from every direction. Beaten back, Farnsworth and a few others turned around and tried to head back the way they had come. In so doing, however, they crossed Plum Run again and collided on the hillside of Big Round Top with the 15th Alabama, which now stood ready to receive them.[15]

Oates had been ordered to come to the aid of Reilly's battery, but he had no time to order a countermarch before Farnsworth and his "squadron" began to bear down on the 15th Alabama skirmish line, which Oates had taken pains to re-form after the first pass of the 1st Vermont. Worse for Oates's men, their position exposed them to canister fire from Reilly's guns to the west, and Oates remarked ominously that the spray of canister balls passing over their heads sounded remarkably like the flutter of bird wings. In the midst of all this confusion, Oates saw Farnsworth coming on—brave, daring, determined. About fifty yards to his front, he threw forward a line of skirmishers. The Union general rode up at a gallop to the 15th Alabama pickets and, pistol in hand, demanded their surrender. Farnsworth's horse reared. Lieutenant John B. Adrian of the 44th Alabama, who had come over to the lines of the 15th Alabama looking for a riderless horse and, in the process, had assumed command of Oates's skirmishers, ordered his men to let loose a volley.[16]

No one knows precisely what happened next, for it all took place—as Oates later admitted—out of his direct line of sight. Only Lieutenant Adrian and a dozen or more skirmishers witnessed the events that next transpired. All agree that Farnsworth and his horse went down in the volley fire from the Alabama skirmish line and that Farnsworth had been struck several times by minié balls. Severely wounded, but with some strength left, Farnsworth—still firmly grasping his pistol—tried to stand. According to Adrian, he approached the wounded general and told him, "Now you surrender." Farnsworth, said Adrian, replied fiercely: "I'll be damned if I do." Then Farnsworth took his pistol, pressed it to his chest, and fired. His body slumped to the ground, dead.

Adrian reported this unusual occurrence to Oates immediately, but the Alabama colonel—who breathed a sigh of relief as he watched the failed Union cavalry charge disintegrate and the remnants of Farnsworth's battalion seek the safety of the woods on Bushman's Hill—was exhausted and sat down to rest for a moment.

Within a few minutes, one of the skirmishers walked up and called out, saying, "Col., don't you want the shoulder-straps of that Yankee Major we killed up there a few moments ago? I pulled them off his coat thinking you'd like to have them."

Oates took the straps and inspected them closely. "A Major, the devil," he cried. "He is a General."

He walked over to where Farnsworth's body lay on the ground. Small groups of Alabamians were taking a look for themselves, many never having seen a dead Union general before. The earth was bloody all around Farnsworth's body. Oates noticed two or three bullet holes "in different parts of his body from which the blood was issuing." He ordered one of his men to search the body, and the soldier extracted some letters from one of the coat pockets. Oates assumed the letters were from Farnsworth's wife. They were clearly addressed to Farnsworth, which was how Oates learned the general's identity. He tore up the letters and threw the pieces away. Putting the shoulder straps in his own pocket, Oates lingered only a few minutes where Farnsworth had fallen (probably in the vicinity of where the monument to the 1st Vermont Cavalry now stands on the slope of Big Round Top), and he soon received orders for his regiment to resume its position on the Confederate right flank.[17]

With Farnsworth dead, Kilpatrick ordered no more assaults against Law's formidable lines. As evening finally descended over the battlefield, General Robert E. Lee and his battered army faced the likelihood of retreating back across the Potomac to the safety of Virginia, Oates and his men spent another dreary night in the vicinity of Big Round Top, and the legend of Farnsworth's suicide began to grow as Alabamians in Law's brigade—and then other Southerners in the Army of Northern Virginia—spread the tale from one campfire to the next.

*　*　*

In the summer of 1868, five years after the incident had taken place, William C. Oates—who had returned to his law practice in Abbeville, Alabama—publicly told the story of Farnsworth's suicide for the first time to Edward Porter Alexander, Longstreet's former artillery chief. "I don't believe I ever related to you an incident which occurred within my observation at Gettysburg on the 3rd day of July," Oates wrote, giving Alexander the impression he had witnessed what he was about to reveal. After briefly describing Farnsworth's charge, Oates told how the Union general—wounded in the leg and shoulder—refused to surrender "and placing his pistol to his own head fired and shot his brains out." In this first telling, Oates claimed to have removed Farnsworth's shoulder straps and some letters, which he assumed were from the Union officer's wife, from the dead man's pockets. He destroyed the letters at the time, but kept the shoulder straps, "which I still have & would be pleased to deliver them to his widow if I knew her address."[18]

From these humble beginnings, the story of the suicide circulated throughout the South, passed along undoubtedly by Alexander, who was corresponding with former Confederates to gather information for an intended history of Longstreet's First Corps that he hoped to write but later abandoned. Eight years later, Oates repeated the Farnsworth suicide story to John B. Bachelder, a former teacher and artist, who had become the leading authority on the battle of Gettysburg and who also corresponded assiduously with veterans from both sides to collect facts that would help him mark troop deployments on the battlefield.

To Bachelder, Oates wrote: "[Farnsworth] reined in his hosse & with his pistol in hand ordered Lt. Adrian who was in command of the skirmish line to surrender; thereupon Adrian & his line or those near enough fired upon him killing his horse & wounding Farnsworth in several places. He fell. Adrian advanced towards him (his few men never halted) and said 'Now you surrender.' Gen. Farnsworth replied 'I'll be damned if I do,' & placing his pistol to his own head fired & shot his brains out. I took from his pocket some private letters (which I read & destroyed) from which I learned who he was." Oates also mentioned that he had taken Farnsworth's shoulder straps and kept them for many years, intending to return them to the Union general's family, but now he regretted that the straps "are now mislaid & cannot be found."[19]

In 1878, Oates made the Farnsworth story truly public by including it in an article, published in the *Southern Historical Society Papers,* on the 15th Alabama's role at Gettysburg. Oates omitted Farnsworth's curse and had him say in response to Adrian's demand for his surrender, "I will not do it." Oates insisted, however, that Farnsworth placed "his pistol to his own head, [and] shot his brains out." Oates did not claim to have witnessed the suicide himself. And, in a slight change, he admitted that one of the 15th Alabama skirmishers had brought him the Union general's shoulder straps.

It is safe to say that the origin of all other Southern accounts of Farnsworth's suicide lay in Oates's article in the *Southern Historical Society Papers.* What's more, Bachelder was deeply impressed by the tragic story of Farnsworth's taking his own life, and in 1882 the self-proclaimed "government historian" of Gettysburg published his own article on Farnsworth's death and, accepting the general's suicide at face value, quoted Oates's 1876 letter at length. Oddly, though, Bachelder claimed that he had first heard of Farnsworth's suicide not from Colonel William Oates, but from Oates's younger brother, Lieutenant John A. Oates, who had fallen mortally wounded on the slopes of Little Round Top during the 15th Alabama's desperate attempts to dislodge the 20th Maine from the hillside on July 2, 1863. Before John Oates died on July 25 in a Union hospital, Bachelder visited him and heard the strange story of Farnsworth's suicide in "full and graphic" detail. According to Bachelder, the young dying Oates "remarked that 'praises of his [Farnsworth's] gallantry and courage were on every lip,' and that many of the officers and men of his regiment possessed themselves of some memento of the event, his brother, Colonel Oates, taking off his shoulder straps, some securing articles of his equipments, others a button, etc."

How John Oates could have known all of this is a pure mystery, since he fell and was left behind on Little Round Top the day *before* Farnsworth's charge and had not witnessed any of the events that transpired near Big Round Top on July 3. Possibly a member of the 15th Alabama captured or wounded *after* Farnsworth's charge on July 3 told the tale of the Union general's death to Lieutenant Oates in the Union hospital before Bachelder interviewed the dying young man. But Bachelder believed that he was gathering eyewitness accounts from the two Oates brothers, not secondhand gossip.[20]

While William Oates's various accounts of Farnsworth's death seem to have gone relatively unnoticed in the North, Bachelder's article, published in a Philadelphia newspaper, did not. Soon came vehement denials from veterans of Farnsworth's brigade that their brave general had committed suicide on the battlefield of Gettysburg. One of the first challenges to Oates's claims came from Dr. Ptolemy O'M. Edson, the former assistant surgeon of the 1st Vermont Cavalry, who wrote to George G. Benedict in 1888 that "General Farnsworth certainly did not blow his own brains out." When he and Lucius P. Woods, the surgeon of the 5th New York Cavalry, examined Farnsworth's body on the field they found five bullet wounds—four in the chest and abdomen and one high up on the thigh—and no head wound. The body had been stripped down to Farnsworth's flannel underwear. Edson could not explain how Oates, whom he thought had witnessed Farnsworth's suicide, could think that the Union general had shot himself in the head. As a possible explanation, Edson suggested that

Farnsworth may have been confused with Captain Oliver T. Cushman of Company E, 1st Vermont, who fell near Farnsworth with a ghastly bullet wound in the face. "But even this," said Edson, "cannot explain the declaration of suicide."

Later that year, Benedict published Edson's letter in a history of Vermont's participation in the Civil War. Around the same time, Henry C. Parsons, former captain of the 1st Vermont, who had led one of the battalions in Farnsworth's Charge, published his own account of the general's death in *Battles and Leaders of the Civil War* and denied the Confederate assertions that Farnsworth committed suicide, suggesting, like Edson, that the enemy may have confused Cushman with Farnsworth.[21]

Bachelder had apparently corresponded with Edson, even before writing his newspaper article, and had learned about Farnsworth's body being stripped but, inexplicably, not about the nature of the general's wounds. When Bachelder read Edson's letter in Benedict's history and Parsons's account in *Battles and Leaders,* he wrote to Oates and asked, somewhat deceitfully given what he now knew about Farnsworth's death, for him to repeat what he knew about the actions on the Confederate right after July 2. Oates replied by narrating as carefully as possible the events as he understood them. Using practically the same words he had in the past, he repeated the Farnsworth suicide story.

Then Bachelder wrote back and revealed that Farnsworth had not been shot in the head. Nor had Farnsworth ever been married. Oates was taken aback. "I perhaps should have been more particular in my statement," he wrote, "and will now give you my statement as though I were making an oath." He retold the story, this time by giving every detail in a step-by-step account of what had taken place, as best as he could remember it. At the time of Farnsworth's death, he admitted, he could not see the place where Adrian confronted Farnsworth or the spot where the Union general fell. Later, he said, it was a skirmisher who brought Farnsworth's shoulder straps to him while he was resting. When he went to examine the body himself, Adrian informed him of what had happened.

He was sure, although he could not be positive, that Adrian had said that Farnsworth had placed his pistol to his head. Oates had one of his men search the dead general's pockets. The one letter—not several as he had previously stated—found on Farnsworth's body had been written by a woman, and Oates had assumed it had been the general's wife, although he now allowed it could have been "some female admirer." Unfortunately, reported Oates, Adrian could not be reached to confirm the story of Farnsworth's suicide—he had died in a later battle. Yet Adrian, affirmed Oates, "was a faithful young officer and regarded as perfectly reliable and I believe he told the truth." Still, Oates could offer no explanation as to why Adrian had claimed that Farnsworth killed himself with a bullet to the head when there were no wounds to confirm the act.[22]

The suicide story would not die, despite the fact that several veterans from Farnsworth's brigade swore that their general had not killed himself on the battlefield. Even as these protests were aired, Confederate veterans adamantly maintained that the Union general had taken his own life, not only as Oates had claimed but also because they themselves, remarkably enough, had witnessed the suicide (or so they said). Inexplicably, several former soldiers in the 1st Texas claimed to have seen Farnsworth shoot himself, and one Texan even asserted that it was one of his comrades who had taken the general's shoulder straps. Another Texan cast a corporal, A. F. Taylor, in Lieutenant Adrian's role, having him do and say practically verbatim what Adrian, according to Oates, had done and said. The same Texan, however, had Farnsworth shooting himself four times—apparently firing his pistol repeatedly until he got it right.[23]

There is no explaining why so many Confederates claimed to have seen Farnsworth shoot himself when it is clear they had not. Nor is it clear why Adrian told Oates that Farnsworth had committed suicide, when it seems almost certain that the Union general did no such thing and died of the wounds he received from the volley Adrian had ordered his skirmishers to fire.

Strange things happen on battlefields. The fog of war often prevents soldiers from seeing things clearly around them and from understanding what they are experiencing as it happens.[24] Multiple eyewitnesses—even reliable ones—never see the same event in quite the same way, as police officers and criminal trial attorneys can readily attest. Some memories can remain sharp over time, but other memories can fade. Details often become blurred as the years go by—or sometimes are entirely forgotten.

But there are other aspects of human behavior, on and off the battlefield, that often defy reasonable explanation. Psychologists do not know for certain what makes some people confess to crimes they have not committed or others believe they are victims of strange occurrences—such as sexual abuse, alien abductions, and spectral encounters—that could not possibly have happened. No one can explain why several individuals, including the famous industrialist Andrew Carnegie, related in separate reminiscences that they rode the same train that Lincoln took to Gettysburg and watched him while he composed his famous address during the journey (which he did not do), when actually these individuals are known to have been somewhere else doing other things. Nor can it be explained why President Ronald Reagan once claimed to have been present when Jews were liberated from a Nazi death camp toward the end of World War II, when in fact he wasn't even in Europe at the time. Equally confounding were the tall tales told by Joseph J. Ellis, a Pulitzer Prize–winning historian and professor at Mount Holyoke College, to his students about his combat experiences in Vietnam, where he also claimed to have served on General William Westmoreland's staff, when in reality he spent the war teaching history classes to cadets at West Point.

These examples, including the story of Farnsworth's suicide, represent something far different from lies. It would seem that some people—for vast and extremely complex reasons—convince themselves from time to time of the impossible, seeing themselves in places they've never been, believing they've done things they've never really done. Besides such illusions (or delusions, as the case might be), our physical powers of perception are also not infallible. Human eyes have an uncanny way of failing to capture every movement—every flutter of a hummingbird's wings—that takes place before them. Sometimes our brains must fill in the blanks, trying to make sense out of the jumbled or incomplete images that are communicated through our feeble and undependable eyes. Maybe Lieutenant Adrian *thought* he saw Farnsworth commit suicide. Maybe Farnsworth *tried* to shoot himself in the head and failed. Maybe he struggled, hoping to get up after falling, and assumed a peculiar posture that convinced Adrian that the man was trying to blow his brains out. Whatever the truth, we will probably never know it.[25]

For his part, Oates did not seem to care much one way or another how Farnsworth had died, but he had no reason to doubt Adrian's word and knew of no apparent motive why Adrian should have fabricated such a story. Oates accepted Adrian's story as reliable because he had no reason to question its validity or the young lieutenant's credibility. Contrary to the instincts he had developed as a trial lawyer, Oates failed to verify the story for himself. When he examined Farnsworth body, as he later admitted, he never paid much attention to the general's wounds, only to the fact that the ground around the body was soaked in blood. But he had no cause to challenge Adrian's account. So he accepted it as it had been told him.

In repeating the story over the years, Oates often slipped into imprecision and sometimes failed to keep his facts straight. Did he personally remove the shoulder straps from Farnsworth's body? Did he take one letter or several letters from the general's pockets? Did he not even touch the body at all but ordered his men to search Farnsworth's coat? Oates contradicted himself on these points in his various accounts, and it's impossible now to know exactly what he did do after he learned of Farnsworth's death, never mind how Farnsworth himself might have met his end. It seems unlikely that Oates ever comprehended that his repeating of Adrian's story of the suicide was the genesis for all other Southern accounts of the Union general's death—no Confederate recounting of Farnsworth's suicide can be found that predates Oates's telling of the story. In fact, not a single Confederate source that could have been independently produced corroborates Adrian's account and Oates's dissemination of it. Oates started the whole thing, but he seems never to have known it.

Despite the Union testimonies that countered Adrian's version of Farnsworth's death, Oates refused to give up believing in what the young Alabama officer had told him at the scene of the Union general's demise on the battlefield. In his combined memoirs and a history of the 15th Alabama regiment that he published five years before his own death, Oates changed his account to fit the facts he had learned years earlier from Bachelder—that is, that Farnsworth had suffered no head wounds. As a result, Oates altered the story so that Farnsworth—instead of pointing his pistol at his head—aimed his gun at his chest and shot himself through the heart. "I had the facts . . . related as to the death of Farnsworth stated to me then and there by Adrian," Oates declared, "and from what I saw at a distance of not more than fifty steps I am satisfied of their truth."[26] To his own dying day, Oates steadfastly believed that Farnsworth had committed suicide because a young subordinate, who had no reason to lie, had told him so. For Oates, that was more than enough to go on.

9 Mr. Lincoln's Victory at Gettysburg

By the spring of 1863, as the Civil War cast a dark shadow across the land, it became more and more evident to soldiers and civilians alike that the terrible conflict between North and South had grown into a behemoth that no one could successfully control or constrain—a leviathan, like Melville's great white whale, that set its own course and moved at its own speed and evaded every attempt to arrest its awesome power. Nothing in this awful war—what Abraham Lincoln called this "great national trouble"—had gone according to plan.[1] The war had grown in intensity, in brutality, in the vastness of misery and loss that went far beyond what any American could have imagined in the passionate years that led up to the fall of Fort Sumter.

When mankind turns to war, as the North and South did in 1861, it sets in motion events that cannot be predicted or harnessed. "War," wrote Thomas Paine in the eighteenth century, "involves in its progress such a train of unforeseen and unsupposed circumstances . . . that no human wisdom can calculate the end."[2] Unanticipated consequences flow out of actions that in retrospect seem tiny and insignificant. The Civil War, like all wars, swept over the land and unleashed itself from the hands of the men who had started it—men who could barely ponder its depth and fury in the wake of all that it had laid to waste.

Yet, in the spring of 1863 there was at least one man who believed that he knew how to end and win the war, one man who seemed to recognize—like Melville's Ahab—the behemoth's weakness, one man who thought it possible to take hold of the monster and slay it once and for all. Abraham Lincoln believed that if the Army of the Potomac could deliver a death blow to the Confederate Army of Northern Virginia, under the command of Robert E. Lee, the conclusion of the Civil War would at last be in sight.

Lincoln grew into his role as commander in chief, just as all presidents must grow into their offices, but Lincoln's conduct as head of the Union's armed forces during the first eighteen months of the war was determined to a great extent by the anguish he experienced trying to get General George B. McClellan to commit himself and the Army of the Potomac to a strategic course of action. At first, trusting in McClellan's expertise as a professional soldier, Lincoln gave his commanding general wide latitude in organizing the army, training its soldiers, and formulating campaign plans. But as McClellan's notorious reluctance to commit his army to battle stretched from weeks to months, and from months to entire campaign seasons, Lincoln—and the rest of the nation—began to wonder if the commanding general of the Union's finest army ever intended at all to fight the enemy on the battlefield.

Throughout his ordeal with McClellan, Lincoln came to see that something more was required of him as commander in chief than simply waiting in Washington for his armies to march and for battles to be fought. As his anger rose steadily over McClellan's recalcitrance, the president received stern urging from his conservative attorney general, Edward Bates, to assert himself more forcefully as commander in chief in accordance with the Constitution. "The Nation requires it," Bates said to Lincoln, "and History will hold you responsible."[3]

Apparently taking this advice to heart, Lincoln assumed a new posture as commander in chief and became increasingly more vocal in expressing his opinions to McClellan and pushing the general toward commencing an actual campaign against the enemy. From where McClellan stood, the president and Secretary of War Edwin M. Stanton were nothing but meddlers in army matters—civilians who knew precious little about how to fight a war or lead an army. To some degree, a good number of historians have also agreed with McClellan on this score, seeing Lincoln as interfering far too much and far too often in the operations of generals and armies in both theaters of the war, east and west.

To be sure, McClellan and Lincoln had diametrically opposite views of how the military was supposed to function within the republic. Expressing a firm opinion held by some military men in his own time and by many other soldiers throughout the course of American history, McClellan believed that the military should be left to the generals—and, in particular, to himself—to command, as if it represented a separate and distinct branch of the government and as if it were on equal footing with the executive, legislative, and judicial branches. Lincoln—perhaps as the result of Edward Bates's prodding or his own growing impatience with McClellan's inactivity—came to understand with intense clarity that the military, as specified in the Constitution, fell entirely under the civilian authority of the president and Congress and, even more specifically, under the powers held by the president as commander in chief.

The difficulties between Lincoln and McClellan constituted an important chapter in the ongoing conflict between the armed forces and civilian control over the military, what has come to be called civil-military relations. As Lincoln saw it, the president as the commander in chief stood at the head of the military chain of command and held all authority over the making of military policy. Based on his understanding of Article II, Section 2, of the Constitution, Lincoln believed that the military was responsible for carrying out the policy established or approved by the president, not the other way around. In Lincoln's opinion, there was little room for interpreting the meaning of the Constitution or the intention of the Founding Fathers: civilian control of the armed forces was a crucial element in a government of the people, by the people, and for the people.

As he grew in confidence as president, Lincoln's role as commander in chief became more distinctly defined. He asserted civilian control over the military just as other presidents—namely James Madison and James K. Polk—had done in time of war. But Lincoln accepted more responsibility and injected himself more fully into military affairs than his predecessors had done as commander in chief, if only because the crisis at hand called for the president to play a larger part in the military contest that would, in the end, determine the fate of the Union and because circumstances demanded that someone provide the necessary leadership.

At the core of his interpretation of how the commander in chief should control the military was Lincoln's broad and nationalist construction of the Constitution, a legal and political view that he had inherited from Alexander Hamilton, the Federalists, and the Whigs. This nationalism amounted to not only a belief, but an absolute faith. Lincoln saw the Constitution as "the charter of our liberties."[4] The wisdom of the Founding Fathers and the brilliance of the Constitution had seen the country through every difficulty in the nation's past, and Lincoln believed that the document would continue to serve the needs of the country and its people. What he recognized, however, is that the Constitution could do so while also sanctioning extreme measures and extraordinary powers. The broad language of the Constitution and the requirements of what Lincoln referred to as political "necessity" were all he needed to buttress his interpretation and his course of action.[5]

In the wake of the Union victory at Antietam in September 1862, Lincoln decided to assert his prerogative as commander in chief by issuing a preliminary draft of the Emancipation Proclamation and by ridding the Army of the Potomac of McClellan once and for all. The two actions were intimately tied together. McClellan had earlier expressed his opinion that the Union war effort should not tamper with the institution of slavery, a piece of unsolicited advice he gave the president in what has become known as the Harrison's Landing Letter.[6] As Lincoln's patience ran out over McClellan's failure to crush Lee's army in the aftermath of Antietam, he also recognized that McClellan was not the general he needed to wage a war that now, by virtue of the Emancipation Proclamation, had been transformed from a limited war into a total war, from a war for the Union into a war for freedom.

So on November 5, 1862, Lincoln relieved McClellan of command and, by so doing, expanded his own role of commander in chief beyond what any previous president had done—not because he fired McClellan and replaced him with Major General Ambrose Burnside, who turned out to be an even worse general than McClellan ever was, but because he had come to comprehend the paramount importance of civilian authority over the military and did not hesitate to define his duties as commander in chief in a way that would enable him—and his successors down through the decades—to ensure that the president would possess supremacy over his generals and over the formulation of what James M. McPherson and military scholars have called "national strategy."[7]

It was not pure dominance, however, that Lincoln sought. Acknowledging that he was not a military strategist, he wanted generals who—unlike McClellan—would be willing to communicate with him along what he considered to be a two-way street. In the ensuing dialogue, as Lincoln envisioned it, he and his generals could establish the best possible strategy by gaining a mutual understanding and, better yet, a consensual agreement as to the correct course to follow, thus fulfilling the letter and spirit of the Constitution in its placing control of the military in the hands of the president. The president would tell his generals what he wanted and describe for them the political realities of the situation; in return, his generals would inform him of the military circumstances they faced and the necessary steps that must be taken to avert disaster or to win victory. Together, Lincoln hoped, he and his generals could run the war by means of consent and concurrence.[8] "All [I] wanted," Lincoln is reported to have said, "was some one who would take the responsibility and act. . . . [I] had never professed to be a military man or to know how campaigns should be conducted and never wanted to interfere with them."[9]

After watching two other commanders of the Army of the Potomac go down in flames—General Burnside, who threw away the lives of his men at Fredericksburg in December 1862, and Major General Joseph Hooker, who lost his nerve in a contest of wills with Lee in the thick woodlands around Chancellorsville in May 1863—Lincoln found himself in a quandary. While he did not sack Hooker immediately in the wake of the Chancellorsville disaster, he could not determine what the general had in mind for a summer campaign. Hooker himself seemed unable to decide whether he had a plan or not. As the days passed, Lincoln grew more concerned that Hooker had missed his best opportunity to strike at Lee and that circumstances now meant that another offensive by the Army of the Potomac across the Rappahannock would prove far too costly.

Lincoln, too, seemed not to know what he really wanted. He was beginning to suspect that Hooker lacked the ability to lead an army and successfully carry out complicated operations. The president's thoughts turned to finding someone else to take charge of the Army of the Potomac, and he offered the job to Major General Darius N. Couch, who declined it because of poor health, and Major General John F. Reynolds, who told Lincoln he didn't want the command either. In turn, Lincoln told Reynolds he would hold on to Hooker for a while longer. He would not throw the gun away simply because it had misfired once.[10]

That decision was a crucial mistake. Sticking with Hooker meant hoping for the best, and the president kept wishing that "Fighting Joe," as the newspapers called the general, would come out swinging sooner or later. That's why, as May slid into June, Lincoln thought that Hooker and his army still had a chance to win a major victory over Lee and the Army of Northern Virginia—in fact, an even better chance than they had gotten at Chancellorsville. When it became apparent that Lee was moving north in another raid across the Potomac, Lincoln's optimism rose into a virtual gleefulness. Despite the leviathan's bulk and deadly course, the president saw that Lee's invasion of the north gave the Army of the Potomac a perfect opportunity to strike like lightning and destroy the Southern army once and for all.

Earlier, when he was wrestling with McClellan's overcautiousness after Antietam, he pointed out that Lee's going into Pennsylvania was something not to dread but to see as a golden opportunity. If Lee moved his whole force into Pennsylvania, Lincoln had told McClellan, he would give up his line of communications, "and you [would] have nothing to do but to follow, and ruin him." Lincoln emphasized that Lee's abandoning of his communications amounted to "a simple truth." "In coming to us, he tenders us an advantage which we should not waive," Lincoln said to McClellan. Now, in the spring of 1863, with Lee's army headed north once more, Lincoln's spirits soared, for he believed that the enemy was creating another opportunity for the Army of the Potomac, another advantage for the Union forces to destroy in detail the Army of Northern Virginia.[11]

No one comprehended this point less than Hooker did. When he realized that Lee's army was marching north toward the Potomac, Hooker proposed crossing the Rappahannock to attack the rear of Lee's army near Fredericksburg. Lincoln replied with the gentle, yet emphatic, advice not to "take any risk of being entangled upon the river, like an ox jumped half over a fence, and liable to be torn by dogs, front and rear, without a fair chance to gore one way or kick the other." Offering some sound strategic "suggestions," Lincoln said that if Lee had indeed come over to Hooker's side of the river, the best thing for the Army of the Potomac to do would be to stay on that same side and fight the enemy.[12]

But Hooker still could not process the notion that he would have to find Lee's army and try to crush it. He sent another plan to Lincoln suggesting a phantasmagorical scheme by which he and the Army of the Potomac would ignore Lee's movements completely and strike forward in an attack on Richmond. After taking the Confederate capital, he proposed heading north to capture Lee. Lincoln must have thought that Hooker had lost his mind. Quickly he replied to the general with a short message that could not be misunderstood: "I think *Lee's* Army, and not *Richmond,* is your true objective point. If he comes towards the Upper Potomac, follow on his flank, and on the inside track, shortening your lines, whilst he lengthens his. Fight him when opportunity offers. If he stays where he is, fret him, fret him."[13]

Finally Hooker began to move his army north in an effort to find out what Lee was truly up to. Understandably Lincoln became more nervous, spending long hours at the telegraph room in the War Department hoping to hear some word of progress from Hooker or learn with more certainty where Lee had taken his army. Lincoln was rapidly loosing faith in Hooker. As he learned that Union garrisons at Winchester and Martinsburg had been invested by the advance elements of Lee's army, Lincoln called on Hooker to help them. He also observed, in a statement that was one of his best as commander in chief, that "if the head of Lee's army is at

Martinsburg and the tail of it on the Plank road between Fredericksburg and Chancellorsville, the animal must be very slim somewhere. Could you not break him?"[14]

Lincoln tried to get his general to focus his efforts. Lee's advance, he said, "gives you back the chance that I thought McClellan lost last fall."[15] The president was actually growing more desperate as the warm days of June wore on. While Lee's forces swept into Pennsylvania without resistance, Hooker spent his time arguing with his superiors over army strengths and garrison deployments rather than addressing the fact that the enemy army had freely crossed the Potomac and moved at will within the Commonwealth of Pennsylvania. When permission was denied for Hooker to subsume the Federal garrison at Harper's Ferry into his army, the general responded in anger and asked to be relieved of command.

Without hesitation, Lincoln approved Hooker's request and appointed Major General George Gordon Meade to assume command of the Army of the Potomac. He was a good choice. Known and respected widely among rank and file in the Army of the Potomac, he had performed well in battle and as a leader of men. The army's command was not offered to Meade; he was ordered to take it. With reluctance, Meade took up the job and tried as quickly as possible to learn the dispositions of the Army of the Potomac, to find Lee's whereabouts, and to ready his troops for battle. From Washington, Meade received instructions to defend the nation's capital from enemy attack while also operating against "the invading forces of the rebels."[16] No explicit mention was made of destroying Lee's army, but Lincoln somehow assumed that Meade should know that such an annihilation should be his highest priority.

Having done what he could, Lincoln waited nervously in Washington for the outcome of Meade's search for Lee's army and the inevitable battle that would take place when the Army of the Potomac and the Army of Northern Virginia collided. After finally learning that a major battle was underway at Gettysburg, Lincoln spent long hours in the War Department telegraph office reading dispatches from the front and pacing the room in anxiety. It must have taken great discipline not to dash off a string of messages to Meade telling him how to fight the battle.

When word finally reached Washington that Meade had won a great victory at Gettysburg, Lincoln was relieved and pleased but not overjoyed. He issued an announcement to the press on Independence Day morning that displayed extreme caution in his choice of words. As of 10:00 PM on July 3, Lincoln said, the news from Gettysburg was such "as to cover that

Army with the highest honor, to promise a great success to the cause of the Union, and to claim the condolence for all of the many gallant fallen." Lincoln did not use the word "victory" in his announcement, and he carefully offered no effusive praise of Meade and his generals. Too often in the past had good news turned sour quickly when what appeared to be victory ended up in ignominious defeat. More significantly, true victory in Lincoln's estimation could only be won by the annihilation of Lee's army, not by the enemy's defeat in battle and retreat back to Virginia.[17]

On July 5, Lincoln read Meade's congratulatory order to the Army of the Potomac, and his heart sank when he realized that his general's goals differed considerably from what the president thought they should be. Meade thanked his army for its courage and gallantry against superior numbers and for utterly defeating the enemy and forcing it to withdraw. There was more to be done, however. He wanted the Army of the Potomac "to drive from our soil every vestige of the presence of the invader." Lincoln was beside himself after reading those words. "Drive the invader from our soil!" he cried out. "My God! Is that all?" In Lincoln's opinion, as he later expressed to John Hay, his secretary, "the whole country is our soil." He couldn't understand why his generals so consistently failed to grasp this fundamental point.[18]

To Henry W. Halleck, the general in chief of the Union armies, Lincoln sent a note saying that he disliked Meade's choice of words and that dispatches were flooding in suggesting that Meade was doing little to prevent Lee's army from escaping. Strangely, given all that was at stake, Lincoln seems to have satisfied himself by wringing his hands rather than taking decisive action as commander in chief. After learning that Vicksburg had surrendered to Grant, Lincoln sent another message to Halleck, urging him to press Meade toward a completion of his work "by the literal or substantial destruction of Lee's army." If this could be done, said Lincoln, "the rebellion will be over."[19]

Remarkably Lincoln did not communicate directly with Meade himself. Having convinced himself that the conclusion of the rebellion might be a simple victory away, Lincoln never personally informed Meade of his belief or, for that matter, of his own anxiety. Halleck dutifully forwarded Lincoln's message to Meade, stressing that "the president is urgent and anxious that your army should move against him [the enemy] by forced marches."[20] But Lincoln sent no word of encouragement to Meade, no indication of his own distress, no forceful direct order for Lee's army to be wiped from the face of the earth.

It was another major error. In dealing with the Army of the Potomac's other commanders, Lincoln had been direct, candid, emphatic, clear, and —in a word—commanding. Now, when the situation demanded such an approach, more than any occasion had demanded it in the past, Lincoln retreated from his duties as commander in chief and left Meade to his own devices. Remaining behind the scenes, pacing in the telegraph office of the War Department or flaring up in anger while in the company of visitors or his own staff, Lincoln failed to apply consistently all the assertive methods he had previously developed in carrying out his responsibilities as commander in chief.

It is possible that Lincoln did send a confidential order to Meade prodding him to attack Lee and offering, if the assault did not succeed, to assume all responsibility for the failure. Robert Todd Lincoln many years later remembered his father telling him of such an order, and the younger Lincoln in turn related his story to several others, including John Nicolay, Lincoln's secretary, twenty years after the president's assassination. Based on circumstantial evidence, it would seem that Hannibal Hamlin, Lincoln's vice president, delivered this confidential order to Meade on July 11.[21] If the story is true, which cannot be definitively established, then Lincoln did at least make an effort to communicate candidly with Meade. But it seems likely that if Meade had received such an order, even a confidential one, he would have acknowledged it, which he never did. In the end, it appears that Lincoln sent no such message and, instead, persisted in fuming about Meade rather than making command decisions by the means he favored most—a direct dialogue between himself and his commanding general that would, in the end, lead to a consensus agreement on the best course to follow.

By the evening of July 12, Meade faced Lee's makeshift lines near Williamsport, and while the Potomac swelled within its banks, blocking the Confederate route of retreat, it appeared as if the Federals had succeeded in trapping the Southern army. At this crucial moment, a council of war of Meade's subordinate generals in the Army of the Potomac voted not to attack Lee until the strength of the Confederate army could be determined. Meade opposed the council's decision, but he decided to delay any assault against the enemy until he could personally inspect the Confederates' lines. Rain and mist prevented him from seeing much, but orders were given for the army to prepare for a reconnaissance in force on the enemy's works during the morning of July 14. When dawn came, however, it revealed that the river had fallen and the Army of Northern Virginia had escaped unscathed to the safety of Virginia.

Predictably, Lincoln was in the telegraph office when the news arrived announcing Lee's escape. To John Hay, the president said: "We had them within our grasp. We had only to stretch forth our hands & they were ours." With his anger boiling over, Lincoln told Gideon Welles, the secretary of the navy, that he believed "there is bad faith somewhere," implying that Meade's lack of aggressiveness was possibly a traitorous act. To those around him, Lincoln's grief and anger were visible, tangible, and shocking to behold. Lincoln exclaimed petulantly to his son, Robert: "If I had gone up there, I could have whipped them myself."[22]

Halleck let Meade know that the president had expressed "great dissatisfaction" with Lee's escape, and the general in chief urged the Army of the Potomac to pursue the Confederates as vigorously as possible and slash them to pieces. Meade sent a sharp reply to the War Department: "Having performed my duty conscientiously and to the best of my ability, the censure of the President conveyed in your dispatch . . . is, in my judgment, so undeserved that I feel compelled most respectfully to ask to be immediately relieved from the command of this army." Halleck, no doubt with Lincoln's approval, dashed off another telegram to Meade and tried to assure the general that his earlier message "was not intended as a censure, but as a stimulus to an active pursuit."[23]

When Lincoln saw Meade's resignation telegram, he sat down and composed a brusque letter of reply to the general. The president assured Meade that he was "very—*very*—grateful to you for the magnificent success you have given the cause of the country at Gettysburg." But Lincoln told him bluntly that he was disappointed by Meade's apparent willingness to let Lee slip away without fighting another battle. All in all, Lincoln believed that Meade did not appreciate "the magnitude of the misfortune involved in Lee's escape." Here was the crux of the matter. Wrote the president, as forcefully as he could: "He was within your easy grasp, and to have closed upon him would, in connection with our other late successes, have ended the war. As it is, the war will be prolonged indefinitely."[24]

Having committed these strong words—these searing words of rebuke and blame—to paper, Lincoln then decided not to send the letter, and Meade never knew that the document existed. The president, after considering the matter, did not want to remove Meade from command, despite his personal anguish over how the general had failed to achieve a total victory. As Lincoln said to Welles, "He has made a great mistake, but we will try him farther." But it was not until the following year that Lincoln was able to tell Meade directly how much he appreciated the victory at Gettysburg and Meade's unfailing devotion to the Union cause. "The country knows that . . . you have done grand service," wrote Lincoln in a personal letter to Meade.[25]

Ironically, Lincoln never tried to establish personal ties between himself and the commander of the Army of the Potomac after Gettysburg. Instead the president's efforts went into cultivating his relationship with General Ulysses S. Grant, with whom Lincoln found communication easier and less distressing. Lincoln and Grant seemed always to be on the same wavelength. The president found that there was little need to prod Grant because the general showed more than enough initiative on his own. Unlike so many of Lincoln's other generals, Grant also understood how a hard war must be fought, and he never wavered from comprehending that the enemy's army, and not its capital, was the ultimate target for destruction. For his part, Grant grasped the crucial importance of civil-military relations in a democracy and never resented Lincoln's involvement in strategic matters or the necessity of answering to civilian authority.

Several weeks after Gettysburg, Meade was called to Washington for meetings with the president and War Department. At one point, Lincoln turned to Meade and asked: "Do you know, general, what your attitude toward Lee for a week after the battle [of Gettysburg] reminded me of?" No, said Meade, he did not. "I'll be hanged," said Lincoln, "if I could think of anything else than an old woman trying to shoo her geese across a creek."[26] It was an unfair comment, and despite its cutting edge, Meade seems not to have been offended by it.

The president never gave up the idea that Meade should have been able to destroy Lee's army after Gettysburg, even though his expectation of such a total victory had been based less on military reality than on hope alone. Over and over again during the long ordeal of the Civil War, the Union and Confederate armies revealed their inability to strike such a decisive blow of destruction against their foes. Even if Meade had thrown his entire army against Lee's defenses at Williamsport, and even if he had miraculously destroyed the enemy, it is doubtful he could have brought about an end to the war. In the summer of 1863, the Confederate will to fight remained strong and vibrant, despite the defeats at Gettysburg and Vicksburg.

Lincoln, of course, turned Gettysburg into a personal victory when he visited the battlefield on November 19, 1863, and dedicated the Soldiers' National Cemetery there with a "few appropriate remarks." With unparalleled eloquence, Lincoln laid forth before the American people the meaning of the war and urged the nation to embrace "a new birth of freedom." Many Northerners were inspired by Lincoln's call for a rededication to American first principles and to winning the war. But few, including Abraham Lincoln himself, could have known that autumn day at Gettysburg that this great war, like a rogue leviathan, would continue to determine its own course for more than a year's time—endless months of death, destruction, and human sorrow. Like Melville's great beast, the Civil War seemed to embody both the absolute power of the Almighty and the demonic power of Satan. No one really could control its actions or its outcome—not Lincoln, not Grant, not Lee. The end would come only when the will of the behemoth was broken.

10 Lincoln and the Gettysburg Awakening

All of our roads lead to Gettysburg. Tragedy and eloquence draw us back to that special place, that crossroads town, and much of what it means to be an American seems to intersect there. We are drawn back by the distant call of trumpets and by the echoes of noble purpose. It is where our greatest gods of war clashed for three days and decided the nation's fate; it is where our most revered president set forth both the promise and the hope of the nation's future. Gettysburg is by any measure America's most hallowed ground. But while we are repeatedly drawn back to those broad fields and rolling hills and to the story they have to tell, and no matter how often we may try to satisfy our longing to understand the meaning of Gettysburg, we are left mostly listening to those distant trumpets and far-off echoes, and we are never quite sure why we should feel an almost spiritual attachment to the bloody battle that was fought there and to the rather spare words that were spoken there.

One reason for that spiritual attachment is obvious. The fierce fighting that occurred at Gettysburg for three days in July 1863, when the Union Army of the Potomac collided with the Confederate Army of Northern Virginia, resulted in more than fifty-one thousand casualties. The soldiers who died there gave the ultimate sacrifice of their lives, the "last full measure of devotion" as Lincoln aptly called it, and it is difficult not to see that act of sacrifice as something precious, something holy, something grandly divine. Thousands of lives were lost on every battlefield in that great and terrible war, and yet Gettysburg resonates with the deepest spiritual connections, hearkening the soul back to the bowers, forging a tangible link with the past that can, for many people, be felt and not just seen. Gettysburg, wrote Bruce Catton, "was, and is, preeminently the great American symbol, and it is not to be touched lightly. It has overtones."[1]

Overtones, indeed. Some of those overtones, the blaring ones that sound like the horns of archangels and that compel us to think of Gettysburg as sacred soil, come from the solemn words that Abraham Lincoln spoke at the dedication of the Soldiers' National Cemetery on November 19, 1863. If it is any wonder that we think of Gettysburg in a spiritual way, it should not be, because it was Lincoln himself who set such thinking in motion. It is fairly commonplace for scholars to point out that the words and phrases Lincoln used in the Gettysburg Address tend, to a great extent, to be religiously charged. One recent historian has even suggested that it was "divine help" that told Lincoln "how to communicate to the people assembling at Gettysburg."[2]

Whether or not such a thunderclap of heavenly intervention can ever be proved or even safely assumed, numerous scholars have, nevertheless, noted the plentiful passages in Lincoln's address that seem to have been borrowed from the Scriptures. Even though Lincoln said that it was beyond our poor power to consecrate the ground of Gettysburg, that is precisely what his speech achieved. Emory M. Thomas has ruefully observed that the "sacred acres" of Gettysburg "have endured an absolutely harrowing degree of hallowing."[3] If we take a closer look at the Gettysburg Address, if we follow the roads that lead us back to Lincoln's supreme moment, we may begin to see that some of the blame for Gettysburg's spiritual aura belongs to Abraham Lincoln and the words he chose for his immortal speech.

To begin with, there is the famous opening phrase of the address, "Fourscore and seven years ago," a fairly ornate method of rendering a particular historical date that Lincoln could have picked up anywhere, but that must have come from his ready command of the Bible and from chapter and verse, in this case from the "threescore years and ten" and the "fourscore years" found in Psalms 90:10. Lincoln's reference to "our fathers" in the first sentence is mindful of the Lord's Prayer. It is also possible that behind Lincoln's clarion call for a "new birth of freedom" was the idea of rebirth set forth in John 3:3–7.

Apart from those specific citations, however, it is difficult to pin down the sources of Lincoln's biblical language in the Gettysburg Address. In his best-selling and Pulitzer Prize–winning study *Lincoln at Gettysburg: The Words That Remade America*, Garry Wills states that the most frequent "scriptural echoes" in the speech are from the Gospel of Luke. Philip B. Kunhardt Jr. argues that Lincoln relied heavily on the style and repetition of the Book of Common Prayer for his couplings of "so conceived and so dedicated," "fitting and proper," and "little note nor long remember." The speech, says Kunhardt, also "flared with sounds and images from the Scriptures." A thoroughly provocative thesis, propounded by William J.

Wolf in 1959, maintains that the central image of the Gettysburg Address is the Christian sacrament of baptism. "Lincoln," says Wolf, "conflates the themes of the life of man in birth, baptismal dedication, and spiritual rebirth with the experience of the nation in its eighty-seven years of history."[4] Wolf may certainly be stretching things a bit, but the point is that Lincoln's speech did have a distinctive "biblical ring." Commentators have variously likened it to a hymn, a prayer, or a benediction.[5]

But there are other, more subtle, reasons why Americans regard Gettysburg as hallowed ground and Lincoln's address as sacred text. It is not only Lincoln's spiritual vocabulary that ties us to Gettysburg with a mystic chord, as Lincoln himself might have called it. There is also something beneath the surface, something emotional and sensational. Magic happened at Gettysburg, but we have long since lost sight of it. Lincoln predicted that the world would not remember what was said over the graves at Gettysburg, and although he was wrong because his words have become immortal, he was correct if he also meant that the full impact of his words would fade over time, like colors that grow dull and dark on an ancient painting. As one historian has recently put it, the Gettysburg Address is "the Lincoln speech that nobody knows."[6]

Historians are not quite sure what actually took place at Gettysburg, and the fact is that we may never know for certain the details of that day. We are left with a multitude of conflicting evidence and eyewitness testimony. Some people swore that Lincoln wrote his remarks on a scrap of paper while riding the train to Gettysburg; others, on the same train, swore that he wrote nothing at all during the entire journey. Some said, too, that Lincoln spoke his words from memory, never once glancing at the sheets of paper he held in his left hand (or was it his right?). Other observers remarked how Lincoln carefully read his text, word for word, from the sheets of paper he held in his right hand (or was it both hands?).[7]

It should come as no surprise that this pivotal event in American history, this great and shining moment in Lincoln's presidency, is clouded in contradictory testimony and murky mythology. In our own lifetime, we have come to see, in the case of President Kennedy's assassination in Dallas, how unreliable and conflicting the memories of witnesses can be. In the place of facts, myths are readily substituted; or, worse, the stuff of legend is interwoven with the truth in so tight a fabric that one thread cannot be distinguished from the other. So, too, with the Gettysburg Address. We know far less than we ought to know about it. And we know far less than we would surely like to know. Sorting it all out strand by strand is almost impossible.

But not entirely impossible. If we are to recapture the magic of the Gettysburg Address, we must try to reconstruct the event itself and get a picture of the moment that can take us beyond the few famous but very fuzzy photographs that were snapped on Cemetery Hill that November day. There is, luckily, enough evidence to give us a pretty good idea of what the scene was like.

By all accounts, the crowds were enormous. People had come from far and wide to attend the dedication ceremonies; for many, it was a journey they would never forget. Streets leading into Gettysburg were clogged to capacity, a newspaper reporter wrote, "by citizens from every quarter thronging into the village in every kind of vehicle—old Pennsylvania wagons, spring wagons, carts, family carriages, buggies, and more fashionable modern vehicles, all crowded with citizens—kept pouring into the town in one continual string." The armies had long since left Gettysburg, but now the town was overwhelmed by a new "invading host" who came by wagon, by train, by horse, and by foot to witness history in the making.[8]

On the night before the dedication of the cemetery, the crowd took over the town and turned it into something resembling a fairgrounds. Along the streets, torches lit the way for the surging mass of people who jammed the avenues and the taverns, the hotels, and the boardinghouses. The noise in the street was almost deafening. Bands played, people sang, and rowdies shouted.[9] There was an oddly festive air, an atmosphere for wild rovers, in Gettysburg that night—not the kind of backdrop one would associate with the solemn occasion of a cemetery dedication. Men were drinking, and some men were getting drunk. Even John Hay and John Nicolay, Lincoln's private secretaries, imbibed a few glasses of whiskey and sang a few songs. Nicolay, said Hay in his diary, "sung his little song of the 'Three Thieves,' and then we sung 'John Brown.'"[10]

Hoping to see Lincoln, the crowd serenaded him that evening at the home of David Wills, where the president was spending the night, and called for him to come out. Lincoln made an appearance, stood in the doorway for a few minutes, and then quietly slipped back inside. Later a larger crowd gathered and made a terrible racket, calling for the president from beneath a window at the Wills house. A military band played a few songs. A group of young women sang "We Are Coming Father Abraham, Three Hundred Thousand More." A male quartet also serenaded. When

Lincoln reappeared, the crowd asked him to say a few words, something he did not like doing without a prepared text. But he did make a few extemporaneous remarks. Lincoln retreated quickly, however, and the crowd moved next door and found William Seward, the secretary of state, who was more than willing to deliver a speech. Lincoln spent the rest of the night writing and briefly conferring with Seward. Around midnight, the president went to bed, but it is hard to imagine anyone getting much sleep that night, given the high spirits and loud revelries of the merry multitudes.[11]

With the daylight it was easier to guess the size of the crowd. Some observers thought that there were as many as twenty thousand people in town, although a more reasonable estimate places the size of the crowd at about fifteen thousand. When the president emerged from the Wills house to join the procession of dignitaries marching to the cemetery, the crowd responded enthusiastically. Lincoln was greeted with "three hearty cheers," and clumps of people surged toward him, arms outstretched, wanting to shake his hand or touch him. At first the mass of people behaved in an orderly fashion, but shortly things got out of control, and people began jostling Lincoln back and forth and cramming in all around him. Finally Ward Hill Lamon, marshal in chief of the day's events and Lincoln's unofficial bodyguard, ordered the crowd to move back. The people slowly retreated, but not before issuing a few more cheers for "Father Abraham" and "honest Old Abe."[12]

It was a perfect day for the ceremony. "The sky was cloudless," remembered a Gettysburg resident, "and the sun shone out in glorious splendor."[13] The procession soon arrived, flowing up Cemetery Hill to the marching tunes of four military bands, and all but one of the honored guests were escorted to their seats on the platform. The program was delayed for half an hour as everyone waited for the principal speaker, Edward Everett, to arrive and take his place on the platform. After he was seated, a little before noon, the proceedings began, and the crowd watched in awe and wonder as the ceremony unfolded—a grand ceremony, the likes of which few had ever seen. Those who witnessed what took place that day at Gettysburg would never forget it. As one observer noted years later, "We had heard very much more that day than we dreamed of."[14]

The crowd was ready for something momentous to occur, and they did not have to wait long. After a dirge was played by Birgfield's Band of Philadelphia, the Reverend T. H. Stockton, chaplain of the House of Representatives, offered a prayer, a soulful entreaty for the nation to remember that "in the freshness of their young and manly life, with such sweet memories of father and mother, brother and sister, wife and children, maiden and friends, they died for us." His words struck a deep chord. The *New York Times* reported that Stockton's invocation, which concluded with the Lord's Prayer, "was touching and beautiful," and the *Philadelphia Press* remarked that "there was scarcely a dry eye in all that vast assemblage." Lincoln was among those noticeably moved, and his "falling tear" was seen as proof of the "sincerity of his emotions."[15]

After a reading of the lengthy regrets of important people who could not attend, the U.S. Marine Band played an appropriate musical selection. Finally, Edward Everett, the nation's most famous orator, was introduced. His address, which lasted nearly two hours, soared in rhetorical flourish as he reviewed the history of the Battle of Gettysburg within the context of the great battles of the ages. The crowd was enraptured and distracted by turns. Everett was a masterly speaker and knew precisely how to hold an audience, but his emotional appeal may have discomforted his listeners. The audience, in fact, began to dwindle, some people wandering away from the immediate area of the platform toward the unfinished gravesites or the slopes of the hillside and the crest of the ridge where the deadly fighting had taken place four months earlier. At last Everett finished his speech, and as he did the strollers drifted back to the platform and waited for the next installment of the program.[16]

A poem composed for the occasion was sung as a hymn by the Baltimore Glee Club. Then Ward Lamon walked to the center of the platform and proudly introduced his friend, "The President of the United States." Precisely what occurred during the next two or three minutes cannot be known. It is certain that Lincoln delivered his brief remarks, or at least a version of what we today know as the Gettysburg Address, but beyond that only the grayness of history seems apparent. As John Hay rather matter-of-factly recorded in his diary, "The President, in a fine, free way, with more grace than is his wont, said his half dozen words of consecration, and the music wailed, and we went home through crowded and cheering streets. And all the particulars are in the daily papers."[17]

We do know that there was more to the Gettysburg Address than that. If indeed there was magic that did take place, a spiritual connection that touched the soul of America, then presumably we should be able to account for it in the reactions of the thousands of people who heard him speak that afternoon. The crowd assembled at Gettysburg had played a major role in the events of this dedication; the crowd's reaction, therefore, should tell us what we need to know about the speech's impact and its significance. Yet the surviving evidence concerning the audience's response is frustratingly—and rather amazingly—in conflict with itself. It is amazingly so only because the testimony of witnesses seems to suggest that the crowd reacted in contradictory ways at once: both enthusiastically and stoically, with great emotion and with great silence. Some observers said that the crowd ardently received Lincoln's words, even to the point of interrupting the address with applause. Benjamin B. French, who wrote the hymn that the glee club had sung that day, claimed that Lincoln's "every word at Gettysburg" had been met by a "hurricane of applause." Someone else remembered that when the president had finished, the crowd lustily gave him three cheers and offered three more for the governors of the states. Joseph L. Gilbert, the Associated Press correspondent who transcribed Lincoln's words verbatim, included in brackets the five places where the crowd interrupted Lincoln with applause, although many years later Gilbert acknowledged that he had arbitrarily inserted the references to the outbursts of applause and that he actually could not remember hearing any hand-clapping at all. Other witnesses, however, were absolutely sure that no applause occurred. W. H. Cunningham, a reporter, maintained that there was perfect silence during and after the speech. He was confident the audience had uttered "not a word, not a cheer, not a shout."[18]

But how could that be possible? How could some witnesses believe there was thunderous applause and others believe there was none? Historians have not helped to solve the contradiction. Generally, they tend to take sides, some favoring the idea of a silent crowd, others believing that the audience erupted in deafening applause. If we consider that both stunned silence and excited applause are acts that express emotion, we may begin to see them as vital clues about the impact of Lincoln's speech.

What the evidence really tells us is that the people who heard Lincoln's speech reacted very differently, but emotionally, to the president's words. Some people clapped wildly during the speech; others regarded the address as a solemn expression of sentiment and stood in silent awe of the man and his eloquence. The emotional response to Lincoln's address that took place was deep and varied. And it was, indeed, very emotional.

Already the day had been filled with emotion. The crowd was in high spirits. The bands played martial tunes. Reverend Stockton's soulful prayer had brought tears to many an eye. Edward Everett's speech had stirred patriotism and sadness, pride and sorrow. And now Lincoln, with a slight 272 words, had finally touched the deepest chord of all.

It went so deep, in fact, that it took many listeners completely by surprise. When Lincoln stopped talking (after fewer than three minutes), some members of the audience were not quite sure he had finished, and, according to one eyewitness, "the awe-struck people, apparently deeply moved, gave no sign of approval or appreciation." Ward Lamon, whose account of the Gettysburg proceedings cannot be entirely trusted, later claimed that "the lack of hearty demonstrations of approval immediately afterward, were taken by Mr. Lincoln as certain proof that it was not well received," although it seems unlikely that Lincoln thought his speech as much a failure as Lamon maintained.[19] In any case, some people were so taken aback by Lincoln's words, because of either the brevity of his speech or the emotional power of what he had said, that they did not applaud and, in fact, did not respond in any outward manner. "It was a sad hour," recalled a Gettysburg man. "Any tumultuous wave of applause would have been out of place."[20]

But there were "roars of applause," as one observer described it, and there was great solemnity all at once.[21] Mostly, the crowd was overcome by a wave of emotion. Some responded with heartfelt silence; others, like church-goers who occasionally wish they could applaud a particularly fine choir performance or a touching sermon (but who restrain themselves and do not), permitted their instincts to control their actions this time and exploded into applause at intervals throughout the president's address.

Members of the audience were touched in a variety of ways. One Union officer was powerfully—and spiritually—moved by Lincoln's remarks. As the president spoke, the officer realized that they all stood "almost immediately over the place where I had lain and seen my comrades torn in fragments by the enemy's cannon-balls—think then, if you please, how these words fell on my ears." For this army officer, Lincoln's address brought forth a moment of pure epiphany: "If at that moment the Supreme Being had appeared to me with an offer to undo my past life, give back to me a sound body free from the remembrance even of sufferings past and those that must necessarily embitter all the years to come, I should have indignantly spurned the offer, such was the effect upon me of this immortal dedication."[22]

When the president told the crowd that the world could never forget what the soldiers of the North had accomplished at Gettysburg, an army captain sobbed openly and then, according to a reporter who saw him, "lifted his eyes to heaven and in low and solemn tones exclaimed 'God Almighty, bless Abraham Lincoln.'" Isaac Arnold—who was not present at Gettysburg but who gained his information from Governor William Dennison of Ohio, who was there—said that "before the first sentence was completed, a thrill of feeling, like an electric shock, pervaded the crowd."[23] Others who were not there agreed nonetheless that the words Lincoln had spoken were positively thrilling. As George William Curtis, editor of *Harper's Weekly,* put it, "The few words of the President were from the heart to the heart. They cannot be read, even, without kindling emotion." Horatio King, who heard Lincoln deliver the address, expressed it simply but passionately. "My God," he said, "it was so impressive!"[24]

Whatever these people had experienced, it was not easily put into words. Nor was it at all what they had anticipated. One modern commentator, Garry Wills, has compared the Gettysburg ceremony to the rituals used in the dedication of rural cemeteries such as Mount Auburn in Cambridge, Massachusetts, in 1831; while that comparison is useful and illustrative, it is not altogether satisfying.[25] What took place at Gettysburg—the thrumming bands, the rowdy crowd, the surprising and touching speech of the president, and the varied emotional reactions to it—was really quite different from the solemn and sedate proceedings of the rural cemetery movement. It is most unlikely, in fact, that an audience at the consecration of any rural cemetery in nineteenth-century America would have ballyhooed three cheers for the dedicatory speaker, as the crowd at Gettysburg did for Lincoln. If the Gettysburg dedication resembled anything at all, it was more like a camp meeting than a cemetery consecration.[26]

I do not mean to suggest that fire and brimstone defined the major elements of the Gettysburg ceremony. Lincoln was no Bible beater, and Gettysburg was no Cane Ridge. Obviously the gyrations and hysteria of converted multitudes, which had given camp meetings a bad reputation among religious conservatives during the early decades of the nineteenth century, were not manifested by the audience at the Gettysburg dedication. But the emotional responses to Lincoln's address do seem to be strikingly similar to the reactions of revival worshipers, particularly those attending the outdoor meetings that, by the 1850s, had matured into carefully organized and orchestrated occasions for prayer, social exchanges, and festivity that downplayed the demonstration of bodily excitement. At the orderly camp meetings of the 1840s and 1850s, including the Methodist revivals in Lincoln's home state of Illinois, some attending souls would maintain a perfect decorum, whereas others might be moved to tears and supplications.[27] Occasionally passions might be heightened by the exhortations of an effective preacher, and "wild-fire songs, processions, blowing of trumpets . . . and other imitations of military operations" would flare up out of the crowd.[28] But the point is that these camp meetings produced a range of emotional responses, some overt and some serene, some blatant and some hushed.

Lincoln himself was familiar with such camp meetings, which were a fixture of the frontier culture in which he had been raised. In New Salem, Illinois, where Lincoln resided in the 1830s, revival meetings were commonplace, although Lincoln belonged to a group of skeptics who preferred to read books by Thomas Paine and other enlightened thinkers rather than listen to the volcanic sermons of backwoods orators.[29]

Generally, Lincoln steered clear of such spiritual gatherings, and he never quite came to grips with the oblations and obligations of any organized religion or Christian denomination, but he did attend camp meetings from time to time, just as he went to church in his later years, on and off.[30] Francis Grierson, an essayist and professional pianist who spent his childhood in rural Illinois (and who knew from firsthand experience what camp meetings were all about), reported that Lincoln had attended at least one revival meeting as a young man. The meeting, said Grierson, had a profound effect on Lincoln, especially when the preacher described the coming inevitable destruction of slavery in a fiery war, and Lincoln, so the story goes, had a vision of himself as an instrument of that destruction.[31] The story is almost certainly apocryphal, but it demonstrates, at the very least, Lincoln's occasional attendance at such meetings. The man was always searching for answers.

He did not find them at these frontier meetings, although he seems to have learned from their example some important lessons about using words for emotional effect. Like the preachers at revival meetings who often took on the role of prophets, stern Jeremiahs warning of God's unforgiving wrath, Lincoln could also at times seem like an Old Testament prophet—which was precisely how many people regarded his deportment at Gettysburg. One minister attending the Gettysburg ceremony remembered how Lincoln and his words seemed to cast a spell over the audience.[32] Isaac Arnold said that Lincoln's charisma mesmerized the crowd: "That mysterious influence called magnetism, which sometimes so affects a popular assembly, spread to every heart. The vast audience was instantly hushed, and hung upon his every word and syllable." A few years after the Gettysburg dedication, a national magazine declared that Lincoln's address "in the light of subsequent events sounds more like inspiration or prophecy . . . than the utterance of mere human lips."[33]

Lincoln seemed like a prophet of old at Gettysburg because what he said possessed profound spiritual force. Simply put, Lincoln offered a new definition of old truths—a new perspective on old traditions—that unlocked deep American emotions, the mystic chords of memory that Lincoln referred to in his First Inaugural Address. Lincoln had once declared, "I have never had a feeling politically that did not spring from the sentiments embodied in the Declaration of Independence."[34] At Gettysburg, his address looked back to those sentiments, which were "dedicated to the proposition that all men are created equal," and then looked forward with hope that those sentiments, those old traditions, could be understood in a new light and could, through a rededication of the American people, produce "a new birth of freedom" in the nation—a rebirth that would be as dramatic and as transforming as the spiritual regeneration of a camp meeting or a great awakening. In this respect, then, Lincoln at Gettysburg resembled the stump preachers whose sermons urged that the old light be shunned and a new light embraced, that each soul find God's new light in the awakening of conversion. With the Gettysburg Address, Lincoln was preaching his own great awakening.[35]

By 1863, at least two religious great awakenings had taken place during America's short history—one in the mid-eighteenth century and the other in the early decades of the nineteenth century—and although they were both marked by religious revivals and an outpouring of enthusiastic piety, historians and anthropologists are careful to point out that a great awakening is really more than just a flood of spiritual intensity. A great awakening, as William McLoughlin has explained, is actually a time of stressful cultural transformation that results in a "profound reorientation in beliefs and values" and the tumultuous alteration of a culture's worldview. Awakenings are the means by which society adjusts itself to new realities and redefines its norms to fit those realities.[36] They are moments when the world is turned upside down.

And so it was in America's worst cataclysm, the Civil War. The war had brought great change with it, and it was plain to see in the autumn of 1863 that the nation, whether divided or reunited, would never be the same. In his annual message to Congress in December 1862, Lincoln had said, "The dogmas of the quiet past, are inadequate to the stormy present. The occasion is piled high with difficulty, and we must rise to the occasion. As our case is new, so we must think anew, and act anew. We must disenthrall ourselves, and then we shall save our country."[37] A deep chasm already separated the old from the new.

Ultimately, what Lincoln envisioned was the need for the nation, even before the fighting was over, to renew itself and refashion its identity as a way of traversing that chasm. He had taken the first step toward that end in January 1863, when he had issued the Emancipation Proclamation, a document that reshaped the cause of preserving the Union into a crusade to make men free. But something else was still required to bridge the gap between the racial oppression of slavery and the promise of equality contained in the Declaration of Independence. The Gettysburg Address was that bridge. Lincoln's speech was a summons for the nation to embrace the principle of equality and, in the process, to transform itself into a new nation, a different America. In Lincoln's mind, such a change would require an act tantamount to spiritual regeneration, an evangelical renewal of what he had earlier called "the political religion of the nation."[38]

Commenting on Lincoln's compelling sense of purpose during the Civil War, Alexander Stephens, vice president of the Confederate States of America, wrote, "The Union with him, in sentiment, rose to the sublimity of a religious mysticism."[39] Stephens was not entirely wrong, but what he did not perceive—perhaps could not see at all—was that Lincoln's political religion, the source of his fervent mysticism, was founded not upon a simple and single-minded devotion to the cause of Union, but rather upon a matrix of interrelated propositions that became the objects of his pure faith—Union, liberty, democracy, and equality.[40]

The Gettysburg Address was Lincoln's supreme expression of that faith. And he used his carefully chosen words to inspire an awakening throughout the nation, a rebirth of old ideas, a plea for his fellow Americans to change their own hearts, just as the Book of Ezekiel in the Old Testament calls upon the faithful to "make you a new heart and a new spirit."[41] There was, Lincoln said at Gettysburg, "unfinished work" and "a great task" remaining before the American people. Through all the applause and silence, cheers and tears, what his emotional audience could not know, and what he probably did not know himself, was that the work would remain unfinished for generations yet to come. Nor did he fully understand that his words would thrill the hearts and touch the souls of millions of Americans down through the years and that his address, by the force of his spiritual plea for the birth of a new America, would compel us forevermore to think of Gettysburg as a sacred place.

11 Memories of Little Round Top

If Lincoln's Address at Gettysburg not only brought forth a call for a "new birth of freedom," but also set the sacrifice of the Union soldiers who died there within the emotional context of the nation's "political religion," it was the veteran soldiers who actually shaped how subsequent generations of Americans would comprehend what took place in the Civil War's most bloody battle. Memories, sometimes faded and sometimes vibrant, would recall the actions of perfect heroes on both sides. Out of their memories, and sometimes using their remembrances as an instrument in the reconstruction of history (and thus of their own glory), the old soldiers forged a new meaning for the war and created its lasting legacies. Often these soldiers could not agree as to precisely what had happened to them and their comrades during the war or at specific places like Gettysburg; in other instances, old enemies, Union and Confederate, took up the fight again, battling over the meaning of the Civil War with words instead of bullets. As they looked to the past, the veterans sometimes softened their accounts, not wanting to upset delicate Victorian sensibilities, but just as often the harsh realities of war—its brutality, its inhumanity, its utter disregard for anything that lay in its path—came through with disturbing clarity. Over time, the veterans' voices grew fainter, less audible, until they finally could no longer be heard at all. In time, too, the landscape of the Civil War changed, so that nothing in our modern world could be found that looked or sounded like it had when the perfect heroes had fought their great war and had given so much of themselves for their causes.

For those who tried to scale Little Round Top's heights at Gettysburg and for those who defended its ledges—including William C. Oates and Joshua Chamberlain and so many others who fought and fell there—this was not a place to be forgotten. But when it came to setting down the history of the battle for all posterity, these veterans could not agree among themselves as to the details or the meaning of the terrible battle in which they had participated. Oliver Norton tried to elevate the memory of his commanding officer, Colonel Strong Vincent, to a place of veneration above all the other perfect heroes of Little Round Top. Oates and Chamberlain, as we have seen, could not agree as to the place where a monument should be raised to the 15th Alabama, and so, in the end, no monument to that regiment was ever erected on the hill at all. It is in the story of Oates's failed efforts to erect that monument, and to get the Gettysburg National Military Park officially to honor his fallen Confederate comrades, that we may begin to understand why the veterans staked so much on their memories and made such a concerted effort after the war to honor their brethren, lost and living, on the old battlefields. It involved much more than Chamberlain's ego, Norton's hero worship of Vincent, or Oates's own feelings of pride or loss. The veterans—like Chamberlain and Oates and Norton—wanted something more than ethereal words, something more tangible than the brief sentences Lincoln spoke at Gettysburg or the sentiments that the veterans themselves expressed on Memorial Day or the Fourth of July, to mark their deeds and validate their memories. They wanted something in stone to salute their courage and acknowledge how their lives had been forever changed in the awful ordeal of battle. The old soldiers, like Oates and Chamberlain, wanted to become immortalized; they wanted monuments that would let them, in a sense, live forever.[1]

*   *   *

When William C. Oates returned to Gettysburg long after the smoke of the battle had cleared, the slopes of Little Round Top looked unfamiliar and strange to him. As he walked the ground where his men had fought for more than an hour trying unsuccessfully to dislodge Chamberlain's regiment from its strong defensive position, he did discover trees still scared by the gashes of bullets, but some of those trees were located in places where Oates could not remember any fighting ever happening. Even after visiting the battlefield four times in the years following Appomattox, he still was forced to admit that the topography of Little Round Top, with all its boulders and ledges and trees, caused him to be "confused in directions" and unsure of where some of the crucial events in his historic confrontation with the 20th Maine had occurred.[2]

Oates was not alone in his confusion. On October 3, 1889, veterans of the 20th Maine regiment, and a sizable number of interested citizens and dignitaries from the State of Maine, gathered on the hillside of Little Round Top to dedicate the regiment's monument and to memorialize its heroic defense of the Union left. When Joshua Lawrence Chamberlain, the great "Hero of Little Round Top," gave his address, he must have created quite a stir in the crowd. As we've seen, he pointed out rather casually—and with some irritability—that the granite memorial was not located where it was supposed to be, at the center of the regiment's line on July 2. As he remembered it, the real center was to the right of the new monument. But he dismissed the error as inconsequential (though his comments said otherwise). The important thing, he asserted, was that the monument fittingly paid tribute to the brave men of the 20th Maine who had so ably defended Little Round Top.[3]

The memories of the participants were imperfect, although not everyone was willing to admit that his own recollections might be hazy or his backward glances might in any way be fallible. The Civil War generation seemed to be convinced that each witness, each man who had shouldered a musket, could recall every detail of the conflict at will, and that every memory was as sharp in their minds as it had been during the moments when they had first experienced it. Inevitably, however, the Civil War veterans discovered that their memories did not coincide with each other's and that often they could not agree about what had taken place.[4]

William Oates was not looking for a fight—or a controversy—when he came up with the idea almost forty years after the battle to erect a monument at Gettysburg that would honor his old regiment, the 15th Alabama, and his younger brother John, who had been mortally wounded during the regiment's repeated assaults against the 20th Maine. For all his years of service in the Army of Northern Virginia, and for all the battles he had been through, it was Gettysburg that still haunted him and tormented his memory.[5] The memory that plagued him the most was of his lost brother. Lieutenant John A. Oates had been a playmate and a friend, a colleague and a student. When the war came, John joined another regiment but later transferred to the 15th Alabama. William Oates spent much of his time worrying about his brother and watching out for his safety.[6]

After John Oates went down on Little Round Top, struck by seven bullets, his brother was forced to withdraw the regiment as the famous assault of the 20th Maine came tumbling down the hillside. John Oates was removed by Federal soldiers, probably sometime on July 3, to a Union Fifth Corps field hospital behind the lines. He was kindly cared for by a nurse named Miss Lightner and a doctor named Reid. Twenty-three days after the battle, he died. His personal effects were transported to his brother under a flag of truce. Many years after John's death, William Oates said: "We were not only brothers, near the same age, but had not been reared together, and no brothers loved each other better."[7] He missed his brother every day for the rest of his life.

So it seemed fitting in 1899, while Oates was serving in Georgia as a brigadier general of the U.S. Army, while the war with Spain was raging in Cuba, that he wanted to remember his lost brother and his brave regiment with a lasting memorial on Little Round Top. In January 1899, Oates wrote to William M. Robbins—a former major in the 4th Alabama Infantry who now served as one of three commissioners charged by the War Department with administering the Gettysburg National Military Park—and inquired about erecting a memorial to the 15th Alabama. Robbins was the Southern member of the commission; the other two members were former Union veterans. Oates received a friendly and noncommittal reply from Robbins, who had forwarded Oates's request along to the commission chairman, John P. Nicholson of Philadelphia.[8]

Nothing seems to have happened for several months, although the commissioners, who were under pressure to demonstrate a willingness to have Confederate troop positions on the Gettysburg battlefield marked in some manner, appear to have looked on Oates's proposal favorably. In June, Oates was asking Robbins to find out for him how much a stone for the monument would cost, and Robbins dutifully collected some estimates from a local Gettysburg stonecutter. More than a year elapsed, however, before the issue of a monument to the 15th Alabama came up again. When it did in the summer of 1900, the commissioners told Oates that they supported his idea of a memorial, but only if it consisted of a single stone at the center of the Alabamians' line on Little Round Top. In September, Robbins sent Oates a diagram of the monument, which had been drawn by the commission's engineer, Captain Emmor B. Cope.[9]

Nothing else happened regarding Oates's monument for more than two years. The hiatus is difficult to explain, and the silence of the extant records only adds more confusion to the story. But the fault for any lack of progress seems to have rested entirely on Oates's shoulders. What the records do reveal is that Oates, a man with a fiery temper, had been greatly offended by the commissioners' decision to allow only a single stone regimental memorial for the 15th Alabama. Indeed, that decision had thrown him into a rage. He had proposed a stone memorial *with* flank markers, and he was unwilling to settle for anything less.

In time, however, his anger subsided and his position softened, so in April 1902 he wrote to Robbins again to say the single stone monument would be fine. "When we do the best we can we must be satisfied," he told Robbins. For the record, Oates reiterated his desire for Robbins to arrange to have the monument cut and inscribed, and he gave Robbins specific instructions on how best to get the job done. Oates, of course, would pay for the work out of his own pocket, but he didn't want Robbins to go overboard when it came to the stone or the craftsmanship of the engraving. "Get it all within $100," he said to Robbins. But whatever the cost, he wanted it done. Oates hoped to dedicate the monument on the thirty-ninth anniversary of the battle in July, after he returned from a European tour with his family.[10]

By the following September, after spending the spring and most of the summer in Europe, Oates had received no word from Robbins or the other Gettysburg commissioners about his monument. Reopening his communication with the commission, but worried that mail had somehow gone astray, he wrote directly to Robbins and asked him for news on the monument. When Robbins received the letter, he began to get nervous. While Oates had been in Europe, something had happened to change the commissioners' opinion about the proposed monument. No longer could Oates count on getting a monument to his regiment or to his dead brother.[11]

What had changed while Oates was off stewing about flank markers and visiting the Continent was that the third member of the commission, Charles A. Richardson of New York, expressed the opinion that the park "should not favor giving any single regt. on either side conspicuous notice and precedence over others by special regimental monument apart from other regiments engaged in substantially the same position." Richardson seems to have believed that recognition should be given to Brigadier General Evander M. Law's Alabama brigade for the assault on Little Round Top rather than singling out the 15th Alabama regiment for recognition. Nicholson, the chairman, agreed with Richardson. And, more tellingly, Robbins himself felt particularly uncomfortable about endorsing a monument to any Alabama regiment that was not his own beloved 4th Alabama.

There was, of course, no hard or fast rule against such regimental monuments, which already populated the landscape of the battlefield along the length of the Union battle lines. Nevertheless, Robbins wrote to inform Oates that the monument to the 15th Alabama would not be approved after all, for the commission's endorsement could be taken as a bad precedent. At the same time, Robbins asked his fellow commissioners to write the formal letter turning down Oates's proposed monument; he did not want his name dragged into the matter any further than it already had been.[12]

Despite his desire to distance himself from the monument's rejection, Robbins did write Oates to say that, even apart from other considerations, it was highly unlikely that the 15th Alabama memorial could be placed where Oates wanted it to go because the commissioners operated under the battle line restrictions that had been set forth by the Gettysburg Battlefield Memorial Association, the local organization and veterans' group that had managed the park before the War Department had taken it over. Robbins did not mention that the rule had been erratically enforced over the years and that a Pennsylvania Supreme Court ruling in 1891 concerning the placement of the 72nd Pennsylvania Infantry's regimental monument had successfully weakened the legal legs upon which the battle line rule was supported in the past. The point was clear: if Oates wanted a monument, it would have to be placed where the Alabama brigade formed in line of battle before its advance across the farm fields that lay in the shadow of the Round Tops. If any monument to the 15th Alabama were to be approved by the commissioners, it would have to be placed on Confederate Avenue, about a mile southwest from Little Round Top.[13]

Given Oates's hair-trigger temper, it didn't take much to set him off. When Robbins's letter arrived suggesting Confederate Avenue as the site of the monument, Oates exploded with rage. He quickly fired back a salvo to Robbins and declared that the battle line rule would effectively mean that Union regiments could place their monuments where they did most of their fighting, since those places tended to be the same as where the Union regiments had formed their lines of battle, and that Confederate units would be banished to remote locations on the battlefield. Blatantly playing his political cards, Oates pointed out that he and other former Confederates had voted in 1890s to approve the enabling legislation for the Gettysburg National Park, but "never with a view to such a rule as that."

Several weeks later, after once more putting his anger aside, Oates submitted a formal application to the commissioners for permission to erect a monument on Little Round Top and enclosed a resolution endorsing the memorial, signed by eighty-nine survivors of the 15th Alabama.[14] When he received no reply to his petition, Oates wrote directly to Colonel Nicholson and asked for prompt action; if the commission did not act speedily, he said, he would be forced to submit his request directly to the attention of the U.S. secretary of war. Nicholson, who seems to have been put off by Oates's threats to go over his head, urged him to send such a formal request to the secretary of war. Probably he knew that any petition to the secretary would be slowed down by the tangle of red tape in Washington and that, ultimately, any document concerning the battlefield would be forwarded by the secretary to the commissioners for their advice and consent. To cover himself, Nicholson—ever the skillful bureaucrat—let Oates know that he, personally, was not to blame for the slow response to his proposal; the commission as a whole, he said, had simply deferred to Major Robbins in dealing with any requests made for Confederate monuments.[15]

Bureaucrats must sometimes take calculated risks, and in this case the price Nicholson paid for covering himself from the effects of any political pressure from outside the War Department resulted in a different kind of unpleasantness closer to home—a divisiveness among his fellow commissioners. Robbins, for one, was furious when he read Nicholson's letter to Oates. He told Nicholson that he resented being cast as the "*main authority* and the *umpire*" in the matter over a monument for the 15th Alabama, which was precisely what he had tried to avoid. As far as he was concerned, his service in the 4th Alabama created a conflict of interest in handling Oates's proposal—not simply because he, like Oates, had served as an officer in Law's brigade, but also because he felt the 4th Alabama deserved a monument on Little Round Top as much as the 15th did.[16]

But what Robbins did not admit was that the division among the commission members had followed a fairly predictable course. As the Southern member, he was being singled out for blame—or if not blame, then at least he was being singled out—by Nicholson and Richardson, the two Northern members of the commission. To Oates, Robbins made the point that if his fellow Alabamian could win the support of the two Northern commissioners and of the secretary of war, the 15th Alabama would get its monument, although Robbins added that he thought such an approval was pretty doubtful.[17] Under the circumstances, it was a peculiar thing to say to Oates. No matter how much Robbins qualified his suggestion, it seemed to Oates like Robbins was saying that with a little persuasion, or perhaps a little political pressure, the monument could become a reality. Yet Robbins must have known that Oates's case had already been decided and that there could be no memorial to the 15th Alabama anywhere other than on Confederate Avenue.

Dutifully, and taking Robbins's encouraging words seriously, Oates forwarded his formal application through his congressman, Aristo A. Wiley, and to the secretary of war, Elihu Root. To clarify matters, Oates noted that he had declined the commissioners' offer to place the monument on Confederate Avenue and that he wanted the stone to be located on Little Round Top. On February 19, 1903, Secretary Root, following routine and the War Department's chain of command, referred the petition to the men who would be responsible in the government bureaucracy for deciding the matter—the three Gettysburg commissioners.[18]

Hoping he might have a chance this time to get favorable results, Oates notified Nicholson that he would change the memorial's inscription later and would get more precise about the wording and the location after the monument had been approved. For the time being, though, Oates wanted Nicholson to know roughly where he intended to put the monument—somewhere along where his left, he said, had pushed back Chamberlain's right—and around the slope some distance from where the 4th Alabama, Major Robbins's regiment, had become separated from Oates's command during the fighting. Thinking that the commissioners might give up their notion of putting the monument on Confederate Avenue if they could grasp what the 15th Alabama had gone through on the second of July, Oates wrote a long account of the Little Round Top assault for Robbins and asked that his request for a monument be considered in light of his regiment's sacrifices and its dead that were left on the hill's bloody slopes. "I mean no disrespect to any other regiment in the brigade," Oates said pleadingly, "but when I am dead and gone, I want to leave a little stone on the spot where my brother and others were killed."[19]

His detailed references to the fight for Little Round Top had some unanticipated consequences. Although the commissioners had previously maintained that their opposition to Oates's proposed monument was based on the battle line rule and their concern over precedents, the issue of conflicting historical memories suddenly dominated the controversy. In response to Oates's description of the battle, Robbins told Nicholson that Oates was mistaken about the relative positions of the Confederate regiments that had attacked Little Round Top. "I'm sure," said Robbins, "I was within about 100 yards of where Gen. O. must have been." Confused by Oates's account, Robbins could not reconcile the fact that Oates somehow believed "he was *far off to himself* in the fight there." A few days later Robbins wrote Nicholson again, this time giving the commission chairman an even more detailed description of the location of the regiments of Law's brigade during the attack on Little Round Top. "All these regiments on both sides [of the hill] were in close touch with each other," Robbins remembered, "and it was a mistake to say that either regiment on either side fought a separate fight off to itself."[20]

In early February, Major Richardson had drafted for the commission a formal reply to Oates's petition, but the letter, for reasons that are unclear, was not sent. During the first week of March, however, the commissioners decided the time was right to let Oates know where they stood, and they forwarded the Richardson draft to the secretary of war for his approbation. The letter granted the commission's approval for Oates to erect a monument to the 15th Alabama, but only if "such a monument is placed on its Brigade line now marked by a Brigade Tablet with an inscription stating what and where its movements and engagements were during the battle." In other words, the commission ruled that Oates's monument could be placed only on Confederate Avenue. There was no mention in the official response to any disagreements over Oates's account of the battle.[21] The commissioners assumed that the War Department would obtain the clearance of the secretary of war and then the letter would be forwarded to Congressman Wiley.[22]

More than two months passed, however, and Oates received no word from the commissioners, the War Department, or Congressman Wiley about his application. Apparently the War Department was as efficient in those days as the Pentagon is today, and somehow the reply to Oates's petition had been lost or forgotten in the office of the secretary of war. When the matter was brought to Secretary Root's attention, he choose not to send the commission's response to Oates and instead had a shorter letter drafted that invited Oates to visit the battlefield and work out his differences with the three commissioners.[23]

Oates took this opportunity to deal directly with Root and wrote the secretary a long letter that repeated a description of his regiment's attack on Little Round Top, its position on the hill and the fact that it had turned the right flank of the 20th Maine during the assault, and his desire to erect a modest memorial to his dead brother and the other heroes of the 15th Alabama. He also observed, with considerable annoyance, that Robbins seemed to be the commissioner who objected the most to his proposal and who insisted on locating the monument on Confederate Avenue. He hoped that the secretary would grant permission for a Confederate marker to be placed where the fighting had actually occurred. If not, said Oates, "it shows that the bitterness engendered by the Civil War has not completely subsided." Root, without replying himself, forwarded Oates's letter for action to the Gettysburg commissioners, the source of the problem.[24] Oates, who had had plenty of experience as a congressman with the federal bureaucracy, seems never to have encountered anything quite like this War Department dance before.

The situation, of course, was right back where it had started, except that conflicting memories of the battle now helped to slow down or impede Oates's application beyond the issue of the battle line rule, making the case even more complicated than it had been when Oates sent his first request to the commissioners in 1899. Oates's version of the Little Round Top fight became a major source of concern for the commissioners, but for none other so much as Robbins, who totally disagreed with Oates's description of the battle. Robbins, in fact, took offense at Oates's most recent letter to Secretary Root. Trying to dissuade Oates from the idea that he was the most vigorous opponent among the commissioners to the monument, Robbins stood by the rules for placing monuments on the field. The truth, Robbins realized, was hard for Oates to accept, but he knew no other course to take. "I have thought it was no more than just & fair to myself to say this much to you as an old comrade," Robbins wrote.[25]

But what Robbins did not say was that he seriously doubted the accuracy of Oates's account of the battle. To Oates, he wrote letters filled with mixed messages that both encouraged and angered his former comrade in arms. To others, particularly to his fellow commissioners, Robbins tried to cast doubt on Oates's memory of the events that had occurred on Little Round Top. Hoping to catch Oates in as many errors as possible, Robbins even dashed off a note to Evander M. Law, the brigade commander who had ordered the 15th and 4th Alabama regiments into action at Gettysburg, asking him to verify Oates's claim that Law had put seven companies of the 47th Alabama under his command prior to Little Round Top. Robbins said that he had "recently heard rumors" to this effect and now wanted to know if the delegation of command had been so ordered by General Law. There is no record that Law ever replied to Robbins, although Oates later maintained that a confirmation of the controversial order came to him in a letter from Law during his disagreement with the commissioners. He never produced any such letter, however, and no copy of it is to be found among his personal papers.[26]

As Oates's irritation with Robbins and the rest of the commissioners grew more intense with each passing week in the summer of 1903, the battlefield commissioners found themselves increasingly annoyed by Oates's threats to take his case to Congress or to write up the controversy in a book on the Civil War he was about to publish. Not willing to be intimidated and wanting somehow to buttress the commission's case, Nicholson sent Joshua Lawrence Chamberlain, who in a month would be seventy-five years old, a copy of Oates's most recent letter to Secretary Root and asked him to comment on whether Oates's statements were, as the commissioners suspected, "at variance with the records."[27] No doubt Nicholson expected Chamberlain's memory of the fight for Little Round Top to be more trustworthy than Oates's recollections—if not, he made sure he led his star witness's reply even before Chamberlain could have a chance to ponder what this was all about. Nicholson was, in a sense, calling on the most expert witness anyone could find.

It did not take long for Chamberlain to reply. His answer, no doubt, at first surprised the commissioners, for he said that he would have no objection to a monument honoring the 15th Alabama on Little Round Top. But, more to their liking, Chamberlain also said that such a memorial would have to be placed "on ground where it [i.e., the 15th Alabama] actually stood at some time during the battle . . . so that it might not only represent the valor of the regiment but the truth of history." And that, of course, was the rub. Chamberlain acknowledged that Colonel Oates's statements about the battle differed widely "from the well established record of facts." After giving a full account of how he recalled the fight, Chamberlain declared that Oates never could have driven the 20th Maine's right wing back upon its left—the most glaring of several discrepancies he could cite in Oates's letter to the secretary of war.[28] Without saying so, Chamberlain made a very forceful point. Oates's memory was wrong about the battle, so it was likely that the place where he wanted to locate his monument would be historically inaccurate as well.

Chamberlain's comments were just what Nicholson had hoped for. Without hesitation, he declared that Chamberlain was right and Oates was wrong about the battle, and he asked Chamberlain if he had any objection to letting Secretary Root see his letter. Chamberlain was more than happy to be of assistance, so Nicholson sent a copy of the letter to the secretary along with an acknowledgment that Oates would have to visit the battlefield to clear up his statements that seemed so far off the historical mark.[29]

Meanwhile, Oates himself was not idle. Making good his threats for political action, Oates succeeded in getting the Alabama legislature to pass a joint resolution in early October 1903 that called upon the state's congressional delegation to look into the monument controversy. Around the same time, a fellow Alabamian, William R. Houghton, a lawyer who had served in a Georgia regiment during the war (but whose brother, Mitchell, had served in the 15th Alabama), wrote a series of newspaper articles complaining about the management of the Gettysburg battlefield and the commission's handling of Southern memorials in the park. "If the government does not allow confederate monuments where the commands fought," said Houghton, "the field will always be one sided history." Houghton also wrote directly to Robbins, enclosing the resolution of the Alabama legislature and asking Robbins to convince his fellow commissioners to reconsider their stand on the 15th Alabama monument and Southern monuments in general. To Nicholson and Secretary Root, Houghton sent copies of his newspaper articles and asked them to abandon the battle line rule.[30] It is likely that Oates put Houghton up to his campaign against the commissioners and their monument policy.

Southern protests to the monument policies were not limited to Oates and his friends alone. Despite Robbins's vigorous efforts as the Southern member of commission to convince former Confederate states to erect memorials at Gettysburg, no Southern state (except for Maryland, which had not joined the Confederacy) had agreed to do so. Southern expectations had been raised by the park's enabling legislation of 1895 that instructed the secretary of war to preserve and mark the battle lines of both Union *and* Confederate forces, and while the battlefield commissioners had gone about that task with alacrity, the strict enforcement of the battle line rule bothered many former Confederates and convinced them that Gettysburg was unlike other national battlefield parks (namely, Chickamauga and Shiloh), where no such restrictions had been placed on the location of memorials. A growing spirit of reconciliation that swept through the country, particularly during the first decade of the twentieth century, argued against the battle line prohibition, but the Gettysburg commissioners and the War Department refused to yield to Southern pressures, even though the park authorities at the same time wished to mark Confederate positions on the battlefield in a more authoritative manner.[31] But the commissioners wanted to do the marking in their own way, not as a reaction to Southern protests and criticisms.

In reply to Houghton's public attacks, Robbins wrote several pieces for the Southern press in which he decried Houghton's erroneous descriptions of the battlefield at Gettysburg and defended the battle line rule. The tablets with inscriptions located along Confederate Avenue, argued Robbins, "are placed where everybody who visits Gettysburg battlefield sees and reads them without inconvenience; whereas if they were placed among the rugged rocks and steeps of Devil's Den and vicinity not one visitor in a hundred would ever know of their existence."[32] Nicholson, proud of his colleague's right thinking, sent copies of Robbins's replies along to Secretary Root. The controversy over Oates's monument was mushrooming rather than shrinking, and now the Alabama legislature, the Alabama congressional delegation, and the press were all involved.[33]

Oates's intensified campaign proved to be very effective, for it caused something of a crisis among the Gettysburg commissioners. Nicholson knew the commission must prepare an answer in some fashion to the resolution of the Alabama legislature, but his fellow commissioners were not quite sure what should be said in reply. By the beginning of the new year, Nicholson came up with a rough draft of a response and circulated it to his colleagues. By mid-January, the commissioners settled on a final text and sent it in the form of a letter to Secretary Root. In this communiqué, the commissioners falsely claimed that Oates had never submitted a request that designated a location of the monument or a design with a proposed inscription for the memorial.[34]

The postulation was not simply disingenuous, it was a blatant lie. Oates had on several occasions indicated the general location of the monument, and he also, in the spring of 1902, had sent Robbins a sketch of the monument and a suggested inscription. Later the commission's own engineer, Captain Cope, had prepared more finished drawings for Oates. Even though Oates had later retracted the early design and inscription, and had reserved the right to postpone pinpointing the precise location of the monument until after the commission approved the memorial on principle, Robbins became concerned when he saw Nicholson's letter, for he knew that Oates had complied with commission rules in this regard. As a result, Robbins warned Nicholson to delete the passages dealing particularly with Oates's alleged failure to submit a design and inscription. Nicholson ignored Robbins's warnings.[35]

By the end of January 1904, Secretary Root approved the reply from the commissioners and sent copies to Oates and the members of the Alabama congressional delegation.[36] Root's action prompted Oates to redouble his efforts, and he turned again for assistance to Alabama Congressman Wiley, who wrote to Nicholson for application papers pertaining to the erection of monuments on the battlefield.[37] Oates opened another front in his campaign by asking the army's adjutant general for information about erecting monuments at Gettysburg. And, in a very formal letter, Oates asked Nicholson directly for applications and instructions about how to gain permission to erect a memorial on the field. Of course, Oates's inquiries, and Wiley's, and the referrals from the adjutant general's office in the War Department all landed on Nicholson's desk.[38] The Oates problem was turning into a bureaucrat's worst nightmare.

Actually, there were no formal application papers for putting up monuments, and Nicholson informed Oates of this fact (which Oates already knew) in mid-April 1904, but only after pointing out to Oates that his first request had not been "turned down" by the commission; instead, Nicholson asserted, Oates had failed to abide by the regulations of the park. Looking back on the whole affair, which had escalated beyond anyone's control, it is probably fair to say that the one thing Oates did accomplish was a small and remarkable miracle—by the spring of 1904, his request for a monument, though resolutely hindered and undetermined by the commission, had not died, and the commissioners (or the secretary of war) still owed Oates an official answer to his petition.

Although it was the commissioners' turn to act, Oates did not want to give them an opportunity to argue that he had failed to abide by the rules of the park. So he decided to visit the battlefield, as Secretary Root had earlier suggested, and resolve his disagreements with the commissioners in person. During the summer of 1904, he arrived at the park and arranged to show the Gettysburg commissioners where he thought the 15th Alabama's monument should be placed, once and for all.[39]

Things did not work out exactly as he had hoped. Oates traveled first to Washington City, where Congressman Wiley and Judge and Mrs. R. B. Kyle of Alabama joined up with him, and the foursome went on to Gettysburg by train. Oates met Robbins and Richardson (Nicholson excused himself for the afternoon) in town, and the party took an omnibus down the Emmitsburg Road and across the park's paved avenues to the saddle between the two Round Tops, just below the place where Oates and his men had fought their desperate fight on July 2, forty-one years before. Oates and Robbins walked up the hill toward the 20th Maine's stone monument. Richardson refused to get out of the vehicle. The two Alabamians, however, strolled over the ground together and talked about what had happened there so many summers ago. Oates pointed out the spot where he wanted the 15th Alabama's monument to be placed—a large boulder behind the lines of the 20th Maine.[40]

Later that evening, at a hotel in town, Nicholson met the group and convened an informal meeting of the battlefield commission, which listened attentively as Oates presented his case in person. But just when everything seemed to be going so well, just when Oates felt that the monument might become a reality after all, Nicholson pulled out a piece of paper from his jacket and announced that it was a letter from Joshua L. Chamberlain, the one that had been sent a year before, in 1903, when the commissioners had asked for Chamberlain's expert opinion. Nicholson emphasized that Chamberlain had raised serious questions about Oates's account of the battle and had denied that the 15th Alabama ever advanced as far up the hillside as Oates had claimed. Oates could not believe what he was hearing. At every turn, Oates had tried to give the commissioners what they had said they wanted—diagrams, inscriptions, a historical narration of the fight for Little Round Top, a personal visit to the battlefield to mark locations in person—but in the end, despite all those efforts made in good faith, the commissioners always seemed to have one last card to play, one additional reason for denying the monument and rejecting Oates's proposal. Understandably Oates was outraged by Nicholson's maneuver, but he knew at once what it meant. While it is not certain how the meeting in the Gettysburg hotel ended, whether in a loud altercation or a quiet hush of resignation, Oates later maintained that his application for a memorial was "turned down" by the commissioners at this time on the basis of Chamberlain's unfavorable testimony.[41] The battle of memories was dashing Oates's hopes for a monument.

Oates, however, did not give up the fight. As soon as he returned to Montgomery—"a little fatigued," he admitted, from the long trip—he wrote to Robbins and noted that Chamberlain was "not accurate in his statements, [and] his memory is at fault in some respects." In Oates's opinion, Chamberlain suffered from an overt case of inflated ego. "He is like many others on both sides at this late date who are disposed to make themselves the whole push," wrote Oates. In other words, Oates accused Chamberlain of pretending to be the perfect hero. Regardless, Oates felt that his application—no matter what Nicholson had stated at the Gettysburg meeting—was still under consideration, and he asked Robbins to send back the old monument sketches and a map so that he could mark the intended location on paper. Robbins, amazingly enough, seems to have complied, or, at the very least, turned the matter over to Captain Cope, the commission's engineer. In a few weeks, Oates was dealing directly—and fruitfully—with Cope on monument designs and blueprints.

As if by magic, Oates's plans were moving forward, and the Gettysburg commissioners—for the first time since 1899 and 1900—seemed willing to cooperate with him and help his dream along. Even Nicholson, who seems to have experienced a complete change of heart, wrote encouragingly to Oates about calling in a Gettysburg "granite man" to get some estimates on the monument's proper size.[42] It is impossible to explain this sea change today, for the extant records simply do not tell us all we would like to know about Oates, the Gettysburg commissioners, the secretary of war, and the other players who took part in this little drama. Oates himself must have felt like a cork bobbing in an open ocean. Up and down, up and down, his tireless efforts to erect a monument looked like they were finally going to pay off.

If he thought this even for a moment while he worked out details with the obliging Captain Cope, he was wrong. Despite all appearances, the question of Chamberlain's doubts persisted among the commissioners. As the summer of 1904 wore on, the commissioners' uncertainty began to surface again, and Oates found himself arguing more vigorously than ever before that Chamberlain's version of the Little Round Top battle was simply unreliable and should not be taken as gospel. Oates was particularly vexed by Chamberlain's fierce denial that his right wing had ever been pushed back during the afternoon of July 2. Oates may have had some lapses of memory in the past, he admitted to Robbins, and even some confusion over where every event had taken place on Little Round Top, but there was one thing of which he was absolutely sure: "Just as sure as your name is Robbins and mine Oates, my regiment not only overlapped his [i.e., Chamberlain's] left flank but drove the 20th Maine from that position back to where I showed you[,] and his right as well as his left was forced back[,] but not too far." Robbins pleaded that he could not resolve this difference of opinion. To Nicholson, Oates said plainly that he was right and Chamberlain was wrong.[43] And he thought that should settle the matter.

It did not. Nicholson was worried about Chamberlain's conflicting account—and conflicting memory—of the fight for Little Round Top. Although Nicholson was now encouraging Oates to work with a Boston stonecutter on the monument, he asked Oates in January 1905 if he would be willing to submit his version of the battle in writing to Chamberlain for review. The commission, Nicholson said with unintentional irony, wished "to avoid any controversy." Oates, who had instructed the Boston firm to cut the monument for six hundred dollars, emphatically declined Nicholson's invitation and observed "that I have no hope of an agreement with General Chamberlain." As far as Oates was concerned, he and Chamberlain would never see eye-to-eye, and there was no sound purpose in trying to reach a consensus. Perfect heroes, in other words, could never agree when it came to conflicting memories. To Oates, one fact was certain: he and his men had pushed Chamberlain's regiment back far enough to reach the boulder along the 20th Maine's left wing, and to underscore the point he sent Nicholson a map showing where the boulder still could be found on Little Round Top. He closed his letter by saying: "I am not vain or boastful enough, if I ever was in my old age[,] to perpetrate a falsehood forty-two years after the occurrence by erecting a monument to the memory of my dead comrades on ground they never reached in their assault."[44]

Nicholson, however, remained in doubt. To ease his own concern, he called on Chamberlain again and sent him a copy of one of Oates's recent letters, the one in which Oates had expressed pessimism over reaching an agreement with Chamberlain about the events on Little Round Top. Surely Nicholson must have calculated what Chamberlain's response would be. It could not have come as any surprise when Chamberlain wrote back and revealed that he had been greatly offended by Oates's remarks. Chamberlain said that Oates "seems to have satisfied himself that I am incorrigible on the point he wishes to establish." Whatever Nicholson's purpose in sending him Oates's letter—and from every angle it would appear that Nicholson was hoping to stir up trouble—Chamberlain wanted to state for the record that he was not going to modify his interpretation of the battle. He repeated his belief that his right wing had never wavered or moved away from the anchor it had established with the 83rd Pennsylvania next to it in line. "I cannot change the facts," Chamberlain said. "The matter of monuments," he told Nicholson sternly, "is in your charge, not mine." All he wanted was for the 15th Alabama monument to be located "in accordance with historic truth."[45]

Nicholson's trouble-making was not finished. When he received Chamberlain's reply, he hurried a copy off to Oates. Again, the response was predictable. No longer willing to restrain himself, and tired of dealing with the commissioners as middle men, he scratched off a passionate reply directly to Chamberlain. "General," Oates wrote in an admonishing tone, "neither of us are as young as we were when we confronted each other on Little Round Top." In the intervening forty-two years, their memories had become less clear and less certain. Oates said he had no desire to dispute Chamberlain's word, "for you are an honorable gentleman." Nevertheless, Oates insisted that the 15th Alabama had driven back the right wing of the 20th Maine and had reached a point behind the 20th's marked lines on the hillside. If Chamberlain was unaware of the fact, perhaps it was because the fog of war had obscured his perspective. "No one man," said Oates, "can see all that occurs in a fight even between two regiments." At any rate, Oates cast aside his belief that he and his former enemy could never agree about what had taken place on Little Round Top and proposed to Chamberlain that the two of them should meet in Gettysburg, where they might be able to reach some mutual understanding of who had done what and where it had occurred on that terrible afternoon four decades before.[46]

Oates was wrong. Their memories divided them deeply, fundamentally, irreparably. Chamberlain answered him with a long letter that essentially delivered a coup de grâce. He insisted, one more time, that he had never objected to Oates's proposal for a monument, but he did express firm belief that it should be placed accurately on ground that the 15th Alabama had actually occupied. Chamberlain said his statements were made independently of the Gettysburg commissioners, and he asserted that Colonel Nicholson had not based any decision on Chamberlain's own "testimony or influence." As for the historical record, Chamberlain stated again that the 15th Alabama had never pushed back the right of the 20th Maine. Oates's statements to the contrary were faulty. "It is really my desire to have your monument set up," Chamberlain said in closing, "only let us make sure of our ground for the sake of the historical fact." Chamberlain sent a copy of his letter to Nicholson, who was overjoyed when he read it. "It is very clear," Nicholson wrote back to Chamberlain with great enthusiasm, "that General Oates has not the slightest idea of admitting the views of any one in the controversy except himself." As far as the commissioners were concerned, the matter rested now in the hands of the secretary of war to decide.[47]

And that's where it remained. The secretary of war took no further action on the monument proposal. Elihu Root never sent Oates a formal reply rejecting the monument, and the Gettysburg commissioners gave Oates only their barest attention through the remaining months of 1905. Inactivity is one of the favorite devices of bureaucrats, next to delay, and the Gettysburg commissioners put both to good use in bringing the Oates controversy to a close. After all the wrangling, after all the angry words that went back and forth between the parties, after all the effort each side expended to gain an advantage or to prove a point, the commissioners, in the end, handled Oates's request for a monument by simply doing nothing at all.

The technique worked. Slowly the controversy slipped from view. William Robbins died in September 1905, and his place on the commission was filled by a Virginian, Major General Lunsford L. Lomax, who had served in J. E. B. Stuart's cavalry at Gettysburg. Oates tried to carry on his crusade with Lomax, but he didn't get very far. Lomax, from the very start of his correspondence with Oates, made much of the fact that Chamberlain's view of the Little Round Top fight differed in important respects from Oates's, and the two conflicting points of view would have to be reconciled before the location of any monument to the 15th Alabama could be finally determined. In the spring of 1906, Oates leaned on the Alabama delegation and other friends in Congress to get behind the monument cause again, but Lomax thwarted the political pressure by raising the Chamberlain specter one more time. "It will be difficult to satisfy the claim," Lomax told Congressman J. F. C. Talbot of Maryland. He did say, however, that Chamberlain was willing to meet Oates on the battlefield and see if agreement could be reached between the two old warriors.[48]

Oates was at the end of his road. He never met Chamberlain on Little Round Top to sort out their differences; in fact, he never returned to Gettysburg before his death in September 1910. Earlier that year, in January 1910, Nicholson succeeded in getting the secretary of war and the president to confirm the battle line rule once and for all, but with one slight modification: henceforth, markers and tablets could be erected on the field in honor of individuals who, in the opinion of the secretary of war, had demonstrated "conspicuous and exceptional" acts of heroism during the battle. President William Howard Taft signed the regulations on January 18. That same day Senator Eugene Hale of Maine sent the secretary of war a blueprint, approved by the Gettysburg battlefield commission, that marked the location on Little Round Top for a proposed statue of Joshua Lawrence Chamberlain.[49]

Gone forever are the memories of Oates and Chamberlain, like voices on the wind. We can never really recapture what they saw, what they think they saw, and all that they could—and could not—remember about Little Round Top. Chamberlain died in 1914. Today there is no statue of him on Little Round Top, and it seems rather doubtful that there ever will be. Nor is there a monument to the 15th Alabama on that hillside, although William Oates certainly tried his level best to put one there. For Chamberlain and Oates, the tide of reconciliation between the North and the South that was sweeping across the nation during the first decade of the twentieth century could not overcome or blunt the sharp personal animosities of former foes, one the victor and the other the vanquished. Unlike their comrades, Union and Confederate, who would shake hands at the High Water Mark when the great Gettysburg reunion of July 1913 commemorated the fiftieth anniversary of the battle, these two old men could not come to terms, could not resolve old differences, could not stop fighting their old war. Some wounds never heal. In the end, it would appear that Chamberlain—with considerable help from the Gettysburg commissioners and from the foggy confusion caused by fallible memories—won as clear a victory in the second battle of Little Round Top as he had won in the first.

And yet, even without any heroic statues on that hill to glorify them, we remember Chamberlain and Oates, perhaps not precisely as they wished to be remembered, but we recall them and honor them nevertheless. They are not gone from us; they have not become dreams that slip easily away. "Life has no memory," said Ralph Waldo Emerson.[50] He was wrong. Life is filled with memories, and sometimes the memories abide long after life ends. Oates, Chamberlain, and the stalwart men who fought on Little Round Top wanted to be perfect soldiers and wanted to be remembered. Perfect they weren't. But we remember them with awe.

12 Ike and Monty Take Gettysburg

Ghosts walk the land at Gettysburg, and anyone who visits the battlefield must come to grips with the fact that the place belongs to the spirits of the past. Nearly forty years ago, Dwight D. Eisenhower and Bernard Law Montgomery, two old generals—perfect heroes in their own right—who had won their own terrible war in Europe, toured the Gettysburg field together and discovered, just as Oates and Chamberlain had some fifty-five years before, that very little can be said about that hallowed ground, that land of honored spirits, without sparking fierce disagreement and igniting great controversy.[1] With a hungry press corps accompanying them and hanging on their every word, Ike and Monty learned that at Gettysburg, where the specters always seem to be listening, one must tread lightly and speak with great care.

The two famous soldiers of World War II had talked about the Battle of Gettysburg from time to time during the war when Montgomery, the commander of the British and Canadian 21st Army Group, served under Eisenhower, the supreme commander of the Allied Expeditionary Force.[2] For years Eisenhower had promised to take Montgomery on a tour of the Gettysburg battlefield, but when no specific invitation was ever made, Monty decided to press the issue. In November 1954, when Montgomery accompanied President Eisenhower, the first lady, and a small party of friends for Thanksgiving in Augusta, Georgia, the British field marshal announced that he would like very much to see the battlefield, and Eisenhower relented by inviting him to visit Gettysburg the following autumn, when renovations on the president's farmhouse would be completed. Ike could not keep his promise, however; a heart attack put him in a Denver hospital in the fall of 1955, and Montgomery's visit was spent at the president's bedside rather than on the battlefield.[3]

It was not until the spring of 1957 that Montgomery, who was then serving as deputy commander of the North Atlantic Treaty Organization, arranged to visit the Eisenhowers at Gettysburg during an American speaking tour. He arrived in New York on Tuesday, May 7, for talks with NATO officials, and the press reported with anticipation that he and Eisenhower would have a great deal to discuss, especially in the wake of the Suez crisis of 1956 and the president's pledge in January 1957 to send U.S. troops to any Middle Eastern nation that asked for assistance against communist aggressors.[4] But when Montgomery gave a speech in Baltimore at the English Speaking Union on Thursday evening, May 9, he complained that "the Western world looked on" and did nothing to prevent Egypt's closing of the Suez Canal, a direct reference to Eisenhower's refusal to endorse the combined invasion by French, British, and Israeli forces in October 1956. The Suez crisis, said Montgomery, was simply another instance of the Soviet Union's successful incursion into the Middle East; that success, he declared, "will go much further unless the Western Alliance quickly comes to its senses—which it shows little sign of doing."[5]

As if Monty's unfavorable comments about the foreign policy of the Eisenhower administration weren't bad enough, he had more to say immediately after his Baltimore speech that would soon enrage the president and a good number of other Americans as well. Explaining to reporters that he was about to visit Eisenhower in Gettysburg, Montgomery remarked that he had read all about the battle and that, in his opinion as a military man, he would have "sacked" General Robert E. Lee, commander of the Confederate Army of Northern Virginia, and Major General George Gordon Meade, commander of the Union Army of the Potomac, for mishandling their forces during the battle that shook the peaceful Pennsylvania countryside in July 1863. When asked by reporters why the generals should have been fired, Monty explained that "Lee did not press his advantage and made a mistake in launching his strongest thrust at the strongest Union position, whereas Meade did not keep Union forces under adequate control."[6]

*   *   *

When Eisenhower learned of Montgomery's comments the following morning, Friday, May 10, he was livid, although it's not entirely clear what angered him the most—Montgomery's attack on his Middle East policy or the field marshal's careless comments about Gettysburg, a cherished American symbol of courage and sacrifice. Whatever the cause, the president was agitated enough to think about canceling Montgomery's visit to Gettysburg, but he realized it was too late to change plans. So he escaped to the golf course, timing it so he would be absent from the White House when Montgomery arrived later that morning.[7]

Frankly, the two men had never really gotten along. As Eisenhower's subordinate during the war, Montgomery held the supreme commander in very low regard and never bothered to hide that fact from anyone, including Ike. From his earliest dealings with Eisenhower during Operation Torch, the Allied invasion of North Africa in 1942, to the final campaigns in France and Germany, Montgomery expressed over and over again his disdain for Ike's ability as a combat general. A few months after the Normandy invasion, Monty wrote to Field Marshal Sir Alan Brooke (later Viscount Alanbrooke), Churchill's chief military adviser: "As a commander in charge of the land operations, Eisenhower is quite useless. There must be no misconception on this matter; he is completely and utterly useless."[8] Knowing that the well-being of the alliance between the United States and Great Britain depended on harmonious relations, Ike showed great patience and restraint in his dealings with Monty. He admitted, however, that "Montgomery's the only man in either army I can't get along with."[9]

The two men were a study in contrasts. Montgomery, with his piercing blue eyes and his birdlike appearance, was a small man with a very large ego. Arrogant and inconsiderate, he paid little attention to the people around him and seemed not to care if he offended them.[10] Loved by his troops, he had very little in common with the rank and file that served under him. Eisenhower, on the other hand, was liked by nearly everyone. He seemed genuinely to care about people—their lives, their dreams, their problems. Despite a fierce temper, which he tried to keep in check, he handled his superiors and subordinates with respect and patience. Inside, he was a bundle of nerves: he often smoked four packs of cigarettes and drank fifteen cups of coffee a day.[11] Outside, though, he was calm and collected.

At bottom, Eisenhower and Montgomery could not agree how the war against Germany should be fought. Slow and cautious, Montgomery favored careful plans and painstaking preparation in his campaigns against the Nazis. Although he had won great acclaim for his victories over General Erwin Rommel in the North African desert, he never could seem to move his troops quickly enough in Sicily, Italy, and the engagements that occurred after the Normandy landings. After D-Day, when Eisenhower ordered the Allied Expeditionary Force to push along a broad front toward the Rhine, Montgomery argued vehemently for a different strategy—a pencil-line thrust along a broad front through Belgium and into the Ruhr by a force placed entirely under his own command. "Monty's suggestion is simply: give him everything, which is crazy," said Eisenhower.[12]

Their arguments over strategy underscored a more fundamental difference between them. In their incompatible styles of command and their conflicting personalities, it seemed as if they were generals from two different epochs of history: Monty epitomized the typical nineteenth-century general who excelled at massing his forces and fighting set-piece battles; Ike, who also embraced many of the old military values and traditions, embodied more the modern general who wages war by managing the movement of large armies, coordinating large-scale campaigns, balancing the delicate relations in sensitive multilateral alliances, and keeping everyone focused on the final objective. In that respect, Montgomery was the direct descendant of the Duke of Wellington; Eisenhower was the immediate forebear of Norman Schwarzkopf. Small wonder they rarely saw eye to eye.

*   *   *

One can only imagine what they talked about in the small, twin-engine Aero Commander that flew them on Saturday morning, May 11, from Washington to the tiny airport outside Gettysburg. If the conversation was strained, there was no evidence of it when they walked down the airplane's stairway to the tarmac. They were surrounded by reporters and photographers. Eisenhower, who seemed relaxed and casual in a sport coat and slacks, was in a "happy mood," according to one newspaper account. But Montgomery, who wore a military cap and khaki uniform (replete with rows of decorations), was annoyed with the photographers and their popping flashbulbs. He asked the president who these people were and what they were doing. Ike grinned and said, "They're making pictures and some of them may get printed." He led the way to a waiting limousine, which whisked them off to the president's farm.[13]

Their tour of the battlefield, a private affair with no members of the press in tow, began an hour later, shortly after 10:00 AM, at the Eternal Light Peace Memorial on the site of the first day's fighting. The monument, a massive obelisk with an eternal flame fed by natural gas, was dedicated by President Franklin D. Roosevelt on July 3, 1938, the seventy-fifth anniversary of the battle. Not far from the memorial, Ike showed Monty a pair of Whitworth breech-loading cannons, which the Confederates had acquired from England.

For the rest of the morning, they drove around the battlefield, stopping at the site of Lincoln's Gettysburg Address in the National Cemetery; the Angle, where Union forces repulsed Pickett's Charge on July 3, 1863;

Meade's headquarters; the monument to the 1st Minnesota Regiment; Little Round Top; and Devil's Den. It was not a whirlwind tour, but they could spend only a short time at each stop. The *New York Times* speculated that Eisenhower and Montgomery discussed "what happened and what might have happened at the battle that marked the turning point of the Civil War and that all military men study as a classic." Perhaps they "reminisced a bit . . . about the campaigns of World War II," surmised the *Washington Post*.[14] Obviously the press thought there was a story here, but no one could quite figure out what it was.

At the end of the day, White House Press Secretary James C. Hagerty met with reporters to tell them what the two old allies had actually said to one another. Some reporters wanted to know if Montgomery still believed that Lee and Meade should have been fired. Hagerty dodged the questions and said the president had "expressed the view, with his guest in agreement, that in studying the Gettysburg battle it was necessary to study also the economic and political pressures on both sides." Without any lengthier explanation, this official comment was nearly incomprehensible, but newspapers and wire services scooped it up and dutifully reported it anyway. Hagerty said the tour of the battlefield would be continued over the course of the weekend.[15]

Eisenhower and Montgomery spent the remainder of Saturday staying at the president's farm and inspecting cattle at some neighboring farms (an odd activity that is not explained in any surviving account of the weekend). They were joined by Mamie Eisenhower, George Allen (one of the president's closest friends in Gettysburg), Major General Howard McC. Snyder (the president's physician), and some other friends of the first family. Apparently the Eisenhowers dined alone at the farm with Montgomery on Saturday evening.[16]

* * *

At 8:15 on Sunday morning, May 12, a press corps comprising twenty-one reporters and sixteen photographers assembled in front of the Gettysburg National Museum, a private facility then owned by the Rosensteel family of Gettysburg. (Today it is the Visitor Center of the Gettysburg National Military Park and the Eisenhower National Historic Site.) The president and the field marshal arrived fifteen minutes later and went inside to see a presentation of the Electric Map, a huge, three-dimensional plaster map of the Gettysburg area that uses flashing colored lights and narration to tell the story of the battle. Mrs. Rosensteel, the wife of the museum's owner, presented Eisenhower and Montgomery with two books about the battle, but the field marshal seemed unimpressed with the electric map or the gift. What caught Monty's attention was a display of Ike and Mamie plates and drinking mugs in the souvenir shop. "I never saw any of those before," the president remarked. Montgomery asked for prices, but he didn't buy any of the items.[17]

As the presidential party climbed into its cars for the tour, the members of the press scurried for their own vehicles. No one wanted to miss one moment of this historic occasion or one word that might be uttered. Reporters and photographers were practically falling over one another to stay as close to Ike and Monty as they could. The *New York Herald Tribune* believed that the tour would be "the most detailed study" of the battle Eisenhower had conducted since being stationed in Gettysburg during World War I, when he commanded a training camp for the tank corps. Although such a thing seemed unlikely, given the frequent visits Eisenhower made to Gettysburg after purchasing and refurbishing the farm, it certainly made good copy. Other newspapers emphasized that the president had actually studied the battle closely. "Before the Viscount leaves," predicted the *Gettysburg Times,* "he will be given a true picture of what happened here by the man who probably knows more about the battle than anyone else."[18]

Through a heavy fog and a persistent drizzle, a murky morning better suited for Gettysburg's ghosts than for any kind of trip around the battlefield, the tour party wound its way up Culp's Hill, the place where the extreme right flank of Meade's Army of the Potomac was defended in desperate fighting on the second and third days of the battle. At the summit was a seventy-foot metal observation tower that had been erected in 1895.

The dense fog obscured the top of the tower, but Montgomery insisted on walking up anyway. He bounded up the steps, a dynamo in motion, and Ike and the reporters trailed behind. They stopped at the fourth landing, where they inspected a map. Although Major General Snyder was worried about his patient, he told reporters that the president was handling the climb pretty well "for a heart man." The reporters and photographers jammed themselves onto the landing, and Monty got annoyed with all the pushing and shoving. "Look here, you chaps," he said to the press corps, "we have too many people up here."[19] Everyone obediently began to file down the steps.

At the base of the tower, one reporter asked Montgomery if he still thought that Lee and Meade should have been "sacked" for their mistakes at Gettysburg. "Well," said the field marshal, pausing for a moment, "I wouldn't have fought the battle that way myself." Without missing a beat, and hoping to put a humorous spin on Monty's remark, the president quipped: "If you had, I would have sacked *you.*" The entire party, according to the press reports, roared with laughter, but no one laughed more loudly than Monty and Ike.[20]

They stopped at the Angle on Cemetery Ridge, where Eisenhower and Montgomery walked through high grass and got their shoes wet and their trousers soaked up to their knees as they inspected an equestrian statue of General Meade. Then the tour party piled back into the cars and ascended the rocky slopes of Little Round Top. On the hilltop, near the spot where a statue of Major General Gouverneur K. Warren stands overlooking a sweeping panorama of nearly the entire battlefield, the two World War II generals walked all around the rocks and discussed the tactics of the battle. Occasionally Eisenhower gestured to key places on the battlefield. Bill Achatz, an Associated Press correspondent who accompanied the press corps that day, remembers that "Ike and Monty occasionally moved out of earshot and continued their conversation" in private—much to the frustration of the newsmen.[21] The two former generals did not visit the spot on the hill where the 20th Maine made its famous charge on July 2, 1863. In those days, Chamberlain and the story of the charge were not widely known and had not yet been elevated to legend.

At the Virginia Memorial on Seminary Ridge, the concluding stop of the tour, the atmosphere became dignified and solemn. The party stood at the base of the monument, an impressive granite edifice that features a group of seven Virginia soldiers standing below a magnificent statue of Lee astride his favorite horse, Traveller. General Lee and his soldiers gaze out forever toward the Copse of Trees on the opposite ridge, where Pickett's grand assault was broken. Half-hidden by the wisps of fog that swirled around the memorial, the bronze figures looked sad and gray and spectral.

Eisenhower and Montgomery stood on the steps of the memorial and quietly pondered the expanse of ground before them. Ike finally broke the silence. "Why Lee would have gone across that field, I don't know," he said. Wondering aloud, he added, "Maybe he got so darned mad he wanted to hit them with a brick." The president pointed to the south, toward the Round Tops in the distance, and said: "Why he didn't go around there, I'll never know."[22]

Montgomery had his own comments to make about the Confederate frontal assault on July 3. "It was a monstrous thing to launch this charge," he said shaking his head. "Monstrous thing. A monstrous thing." When the reporters asked what he would have done if he had been the commander of the Army of Northern Virginia, he was ready with an answer: "I would have thrown a right hook around Little Round Top where you had plenty of cover. I would have used a little feint here to draw the Union's attention." Montgomery also pointed out that Meade, the Union commander, had made his own share of errors, particularly at the end of the battle when he let "that guy" (meaning Lee) get away. When asked who did the worse job at Gettysburg, Lee or Meade, Monty said, "Oh, I think Lee."[23]

∗   ∗   ∗

Several news stories published the next day remarked that Eisenhower was "in a gay mood" throughout the tour and that he and Montgomery were having "a wonderful time and thoroughly enjoyed every minute." But that's not how everyone remembered it. Bill Achatz, the AP reporter, recalls that "there was a lot of tension in the air." Despite Ike's attempts at humor and Monty's breezy manner, it was quite evident to everyone in the press corps that "these two men had not gotten along well during the war" and that some of those feelings had not changed over the subsequent decade. The comments offered by Eisenhower and Montgomery, says Achatz, and especially the assertion made by Montgomery that Lee and Meade should have been relieved of their commands, created "quite an emotional scene."[24]

Anger was the emotion Ike felt. "Monty can never resist a newspaper reporter nor a camera," the president wrote in a letter to his old friend Leonard Gerow in November 1958. At the Virginia Memorial, wrote Eisenhower in the letter, Montgomery kept raising his voice so the reporters wouldn't miss a word. Ike walked to the car, feeling more and more as if Montgomery were turning the tour into a circus, and at that moment the field marshal declared one more time in his loudest voice that "both Lee and Meade should have been sacked." Then, wrote Eisenhower, Monty added something about incompetence and called over to him, "Don't you agree, Ike?" The president replied carefully, directing his comments to the press: "Look, I live here. I represent both the North and the South. He can talk."[25] Obviously Eisenhower was not amused. As he later told Gerow, "I was resentful of Monty's obvious purpose and his lack of good taste."[26]

But the reporters pushed the president on the issue of whether he agreed with Montgomery's view of the battle and its commanders. Eisenhower tried to shift the focus by saying that General J. E. B. Stuart, the Confederate cavalry officer, let Lee down by failing to keep in touch with the Army of Northern Virginia while he rode a reconnaissance mission around the Union army. He called Stuart "a lover of headlines." Trying to soften the blow of Montgomery's remarks, the president told reporters that "some of the finest troop movements in military history" took place on the Gettysburg battlefield, "but everything seemed to break to pieces on coordination, unfortunately, on the Southern side." He turned to Montgomery and said: "If some of the generals who fought here were alive today, they probably would have criticized the way we fought." Montgomery nodded.[27]

The tour was over. By 10:18 AM, the president and his party had returned to the farm. All in all, Eisenhower and Montgomery had spent less than an hour on the battlefield—certainly not enough time for the in-depth study of events so many of the newspapers had predicted. In fact, it's hard to avoid the conclusion that the tour was rushed to completion.[28]

For the rest of the day, Montgomery hung on as the Eisenhowers attended church services at the Presbyterian Church, stopped briefly at a museum to view a diorama of the battle, and went to Thurmont, Maryland, where the president spent the rest of the day fishing—without Monty.[29] At 11:00 AM the following day, Montgomery left Gettysburg for Washington. Ike stayed on at the farm and played eighteen holes that afternoon at the Gettysburg Country Club.[30]

* * *

The ghosts of Gettysburg began to howl on Monday morning, May 13, and it soon became evident that the spirits of the battlefield were not about to let Eisenhower and Montgomery have the last word. Across the front pages of newspapers from New York to New Orleans, the headlines were pretty much the same: "Eisenhower Joins Montgomery in Criticizing Meade and Lee"; "Lee, Meade Deserved 'Sacking,' Ike and Monty Say at Gettysburg"; "Battle of Gettysburg Gets a Going-Over."[31] The news stories gave all the details of the tour, describing what the two old generals had said and what had caught their attention on the battlefield. Eisenhower's attempts to distance himself from Montgomery's tactless remarks had not succeeded. Most of the new accounts lumped Ike and Monty together as having equally—and blatantly—condemned the Union and Confederate commanders at Gettysburg.

All at once, there was an enormous outcry, North and South. The *New York Herald Tribune* complained that "the World War II comrades couldn't seem to find anything that went right in the bloody three-day battle ninety-four years ago." *Time* magazine commented that when the two generals agreed that Lee and Meade should have been fired, "they committed themselves irrevocably to battle." A number of critics suggested that Ike and Monty should have been sacked for the way they led their armies in World War II. A Scripps-Howard editorial took the ghosts of Lee and Meade on a jeep trip through the Ardennes to retrace the Battle of the Bulge; to no one's surprise, the editorial quoted Meade as saying the battle was "an absolutely monstrous thing" and Lee as declaring that the responsible generals should have been sacked.[32]

The fiercest protests came from the South, where, as the *Washington Star* put it, "the cotton really hit the fan." In Mississippi, the *Jackson News* screamed: "Southern Blood Boils!" Mrs. Robert E. Lee III, widow of the general's grandson, said the comments by Eisenhower and Montgomery at Gettysburg were "disgusting." Mrs. John L. Harper, president of the Atlanta Ladies Memorial Association, a group that had decorated Confederate graves since 1866, called their remarks about Lee "uncouth." Senator Sam Ervin of Georgia, one of several prominent Southern politicians who spoke out in the wake of the Gettysburg tour, believed that Lee had ably demonstrated "that he was a greater general than either the President or Montgomery."[33]

Much of the response in the Southern press took issue with the military achievements of Ike and Monty. "President Eisenhower may have forgotten his own Kasserine Pass defeat and the breakthrough in the Bulge; Marshal Montgomery his excruciating slowness in hitting the Germans after the initial Rhine crossings," stated the *Staunton News-Leader*, a Virginia newspaper. In South Carolina, a columnist argued in the *Charleston News & Courier* that Eisenhower was not "an actual battle leader [but] a sort of super military executive director." Colonel Allen P. Julian, the president of the Atlanta Historical Society, was more forceful in his reply to Montgomery's suggestion that Lee should have been fired: "That's a helluva remark to come from a man who claims he was 'too busy tidying up his front' to aid Eisenhower in the Battle of the Bulge."[34]

The generalships of Eisenhower and Montgomery were also challenged outside the South. In a blistering editorial, the *National Review* declared: "Monty, though victorious like Meade, never did manage to exploit his successes by getting his mitts on Rommel. Nor did Ike get any better cooperation before the Bulge from his G2 [Intelligence Division] than Lee got from Jeb Stuart. By their own standards maybe Ike and Monty should have been sacked too." *Newsweek* reminded its readers that "of all the topflight British generals who helped to lead the Allied forces to victory in Europe in World War II, there was none who managed to irritate the Americans more (and more often) than Montgomery." A few publications could not resist mentioning that Viscount Alanbrooke had been recently quoted as saying that Eisenhower lacked combat experience during the war and that his leadership had suffered as a result.[35]

Professional historians seemed to be divided in their reactions to Ike and Monty's remarks. Bell I. Wiley, an authority on the experiences of common soldiers during the Civil War, agreed that the tactics of Lee and Meade at Gettysburg were "deplorable," but he pointed out that it would be unfair to judge those generals by modern standards, when in fact they could not possibly have known at the time everything that historians have subsequently learned about the battle. At Gettysburg National Military Park, J. Walter Coleman, the superintendent, told reporters that he couldn't imagine anyone suggesting that Lee and Meade should have been fired. Who would have replaced them if they had been sacked? Coleman wondered.[36]

At first Bruce Catton, the celebrated Civil War historian, concurred with the analysis made by Eisenhower and Montgomery. "There is no question," said Catton in a newspaper interview, "that Lee should have gone around Little Round Top" instead of mounting a frontal assault against Cemetery Ridge on July 3. A month later, however, Catton changed his mind and argued in a special article written for the *Saturday Review* that Ike and Monty obviously did not "understand what Gettysburg was all about." The battle, Catton wrote, cannot be reduced "to terms of who made the worse mistakes there." The important thing to remember, he said, was that the battle was won by the men in the ranks who fought it.[37]

A number of commentators actually agreed with Eisenhower and Montgomery and found it difficult to believe that anyone had criticized the old generals for what they had said. Colonel Willard Webb, a past president of the Civil War Round Table (Chicago), called the Ike-Monty view of the battle "standing operating procedure" and agreed that Lee and Meade could each have done a better job. Surprised by all the fuss, Major General H. W. B. Lakely, a retired army officer, said that "almost everything the President said is what has been taught to generations of American professional soldiers." Columnist Pie Dufour observed in the *New Orleans States* that Eisenhower and Montgomery were both "on solid ground, believe it or not."[38]

And indeed they were. Taking Meade and Lee to task for their short-comings at Gettysburg was actually nothing new. The criticism, in fact, began as soon as the battle was over.

Lincoln, as we've seen, was nearly beside himself when he learned that Meade had let Lee's army slip back into Virginia after the battle, and Meade was informed of the president's distress. In response, the Union general decided to sack himself—he submitted his resignation, but Lincoln refused to accept it. Nevertheless, Meade was summoned in 1864 to appear before the Joint Congressional Committee on the Conduct of the War to explain why he had not done a better job at Gettysburg. While nothing ever came of the congressional investigation, it did leave a stain on Meade's military record.

As for Lee, he told his troops that the failure of Pickett's Charge was entirely his fault. He was so distraught by the outcome of Gettysburg that he also wanted to fire himself, and he wrote offering his resignation to President Jefferson Davis. The offer was declined. Davis, like later historians, recognized that Lee could not be replaced and that his victories in Virginia outweighed the defeat in Pennsylvania.

Even today the battle remains a minefield of controversy. When Eisenhower and Montgomery criticized the Union and Confederate commanders at Gettysburg, they were hardly venturing into uncharted territory. The fields of Gettysburg have been well trodden in more ways than one.[39]

*   *   *

In the days immediately following the Gettysburg tour, Montgomery was bewildered by the furor his comments had caused. He hoped, however, that the public firestorm would die down before he traveled to Montgomery, Alabama, the final stop on his speaking tour (and a place he remarkably thought had been named after him, in honor of his war achievements). In Washington, D.C., where Montgomery stayed for a few days to meet on NATO business, General Maxwell D. Taylor, the army's chief of staff, told him in jest that his derogatory remarks about Lee might get him lynched in the South; but the field marshal did not get the joke and wondered why so many Americans were upset with him. Montgomery continued to appear undaunted in public, even though he admitted that "the women of the South are after me." Still failing to grasp the symbolic importance of Gettysburg to Americans, or how extensively the battle had been studied by historians, Montgomery declared, "I suppose that battle never had so much publicity since it was fought."[40]

The field marshal headed South, passing through Georgia on his way to Alabama. Reporters accosted him at the Atlanta airport with questions about Lee and Gettysburg, but Montgomery shooed them away. The press in the South, however, did not remain silent. One Georgia newspaper tried to put Montgomery in his place by asserting that "a lot of American survivors of World War II" wished he had been sacked "before the United States was drawn in." Montgomery responded, "I'm finished talking about the Battle of Gettysburg." He gave his Alabama speech and then flew to Santiago, Chile, where he spent a few days visiting his only son before returning home to England via New York.[41]

In Washington, Eisenhower had to deal with the fallout from Montgomery's bombasts and his own misunderstood remarks about Lee's role at Gettysburg. At a regularly scheduled news conference held on Wednesday, May 15, when most of the questions from the press predictably dealt with weightier foreign and domestic matters (including the president's proposed federal budget), one reporter asked Eisenhower if, in light of his comments at Gettysburg, he thought the Allies could have handled things better during World War II. Stumbling through his answer, the president said some phases of the war could have been managed differently, but he observed that "it is hard to quarrel with victory." Eisenhower tried to clear the air about the Gettysburg tour and explained, very defensively, that he had a great deal of affection for Lee and even kept the general's portrait on prominent display in his office.[42]

Then another reporter wanted to know how the president thought his remarks about Lee would be received in the South, particularly since Eisenhower had spoken recently in Kentucky and had predicted Republican gains in congressional seats and governorships throughout the Southern states in the 1958 off-year election. Before Eisenhower could answer, the reporter wondered if the president's support of the civil-rights bill, which had been introduced in Congress earlier that year, would hurt Republican chances in the South. The point was clear: unfavorable comments about Robert E. Lee and a presidential endorsement of civil-rights legislation did not play very well in Dixie.[43]

Eisenhower quickly pointed out that the civil-rights bill was "a very moderate thing," and he couldn't believe that his support for it would have any significant impact one way or another on the election of Republicans in the South. But he must have realized at that moment, if it hadn't occurred to him before, that the Gettysburg tour had become not only controversial, but a real political liability. Suddenly Eisenhower's "southern strategy" was on the line. An editorial in the *Washington Star* proclaimed, "It is difficult to comprehend the strategy of a commander-in-chief who sets out on a Friday to woo the South with sweet talk about the virtues of modern Republicanism and winds up on Sunday saying that General Lee bungled the battle of Gettysburg and should have been sacked." The newspaper concluded that any chance for gaining Republican votes in the South "was surely lost."[44]

To be sure, the Republicans were badly trounced at the polls in November 1958, but the party's defeat had less to do with the Gettysburg tour than it did with the racial crisis in Little Rock, Arkansas, the launching of the Soviets' Sputnik satellite, allegations of a "missile gap" between the United States and the Soviet Union, and the scandal involving Sherman Adams, Eisenhower's White House chief of staff, who was forced to resign after being accused of influence peddling. The election outcome also had something to do with a vigorous and effective Democratic campaign.[45]

In the vortex of national politics, the remarks Eisenhower and Montgomery made at Gettysburg were swiftly overtaken by other events. In assessing the significance of the tour, an editorial in a North Carolina newspaper seemed to hit the bull's-eye: the dispute over what they had said was "one of those tempests in a teapot in which Americans delight to engage." Such controversies enabled people "to argue without having to decide, to debate without some vital result depending on the outcome."[46]

Yet there were some measurable consequences of the Gettysburg tour. The weekend put an added strain on the already difficult relationship between Eisenhower and Montgomery—especially since the American general whom Montgomery probably wished he really could have sacked was his old boss, Ike.

That desire came out forcefully in Montgomery's memoirs, which were published in late 1958, more than a year after the Gettysburg visit. Among the uncomplimentary things that the field marshal had to say about Eisenhower as a general (although his comments about Ike's character were much more favorable), the worst was certainly his statement that the war could have been won—and thousands of lives could have been saved—by December 1944 if only Eisenhower had allowed him to make his pencil-strike across the Rhine. The president was furious. To a friend, Ike wrote: "My opinion [of Montgomery's book] is probably so much lower than yours that I would not like to express it, even in a letter."[47]

What really hurt, remembers David Eisenhower, the president's grandson and biographer, was the realization that Monty had already finished writing his book when he visited Gettysburg in 1957 and when he stayed at the White House for three days in May 1958. On the face of it, Montgomery's willingness to accept the president's hospitality seems hypocritical, but Ike's grandson suspects that Montgomery may have wanted to use the Gettysburg visit to cause some further "personal distance between himself and DDE," knowing how injurious his book would be when it finally came out.[48] Whatever Montgomery's motives, his memoirs made him appear particularly ungrateful for the kindnesses Eisenhower had extended to him in 1957 and 1958. More than anything, though, the memoirs made Monty look mean-spirited.

For Eisenhower, Montgomery's book was the last straw. A Reuters correspondent quoted a White House source as saying, "Monty won't get invited up to Gettysburg again." John S. D. Eisenhower, the president's son, recalls that his father "was always willing to defer to Monty and his antics, long after the end of the war." With the publication of Monty's memoirs, however, the president refused to have anything more to do with him ("understandably," says his son).[49] All ties were severed. In the president's final judgment, Montgomery was "just a little man, he's just as little inside as he is outside."[50]

When Eisenhower and Montgomery attempted to break through the myths of the Gettysburg battle and offer historical opinions that differed not so much from the accepted scholarly wisdom of their day as they did from the entrenched popular notions of what Gettysburg and its perfect heroes mean to America, they were thwarted, beaten back, driven off—repulsed, in fact, as decisively as Lee's men were in Pickett's Charge. A belief in spectral evidence is not required to know that at Gettysburg, the nation's most hallowed ground, the ghosts of history are always around—and watching.

13 The Many Meanings of Gettysburg

Perhaps it is enough to say that Gettysburg has captured the American imagination because the battle brought forth, in one monstrous moment of violence, a great victory and a great defeat. But does that fully explain why nearly 2 million Americans annually visit the battlefield? Does it really tell us why so many books are written about the battle every year, why so many questions still persist about the events that shaped the contest and the men who fought it? Eisenhower and Montgomery both learned the hard way that Gettysburg means something special to the American people. "The Past," wrote Herman Melville in his novel *White-Jacket* (1850), "is dead, and has no resurrection."[1] At Gettysburg, though, the past and present always seem to be the same thing.

Since the summer of 1863, when the largest battle on American soil was fought across the gentle fields and hills of Gettysburg, we have sought to know its deeper meaning. The battle and the place, now enshrined in the American memory, have come to mean many different things to different people.

Historians, in particular, have struggled endlessly to determine the real importance of Gettysburg, what larger significance the battle, which claimed fifty-one thousand American casualties during three days of fierce fighting, could possibly have beyond its gore, its destruction, and the defeat of General Robert E. Lee's Army of Northern Virginia. Many historians have assumed that there must be a single, overarching importance to the battle of Gettysburg—that it was a turning point in the Civil War or that it marked the so-called High Water Mark of the Confederacy.

The soldiers who experienced the horror of the battle and lived to tell about it had their own ideas about the meaning of Gettysburg. Many of these veterans believed that Americans who had not witnessed the battle themselves could never fully understand what had taken place on those bloodstained fields. Lieutenant Frank A. Haskell, as we've already seen, was convinced that no one except the soldiers who had fought at Gettysburg would ever comprehend it: "By and by, out of the chaos of trash and falsehood that newspapers hold, out of the disjointed mass of reports, out of the traditions and tales that come down from the field, some eye that never saw the battle will select[,] and some pen will write[,] what will be named *the history*. With that the world will be—and if we are alive we must be—content."[2]

Many men on both sides, like Haskell and William C. Oates, firmly believed that the battle was the turning point of the war. "I recognized then and there," wrote Levi Baker, a Union artillerist, in his later years, "that this battle was to be, in all probability, regarded as a great turning point in history."[3] Others thought that Gettysburg had decided very little. General Lee dismissed the idea that the Union army had won a great victory at Gettysburg and emphasized in his official reports that his goals for invading the North had been fully accomplished. Said Lee to one acquaintance: "We did whip them at Gettysburg, and it will be seen for the next six months that *that army* [i.e., the Army of the Potomac] will be as quiet as a sucking dove"—a prediction that did not come to pass.[4]

For the residents of Gettysburg, who had evacuated the town or run to their cellars for shelter when the two colossal armies came crashing into their community, the battle forged in them their own personal understanding of its meaning. The havoc caused by the fighting that erupted in and all around Gettysburg did great damage to crops, buildings, and other property. Across the battlefield and throughout the town nothing seemed to have gone unscathed. When the battle was over, one young woman civilian declared: "We were glad that the storm had passed and that victory was perched on our banners. But oh! the horror and desolation that remained."[5]

Gettysburg citizens, however, were instrumental in solving their own problems caused by the battle, particularly the disposal of dead bodies that littered their meadows and pastures. Out of the separate efforts of two Gettysburg attorneys, David Wills and David McConaughy, the idea took root of purchasing property adjacent to the town's Evergreen Cemetery for the sole purpose of burying Gettysburg's fallen Union soldiers and designating the place a national cemetery.

The Soldiers' National Cemetery gave Gettysburg an even greater distinction than it had already achieved as the site of a great Union victory. At the dedication of the Soldiers' Cemetery on November 19, 1863, as I have earlier discussed, Abraham Lincoln delivered a short address that, in its power and its eloquence, altered every American's understanding of the meaning of Gettysburg for all time. In his dedication speech, Lincoln held forth a promise that the war would not be fought in vain. He saw a new America emerging out of the old, a country more dedicated to its most cherished ideals, a nation reborn out of the fire and ashes of war.

His words elevated the significance of Gettysburg. Confronting the dreadful reality of the battle—those grisly remains that still awaited re-burial on the day of the cemetery's dedication—Lincoln honored the men "who here gave their lives" for the sake of their country, but in so doing he helped Americans, then and now, focus on the ideal of the warrior's sacrifice rather than the reality of the soldier's suffering.[6] The ground at Gettysburg, as Lincoln said, had been duly consecrated, as if gods, rather than ordinary soldiers, had spilled their blood there. His heroic image of the dead at Gettysburg did not, at the time, diminish the awful reality of the battle and the war. But as Lincoln's speech gained in popularity after his death, his words were increasingly understood as accomplishing something he claimed they could not: hallowing the ground at Gettysburg. In timeless prose, Abraham Lincoln gave the nation its greatest political speech and turned a bloody battle into a sacred American symbol.

While Lincoln spoke to the nation and offered his understanding of the war's meaning, an effort was already underway in Gettysburg to preserve the ground that the president's words had sanctified. In September 1863, the Gettysburg Battlefield Memorial Association (GBMA) was founded by local leaders, such as David McConaughy, to preserve portions of the battlefield in the "exact form and condition" as it had existed during the battle.[7] Over the next thirty years, the GBMA purchased tracts of land around Gettysburg where the battle's hottest fighting had taken place. Visitors began flocking to Gettysburg, some to satisfy their curiosity, others to determine where their loved ones had fought and died, and still others to remember where they had stood during those three hot summer days in July.

Many veterans sought to memorialize in some permanent manner the brave deeds of their regiments and brigades. Before 1878, monuments commemorating the Union dead were raised only in the Soldiers' Cemetery. During the next ten years, the monuments on the Union side of the field multiplied to more than three hundred in number (today, there are more than nine hundred monuments on the battlefield). The Gettysburg battleground was described by a local newspaper as a "forest of marble and granite, iron and bronze."[8]

The GBMA developed guidelines for the design and placement of monuments on the battlefield, and Northern states increasingly appropriated tax dollars to pay for regimental memorials, including the gigantic and elaborate Pennsylvania Memorial, located not far from the Angle on Cemetery Ridge. In time, it became increasingly apparent that the field dotted with monuments could no longer be regarded as a perfectly preserved battleground, as the GBMA had once intended to create. Monuments would now change the appearance of the battlefield to something the veterans themselves had not seen during the battle. As the landscape of Gettysburg changed, so too did its meaning.

New roads and paths were cut along the locations of the monuments. Soon the roads began to dictate where monuments would be placed, and, to some extent, how the battle would be understood by tourists. Before the end of the century, an electric railway was built so visitors could see the battlefield up close; the railway ran its tracks along the Emmitsburg Road, down to the Wheatfield, over to Devil's Den, and back through the Valley of Death. Obviously the landscape of the battlefield was changing, and as the transformation took place, Gettysburg became less connected with the fire and smoke of battle and instead assumed a more lasting identity as a symbolic memorial and a tourist attraction in its own right.

No monuments, however, were raised to Confederate units or states in the several decades that followed the war—a fact that irritated some Southerners, like, as we've seen, William Oates. But many former Confederates did not long to place monuments on the field at Gettysburg. Not wanting to emphasize one of the Confederacy's worst military defeats in the Civil War, these Southerners felt the battlefield had become nothing more than a park that blatantly celebrated Union victory, both over Lee's army and over the Confederacy itself. Sectional animosities still ran deep in the hearts of both Northerners and Southerners, and particularly among some veterans of both sides, who could not readily forgive their enemies for all the hardship and suffering the war had brought to nearly every household in the land. Clearly the battlefield at Gettysburg meant something far different to former Confederates than it did to Union veterans and the Northern public.

Yet even as Southerners complained about Gettysburg as a shrine to Northern victory, many Americans began to consider the war in a new light and longed to embrace the emotional bonds of brotherhood that had tied the nation's sections together before the Civil War. As memories of the ghastly horrors of war faded, a spirit of reconciliation flowed through the land, and a desire to forgive former enemies inspired a growing number of Northerners and Southerners to discard their hatreds, toss off their bitterness, and join together to honor the courage each section had displayed during America's worst cataclysm. The end of Reconstruction in the South helped to accelerate such feelings, but there were other forces at work that bolstered the spirit of reconciliation throughout the country and at Gettysburg. Some Americans, like Oates and Chamberlain, held onto some of their old sectional animosities. But most of their countrymen seemed carried away by the spirit of reconciliation.

By the advent of the twentieth century, the racism that had stood as a bastion protecting white freedom in America on both sides of the Mason-Dixon line for the entire course of the country's history sprang forth with a vengeance and, in some places, in acts of violence against African Americans. Northerners readily accepted Southern perceptions of blacks, and among the veterans of the Civil War, the spirit and rituals of reconciliation proved to be, as one historian has explained, "rituals of exclusion that ignored the history of black Americans . . . and prevented [them] from taking part in the healing process."[9]

The social amnesia that allowed Americans to forget why the Civil War had been fought had a profound bearing on the many meanings of Gettysburg. The equality that Abraham Lincoln had enshrined with his eloquence at Gettysburg was completely overpowered by the rhetoric and rituals of reconciliation, so much so that equality became twisted and distorted even in the ledgers of our nation's fundamental laws. In 1896, the Supreme Court of the United States established the "separate but equal" doctrine, which made segregation the law of the land and an accepted racial policy throughout the nation. Equality as an ideal still flamed in the hearts of many Americans; but equality as a reality had been doused by an ocean of racial bigotry and prejudice. Gone, too, was Lincoln's hope for a rebirth of the nation, for a new America to be created out of the highest dreams and aspirations of the old. A new freedom *had* emerged in the United States, but it was stillborn from the start. Lincoln's new birth of freedom had been transmuted into a new birth of *white* freedom.

Not surprisingly, as a result of these events, a different meaning could now be applied to Gettysburg. No longer was it simply the site of a horrible battle, or the place where Lee had suffered a devastating defeat, or even the spot where Abraham Lincoln had tried to ennoble the sacrifices of Gettysburg and of the war itself by elevating the struggle to a higher purpose—the fulfillment of equality once promised by the Declaration of Independence. Instead, Gettysburg became the nation's primary symbol of reconciliation, a place that signified the peaceful coming together of North and South, a park that memorialized the magnificent—and equivalent—bravery of soldiers on both sides and, at the same time, the tacit forgetfulness that allowed these once bitter enemies to become close bosom friends.

In 1913, twenty years after the War Department took over the administration of the Gettysburg National Military Park, the culmination of reconciliation sentiment rose to a crescendo when the fiftieth anniversary of the battle was celebrated on the old battlefield. More than fifty-five thousand Union and Confederate veterans attended the commemoration, which was held from the first to the fourth of July. Speeches and tours, dinners and campfire chats, all emphasized the heroism of both sides and the healing of sectional wounds.

"We both fought for principles," said Bennett H. Young, commander of the United Confederate Veterans, "and you won, not because we lacked courage, but because we lacked further resources."[10] Moved by the romantic mood of brotherhood that pervaded the anniversary celebration, Champ Clark, speaker of the U.S. House of Representatives, proclaimed: "Cold must be the heart of that American who is not proud to claim as countrymen the flower of the Southern youth who charged up the slippery slopes of Gettysburg with peerless Pickett, or those unconquerable men in blue, who through three long and dreadful days held these . . . heights in the face of fierce assaults. It was not Southern valor nor Northern valor. It was, thank God, American valor."[11]

After the fiftieth reunion, Gettysburg would forevermore be a cenotaph to American bravery—a proud memorial to an honorable and a uniquely remarkable people who could, in the blink of any eye, kill each other mercilessly and then, in another blink, forget their differences and reunite under a single banner. No longer would it really matter who fought for the Union or who fought for the Confederacy. Since the great reunion of 1913, Gettysburg has stood for valor and honor, for men willing to fight for what they believed in, for country, for nation, for flag, for the defense of rights, and for the defense of freedom.

The patriotic meaning of Gettysburg has been advanced and emphasized by the National Park Service, which assumed management of the military park from the War Department in 1933. Under the Park Service's charge, Gettysburg became an extremely popular tourist attraction, especially during the decades after World War II. Awash in this flood of tourism, Gettysburg National Military Park took on a new meaning for modern Americans. While patriotism and the spirit of reconciliation still gave Gettysburg its symbolic importance, the explosion of visitors to the park transformed the community—at least during the summer season—into a bustling mecca of crowds and families, buses and trailers, cars and trucks.

To provide for all these tourists, commercial facilities and services expanded within the town and around the boundaries of the park. The National Park Service and good-hearted preservationists, such as the Gettysburg Battlefield Preservation Association, and later, the Friends of the National Parks at Gettysburg (now known as the Gettysburg Foundation), did what they could to stop commercial development from encroaching onto the historic battlefield. But as the stream of tourists increased in the 1950s, and as even greater numbers of visitors arrived during and after the Civil War centennial in the early 1960s, the preservation of the field and its monuments became more difficult to maintain under the crunch of Gettysburg's soaring popularity and the area's own growing population. Local residents and the National Park Service administrators often could not see eye to eye. Tourism had become one of the bastions of Gettysburg's local economy. But at the same time, the Park Service seemed set on buying up more and more land to add to the battlefield and to take off the local tax rolls.

For some, Gettysburg was the place they called home, and they resented the intrusion of tourists in the summer and the cavalier ways of the Park Service, which officiously presumed that Washington, in the end, knew what was best for the community. Meanwhile, the Park Service hurt its own cause—and credibility—when it committed a number of egregious errors during the late twentieth century. In the early 1960s, the construction of a new visitor center—a huge, white, futuristic structure, looking like a drum laid on its side—to house the famous Cyclorama painting proved to be a costly blunder and an embarrassment, seeing as it was built on Cemetery Ridge just yards away from where Pickett's Charge had been repulsed. Another blunder was the government's approval in the early 1970s of the National Tower, a privately owned eyesore that resembled an Erector set project from hell. Thirty years later, the Park Service persuaded the federal government to condemn the property and to raze the tower. But the edifice never should have been built in the first place, and the Park Service's tactic of forcing the property's condemnation convinced local residents that their own lands and businesses might easily fall victim to the park's machiavellian policies. As if all this were not bad enough, the

Park Service in 1990 also agreed to swap land with Gettysburg College and, as a result, gave away a portion of the fabled Railroad Cut, which the college then bulldozed into oblivion.

For all its patriotic symbolism and its variety of meanings, modern Gettysburg—as a place, a battlefield, a community—seems to have very little to do with the battle that was fought there or the words that Lincoln spoke there. Recently, the National Park Service has proposed constructing new visitor center facilities at a location outside the park boundaries. If that is accomplished, the Park Service would demolish the present Visitor Center (the former privately owned National Museum) and the white Cyclorama Center and would restore Cemetery Ridge to the way it looked in 1863. Never mind that the ridge can never truly be restored to its historical appearance, for to do so would actually require removing hundreds of monuments, removing roads and modern signs and exhibits, dynamiting the largest monument on the battlefield (the Pennsylvania Memorial), and trucking in tons of manure and mud for the right historical effect. Understandably, some local residents believe the Park Service is simply repeating its pattern of mistakes and bad decisions. Others believe that relocating the visitor center will hurt local business. Preservationists and historians argue both ways: the visitor center should go for aesthetic reasons, or should stay for practical ones (such as traffic and accessibility). Whatever the Park Service does, whatever the outcome of this current dispute, there will be very loud protests from all sorts of people who believe that their particular understanding of the meaning of Gettysburg has been wantonly violated.

So we have come a long way from how the soldiers who fought at Gettysburg understood the meaning of the battle and an equally formidable distance from what Lincoln said should be Gettysburg's great meaning for the nation and for all its people. As Gettysburg has come to mean different things to different people over the last 140 years, it has also slipped more and more from our grasp. The changing meanings of Gettysburg for more than a century have meant that we have lost sight of what the battle *should* mean to us, and it would seem that we no longer hear, on the wind or in our hearts, the words that Lincoln spoke there on the eve of what he hoped would become America's new birth of freedom.

If we are ever to reach an understanding of the true meaning of Gettysburg we must make more of an effort, not only as individuals but also as a nation, to confront our history directly and honestly. We, as a nation and as a people, have avoided such a confrontation with our past because it is difficult and painful to do. It is easy to get caught up in the drama and romance of Gettysburg—even easier, in fact, to forget why these two armies, Union and Confederate, fought against each other in the first place. Facing the past means facing ourselves, and we are afraid of what we may discover buried away in the dust of the archives or, worse yet, down deep in our hearts.

What we have lost in refusing to confront our past is what Abraham Lincoln told us Gettysburg was really all about. He said that the nation needed to press ahead and complete the unfinished work that the Founding Fathers had begun—and that the soldiers at Gettysburg, through their sacrifice, had carried on. He called for a new birth of freedom, the fulfillment of equality for every person throughout the land, so that, when the war was finally over, the United States could face its future and live on, striving for a higher goal, a more noble purpose, than the mere political ones of union and re-union. Today we often forget his words. They are drowned out by the lilting sounds of romance and blotted out by the radiant images of glory.

If white Americans don't seem to comprehend this, African Americans do. While it is almost impossible to find black tourists at Gettysburg, some African Americans have written about their perceptions of the place and their own understanding of what Gettysburg means to them. In 1994, Acel Moore, then associate editor of the *Philadelphia Inquirer*, toured the battlefield and realized that his experience "was just as Abraham Lincoln described it in his Gettysburg Address."[12] Moore, an African American, said he believed that Gettysburg *was* hallowed ground, despite the inequality that divides whites and blacks, despite the hollow promise of equality that still echoes across the land. Four years later, Allen B. Ballard, an African American and a history professor at the New York State University at Albany, admitted that he had always been put off "by the commercial atmosphere" of Gettysburg, but also "by a feeling of emotional detachment from the battle." Worse, he felt "like an uninvited guest" when he visited the battlefield one Memorial Day. The monuments to "slave-spreading" Confederates particularly offended him.[13]

If we could confront our history as a nation, Gettysburg's exclusion of black Americans could change. The place could become a shrine to equality instead of a symbol of white patriotism. Recently the National Park Service has announced its intention to do just that, to begin launching an interpretive effort that will emphasize slavery as the cause of the war, not only at Gettysburg, but at all its Civil War battlefields and sites.

Not surprisingly, this interpretive plan has unleashed a howl of protest, especially from Southerners and those sympathetic to the Lost Cause who believe that states' rights and not slavery was the true cause of the war. Their ranks have been joined by others who think that military history alone should be interpreted at battlefields, not the social context within which those battles took place.

Yet if we are ever to make Lincoln's great vision a reality, if we are ever to embrace the ideal of equality as he expressed it in the Gettysburg Address, we must somehow face up to our history. America, wrote Gunnar Myrdal in the early 1940s, "is continually struggling for its soul."[14] At Gettysburg, and elsewhere, the nation is still at war with itself, particularly when it comes to the issue of race. In our own heart of hearts, perhaps we may finally come to realize that the real meaning of Gettysburg is, after all, to be found in the hidden recesses of our souls, somewhere in the glory and in the pain, in the ecstasy and in the despair, in the light and in the darkness, of what it truly means to be an American.

14 Feeling the Past at Gettysburg

Something that Bruce Catton wrote many years ago about Gettysburg comes to mind every time I visit the battlefield. "The battle was here and its presence is felt," Catton said, "and you cannot visit the place without feeling the echoes of what was once a proving ground for everything America believes in."[1] Although I've long wondered about Catton's curious choice of words (most people *hear* echoes rather than *feel* them), I think he meant precisely what he said.

Despite the garish commercialism that for years has threatened to overwhelm the now peaceful battlefield at Gettysburg, it is still possible to feel the past there. I collided with those feelings several years ago when my youngest daughter, Sarah, and I visited the battlefield on a cloudy and misty day in May to conduct a historical experiment in the style of Francis Parkman and Samuel Eliot Morison, two historians who insisted on visiting the places they wrote about. This was the dad-and-daughter outing I mentioned in an earlier chapter. My intent was that my daughter and I could trace the route Colonel William C. Oates and the 15th Alabama took in launching their doomed attack against Little Round Top. The day turned out to hold much more in store for us than I had imagined.

Like Parkman and Morison, I wanted to see the ground where history had happened. More than that, I hoped to walk the same paths Oates and his men had traversed and, perhaps, gain some insight into what they might have experienced that awful—and dreadfully hot—afternoon when they tried with all their might to take a hill that, in the end, could not be taken. Sarah and I would have some advantages that Oates and his men did not, namely good footwear in the form of hiking boots and the fact that we had not already marched twenty-five miles from the vicinity of Chambersburg, Pennsylvania to the battlefield.

Although my daughter and I traveled up from Virginia, as Oates's Alabamians and the rest of Lee's Army of Northern Virginia did in the summer of 1863, it was our trusty gas-guzzling minivan that got us to Gettysburg without incident on a spring day when a very light rain was falling. Fourteen-year-old Sarah, brave soul, was willing to accompany me on this odd adventure. Besides, she would miss a day of school, and that made this historical expedition all the more appealing to her.

It was not our first visit to Gettysburg, by any means. Since the 1950s, when I first saw the battlefield on vacations with my parents, I have returned to Gettysburg over and over again, a swallow drawn back to his Capistrano. For my wife, Donna, and me, Gettysburg is a place of fond memories. With our children (Sarah is the youngest of three), we have visited Gettysburg many times, often touring the battlefield or seeking out antiques and books in the village's many shops. We lived at that time on a small farm in the Blue Ridge Mountains of Virginia, and it took us only two hours to get to Gettysburg by car. We needed few excuses to make the trip.

So Sarah and I came armed with maps and some photocopies of Oates's writings about the battle, and we set out to reconstruct a faded moment in history. We started where the 15th Alabama had begun its assault, on Warfield Ridge, about a mile southeast of the Round Tops. The ridge is a quiet corner of the park, a place where few tourists gather. In fact, I had never bothered to explore it before.

When I visited Gettysburg as a child, my family never investigated any of the relatively remote edges of the battlefield, like Warfield Ridge. In those days, my father liked pulling the Studebaker over on the Emmitsburg Road in front of Cemetery Ridge and contemplating the famous copse of trees, the High Water Mark, where the Union army repulsed the gray tide of Pickett's Charge on July 3, 1863. Why my father was so intrigued by that landmark, I really can't say. My recollection is that he actually knew very little about the details of the battle. Maybe he could feel an echo of the past that the rest of us in the car could not.

Or perhaps he was drawn back to that place because he realized that Gettysburg had come to mean something to me, that it had captured my imagination, despite my youth and the fact that the only thing I had ever read about the battle was a Landmark series book on Gettysburg by MacKinlay Kantor, the first chapter of which, by the way, was provocatively—and rather weirdly—entitled, "*Ja,* the Rebels Eat Babies!"[2] In any event, my father kept taking the family back to Gettysburg—I'd guess at least a half dozen times during my childhood. We could make the trip in about ten hours from our home in Rhode Island, thanks to "superhighways" like the Merritt Parkway in Connecticut and the Pennsylvania Turnpike. Often we stayed overnight in one of the many motels that still line the long straightaway of Steinwehr Avenue, which connects the battlefield with the town. The next day we would take the Park Service's self-guided auto tour. Other times, when we were just passing through on our way to some other vacation destination, my father would ritualistically pull the car over in front of the High Water Mark and stare at the small grove of trees. Then, without saying a word, he would drive on.

*　*　*

Almost at once Sarah and I hit an obstacle that Oates and his Alabamians didn't encounter—a modern wire fence that was too high to climb easily and that we had to follow along its length until we reached a gate that could be surmounted. But while we had a fence to clamber over, Oates had considerably more to worry about when his men rushed down the slopes from Warfield Ridge at the quick step. For one thing, Union artillery at Devil's Den pounded the Alabama brigade to bits as it rushed toward the Round Tops. For another thing, Oates had sent off a detail of men, carrying the 15th Alabama's canteens, to find water. The order to advance came before the water detail could return, so Oates and his Alabamians began their attack with a prodigious thirst that would only get worse as the afternoon wore on. "It would have been infinitely better to have waited five minutes for those twenty-two men and the canteens of water," mused Oates after the war, "but generals never ask a colonel if his regiment is ready to move."[3]

As if that were not enough, Oates had his younger brother, John A. Oates, to worry about as well. The senior Oates knew that his brother was suffering terribly from rheumatism—an illness that had laid John low the previous spring and had only gotten worse over the past few months. The march to Gettysburg didn't help John's condition, and older brother William had told him to report to the rear on sick call. John refused to stay behind while his regiment went into battle. "I am an officer and will never disgrace the uniform I wear," he declared. "I shall go through, unless I am killed, which I think is quite likely."[4]

After clearing the fence, Sarah and I tried to approximate a Civil War quick step, but in only a few minutes we were too fatigued to keep it up. The field that carried us down into Plum Run valley, in the shadow of Big Round Top, was furrowed and contained the stubble of last year's corn crop. When we successfully passed through the lumpy field, we came over a low ridge and entered a thicket of brambles and tangled nettles and thistles. Every few feet we stopped to help each other unsnag our clothes. Despite the historical maps I carried, we actually had only a general idea of where we were headed. Oates and his men must have experienced the same feeling. We could no longer see the Round Tops in front of us, nor could we see Warfield Ridge behind us. All we could see were the tops of trees. We then came through a woodlot and emerged into a large, marshy field.

It was here, before the 15th Alabama reached Plum Run at the base of Big Round Top, that Brigadier General Evander M. Law galloped up to Oates and told him to "hug the base of Great Round Top and go up the valley between the two mountains."[5] As soon as Oates found the Union left flank, said Law, his Alabamians were to turn the flank and "do all the damage" they could. If the 15th Alabama and the 47th Alabama to its left became separated from the rest of the brigade, Law gave Oates the authority to assume command over both regiments—the command that Major William Robbins of the 4th Alabama, forty years later, would doubt had been issued. With that, Law rode off as quickly as he had arrived and left Oates to carry out his orders.

As Sarah and I stood at this spot, our feet getting wet in the soggy meadow, we could see ahead of us, and off the left some three hundred yards or so, a group of stone and wooden farm buildings—the Slyder farm—that also stood there at the time of the battle. This place is a pristine pocket of the battlefield, and it is not hard to imagine how things actually looked 140 years ago, when the Slyders evacuated their homestead, and the buildings stood as silent sentinels to the approaching Confederate waves. We pressed forward, hopping from one tuft of grass to the next to avoid the mire (which Oates and his men could *not* have evaded as they advanced in battle line), and we soon stood on the banks of Plum Run, a small stream running through a deep cut that divided the Slyder farm fields from the wooded base of Big Round Top.

The stream gave us pause, for there was no apparent way by which we could move ahead—the cut was too wide too jump, the run was too deep to ford without soaking our feet. Our situation required some thought; Oates, standing in the same place, had no such luxury of contemplation. As his lines approached Plum Run, a sudden ripple of musket fire, coming from under the trees on the steep slopes of Big Round Top, caught him and his men off guard. Behind a stone wall on the opposite side of the creek, marksmen from the 2nd U.S. Sharpshooters sent cutting volley fire into the Alabamians. Despite the surprise, Oates swiftly got his men across the steam—no worries about wet feet—and led them forward toward the saddle between the two hills. Another volley from the Yankees, dressed in their distinctive green uniforms, convinced Oates that he could not leave this Federal force on his flank or in his rear, so he ordered the 15th and 47th Alabama regiments to change direction to the right, face the stone wall, and get ready to charge the enemy. As the Alabamians moved into position, the Union sharpshooters decided that they could not possibly hold back two Confederate regiments, so they quickly withdrew from the wall, dispersing into the cover of the woods.

My daughter and I solved the problem of crossing Plum Run by finding a dilapidated wooden bridge downstream and inching our way across the rotting beams. We did not come under fire from sharpshooters or, for that matter, from wandering tourists, for there was no one in sight. The drizzle had stopped, the day was getting slightly warmer, and we now faced our most formidable challenge—scaling the steep and rocky slopes of Big Round Top. On July 2, Oates had responded quickly to the sharpshooters' withdrawal by ordering the regiments under his command to pursue the Federals up the hill. For Oates and his men, or for us trying to follow in their footsteps, the climb was no cakewalk. After the war, Oates remembered: "In places the men had to climb up, catching to the rocks and bushes and crawling over the boulders in the face of the fire of the enemy, who kept retreating, taking shelter and firing down on us from behind rocks and crags which covered the side of the mountain."[6]

Without dodging minié balls, Sarah and I had a hard enough time just pushing our way through the natural barriers of brambles, fallen limbs, downed trees, deep depressions in the ground, exposed roots, and, of course, the huge rocks—boulders that Oates thought were more plentiful than "grave-stones in a city cemetery."[7] He later reported that many of his men fainted from the heat and the exertion required to climb the hill. We didn't faint, my daughter and I, although we became quickly winded and discovered that we could not walk steadily up the hill without stopping every fifty yards or so to catch our breath and muster the energy to go on. Passing through a clearing where today a monument to the 1st Vermont Cavalry is located, we veered a bit toward Big Round Top's southern slopes, crossed a modern park road, entered woods again, and came upon something we had not expected to find—a high, jagged, cliff. Oates never mentioned the cliff in his account, but he and his men must have encountered it, just as we had done—by complete surprise. Huffing and puffing, and watching out for slippery rocks and wet leaves, Sarah and I went straight up the precipice, my leading the way and often reaching back to pull her up the rock face.

So far our feeling the past at Gettysburg had produced but one feeling alone: exhaustion. We kept going, however, watching as the sky above the trees became noticeably brighter, and finally we reached the summit—a broad, rocky crest with a view that is now obscured by high oak trees and impenetrable foliage. Grateful for not having to climb another foot, we sat down on a massive slab of shale, the highest rock formation on the hill-top, near the place where a steel observation tower used to stand. While we rested, I read aloud Oates's account of reaching the summit with his men.

Standing on this "highest point of rocks," he had a clear view of Little Round Top just below him and, in fact, he could see all the way to Gettysburg, three miles to the north. He could also hear the rumbling sounds of battle rising from below the hill. While Oates gave his men ten minutes or so to recover from their climb, a staff officer approached the summit—no small feat on horseback—and told Oates that the Alabamians had gone off course by climbing to Big Round Top's crest and that they must come off the hill immediately and assault the Union left. Oates, however, thought Big Round Top was strategically important, a "key-point on the field," and he urged the officer to allow him to hold this position until Confederate artillery could be moved to the top. The staff officer informed Oates that he had no authority to alter General Law's orders; the Alabamians, he said, must "press on, turn the Union left, and capture Little Round Top, if possible, and . . . lose no time."[8]

Oates knew his duty, and he called for his men to re-form their ranks. Coming down the hill would be a challenge, however, for a cliff on the northern face—not unlike the one scaled by the Alabamians (and by Sarah and me) on the southern face—blocked any possibility of Oates's regiments descending the hill with ease. To avoid the cliff, Oates "caused both regiments to face to the left and [they] moved to the left, so as to avoid the precipice in our front."[9] What this meant, as Sarah and I found out, was that the Alabamians had to backtrack about fifty yards, come around the edge of the cliff, and scramble down some boulders until solid ground could be found at the base of the precipice. Oates must have then reformed his lines, which the terrain most certainly had torn asunder, and advanced down the heavily wooded northern slope of the hill. Sarah and I followed their route, stumbling through the thick woods, admiring the jack-in-the-pulpits sprinkled across the forest floor, and rejoicing that the walk down was nothing like the climb up.

When Oates and his lines emerged from the woods into the narrow valley that divides Big Round Top and Little Round Top, they were greeted by a heavy rolling volley from above, and Oates for the first time saw in front of him the men of the 20th Maine, crouched behind piled rocks and boulders and trees, about half way up the cragged slopes of Little Round Top. It was, he later said, "the most destructive fire I ever saw." All along the gray lines, the men of the 15th Alabama and the 47th Alabama crumpled to the ground, dead and wounded, but the lines closed up, filling the gaps, and the Alabamians returned the enemy fire "most spiritedly."[10]

Out of woods came Sarah and I, finding ourselves at the spot where Oates and his men had been surprised by the volley fire. Across a paved park road, and about half way up the slope of Little Round Top, we could see the white granite monument of the 20th Maine, perched atop a rock ledge, near the spot where Colonel Chamberlain had placed his colors. In 1863, the terrain was different than it is now, for the southern slope of Little Round Top was altered considerably when the park roads were constructed around 1900. Today a small parking area has been carved out of the hillside below the 20th Maine monument, a necessity given the amount of visitors who now make the pilgrimage to see where Chamberlain and his famous regiment performed their heroic deeds.

Standing at the edge of the woods below the monument, I told Sarah the story of how the Alabamians struggled with Chamberlain's 20th Maine for possession of this hill. Oates, I explained, had determined that the weakest point in the Union line was its left flank. So he tried to maneuver his Alabamians to the right, hoping to roll up the Federal defensive line. Chamberlain, seeing the threat, refused his line—a tactical step by which he extended his front and formed it into a salient. For an hour, the bloody battle raged up and down these rocky ledges and treacherously steep slopes. Five times Oates drove his men against the Union defenders. Each time, Oates was in front of the advancing men, waving his sword in one hand and a pistol in the other. The battlefront, he remembered, surged back and forth like a wave.

While Oates directed the fighting on his right, desperately attempting to swing around the Union left, the battle over on his own left wing was going just as badly. On this flank his men were caught in a deadly crossfire. Years later he described the slopes of the hill as being "soaked with the blood of as brave men as ever fell on the red field of battle."[11]

It was along this left flank, amid the boulders and the trees, that Lieutenant John Oates urged his men forward, inch by inch. He was no longer on horseback, having abandoned his mount before crossing Plum Run near the Slyder farm, and he moved his men steadily up the hill and over the rocks, despite the burning pain in his hip and legs. Along this section of the line, below the ledges where the Maine monument stands today, he and his men could find little cover. Suddenly a sharp plunging fire came down the hill, and John Oates fell with seven bullet wounds. A fellow officer quickly pulled him to cover between two huge boulders.

In the meantime, William Oates was preoccupied trying to get his men up the difficult slope. The battle was swirling around him, the blood was flowing into puddles on the rocks, and the Alabamians were running out of steam and ammunition. There was no time for Oates to care for his wounded brother; precious little time, even, to decide what he should do next.

His officers urged him to retreat, but Oates hesitated. A flaming volley of musket fire from the rear made up his mind for him, and he turned around to see a detachment of Union soldiers—including Company B of the 20th Maine and remnants of the sharpshooters the 15th Alabama had earlier chased up Big Round Top—firing from behind a stone wall. Outflanked, low on ammunition, his casualties mounting, Oates realized he had no choice but to withdraw.

He called out the order at a crucial moment. As he did so, while the crashing clamor of battle drowned out his words, Chamberlain—who was also facing an untenable situation of heavy losses and depleted ammunition—decided to order a bayonet charge against the Confederates. As the 20th Maine came rolling like a rockslide down the hill, it struck the disorganized Alabamians as they were trying to pull back and begin their own retreat. As a result, the collision was tremendous—and disastrous for Oates and his men. Oates put it as plainly and as honestly as he could: "We ran like a herd of wild cattle."[12] He could not rescue John. The young lieutenant was left behind, wounded and dying in a crevice between two boulders.

*　*　*

We stood there for a long time, my daughter and I, just looking at the 20th Maine monument from a distance. We were alone at the base of Little Round Top—no tourists or bus groups milled about, as they do so prolifically in the summertime. Everything was still, except for a few songbirds and the faint sounds of water dripping off the leaves in the woods.

Then Sarah broke the silence. "Can you feel that?" she asked. I had no idea what she was talking about, and I told her so. "I can feel something," she said. When I asked her what it was, she shrugged and looked puzzled. "I thought for sure you would have felt it," she asserted, but she couldn't describe what she herself had felt. It was something intangible, like a fog or a shadow. She said it made her feel sad. But beyond that she could not put a name to what she had just experienced.

Later, when I happened to remember this odd incident, my mind unexpectedly started making connections between what Sarah had felt at Little Round Top and what I had once felt many years earlier when I was a young high school student on a visit to the battlefield. On that earlier trip, I had gone to Gettysburg alone during spring break to roam the battlefield. My father had died the previous autumn. It was during that visit, when the dogwood was in full bloom and the robins were darting from tree to tree—on the day after the evening that I had stood at the Cyclorama Center listening to the Civil War chimes—that I felt for the first time what Sarah later experienced on our hike.

On a cloudy April day, I had walked nearly the entire length of the battlefield. Toward late afternoon, as the sun was beginning to squint through the leaden sky, I ended up on Little Round Top, standing beside the monument to the 20th Maine. I knew next to nothing about the regiment and its brave commander. I certainly knew absolutely nothing about William Oates, his brother John, and the luckless 15th Alabama. So I stood in front of the monument and read its inscriptions, including the names of all the Maine soldiers who had defended this hill.

All at once, and without warning, a wave of emotion came crashing over me, and I felt remarkably connected to these courageous Maine boys and what they had done on this famous hillside. I thought about the men who had died there, all the lost souls. I thought about the poor families whose own lives were shattered when they learned the news about loved ones they had lost on a rocky hill in Pennsylvania. I thought about how those families must have felt cheated, bereft, and alone. And then I thought about my father, buried on a grim hilltop in Rhode Island, and it was then—more than at any time since his unexpected death at the age of forty-six—that I understood how much I missed him.

So what, precisely, had Sarah felt at Little Round Top? Perhaps she had encountered the lingering spirits of William and John Oates, Joshua Chamberlain, and all the men of Maine and Alabama who had fought like demons for possession of this little hill. Chamberlain, after one of his own visits back to Little Round Top after the war, once wrote:

In great deeds something abides. On great fields something stays. Forms change and pass; bodies disappear; but spirits linger, to consecrate ground for the vision-place of souls. And reverent men and women from afar, and generations that know us not and that we know not of, heart-drawn to see where and by whom great things were suffered and done for them, shall come to this deathless field, to ponder and dream, and lo! the shadow of a mighty presence shall wrap them in its bosom, and the power of the vision pass into their souls.[13]

Perhaps Sarah had even felt the trace of her own father, who, many years before, had come to this place and found something he had missed, something he had lost.

A few weeks after the battle, when Lee's army had safely returned to Virginia, Oates learned of his brother's death and met a Union courier who, under a flag of truce, returned John's personal effects—a gold watch, a little money, and a small bloodstained book. According to Oates, their mother knew that her boy was dead long before reading any casualty lists. She awoke with a start "at the very hour" of John's death and declared "that he had been wounded in a great battle and had just died." Oates's father tried to comfort her, saying it was all a dream, but she knew better. She wept all night long, insisting that "she had seen her dear child die and saw him laid out."[14]

In July 1910, after decades of searching, William Oates finally learned that his brother's remains had been laid to rest in Hollywood Cemetery in Richmond, after having been reinterred and transferred from a temporary grave located less than two miles from Little Round Top. Two months later, Oates died at the age of seventy-seven. His own personal Gettysburg nightmare was finally over.

Sarah and I walked back to our minivan along Confederate Avenue, which by means of a winding route—but one more easily negotiated than the brambles and rocks of Big Round Top—leads directly to Warfield Ridge, where we had begun our little journey through history. We left Gettysburg that evening before sundown, driving south from the town along the Emmitsburg Road, which took us past Warfield Ridge one last time. Just for a moment, I pulled the car over onto the dirt shoulder. There in the gathering twilight, we could see Big Round Top, its dark form silhouetted against the shimmering sky. We stayed long enough to watch the outline of the hill fade in the falling darkness. Without saying a word, I pulled the car back on the road and headed for home.

Our pasts are locked up inside us. Sometimes, when we least expect it, they come spilling forth and intersect with other parts of our lives. On this day of discovery in Gettysburg, Sarah and I happened on several converging pasts, not all of them our own. Our journey had brought us to a personal understanding of the many meanings of Gettysburg. The past is not always tangible or even knowable. But sometimes it can been seen, and sometimes it can be felt. On a misty spring day, across the lush fields and hills of Gettysburg, my daughter and I felt the far-reaching echoes of our past.

Notes

Introduction

1. Gregory A. Coco tells a version of this story in *On the Bloodstained Field* (Gettysburg, Pa., 1987), 50–51.

2. John S. Patterson, "Zapped at the Map: The Battlefield at Gettysburg," *Journal of Popular Culture* 7 (1974): 825–837; Patterson, "From Battle Ground to Pleasure Ground: Gettysburg as a Historic Site," in Warren Leon and Roy Rosenzweig, eds., *History Museums in the United States: A Critical Assessment* (Urbana and Chicago, 1989), 128–157; Edward Tabor Linenthal, *Sacred Ground: Americans and Their Battlefields*, 2nd ed. (Urbana and Chicago, 1993), 87–126; Amy J. Kinsel, " 'From These Honored Dead': Gettysburg in American Culture, 1863–1938" (Ph.D. diss., Cornell University, 1992); Jim Weeks, *Gettysburg: Memory, Market, and an American Shrine* (Princeton, N.J., 2003); Thomas A. Desjardin, *These Honored Dead: How the Gettysburg Story Shaped American Memory* (Cambridge, Mass., 2003).

3. Oliver Willcox Norton, "Our Fallen Comrades," Address at the Dedication of the Monument of the Eighty-Third Regiment, Sept. 12, 1889, in *Army Letters, 1861–1865* (Chicago, 1903), 341.

4. Robert Littell, "Ghosts Speak at Gettysburg," *Reader's Digest* 33 (July 1938): 54. On Gettysburg as a turning point, see Amy Kinsel, "From Turning Point to Peace Memorial: A Cultural Legacy," in Gabor Boritt, ed., *The Gettysburg Nobody Knows* (New York, 1997), 203–222.

5. "Killer angels," of course, refers to Michael Shaara's very popular novel, *The Killer Angels* (New York, 1974).

6. For example, Harry Roach, *Gettysburg: Hour by Hour* (Gettysburg, Pa., 1993); Blake A. Magner, *Traveller and Company: The Horses of Gettysburg* (Gettysburg, Pa., 1995). On ghosts: Mark Nesbit, *The Ghosts of Gettysburg: Spirits, Apparitions, and Haunted Places of the Battlefield* (Gettysburg, Pa., 1991); Nesbit, *More Ghosts of Gettysburg: Spirits, Apparitions, and Haunted Places of the Battlefield* (Gettysburg, Pa., 1992); Nesbit, *Ghosts of Gettysburg III: Spirits, Apparitions, and Haunted Places of the Battlefield* (Gettysburg, Pa., 1996); Nesbit, *Ghosts of Gettysburg IV: Spirits, Apparitions, and Haunted Places of the Battlefield* (Gettysburg, Pa., 1998); Nesbit, *Ghosts of Gettysburg V: Spirits, Apparitions, and Haunted Places of the Battlefield* (Gettysburg, Pa., 2000); Nesbit, *Ghosts of Gettysburg VI: Spirits, Apparitions, and Haunted Places of the Battlefield* (Gettysburg, Pa., 2004); Nesbit, *The Ghost Hunter's Field Guide: Gettysburg and Beyond* (Gettysburg, Pa., 2005); Dave R. Oester and Sharon Gill, *America's Hauntings: The Ghosts of Gettysburg* (Port Orchard, Wash., 2006); Philip N. Rogone, *The Gettysburg Ghost* (Hesperia, Calif., 2005); Trish Kline, *The Ghost Hunter and the Ghost of Gettysburg* (Helena,

Mont., 2002). Some Gettysburg fiction: MacKinlay Kantor, *Long Remember* (New York, 1934); Joseph A. Altsheler, *The Star of Gettysburg* (New York, 1943); Don Robertson, *The Three Days* (Englewood Cliffs, N.J., 1959); Shaara, *The Killer Angels* (New York, 1974); Joseph E. Persico, *My Enemy, My Brother* (New York, 1977); William A. Williams, *Days of Darkness: The Gettysburg Civilians* (Shippensburg, Pa., 1986); Newt Gingrich and William R. Forstchen, *Gettysburg: A Novel of the Civil War* (New York, 2003); James Reasoner, *Gettysburg: A Novel* (Nashville, 2001); James Walker, *Murder at Gettysburg* (Nashville, Tenn., 1999); Leslie Wheeler, *Murder at Gettysburg* (Waterville, Me., 2005); Jane Langton, *The Deserter: Murder at Gettysburg* (New York, 2003). On women and Freemasons: E. F. Conklin, *Women at Gettysburg* (Gettysburg, Pa., 1993); Sheldon A. Munn, *Freemasons at Gettysburg* (Gettysburg, 1996). For "alternate" or "counterfactual" histories of the battle, see Winston Churchill, *If Lee Had Not Won at Gettysburg* (New York, 1930); Peter G. Tsouras, *Gettysburg: An Alternate History* (London, 1997); Brian M. Thomson and Martin H. Greenberg, eds., *Alternate Gettysburg* (New York, 2002).

7. On the American military tradition, see John M. Carroll and Colin F. Baxter, eds., *The American Military Tradition from Colonial Times to the Present* (Wilmington, Del., 1993); Bruce Catton, *U.S. Grant and the American Military Tradition* (Boston, 1954); Walter Millis, *Arms and Men: A Study of American Military History* (New York, 1956); Samuel P. Huntington, *The Soldier and the State: The Theory and Politics of Civil-Military Relations* (Cambridge, Mass., 1957); Marcus Cunliffe, *Soldiers and Civilians: The Martial Spirit in American, 1775–1865* (Boston, 1968); Russell F. Weigley, *The American Way of War: A History of U.S. Military Strategy and Policy* (Bloomington, Ind., 1973); Robert M. Utley, "The Contribution of the Frontier to the American Military Tradition," *Harmon Memorial Lectures in Military History* 19 (1977): 1–16; F. N. Boney, "The Military Tradition in the South," *Midwest Quarterly* 21 (1980): 163–174; Don Higgonbotham, "George Washington and George Marshall: Some Reflections on the American Military Tradition," *Harmon Memorial Lectures in Military History* 26 (1984): 1–22; Allan R. Millett and Peter Maslowski, *For the Common Defense: A Military History of the United States of America* (New York, 1984); Don Higgonbotham, *George Washington and the American Military Tradition* (Athens, Ga., 1985); William B. Skelton, "Samuel P. Huntington and the Roots of the American Military Tradition," *Journal of Military History* 60 (1996): 325–338; Edward M. Coffman, "The Duality of the American Military Tradition: A Commentary," *Journal of Military History* 64 (2000): 967–980.

8. Ketchum and Bierce quoted in Earl J. Hess, *The Union Soldier in Battle: Enduring the Ordeal of Combat* (Lawrence, Kans., 1997), 74–75, 83. On Civil War courage, see also Gerald F. Linderman, *Embattled Courage: The Experience of Combat in the American Civil War* (New York, 1987); James M. McPherson, *For Cause and Comrades: Why Men Fought in The Civil War* (New York, 1997), 58–60, 77–82. See also Mark Grimsley, "In Not So Dubious Battle: The Motivations of American Civil War Soldiers," *Journal of Military History* 62 (Jan. 1998): 175–188.

9. Linderman, *Embattled Courage,* 266–275. See Linderman's claims that the soldiers went through considerable difficulties readjusting to civilian life, although

other historians—including Earl J. Hess and James M. McPherson—have argued the point by demonstrating that the veterans did not experience an overwhelming disillusionment and did well in resuming their former lives as private citizens. See Hess, *Union Soldier,* 158–190; McPherson, *For Cause and Comrades,* 163–178. Similarly, a recent study shows that Gettysburg veterans lived on average three years longer than other Civil War veterans, which suggests they actually flourished during the postwar period rather than withered in a war-provoked despair. Two scholars who conducted the study, Peter Blanck and Chen Song, surmise that Gettysburg veterans might have enjoyed a longer life span because during the war they developed a stronger resilience to hardship and suffering, a dubious assumption that can never be proved or disproved. See Peter Blanck and Chen Song, " 'Never Forget What They Did Here': Civil War Pensions for Gettysburg Union Army Veterans and Disability in Nineteenth-Century America," *William and Mary Law Review* 44 (Feb. 2003): 1109–1171.

10. On the connections between the Philadelphia Exposition of 1876 and the Civil War, see Susanna W. Gold, "Imagining Memory: Re-presentation of the Civil War at the 1876 Centennial Exhibition" (Ph.D. diss., University of Pennsylvania, 2004). For the exposition and its celebration of American innovation, see Robert W. Rydell, *All the World's a Fair: Visions of Empire at American International Expositions, 1876–1916* (Chicago, 1984), 9–37; Dee Alexander Brown, "The Great Centennial," *American History Illustrated* 6 (May 1971): 4–9, 44–49; Thomas J. Schlereth, *Victorian America: Transformations in Everyday Life* (New York, 1991), 1–5. Among the earliest Civil War memoirs to be published by prominent Union and Confederate generals were: Joseph E. Johnston, *Narrative of Military Operations during the Civil War* (New York, 1874); William T. Sherman, *Memoirs of General William T. Sherman,* 2 vols. (New York, 1875); Ulysses S. Grant, *Personal Memoirs,* 2 vols. (New York, 1885); George B. McClellan, *McClellan's Own Story* (New York, 1887). On the Southern Historical Society Papers, see Richard D. Starnes, "Forever Faithful: The Southern Historical Society and Confederate Historical Memory," *Southern Cultures* 2 (Winter 1996): 177–194. The formal title of the *Official Records* is *The War of the Rebellion: A Compilation of the Official Records of the Union and Confederate Armies,* 4 series, 127 vols. (Washington, D.C., 1880–1901). The volumes were compiled and published by the War Department. On this massive publication project, see Dallas D. Irvine, "The Genesis of the *Official Records,*" *Mississippi Valley Historical Review* 24 (1937): 221–229; Joseph L. Eisendrath, "The Official Records: Sixty-Three Years in the Making," *Civil War History* 1 (1955): 89–94; Harold E. Mahan, "The Arsenal of History: *The Official Records of the War of the Rebellion,*" *Civil War History* 29 (1983): 5–27. For *Battles and Leaders,* see Robert U. Johnson and Clarence C. Buel, eds., *Battles and Leaders of the Civil War,* 4 vols. (New York, 1884–1889). See also Bruce Catton, "Foreword," in Stephen W. Sears, ed., *The American Heritage Century Collection of Civil War Art* (New York, 1974), 8–9. On the editing and publishing of the *Battles and Leaders* series, see Stephen Davis, " 'A Matter of Sensational Interest': The *Century* 'Battles and Leaders' Series," *Civil War History* 27 (1981): 338–349. For the Grand Army of the Republic, see Stuart McConnell, *Glorious Contentment: The Grand Army of the Republic, 1865–1900* (Chapel Hill, 1992). On the United Confederate Veterans, see

Gaines M. Foster, *Ghosts of the Confederacy: Defeat, the Lost Cause, and the Emergence of the New South, 1865–1913* (New York, 1987), 109–140.

11. For Grant's address, see *Philadelphia Inquirer*, May 11, 1876. On "Old Abe," see Bruce Catton, " 'Old Abe': The Battle Eagle," *American Heritage* 14 (Oct. 1963): 32–33, 106–107.

12. Amazingly enough, there is no modern history of the centennial celebrations held around the nation, but see Frederick Saunders, ed., *National Centennial Jubilee: Orations, Addresses and Poems Delivered on the Fourth of July, 1876* (New York, 1877). For the centennial and reconciliation, see Nina Silber, *The Romance of Reunion: Northerners and the South, 1865–1900* (Chapel Hill, 1993), 63, 127, 129; David W. Blight, *Race and Reunion: The Civil War in American Memory* (Cambridge, Mass., 2001), 132–134; Newton J. Jones, "The Washington Light Infantry at the Bunker Hill Centennial," *South Carolina Historical Magazine* 65 (1964): 195–204; Huber W. Ellingsworth, "The Confederate Invasion of Boston," *Southern Speech Journal* 35 (1969): 54–60. See also Philip S. Foner, "Black Participation in the Centennial of 1876," *Phylon* 39 (Winter 1978): 283–296. On the significance of parades in early American history, see Simon P. Newman, *Parades and the Politics of the Street: Festive Culture in the Early American Republic* (Philadelphia, 1997); Len Travers, *Celebrating the Fourth: Independence Day and the Rites of Nationalism in the Early Republic* (Amherst, Mass., 1997); David Waldstreicher, *In the Midst of Perpetual Fetes: The Making of American Nationalism, 1776–1820* (Chapel Hill, 1997).

13. Elbridge H. Goss, *The Centennial Fourth: Historical Address* (Melrose, Mass., 1876), 33–34; "The Centennial Era—Good to Come Out of It," *Macon Weekly Telegraph*, July 4, 1876. On the end of Reconstruction, see Eric Foner, *Reconstruction: America's Unfinished Revolution, 1863–1877* (New York, 1988), 564–601. See also C. Vann Woodward, *Reunion and Reaction: The Compromise of 1877 and the End of Reconstruction,* rev. ed. (Garden City, N.Y., 1956); Keith I. Polakoff, *The Politics of Inertia: The Election of 1876 and the End of Reconstruction* (Baton Rouge, 1973); William Gillette, *Retreat from Reconstruction, 1869–1879* (Baton Rouge, 1979).

14. William J. Black Diary, Oct. 19, 1864, Special Collections, Virginia Military Institute, Lexington, Virginia; Abbott Spear et al., eds., *The Civil War Recollections of General Ellis Spear* (Orono, Me., 1997), 318; J. M. Polk, *The North and South American Review* (Austin, 1914), 29.

15. On Bachelder, see Richard A. Sauers, "John B. Bachelder: Government Historian of the Battle of Gettysburg," *Gettysburg Magazine* 3 (1990): 115–127; Linenthal, *Sacred Ground,* 87–126; Weeks, *Gettysburg,* 23–43; Desjardin, *These Honored Dead,* 83–108. For Bachelder's battle history, see David L. Ladd and Audrey J. Ladd, eds., *John Bachelder's History of the Battle of Gettysburg* (Dayton, Ohio, 1997). The extensive eyewitness accounts Bachelder collected are in the Bachelder Papers, New Hampshire Historical Society, Concord. Most of these records have been published in David L. Ladd and Audrey J. Ladd, eds., *The Bachelder Papers,* 3 vols. (Dayton, Ohio, 1994–1995). On the monumentation of the Gettysburg battlefield, see also Amy J. Kinsel, "History Cast in Stone: Union Regimental Monuments at Gettysburg," paper presented at the Annual Meeting of the American Historical Association, Jan. 11, 1998, Seattle, Washington.

16. Vindication as an element in the writings of Civil War veterans after the war is discussed in Blight, *Race and Reunion,* 149–168. Blight's book also reveals with eloquence and pathos how whites in the half-century after the Civil War pushed African Americans and the part they played in the war to the margins of the American memory. On the many disputes between Gettysburg veterans, see Richard A. Sauers, "Gettysburg Controversies," *Gettysburg Magazine* 4 (Jan. 1991): 113–125; Weeks, *Gettysburg,* 58–64; Desjardin, *These Honored Dead,* 53–176. For Southerners, Longstreet became their favorite Gettysburg scapegoat, although Richard Ewell, J. E. B. Stuart, and Ambrose Powell Hill also came in for their share of criticism by former Confederates.

17. Norton, "Our Fallen Comrades," 338, 342–344. Some historians have begun to challenge Norton's credibility in his accounts of the fight for Little Round Top, especially his compilation of eyewitness records, which he uses to extol the heroic virtues of Strong Vincent, in his book, *The Attack and Defense of Little Round Top* (New York, 1913). See Desjardin, *These Honored Dead,* 24–32. Desjardin, however, is a bit too hard on Norton.

18. "United at Gettysburg," *New York Times,* July 3, 1888; Blanck and Song, "'Never Forget What They Did Here,'" 1146–1165.

19. Thomas J. Grier to John B. Bachelder, June 1, 1888, in Ladd and Ladd, *Bachelder Papers,* 3:1553; John Fletcher Treutlen to William C. Oates, Aug. 24, 1879, in the possession of Dr. Jack Anderson, Enterprise, Alabama (1994); Byron M. Cutcheon to J. C. Johnson, Jan. 25, 1889, in Ladd and Ladd, *Bachelder Papers,* 3:1601; Norman H. Camp to Bachelder, Dec. 3, 1889, in ibid., 3:1682–1683.

20. William Thomas Fluker Jr., A Graphic Account of the Battle of Little Round Top at Gettysburg, ca. 1890–1900, 15th Georgia Infantry File, Gettysburg National Military Park (GNMP); Norton, "Fallen Comrades," 337, 340, 344, 341.

21. Alexander quoted in Gary W. Gallagher, *The Confederate War: How Popular Will, Nationalism, and Military Strategy Could Not Stave Off Defeat* (Cambridge, Mass., 1997), 105; C. H. Salter to Isabella Duffield, Burton Historical Collection, Detroit Public Library; Recollections of Captain Frank J. Bell, July 2nd [no year]: Pennsylvania Reserves File, GNMP.

22. Fluker, A Graphic Account, ca. 1890–1900, 15th Georgia Infantry File, Gettysburg National Military Park (GNMP); William H. Owen to Sister, May 26, 1863, Owen Letters, in the private possession of Harold M. Owen, Milo, Maine (1995); William C. Oates to Joshua L. Chamberlain, March 8, 1897, Schoff Civil War Collection, William L. Clements Library, University of Michigan, Ann Arbor. On Union and Confederate soldiers as friendly enemies, see Reid Mitchell, *Civil War Soldiers* (New York, 1988), 36–44; James I. Robertson Jr., *Soldiers Blue and Gray* (Columbia, S.C., 1988), 139–144; Daniel N. Rolph, *My Brother's Keeper: Union and Confederate Soldiers' Acts of Mercy during the Civil War* (Mechanicsburg, Pa., 2002); James McIvor, *God Rest Ye Merry, Soldiers: A True Civil War Christmas Story* (New York, 2005). For veterans and the process of reconciliation, see Blight, *Race and Reunion,* 140–210. Since 1861, Americans have often described the Civil War as a conflict that pitted "brother against brother." In a few cases that was literally true. See, for example, Bruce Catton, "Brother against Brother," *American Heritage* 12 (April 1961): 4–7, 89–93; Frank Otto Gatell, "The Slaveholder and the Abolitionist:

Binding Up a Family's Wounds," *Journal of Southern History* 27 (Aug. 1961): 368–391; Cruce Stark, "Brothers at/in War: One Phase of Post–Civil War Reconciliation," *Canadian Review of American Studies* 6 (Fall 1975): 174–181; Annette Tapert, ed., *The Brothers' War: Civil War Letters to Their Loved Ones from the Blue and Gray* (New York, 1989); J. Power Tracey, "'Brother against Brother': Alexander and James Campbell's Civil War," *South Carolina Historical Magazine* 95 (1994): 130–141; Bruce Chadwick, ed., *Brother against Brother: The Lost Civil War Diary of Lieutenant Edmund Halsey* (Secaucus, N.J., 1997); James M. McPherson, *Ordeal by Fire: The Civil War and Reconstruction,* 3rd ed. (New York, 2001), 167–168, 196; Amy Murrell Taylor, *The Divided Family in Civil War America* (Chapel Hill, N.C., 2006).

23. Oliver W. Norton to Friends at Home, July 17, 1863, in Norton, *Army Letters,* 165; Gary W. Gallagher, ed., *Fighting for the Confederacy: The Personal Recollections of General Edward Porter Alexander* (Chapel Hill, N.C., 1989), 404; Edward Porter Alexander, *Military Memoirs of a Confederate: A Critical Narrative* (New York, 1907), 53; Charles Francis Adams Jr. to Henry Adams, July 27, 1864, in Worthington C. Ford, ed., *A Cycle of Adams Letters, 1861–1865,* 2 vols. (Boston and New York, 1920), 2:168. On the war as a holocaust of bloodletting and destruction, see Charles Royster, *The Destructive War: William Tecumseh Sherman, Stonewall Jackson, and the Americans* (New York, 1991). Some scholars are not convinced that the Civil War was a "total war," although the consensus seems to be that it was. As Mark Grimsley explains, the term "total war," when used in the context of the Civil War, has been defined in two ways: "to indicate a no-holds-barred conflict that targets civilians as readily as soldiers, or to describe a war in which one side or both mobilize their populations and economies to a high degree and conduct large-scale attacks on their opponent's war resources." I agree with his assessment that "the American Civil War fits the second definition but not the first." Grimsley, "Surviving Military Revolutions: The U.S. Civil War," in MacGregor Knox and Williamson Murray, eds., *The Dynamics of Military Revolution, 1300–2050* (Cambridge and New York, 2001), 75n. See also Grimsley, "Modern War / Total War," in Steven E. Woodworth, ed., *The American Civil War: A Handbook of Literature and Research* (Westport, Conn., 1996), 379–389. Several historians implicitly accept Grimsley's second definition as their own. See, for example, James M. McPherson, "From Limited to Total War, 1861–1865," in McPherson, *Drawn with the Sword: Reflections on the American Civil War* (New York and Oxford, 1996), 66–86; Daniel E. Sutherland, "Abraham Lincoln, John Pope, and the Origins of Total War," *Journal of Military History* 56 (Oct. 1992): 567–586; Lance Janda, "Shutting the Gates of Mercy: The American Origins of Total War, 1860–1880," *Journal of Military History* 59 (1995): 7–26; James M. McPherson, "No Peace without Victory, 1861–1865," *American Historical Review* 109 (2004): 1–18. In an argument that is outweighed by compelling evidence to the contrary, Mark Neely avers that the Civil War could not possibly have been a total war. But his insistence is based on an obstinate adherence to Grimsley's first definition of "total war." See Neely, "Was the Civil War a Total War?" *Civil War History* 37 (1991): 5–28; Neely, "'Civilized Belligerents': Abraham Lincoln and the Idea of 'Total War,'" in John Y. Simon and Michael E. Stevens, eds. *New Perspectives on the Civil War:*

Myths and Realties of the National Conflict (Madison, Wis., 1998), 3–23. Insightfully and eloquently, Bruce Catton first made the case that the Emancipation Proclamation was the real turning point of the Civil War and that the document, by means of its military purpose, transformed the limited war into a total war and, all at once, changed what had been up until that time a war for the Union into a war for freedom. See, for example, Bruce Catton, *Terrible Swift Sword* (Garden City, N.Y., 1963), 461–470; Catton, *Never Call Retreat* (Garden City, N.Y., 1965), 49–50, 276–277. See also James M. McPherson, *Crossroads of Freedom: Antietam* (New York, 2002).

24. Quoted in Weeks, *Gettysburg*, 216.

1. Lee's Old War Horse

This is a revised version of my article "Considering Longstreet's Legacy," in *MHQ: The Quarterly Journal of Military History* 11 (Winter 1999): 60–69, and is used with permission.

1. James Longstreet, *From Manassas to Appomattox: Memoirs of the Civil War in America* (Philadelphia, 1896), 638.
2. Lafayette McLaws to Wife, July 7, 1863, McLaws Papers, Southern Historical Collection, University of North Carolina, Chapel Hill.
3. Robert K. Krick, "'If Longstreet . . . Says So, It Is Most Likely Not True': James Longstreet and the Second Day at Gettysburg," in Gary W. Gallagher, ed., *The Second Day at Gettysburg: Essays on Confederate and Union Leadership* (Kent, Ohio, 1993), 57–58.
4. Longstreet, *From Manassas to Appomattox*, 15.
5. G. Moxley Sorrel, *Recollections of a Confederate Staff Officer* (New York, 1905), 23.
6. Quoted in Gamaliel Bradford, *Confederate Portraits* (Boston and New York, 1914), 65.
7. Arthur James Lyon Fremantle, *Three Months in the Southern States: April–June 1863* (New York, 1864), 266; Thomas W. Cutrer, ed., *Longstreet's Aide: The Civil War Letters of Major Thomas J. Goree* (Charlottesville and London, 1995), 26.
8. Fremantle, *Three Months*, 261; Cutrer, *Longstreet's Aide*, 39.
9. Robert U. Johnson and Clarence C. Buel, eds., *Battles and Leaders of the Civil War*, 4 vols. (New York, 1884–1889), 3:81.
10. John C. West, *A Texan in Search of a Fight* (Waco, Tex., 1901), 115.
11. Jeffry D. Wert, *General James Longstreet: The Confederacy's Most Controversial Soldier—A Biography* (New York, 1993), 152, 200.
12. *New York Times*, Aug. 19, 1894.
13. Wert, *General James Longstreet*, 52.
14. Ibid., 54.
15. Helen D. Longstreet, *Lee and Longstreet at High Tide: Gettysburg in the Light of the Official Records* (Gainesville, Ga., 1904), 83–84.
16. Longstreet to Joseph E. Johnston, Oct. 6, 1862, Longstreet Papers, Duke University.
17. Bradford, *Confederate Portraits*, 69.
18. Cutrer, *Longstreet's Aide*, 60.

19. Wert, *General James Longstreet*, 133.

20. C. Vann Woodward, ed., *Mary Chesnut's Civil War* (New Haven and London, 1981), 509.

21. Johnson and Buel, *Battles and Leaders*, 3:246.

22. John Bell Hood, *Advance and Retreat: Personal Experiences in the United States and Confederate States Armies* (New Orleans, 1880), 57.

23. Longstreet, *From Manassas to Appomattox*, 386–387.

24. *Annals of the War Written by Leading Participants* (Philadelphia, 1879), 430.

25. Fremantle, *Three Months*, 269.

26. *Southern Historical Society Papers* 5 (1878): 71.

27. Johnson and Buel, *Battles and Leaders*, 2:524.

28. Quoted in William Garrett Piston, *Lee's Tarnished Lieutenant: James Longstreet and His Place in Southern History* (Athens, Ga., 1987), 74.

29. Wert, *General James Longstreet*, 410–411.

30. Cutrer, *Longstreet's Aide*, 175.

31. Sorrel, *Recollections*, 26, 79.

2. Frank A. Haskell

This is a revised version of an article that first appeared in *Columbiad* 3 (Fall 1999): 39–55, and is used with permission.

1. Glenn W. LaFantasie, ed., *Gettysburg: Lt. Frank A. Haskell, U.S.A., and Col. William C. Oates, C.S.A.* (New York, 1992), 213–214. There are several brief biographies of Haskell, most of them published as introductions to the various editions of his account of Gettysburg, but the most complete and authoritative is by Frank L. Byrne and Andrew T. Weaver, eds., *Haskell of Gettysburg: His Life and Civil War Papers* (Kent, Ohio, 1989).

2. Bruce Catton, introduction to Frank A. Haskell, *The Battle of Gettysburg* (Boston, 1958), xvii. There have been more than a dozen different editions of Haskell's long letter, the first of which was published in pamphlet form by his brother, Harvey Haskell, around 1881. The original manuscript of Haskell's letter is located in the collections of the Pennsylvania State Archives, Pennsylvania Historical and Museum Commission, Harrisburg.

3. Harrison S. Haskell, "Biographical Sketch of Frank A. Haskell," n.d., Frank A. Haskell Papers, State Historical Society of Wisconsin, Madison (hereafter SHSW). For information about the Haskell family, see Ira J. Haskell, *Chronicles of the Haskell Family* (Lynn, Mass., 1943).

4. Haskell, "Biographical Sketch," Haskell Papers, SHSW.

5. Ibid.

6. The statement was made by Edwin David Sanborn, professor of Latin at Dartmouth. The quote is taken from Byrne and Weaver, *Haskell of Gettysburg*, 1.

7. Frederick A. Stare, "Sketch of Frank A. Haskell," March 1965, Haskell Papers, SHSW.

8. Elisha Keyes quoted in Byrne and Weaver, *Haskell of Gettysburg*, 13.

9. Rufus R. Dawes, *Service with the Sixth Wisconsin Volunteers* (Marietta, Ohio, 1890), 21.

10. Ibid., 23.
11. Frank A. Haskell to brothers and sisters, Sept. 22, 1862, in Byrne and Weaver, *Haskell of Gettysburg,* 50.
12. Ibid., 49–50.
13. Ibid., 44.
14. Ibid., 44–45.
15. Ibid., 48–49.
16. During the fighting at the battle of Fredericksburg, Lee remarked to Longstreet, "It is well that war is so terrible—we should grow too fond of it." Quoted in Douglas Southall Freeman, *R. E. Lee: A Biography,* 2 vols. (New York, 1934), 2:462.
17. Haskell to family, April 23, 1863, in Byrne and Weaver, *Haskell of Gettysburg,* 60.
18. Haskell to family, June 11, 1863, Haskell Papers, SHSW. Inexplicably this letter was not published in the Byrne and Weaver collection.
19. Haskell to [Harvey Haskell?], July 16, 1863, in LaFantasie, *Gettysburg,* 201. Although the manuscript is dated July 16, it is clear from internal evidence that Haskell was still working on the letter—which might be more properly described as an essay—as late as the following November. See LaFantasie, *Gettysburg,* 32–34.
20. Haskell to [Harvey Haskell?], July 16, 1863, in LaFantasie, *Gettysburg,* 204, 205.
21. Ibid., 211.
22. Ibid., 213.
23. Ibid., 216.
24. Ibid.
25. Ibid., 223–224.
26. Ibid., 218.
27. Ibid., 217.
28. On the controversy, see LaFantasie, *Gettysburg,* 41–42; Daniel Bauer, "The Long Fight over the Bloody Angle," *Civil War* 17 (April 1989): 37–43; Richard A. Sauers, "Gettysburg Controversies," *Gettysburg Magazine* 4 (Jan. 1991): 122. The Philadelphia Brigade answered Haskell's disparagement with a publication of its own. See John W. Frazier, ed., *Reply of the Philadelphia Brigade Association to the Foolish and Absurd Narrative of Lieutenant Frank A. Haskell* (Philadelphia, n.d.).
29. Haskell to [Harvey Haskell?], July 16, 1863, in LaFantasie, *Gettysburg,* 226.
30. Ibid.
31. Haskell to family, Nov. 20, 1863, in Byrne and Weaver, *Haskell of Gettysburg,* 232–236.
32. Haskell to Harrison S. Haskell, Jan. 17, 1864, in ibid., 238.
33. Gibbon and Hancock quoted in Reuben G. Thwaites, introduction to *Frank Aretas Haskell* (Madison, Wis., 1908), xx; Hudson quoted in Byrne and Weaver, *Haskell of Gettysburg,* 246.

3. Becoming Joshua Lawrence Chamberlain

This is an expanded version of an essay first published in *North & South* 5 (Feb. 2002): 28–38, and is used with permission.

1. The standard biographies are Willard M. Wallace, *Soul of the Lion: A Biography*

of Joshua L. Chamberlain (New York, 1960); Alice Rains Trulock, *In the Hands of Providence: Joshua L. Chamberlain and the American Civil War* (Chapel Hill and London, 1992); Michael Golay, *To Gettysburg and Beyond: The Parallel Lives of Joshua Lawrence Chamberlain and Edward Porter Alexander* (New York, 1994); Mark Perry, *Conceived in Liberty: Joshua Chamberlain, William Oates, and the American Civil War* (New York, 1997); John J. Pullen, *Joshua Chamberlain: A Hero's Life and Legacy* (Mechanicsburg, Pa., 1999); Edward G. Longacre, *Joshua Chamberlain: The Soldier and the Man* (Conshohocken, Pa., 1999).

2. Chamberlain Autobiography, 3–5, National Civil War Museum, Harrisburg, Pennsylvania; George Thomas Little, ed., *Genealogical and Family History of the State of Maine,* 4 vols. (New York, 1909), 1:132–133; Diana Halderman Loski, *The Chamberlains of Brewer* (Gettysburg, Pa., 1998), 1–2. Chamberlain's unpublished autobiography exists in two copies: the more complete copy is to be found among the Chamberlain Letters, National Civil War Museum, Harrisburg, Pennsylvania; the second copy, which is missing even more pages, is among the Chamberlain Papers at Bowdoin College, Brunswick, Maine. Both are copies of the same typescript—the Harrisburg version includes pages 1–10, 21–77; the Bowdoin version consists of only pages 41–77. Pages 11–20 are apparently not extant. For purposes of convenience, the Harrisburg copy is the one cited in these notes. Chamberlain never completed his autobiography. It ends, on p. 77, with his departure for war with the 20th Maine in 1862. It is not evident if the typescript is, in fact, the original autobiography written by Chamberlain, or if it had been copied from a handwritten manuscript that has not been found.

3. Little, *Genealogical and Family History,* 1:133; Chamberlain Autobiography, 5–6. Some sources insist that Chamberlain was named Lawrence Joshua at birth and that he later reversed the order of his first and middle names. See Trulock, *In the Hands of Providence,* 26–27. However, he explicitly states in his autobiography that his parents named him simply Lawrence (no middle name) and that his mother added Joshua as a "prefix" long after his birth. Chamberlain Autobiography, 6.

4. Mildred N. Thayer and Mrs. Edward M. Ames, *Brewer, Orrington, Holden, Eddington: History and Families* (Brewer, Me., 1962), 185, 244–245; Little, *Genealogical and Family History,* 1:133; Chamberlain Autobiography, 4.

5. Chamberlain Autobiography, 45–46; "He Was A Nice Old Man" (Interview of Catherine T. Smith), *Brunswick Times Record,* Sept. 7, 1976. Smith was Chamberlain's secretary in his later years.

6. Chamberlain Autobiography, 6, 29–30, 42–43, 46–48; Chamberlain Association of America, *Joshua Lawrence Chamberlain: A Sketch* (n.p., [1906]), 4–5; Catherine T. Smith, "Brunswick's 'Soldier Statesman,'" *Brunswick Times Record,* Sept. 7, 1976. It is likely that Chamberlain himself wrote the sketch published by the Chamberlain Association of America.

7. Chamberlain Autobiography, 29, 42.

8. Chamberlain Autobiography, 25–26, 60–61; Chamberlain Association, *Sketch,* 4.

9. Chamberlain Autobiography, 27; Chamberlain Association, *Sketch,* 6.

10. Chamberlain Autobiography, 28–30, 34–36; Chamberlain Association, *Sketch,* 6.

11. Chamberlain Autobiography, 36–40; Chamberlain Association, *Sketch,* 7–8.

12. Chamberlain Autobiography, 41–42.
13. Ibid., 49–52.
14. Ibid., 54–55, 60–65; Chamberlain Association, *Sketch,* 8.
15. Chamberlain Autobiography, 55, 57–60, 63–64.
16. Ibid., 65–69.
17. Charles Edward Stowe, *Life of Harriet Beecher Stowe* (Boston, 1889), 131, 137, 139–162; David McCullough, "The Unexpected Mrs. Stowe," *American Heritage* 24 (Aug. 1973): 4–9, 76–80; Chamberlain Autobiography, 67, 69.
18. Chamberlain Autobiography, 69–70; Trulock, *In the Hands of Providence,* 43–46; Wallace, *Soul of the Lion,* 23.
19. Thompson Eldridge Ashby, *A History of First Parish Church of Brunswick, Maine* (Brunswick, Me., 1969), 234–235; Trulock, *In the Hands of Providence,* 44–45.
20. Frances (Fanny) C. Adams to Joshua L. Chamberlain, Jan. 1, 1852, Chamberlain Letters, National Civil War Museum, Harrisburg, Pennsylvania; S. M. Allen to Frances (Fanny) C. Adams, Jan. 9, 1852, Chamberlain–Adams Family Correspondence, Radcliffe College. On their relationship, see also Diane Monroe Smith, *Fanny and Joshua: The Enigmatic Lives of Frances Caroline Adams and Joshua Lawrence Chamberlain* (Gettysburg, Pa., 1999), which draws quite different conclusions than my own.
21. Chamberlain to Frances (Fanny) C. Adams, May 16, 1852, Chamberlain–Adams Family Correspondence, Radcliffe College.
22. Frances (Fanny) C. Adams to Chamberlain, undated ("Sunday P.M."), Chamberlain Letters, National Civil War Museum, Harrisburg, Pennsylvania; Fanny Adams to Chamberlain, undated ("Sun. eve"), ibid.
23. Frances (Fanny) C. Adams to Chamberlain, Feb. 9, 1852, Chamberlain Letters, National Civil War Museum, Harrisburg, Pennsylvania; Adams to Chamberlain, May 1, 1852, ibid.; Chamberlain to Adams, May 16, 1852, Chamberlain–Adams Family Correspondence, Radcliffe College; Chamberlain to Adams, May 28, [1852], Chamberlain Papers (Collection 10), Maine Historical Society; Adams to Chamberlain, Nov. 14, 1852, Chamberlain Letters, National Civil War Museum, Harrisburg, Pennsylvania. In an excellent study of Victorian mores and manners during the era of the Civil War, Anne C. Rose notes that it was fairly common for women to stand back "from the demonstrative sentimentality of men, as they sensed their vulnerability implicit in the inequality hidden in effusive emotion." Rose, *Victorian America and the Civil War* (New York, 1992), 150–151.
24. Chamberlain to Frances (Fanny) C. Adams, June 7, 1852, Chamberlain Papers (Collection 10), Maine Historical Society. Fanny's troubled relationship with her adoptive father had less to do with her affection for Chamberlain than it did with her reactions to his second marriage and his stern ways with her. Essentially Fanny believed that the Reverend Adams had "thrown me away." See Frances (Fanny) C. Adams to Chamberlain, Sept. 11, 1853, Chamberlain Letters, National Civil War Museum, Harrisburg, Pennsylvania; Chamberlain to Frances (Fanny) C. Adams, Oct. 23, 1853, ibid.
25. Chamberlain Autobiography, 69–71; Chamberlain Association, *Sketch,* 8, 29; Trulock, *In the Hands of Providence,* 46; Golay, *To Gettysburg and Beyond,* 37.

26. Trulock, *In the Hands of Providence,* 47; Chamberlain Autobiography, 71.
27. Chamberlain Association, *Sketch,* 3, 7; Chamberlain Autobiography, 51, 57. On the German roots of American transcendentalism, see Octavius Brooks Frothingham, *Transcendentalism in New England* (Gloucester, Mass., 1965), 1–59.
28. Chamberlain Autobiography, 71–72; Chamberlain Association, *Sketch,* 8; Smith, "Brunswick's 'Soldier Statesman,'" *Brunswick Times Record,* Sept. 7, 1976; Chamberlain to Frances (Fanny) C. Adams, [Autumn 1852], Chamberlain Papers (Collection 10), Maine Historical Society. On Victorian courtship practices, see Daniel E. Sutherland, *The Expansion of Everyday Life, 1860–1876* (New York, 1989), 114–117; Rose, *Victorian America,* 148–149. Rose observes that "the Victorians' search for emotional engagement was mediated by an attachment to individuality that injected alternative notes of assertiveness and reserve into interpersonal ties." Rose, *Victorian America,* 147.
29. Frances (Fanny) C. Adams to Charlotte Adams, Jan. 10, 1853, Chamberlain Papers (Collection 10), Maine Historical Society; Frances (Fanny) C. Adams to Chamberlain, Sept. 11, 1853, Chamberlain Letters, National Civil War Museum, Harrisburg, Pennsylvania; Golay, *To Gettysburg and Beyond,* 37. For examples of Fanny Adams's rebellious streak, see Frances (Fanny) C. Adams to Chamberlain, Jan. 1, 1852, Chamberlain Letters, National Civil War Museum, Harrisburg, Pennsylvania; Adams to Chamberlain, Nov. 21, 1852, ibid.; Deborah G. Folsom to Adams, Feb. 17, 1853, Chamberlain Papers (Collection 10), Maine Historical Society. On the woman's sphere and the ideal of domesticity in nineteenth-century America, see Barbara Welter, "The Cult of True Womanhood: 1820–1860," *American Quarterly* 18 (Summer 1966): 151–174; Nancy F. Cott, *The Bonds of Womanhood: "Woman's Sphere" in New England, 1780–1835* (New Haven and London, 1977); Carl N. Degler, *At Odds: Women and the Family in America from the Revolution to the Present* (New York, 1980). Fanny Adams has been unfairly portrayed and criticized by Chamberlain's biographers, most notably Wallace and Trulock, who fail to place her behavior within its historical context. Historians have shown, for instance, that emotional upheaval in connection with marriage plans was not uncommon among women in the nineteenth century. See, for example, Cott, *Bonds of Womanhood,* 80. For two assessments that see Fanny Chamberlain in a much more favorable light, see Smith, *Fanny and Joshua;* Jennifer Lund Smith, "The Reconstruction of 'Home': The Civil War and the Marriage of Lawrence and Fannie Chamberlain," in Carol K. Bleser and Lesley J. Gordon, eds., *Intimate Strategies of the Civil War: Military Commanders and Their Wives* (New York and Oxford, 2001), 157–177.
30. Frances (Fanny) C. Adams to Chamberlain, no date ("Sunday, P.M."), Chamberlain Letters, National Civil War Museum, Harrisburg, Pennsylvania; Adams to Chamberlain, Sept. 14, 1851, ibid.; Adams to Chamberlain, May 27, 1852, ibid.; Adams to Chamberlain, Oct. 24, 1852, ibid.; Chamberlain to Adams, Dec. 26, 1852, ibid.; Chamberlain to Adams, Feb. 9, 1853, ibid.; Adams to Chamberlain, Sept. 11, 1853, ibid.; Chamberlain to Adams, Jan. 18, 1854, ibid.; Chamberlain to Adams, April 6, 1855, Chamberlain–Adams Family Correspondence, Radcliffe College; Chamberlain to Adams, June 19, 1855, Chamberlain Letters, National Civil War Museum, Harrisburg, Pennsylvania.

31. Chamberlain Autobiography, 72–73; Chamberlain Association, *Sketch,* 9; Trulock, *In the Hands of Providence,* 52–54.

32. Chamberlain Autobiography, 73–74; Joshua L. Chamberlain to Frances (Fanny) A. Chamberlain, May 20, 1857, Chamberlain Papers (Collection 10), Maine Historical Society; Frances (Fanny) A. Chamberlain to Joshua L. Chamberlain, [Feb. 1857], Chamberlain–Adams Family Correspondence, Radcliffe College; Trulock, *In the Hands of Providence,* 54–55.

33. Chamberlain Autobiography, 74–75; Trulock, *In the Hands of Providence,* 56–57, 414n; Golay, *To Gettysburg and Beyond,* 61; Loski, *Chamberlains of Brewer,* 11–12. After the end of the Civil War, the Chamberlains lost another infant daughter, Gertrude Loraine, who was only seven months old when she died. See Trulock, *In the Hands of Providence,* 331.

34. Frances (Fanny) C. Adams to Charlotte Adams, Jan. 10, 1853, Chamberlain Papers (Collection 10), Maine Historical Society; Frances (Fanny) C. Adams to Chamberlain, Sept. 11, 1853, Chamberlain Letters, National Civil War Museum, Harrisburg.

35. Chamberlain Autobiography, 75–76. When Chamberlain did finally enlist, it was for reasons quite similar to those expressed by most Northern soldiers who became fighting men on the front lines: duty, honor, patriotism, liberty, and Union. See, for example, James M. McPherson, *For Cause and Comrades: Why Men Fought in the Civil War* (New York, 1997), 17–28; Earl J. Hess, *The Union Soldier in Battle: Enduring the Ordeal of Combat* (Lawrence, Kans., 1997), 94–109.

36. Joshua Chamberlain Jr. to Joshua L. Chamberlain, [early Sept. 1862], Chamberlain–Adams Family Correspondence, Radcliffe College; "Chamberlains, Maine History Fame, Were Opposed in Politics," *Lewiston Journal,* Oct. 31, 1942; Trulock, *In the Hands of Providence,* 8–9.

37. Louis C. Hatch, *The History of Bowdoin College* (Portland, Me., 1927), 117–118; Chamberlain Autobiography, 76; Chamberlain Association, *Sketch,* 9–10; Joshua L. Chamberlain, *The Passing of the Armies* (New York, 1915), 385–386.

38. Chamberlain Autobiography, 76; *Annual Report of the Adjutant General of the State of Maine for the Year Ending December 31, 1862* (Augusta, Me., 1863), 5–10 (hereafter *Maine Adjutant General Report,* 1862); Chamberlain to Israel Washburn Jr., July 14, 1862, Maine State Archives; Chamberlain to Washburn, July 17, 1862, ibid.; Chamberlain to Washburn, July 22, 1862, ibid. In his unpublished autobiography, Chamberlain maintained that he had initially requested a staff—not a field—officer's position from the governor, but the evidence proves him wrong. See Chamberlain Autobiography, 76; Chamberlain to Washburn, July 14, 1862, Maine State Archives.

39. Josiah Drummond to Israel Washburn, July 21, 1862, Maine State Archives; Chamberlain Autobiography, 76–77; William E. S. Whitman and Charles S. True, *Maine in the War for the Union* (Lewiston, Me., 1865), 490; Chamberlain to Washburn, Aug. 8, 1862 (first letter), Maine State Archives; Chamberlain to Washburn, Aug. 8, 1862 (second letter), ibid.; Chamberlain Association, *Sketch,* 10; *Maine Adjutant General Report,* 1862, Appendix D, 653; Nehemiah Cleaveland, *History of Bowdoin College with Biographical Sketches of Its Graduates from 1806 to 1879* (Boston, 1882), 671; Trulock, *In the Hands of Providence,* 12.

40. Chamberlain to Loring [?], Aug. 11, 1862, Chamberlain Papers, Bowdoin College; Chamberlain to Eugene Hale, 15 Aug. 1862, Maine State Archives; Chamberlain to [?], Aug. 15, 1862, ibid.; Ellis Spear, "The Story of the Raising and Organization of a Regiment of Volunteers in 1862," in Military Order of the Loyal Legion of the United States, Commandery of the District of Columbia, *War Papers* (1903), 5–6; Thomas A. Desjardin, *Stand Firm Ye Boys from Maine: The 20th Maine and the Gettysburg Campaign* (Gettysburg, Pa., 1995), 3; Trulock, *In the Hands of Providence*, 12–13. In assessing the overall experiences of Civil War soldiers, Reid Mitchell observes: "The distance between a soldier and his home helped encourage drastic changes in his behavior, even to the point of helping him create a new identity more appropriate to the conditions of war than of peace." Reid Mitchell, "The Northern Soldier and His Community," in *Toward a Social History of the American Civil War,* ed. Maris Vinovskis (Cambridge, 1990), 88. For a fuller discussion, see also Mitchell, *Civil War Soldiers,* 56–89. Chamberlain's transformation seemed to be a release from a former identity into a more comfortable new persona.

41. Trulock, *In the Hands of Providence,* 13; Desjardin, *Stand Firm Ye Boys from Maine,* 3; Spear, "Story of the Raising," 7–8; Diary of Samuel Keene, Aug. 14, Aug. 18, 1862, in the possession of Abbott Spear, Warren, Maine (1995); Diary of Nathan Clark, 3–4, Maine State Archives; William P. Lamson Jr. to Jennie H. Lamson, Aug. 20, 1862, in Roderick Engert, ed., *Maine to the Wilderness: The Civil War Letters of Pvt. William Lamson, 20th Maine Infantry* (Orange, Va., 1993), 18; Lamson to Jennie H. Lamson, Aug. 24, 1862, ibid., 20.

42. Spear, "Story of the Raising," 9–11; Trulock, *In the Hands of Providence, 77–78;* Golay, *To Gettysburg and Beyond,* 65; John J. Pullen, *The Twentieth Maine: A Volunteer Regiment in the Civil War* (Philadelphia, 1957), 1–17; Joshua L. Chamberlain to Frances (Fanny) A. Chamberlain, Oct. 26, 1862, Chamberlain Papers, Library of Congress.

43. Seldon Connor et al., *In Memoriam: Joshua Lawrence Chamberlain,* Circular No. 5, Whole Number 328, Military Order of the Loyal Legion of the United States, Commandery of the State of Maine (Portland, Me., 1914), 3; Spear, "Story of the Raising," 13–14; Clark Diary, 4–5; Joshua Chamberlain Jr. to Joshua L. Chamberlain, [early Sept. 1862], Chamberlain–Adams Family Correspondence, Radcliffe College; Keene Diary, Sept. 2, 1862; Diary of William Livermore, Sept. 2, Sept. 3, 1862, Fogler Library Special Collections, University of Maine, Orono; Theodore Gerrish, *Army Life: A Private's Reminiscences of the War* (Portland, Me., 1882), 13–15; Joshua L. Chamberlain to Frances (Fanny) A. Chamberlain, Sept. 3, 1862, Chamberlain Letters, National Civil War Museum, Harrisburg, Pennsylvania; Joshua L. Chamberlain to Frances (Fanny) A. Chamberlain, Sept. 4, 1862, ibid.; Smith, "Brunswick's 'Soldier Statesman,'" *Brunswick Times Record,* Sept. 7, 1976; Trulock, *In the Hands of Providence,* 20.

44. Joshua L. Chamberlain to Frances (Fanny) A. Chamberlain, Sept. 4, 1862, Chamberlain Letters, National Civil War Museum, Harrisburg, Pennsylvania; Chamberlain Association, *Sketch,* 10.

45. The reference is, of course, to Shaara's novel *The Killer Angels* (New York, 1974).

4. Joshua Lawrence Chamberlain and the American Dream

This chapter is a slightly revised version of my essay in Gabor Boritt, ed., *The Gettysburg Nobody Knows* (New York, 1997), 31–55, and is used with permission.

1. "The Battle of Gettysburg," Nov. 1868; "Gen. Chamberlain's Lecture—The Battle of Gettysburg," Nov. 1868; "The Bay State Lecture"—all newspaper clippings, Scrapbook, Chamberlain Papers, Library of Congress, Washington, D.C. (hereafter LC).

2. Chamberlain to Frances (Fanny) A. Chamberlain, Oct. 10, 26, Nov. 3, 1862, Chamberlain Papers, LC; Chamberlain, "My Story of Fredericksburg," in "*Bayonet! Forward*": *My Civil War Reminiscences*, ed. Stan Clark Jr. (Gettysburg, 1994), 7. The article was originally published in *Cosmopolitan Magazine* 54 (Dec. 1912): 148–159.

3. Chamberlain, *The Passing of the Armies* (New York, 1915), 19–20, 76, 331.

4. Ibid., 260–261. See also John B. Gordon, *Reminiscences of the Civil War* (New York, 1903), 444–445. Chamberlain's honesty in telling this story of the surrender—and the role he actually played at Appomattox—has been recently challenged by historians. See, for example, William Marvel, *A Place Called Appomattox* (Chapel Hill, 2000), 358–359.

5. Chamberlain, *Passing of the Armies*, 386.

6. Chamberlain, "Address of Gen. Chamberlain at the Springfield City Hall," *Springfield Republican*, June 4, 1897; Chamberlain, "Oration on the One-Hundredth Anniversary of the Birth of Abraham Lincoln" (1909), in "*Bayonet! Forward*": *My Civil War Reminiscences*, ed. Stan Clark Jr. (Gettysburg, 1994), 244.

7. Chamberlain Association of America, *Joshua Lawrence Chamberlain: A Sketch* (n.p., [1906]), 15–16. On Grant's field promotion of Chamberlain, see Ulysses S. Grant, *Memoirs and Selected Letters* (New York, 1990), 601–602.

8. G. W. Carleton to A. B. Farwell, Jan. 6, 1866, Frost Family Papers, Yale University Library, New Haven, Connecticut; Gordon, *Reminiscences*, 444; Theodore Gerrish, *Army Life: A Private's Reminiscences of the Civil War* (Portland, Me., 1882), 347.

9. Chamberlain, "Address of Gen. Chamberlain at the Springfield City Hall," *Springfield Republican*, June 4, 1897. Chamberlain wrote during the war: "I believe in destiny—one, I mean, divinely appointed." Chamberlain to Sarah D. B. Chamberlain, [Autumn 1864], Chamberlain Collection, Bowdoin College.

10. Chamberlain, "Joshua as a Military Commander," *Sunday School Times*, Dec. 1, 1883.

11. Report of Colonel Joshua L. Chamberlain, July 6, 1863, U.S. War Department, *The War of the Rebellion: A Compilation of the Official Records of the Union and Confederate Armies*, 128 vols., index, and atlas (Washington, D.C., 1880–1901), Ser. 1, 27, Pt. 1, 622–626 (hereafter *O.R.*, with all references to Ser. 1). Actually this report, although dated just after the battle, was written by Chamberlain in 1884, after the editors of the *O.R.* informed him that his original report was missing from the War Records files and asked him to supply a replacement. He did so by trying to reconstruct his original report from memory. See Joshua L. Chamberlain to George B. Herenden, July 6, 1863 [ca. March 15, 1884], Records of the War

Records Officer, Entry 729, "Union Battle Reports," RG 94 (Records of the Adjutant General's Office), National Archives, Washington, D.C. (hereafter NA). One can only guess how much of this report can be attributed to Chamberlain's hazy memory or wishful thinking. Another battle report by Chamberlain does exist, also dated July 6, 1863, and this one seems to be a copy of the original lost report. See Chamberlain to Herenden, July 6, 1863, Maine State Archives, Augusta, Maine. My thanks to Thomas A. Desjardin for graciously sharing with me his discovery of when Chamberlain actually wrote his published official report.

12. Chamberlain to Frances (Fanny) A. Chamberlain, July 4, 1863, July 17, 1863, Chamberlain Papers, LC; Chamberlain to Governor Abner Coburn, July 21, 1863, Maine State Archives. It is not true that the 20th Maine actually defeated an entire Confederate brigade, as Chamberlain had claimed. For an examination of the numbers of troops involved in the Little Round Top fight, see Thomas A. Desjardin, *Stand Firm Ye Boys from Maine: The 20th Maine and the Gettysburg Campaign* (Gettysburg, 1995), Appendix 1.

13. Chamberlain to Frances (Fanny) A. Chamberlain, Chamberlain Papers, LC; Report of Colonel James C. Rice, July 31, 1863, *O.R.,* 27, pt. 1, 618, 620; Report of General James Barnes, Aug. 24, 1863, ibid., 603–604; Chamberlain to Frances (Fanny) A. Chamberlain, July 4, 1863, Chamberlain Papers, LC.

14. Chamberlain to Frances (Fanny) A. Chamberlain, Nov. 3, 1862, Chamberlain Papers, LC; *Bridgton News,* April 29, 1898; James Barnes to Chamberlain, Sept. 1, 1863, Maine State Archives; Chamberlain to Barnes, Sept. 3, 1863, Barnes Papers, New York Historical Society, New York; James Rice to William Pitt Fessenden, Sept. 8, 1863, Maine State Archives.

15. Charles H. Howard to Chamberlain, Sept. 14, 1863, Joshua L. Chamberlain Personnel File, Letters Received by the Commission Branch of the Adjutant General's Office, 1863–1870, RG 94, NA; Adelbert Ames to Edwin S. Stanton, Sept. 21, 1863, ibid.; John H. Rice to Abraham Lincoln, Sept. 26, 1863, ibid.; Israel Washburn to Stanton, Sept. 27, 1863, ibid.; Charles Griffin to Seth Williams, Oct. 7, 1863, Maine State Archives; Charles Gilmore to Abner Coburn, Oct. 8, 1863, ibid.; Hannibal Hamlin to Lincoln, Oct. 16, 1863, ibid.; E. B. French to Stanton, Oct. 29, 1863, Chamberlain Military Personnel File, NA.

16. Joseph B. Mitchell, *The Badge of Gallantry: Recollections of Civil War Congressional Medal of Honor Winners* (New York, 1968), 130; Chamberlain, *Passing of the Armies,* xiv, 255.

17. Chamberlain Association, *Sketch,* 12–14; Willard M. Wallace, *Soul of the Lion: A Biography of Joshua L. Chamberlain* (New York, 1960), 128–136; Alice Rains Trulock, *In the Hands of Providence: Joshua L. Chamberlain and the American Civil War* (Chapel Hill and London, 1992), 198–218, 229–286, 301–311; "Gov. Chamberlain's Lecture" [at G.A.R. Post No. 9], n.d.; "A Lecture from Gen. Chamberlain," ca. 1866; "The Military Career of General Chamberlain," ca. 1866; "Four Years Ago—and Now," ca. 1867; "Gen. Joshua L. Chamberlain in the Battle of Gettysburg," ca. 1884—all unidentified newspaper clippings, Scrapbook, Chamberlain Papers, LC.

18. "General Chamberlain at Lake Forest," ca. 1868; [Political Meeting at Calais], ca. Oct. 1868; "The Battle of Gettysburg," Nov. 1868; "Gen. Chamberlain's Lecture—

The Battle of Gettysburg," Nov. 1868; "The Left at Gettysburg," ca. 1869; "Gen. Joshua L. Chamberlain in the Battle of Gettysburg," ca. 1884—all unidentified newspaper clippings, Scrapbook, Chamberlain Papers, LC.

19. Trulock, *In the Hands of Providence,* 176; John B. Bachelder to Chamberlain, Nov. 16, 1865, Aug. 1869, Aug. 14, 1869, Chamberlain Papers, LC; Report of the Reunion of Officers of the Army of the Potomac, Aug. 22–28, 1869, John P. Nicholson Papers, Huntington Library, San Marino, California.

20. Chamberlain, "General Chamberlain's Address," in *Dedication of the Twentieth Maine Monuments at Gettysburg, Oct. 3, 1889* (Waldoboro, Me., 1891), 26–31; Chamberlain, "General Chamberlain's Address," in Charles Hamlin et al., eds., *Maine at Gettysburg: Report of the Commissioners* (Portland, Me., 1898), 546–559. On the "over-soul," see Ralph Waldo Emerson, "The Over-Soul," in *Essays and Lectures,* ed. Joel Porte, Library of America (New York, 1983), 383–400.

21. See, for example, Amos M. Judson, *History of the Eighty-Third Regiment of Pennsylvania Volunteers* (Eire, Pa., 1865), 123–141; William C. Oates, "Gettysburg—The Battle on the Right," *Southern Historical Society Papers* 6 (1878): 172–182; An Old Private [Theodore Gerrish], "The Twentieth Maine at Gettysburg," *Portland Advertiser,* Mar. 13, 1882; James H. Nichols, "Letter of Theodore Gerrish," *Lincoln County News,* April 1882; Gerrish, *Army Life,* 100–119; Holman S. Melcher, "The 20th Maine at Gettysburg," *Lincoln County News,* March 13, 1885; Spear, "Memorial Day Speech Given at Warren, Maine," May 30, 1888, in possession of the late Abbott Spear, Warren, Maine (1994).

22. Chamberlain, "Gen. Chamberlain's Address," in *Dedication,* 27–29; Carswell McClelland to Chamberlain, May 12, 22, 1891, Chamberlain Papers, LC.

23. Thomas Hubbard to the Secretary of War, Feb. 15, 1893; Fitz John Porter to the Secretary of War, May 19, 1893; Alexander S. Webb to the Secretary of War, May 23, 1893; Henry B. Cleaves to the Secretary of War, June 7, 1893—all Chamberlain Military Personnel File, NA. On the 20th Maine Regimental Association, founded in 1876, see William B. Styple, ed., *With a Flash of His Sword: The Writings of Major Holman S. Melcher, 20th Maine Infantry* (Kearny, N.J., 1994), 245–291.

24. Memorandum, Aug. 11, 1893, Chamberlain Military Personnel File, NA; F. C. Ainsworth to Chamberlain, Aug. 17, 1893, William C. Oates Correspondence, Gettysburg National Military Park, Gettysburg, Pennsylvania (hereafter GNMP); Chamberlain to Ainsworth, Sept. 16, 1893, Chamberlain Military Personnel File, NA; Memorandum, March 21, 1897, ibid.; Chamberlain to Ainsworth, Sept. 24, 1907, ibid.; Ainsworth to Chamberlain, Sept. 30, Oct. 19, 1907, ibid.; Chamberlain to Ainsworth, Oct. 21, 1907, ibid.; Chamberlain, *Passing of the Armies,* 390. The official citation reads: "Daring heroism and great tenacity in holding his position on the Little Round Top against repeated assaults, and carrying the advance position on Great Round Top." U. S. Army, *The Medal of Honor of the United States Army* (Washington, D.C., 1948), 139.

25. For example, see William E. S. Whitman and Charles H. True, *Maine in the War for the Union: A History* (Lewiston, Me., 1865), 493–494; William Swinton, *Campaigns of the Army of the Potomac* (New York, 1882 [orig. publ. 1866]), 346–347; Samuel P. Bates, *The Battle of Gettysburg* (Philadelphia,1875), 117–120; Louis Philippe Albert d'Orleans, Comte de Paris, *The Battle of Gettysburg* (Philadel-

phia, 1886), 167, 171, 177–178, 182; Jacob Hoke, *The Great Invasion, or, General Lee in Pennsylvania* (Dayton, 1887), 332–333; James H. Stine, *History of the Army of the Potomac* (Philadelphia, 1892), 511–512; William H. Powell, *The Fifth Army Corps (Army of the Potomac)* (New York, 1896), 525–531; John M. Vanderslice, *Gettysburg: Then and Now* (New York, 1899), 155.

26. Bachelder to Chamberlain, Dec. 21, 1892, Chamberlain Papers, LC; Hubbard to the Secretary of War, Feb. 15, 1893, Chamberlain Military Personnel File, NA; Chamberlain Association, *Sketch*, 30. Chamberlain Avenue no longer exists on Little Round Top; it was torn up and removed many years ago, although the old roadbed is still plainly visible.

27. Holman S. Melcher to Chamberlain, March 4, May 15, 1895; Samuel L. Miller to Chamberlain, May 21, 1895; Spear to Chamberlain, May 22, 1895; Charles Hamlin to Chamberlain, May 23, 1895; George W. Verrill to Chamberlain, June 11, 1896; Hamlin to Chamberlain, July 3, 6, 7, 1896—all Chamberlain Papers, LC. For the articles, see "Twentieth Maine Regiment, Third Brigade, First Division, Fifth Army Corps, at the Battle of Gettysburg," in Hamlin et al., *Maine at Gettysburg*, 252–262; "Historical Sketch by an Officer of the Regiment," in ibid., 273–285.

28. Chamberlain to William C. Oates (incomplete draft), Feb. 27, 1897, Chamberlain Collection, Bowdoin College; Oates to Chamberlain, March 8, 1897, William Clements Library, University of Michigan, Ann Arbor.

29. Oates to William M. Robbins, April 1, 1902; Oates to Root, June 2, 1903; Nicholson to Chamberlain, Aug. 6, 1903; Chamberlain to Nicholson, Aug. 14, 1903; Nicholson to Chamberlain, Aug. 21, 1903; Nicholson to Chamberlain, Aug. 24, 1903; Oates to Robbins, July 18, 1904—all Oates Correspondence, GNMP.

30. Oates to Nicholson, March 1, 1905; Oates to Chamberlain, April 14, 1905; Chamberlain to Oates, May 18, 1905; Nicholson to Chamberlain, May 22, 1905—all Oates Correspondence, GNMP. Oates's Civil War recollections, which contain a full account of the attack on Little Round Top, were published in 1905. See Oates, *The War between the Union and the Confederacy and Its Lost Opportunities* (New York and Washington, D.C., 1905), 206–209.

31. Ellis Spear, "The 20th Maine at Gettysburg," n.d., newspaper clipping, pasted in Diary of John Chamberlain, Pejepscot Historical Society, Brunswick, Maine; Spear to Chamberlain, July 2, 1882, Chamberlain Papers, LC; Spear, "Memorial Day Speech"; Spear to Bachelder, Nov. 15, 1892, Bachelder Papers, New Hampshire Historical Society, Concord, New Hampshire; Spear to Chamberlain, May 22, 1895, Chamberlain Papers, LC.

32. Styple, *With a Flash of His Sword*, 294; W. F. Beyer and O. F. Keydel, eds., *Deeds of Valor: How America's Heroes Won the Medal of Honor*, 2 vols. (Detroit, 1905), 1:246–248.

33. Chamberlain, "My Story of Fredericksburg," 1–15; Chamberlain, "Through Blood and Fire at Gettysburg," *Hearst's Magazine* 23 (June 1913): 894–909; Trulock, *In the Hands of Providence*, 528n; Spear, "The Hoe Cake of Appomattox," in *War Papers, No. 93, Read before the Military Order of the Loyal Legion of the United States, Washington, D.C., Commandery*, May 7, 1913; Abbott Spear, *The 20th Maine at Fredericksburg: The 1913 Accounts of Generals Chamberlain and Spear* (Warren,

Me., 1987); Spear, "The Left at Gettysburg"; Spear, "Recollections" (typescript), n.d., 20th Maine Infantry folder, GNMP. Chamberlain expressed displeasure with the way his article in *Hearst's Magazine* had been "mutilated" and "corrected" by its editors. See Chamberlain to Mrs. Eckstrom, May 28, 1913, Fogler Library Special Collections, University of Maine, Orono. My thanks to Thomas A. Desjardin for bringing this letter to my attention.

34. Norton to Spear, Jan. 12, 1916, in the possession of the late Abbott Spear; Spear to Norton, Jan. 18, 1916, Feb. 1, 1916, both in Styple, *With a Flash of His Sword*, 297–299; Oliver Willcox Norton, *The Attack and Defense of Little Round Top: Gettysburg, July 2, 1863* (New York, 1913).

35. See, for example, Henry Sweetser Burrage, *Gettysburg and Lincoln: The Battle, the Cemetery, and the National Park* (New York and London, 1906), 42–43; E. A. Nash, *History of the Forty-Fourth Regiment New York Volunteer Infantry in the Civil War, 1861–1865* (Chicago, 1911), 143–148; Jesse Bowman Young, *The Battle of Gettysburg: A Comprehensive Narrative* (New York and London, 1913), 237–238.

36. Trulock, *In the Hands of Providence*, 374–376; Wallace, *Soul of the Lion*, 310; Bruce Catton, "Survivor," *American Heritage* 30 (Dec. 1978): 111.

37. Kenneth Roberts, *Trending into Maine* (Boston, 1938), 42–51; Earl Schenk Miers and Richard A. Brown, eds., *Gettysburg* (New Brunswick, N.J., 1948), 145–151; Bruce Catton, *Glory Road* (Garden City, N.Y., 1952), 292–293; John J. Pullen, *The Twentieth Maine: A Volunteer Regiment in the Civil War* (Philadelphia, 1957), 3; Wallace, *Soul of the Lion*.

38. Michael Shaara, *The Killer Angels* (New York, 1974), 250.

39. Ibid., 126, 229, 239.

40. [Boyd M. Harris], *Field Manual 22–100: Military Leadership (October 1983)* (Washington, D.C., 1983), 4–17, 56–62, 71–72, 82, 90–91, 121–127, 138–139, 148–149, 168–170, 174–175, 190–191, 265–266. Army personnel who attend "staff rides" on the Gettysburg battlefield usually hear about Chamberlain as well. See Jay Luvaas and Harold W. Nelson, eds., *The U. S. Army War College Guide to the Battle of Gettysburg* (Carlisle, Pa., 1986), 84–88.

41. See, for instance, Richard Pindell, "Fighting for Little Round Top: The 20th Maine," *Civil War Times Illustrated* 21 (Feb. 1983): 12–20; Champ Clark et al., eds., *Gettysburg: The Confederate High Tide* (Alexandria, Va., 1985), 83–84; Harry W. Pfanz, *Gettysburg—The Second Day* (Chapel Hill and London, 1987), 232–236, 402–403; Richard Wheeler, *Witness to Gettysburg* (New York, 1987), 190–197; David F. Cross, "Mantled in Fire and Smoke," *America's Civil War* 4 (Jan. 1992): 39–44; Eric J. Wittenberg, "The Fighting Professor: Joshua Lawrence Chamberlain," *Civil War* 10 (July–Aug. 1992): 8–14; James M. McPherson, *Gettysburg* (Atlanta, 1993), 56–63; Kent Gramm, *Gettysburg: A Meditation of War and Values* (Bloomington, Ind., 1994), 135–141.

42. "A 'Civil War' for the Masses," *Los Angeles Times*, July 22, 1990; "'Civil War': A Triumph on All Fronts," *Washington Post*, Oct. 2, 1990; Geoffrey C. Ward, with Ric Burns and Ken Burns, *The Civil War: An Illustrated History* (New York, 1990).

43. "When War Was All Glory and Bands and Death," *New York Times*, Oct. 8, 1993. See also C. Peter Jorgensen, "Gettysburg: How a Prize-Winning Novel Became a

Motion Picture," *Civil War Times Illustrated* 32 (Nov.–Dec. 1993): 40–49, 92. The film has since been shown in several foreign countries, broadcast on cable television, and released on videocassette and DVD.

44. Geoffrey C. Ward, "Hero of the 20th," *American Heritage* 43 (Nov. 1992): 14; Trulock, *In the Hands of Providence.*

45. Michael Golay, *To Gettysburg and Beyond: The Parallel Lives of Joshua Lawrence Chamberlain and Edward Porter Alexander* (New York, 1994); Desjardin, *Stand Firm Ye Boys from Maine.*

46. Spear to Norton, Feb. 1, 1916, in Styple, *With a Flash of His Sword,* 299.

5. Finding William C. Oates

1. The manuscript was published by Bantam Books as part of its Eyewitness of the Civil War Series in 1992. See Glenn W. LaFantasie, *Gettysburg: Lt. Frank A. Haskell, U.S.A., and Col. William C. Oates, C.S.A.* (New York, 1992).

2. Oates's three chapters on Gettysburg were extracted and published in the Bantam edition along with Haskell's account of the battle.

3. Krick's introduction, which is unpaginated, is published in William C. Oates, *The War between the Union and the Confederacy and Its Lost Opportunities* (1905; Dayton, Ohio, 1985).

4. Oates's notation was found in William T. Sherman, *Memoirs of General William T. Sherman,* 2 vols. (New York, 1875), vol. 1.

5. Paul Murray Kendall, "Walking the Boundaries," in Stephen B. Oates, ed., *Biography as High Adventure: Life-Writers Speak on Their Art* (Amherst, Mass., 1986), 32–49, quotation at 33.

6. Quoted in Albert Burton Moore, *History of Alabama* (University, Ala., 1934), 633.

6. An Alabamian's Civil War

A different version of this chapter was given as the J. C. C. Sanders Lecture at the Alabama Department of Archives and History, Montgomery, Sept. 12, 2006. Some passages also derive from "Who Was William C. Oates, and Why Should Anyone Care?" *North & South* 9 (Dec. 2006): 34–41, and are used with permission.

1. *Montgomery Advertiser,* Sept. 10, 1910; *New York Tribune,* Sept. 10, 1910.

2. Geoffrey Wolff, "Minor Lives," in Wolff, *Black Sun: The Brief Transit and Violent Eclipse of Harry Crosby* (New York, 2003), 318.

3. Oates unpublished autobiography, chapter 1, Oates Family Papers, Alabama Department of Archives and History, Montgomery, Alabama. I used these papers when they were in the possession of Oates's granddaughter, Mrs. Robert H. Charles, of Washington, D.C., and Newport, R.I.

4. Ibid.

5. William A. McClendon, *Recollections of War Times by an Old Veteran While under Stonewall Jackson and Lieutenant General James Longstreet* (Montgomery, Ala., 1909), 14.

6. William C. Oates, *The War between the Union and the Confederacy and Its Lost Opportunities* (New York and Washington, D.C., 1905), 115.

7. Ibid., 138, 143.

8. McClendon, *Recollections,* 117; Oates, *War,* 151.

9. Oates, *War,* 140.

10. Quoted in Robert K. Krick, "Introduction," William C. Oates, *The War between the Union and the Confederacy and Its Lost Opportunities* (1905; Dayton, Ohio, 1985), unpaginated.

11. Edmund Cody Burnett, ed., "Letters of Barnett Hardeman Cody and Others, 1861–1864," *Georgia Historical Quarterly* 23 (1939): 288.

12. Oates, *War,* 227.

13. Ibid., 220.

14. Quoted in Krick, "Introduction."

15. Oates, *War,* 277.

16. Ibid., 346, 350.

17. Ibid., 367.

18. Ibid., 376.

19. Oates to Edward Porter Alexander, Aug. 25, 1868, E. P. Alexander Papers, Southern Historical Collection, University of North Carolina, Chapel Hill.

20. Albert Burton Moore, *History of Alabama* (University, Ala., 1934), 633.

21. *Official Proceedings of the Constitutional Convention of the State of Alabama, May 21st, 1901, to September 3rd, 1901,* 4 vols. (Wetumpka, Ala., 1940), 3:2789.

22. Walter B. Jones, "William Calvin Oates," *Alabama Historical Quarterly* 7 (Fall 1945): 343.

23. *Official Proceedings,* 4:4441.

24. Oates, *War,* 675.

25. Ibid., 231.

26. *Birmingham Ledger,* Sept. 9, 1910.

27. Thomas Carlyle, *On Heroes, Hero-Worship, and the Heroic in History,* ed. Michael K. Goldberg et al. (Berkeley, Calif., 1993), 13.

7. Hell in Haymarket

This chapter, which I have slightly revised, was first published as "Decimated by Disease," in *MHQ: The Quarterly Journal of Military History* 16 (Spring 2004): 86–92, and is used with permission.

1. William C. Oates, *The War between the Union and the Confederacy* (New York and Washington, D.C., 1905), 67–75.

2. Oates, *War,* 76; James Cantey to Wife, Aug. 21, 1861, in Ray Mathis, *In the Land of the Living: Wartime Letters by Confederates from the Chattahoochee Valley of Alabama and Georgia* (Troy, Ala., 1981), 14; [William A. McClendon], *Recollections of War Times* (Montgomery, Ala., 1909), 30–31 (hereafter McClendon, *Recollections*); W. E. Wight, ed., "Sam Lary's 'Scraps From My Knapsack,'" *Alabama Historical Quarterly* 18 (1956): 511.

3. McClendon, *Recollections,* 31; Oates, *War,* 76; Cantey to Samuel C. Benton,

Aug. 26, 1861, in Mathis, *In the Land of the Living,* 15; Writers Program (Virginia) of the Works Progress Administration, *Prince William: The Story of Its People and Its Places* (Manassas, Va., 1961), 160–161 (hereafter *Prince William*).

4. Cantey to Samuel C. Benton, Aug. 26, 1861, in Mathis, *In the Land of the Living,* 15; McClendon, *Recollections,* 32, 35; Wight, "Sam Lary's 'Scraps,'" 511; Oates, *War,* 76–77.

5. Oates, *War,* 76; Caspar W. Boyd to parents, Sept. 2, 1861, Boyd Letters, Simon Schwob Memorial Library, Columbus College, Columbus, Ga.; McClendon, *Recollections,* 32–34.

6. Oates, *War,* 76; McClendon, *Recollections,* 32–33.

7. McClendon, *Recollections,* 34–35.

8. Wight, "Sam Lary's 'Scraps,'" 511–512; Cantey to Samuel C. Benton, Aug. 26, 1861, in Mathis, *In the Land of the Living,* 15; Oates, *War,* 77; Jeffrey S. Sartin, "Infectious Diseases during the Civil War: The Triumph of the 'Third Army,'" *Clinical Infectious Diseases* 16 (1993): 580–584.

9. H. H. Cunningham, *Doctors in Gray: The Confederate Medical Service* (Baton Rouge, 1958), 188–190; Paul E. Steiner, *Disease in the Civil War: Natural Biological Warfare in 1861–1865* (Springfield, Ill., 1968), 12, 13, 28, 29; Sartin, "Infectious Diseases during the Civil War," 580–584; Centers for Disease Control and Prevention, "Measles," http://www.babybag.com/articles/cdc_meas.htm, June 11, 2001 [*note:* dates in Internet citations refer to date the source was accessed, not when it was created].

10. Oates, *War,* 76, 732; Wight, "Sam Lary's 'Scraps,'" 512–513.

11. Wight, "Sam Lary's 'Scraps,'" 514; William A. Edwards to W. R. Painter, Nov. 11, 1915, unidentified news clipping, 15th Alabama Regimental File, Alabama Department of Archives and History, Montgomery; McClendon, *Recollections,* 35–36.

12. Oates, *War,* 77–78.

13. Oates, *War,* 79–80, 82; Wight, "Sam Lary's 'Scraps,'" 514, 518–519; Barnett H. Cody to Henrietta S. Cody, Sept. 20, 1861, in Edmund Cody Burnett, ed., "Letters of Barnett Hardeman Cody and Others, 1861–1864," *Georgia Historical Society* 23 (1939): 292–293; McClendon, *Recollections,* 28–29.

14. Oates, *War,* 80–81; Wight, "Sam Lary's 'Scraps,'" 518; McClendon, *Recollections,* 36.

15. *Prince William,* 174–175; Robert L. Crewdson, *Crossroads of the Past: A History of Haymarket, Virginia* (Prince William, Va., n.d.), 6–8.

16. *Prince William,* 175–176; Crewdson, *Crossroads of the Past,* 8–9.

17. *Prince William,* 175–177; Crewdson, *Crossroads of the Past,* 9–10; "The Story of St. Paul's Church," in *St. Paul's Episcopal Church, Haymarket, Virginia,* 150th Anniversary Booklet ([Haymarket, Va., 1984]), 27.

18. *Prince William,* 176–177; Crewdson, *Crossroads of the Past,* 10–12; Alice Maude Ewell, "St. Paul's Church, Haymarket, Va." (1930), in *St. Paul's Episcopal Church,* 2–3.

19. Oates, *War,* 80–81; Wight, "Sam Lary's 'Scraps,'" 518; McClendon, *Recollections,* 36; *Prince William,* 176–177. On St. Paul's "heavenly trees" in its churchyard, see "The Story of St. Paul's Church," 30.

20. Oates, *War,* 82.

21. Ibid., 81. Across from the Confederate marker, on the other side of the church's front doors, another stone tablet reads: "In memory of the wounded Union soldiers who died in St. Paul's while it was a hospital during the Civil War, 1861–1865."

22. *Prince William*, 176; Crewdson, *Crossroads of the Past*, 13–17; Ewell, "St. Paul's Church, Haymarket, Va." 3.

23. It is also quite possible that the dead of the 15th Alabama were originally buried in the fields and woods across from the entrance of St. Paul's Church. If so, it would not be the first time in Virginia that a greedy developer, not wanting to risk costly delays in a project, kept a Civil War site, valuable artifacts, or bodily remains a secret from the public, unsuspecting buyers, or local authorities. One secondary source—basing its statement on local oral tradition—says that the 15th Alabama, which it incorrectly identifies as the 11th Alabama, buried its dead "on the south side of the churchyard." See "The Story of St. Paul's Church," 28.

8. William C. Oates and the Death of General Farnsworth

This is a slightly expanded version of my article in *North & South* 8 (Jan. 2005): 48–55, and is used with permission.

1. William C. Oates, *The War between the Union and the Confederacy and Its Lost Opportunities* (New York and Washington, D.C., 1905), 225–226, 235; Thomas L. Elmore, "A Meteorological and Astronomical Chronology of the Gettysburg Campaign," *Gettysburg Magazine* 13 (July 1995): 14.

2. For a full account of the fight for Little Round Top, see Glenn W. LaFantasie, *Twilight at Little Round Top: July 2, 1863, The Tide Turns at Gettysburg* (Hoboken, N.J., 2005); LaFantasie, *Gettysburg Requiem: The Life and Lost Causes of Confederate Colonel William C. Oates* (Oxford, N.Y., 2006), 69–109. For the federal side of the story, see also Thomas A. Desjardin, *Stand Firm Ye Boys from Maine: The 20th Maine and the Gettysburg Campaign* (Gettysburg, Pa., 1995), esp. chapter 2.

3. William C. Oates to John B. Bachelder, Sept. 16, 1888, in David L. Ladd and Audrey J. Ladd, eds., *The Bachelder Papers*, 3 vols. (Dayton, Ohio, 1994–1995), 3:1556. The stone wall is still standing on the southwestern slope of Big Round Top, although West Confederate Avenue now bisects it. For the movement and position of the 20th Maine on the evening of July 2 and the morning of July 3, see Desjardin, *Stand Firm Ye Boys From Maine*, 79–96.

4. Evander M. Law to John B. Bachelder, June 13, 1876, in Ladd and Ladd, *Bachelder Papers*, 1:495; Oates to Bachelder, Sept. 16, 1888, in ibid., 3:1556–1557; Evander M. Law, "The Struggle for 'Round Top,'" in Robert U. Johnson and Clarence C. Buel, eds., *Battles and Leaders of the Civil War*, 4 vols. (New York, 1884–1889), 3:327; Paul M. Shevchuk, "The 1st Texas Infantry and the Repulse of Farnsworth's Charge," *Gettysburg Magazine* 2 (Jan. 1990): 83; J. Gary Laine and Morris M. Penny, *Law's Alabama Brigade in the War between the Union and the Confederacy* (Shippensburg, Pa., 1996), 112.

5. George G. Benedict, *Vermont in the Civil War*, 2 vols. (Burlington, Vt., 1886–

1888), 2:596; Eric J. Wittenberg, *Gettysburg's Forgotten Cavalry Actions* (Gettysburg, Pa., 1998), 7, 20; Edward G. Longacre, *The Cavalry at Gettysburg: A Tactical Study of Mounted Operations during the Civil War's Pivotal Campaign, 9 June–14 July 1863* (Rutherford, N.J., 1986), 235. On Kilpatrick, see Longacre, "Judson Kilpatrick," *Civil War Times Illustrated* (June 1998), http:// www.thehistorynet.com/ CivilWarTimes/articles/1998/06982_text.htm, July 26, 2001.

6. Law, "The Struggle for 'Round Top,'" 326–327; Oates, *War*, 231–232.

7. Law to Bachelder, June 13, 1876, in Ladd and Ladd, *Bachelder Papers*, 1:495; Laine and Penny, *Law's Alabama Brigade*, 112–113; Shevchuk, "The 1st Texas Infantry," 83.

8. Law, "The Struggle for 'Round Top,'" 327; Laine and Penny, *Law's Alabama Brigade*, 113.

9. H. C. Parsons, "Farnsworth's Charge and Death," in Johnson and Buel, *Battles and Leaders*, 3:394. Precisely when this exchange took place between Kilpatrick and Farnsworth is not known. Different sources place it as occurring at different times. Some eyewitness accounts, along with some secondary reconstructions of the event, state that it happened after the cavalry charge of the 1st West Virginia against the defensive line of the 1st Texas Infantry. Other accounts claim that the argument was going on while the 18th Pennsylvania and the 5th New York cavalry were making the second-wave attack against the Texans. Most accounts seem to imply that the exchange took place immediately before the charge of the 1st Vermont, under Farnsworth's direct command. I have assumed that the conversation must have happened before any cavalry attack emerged from the woods, if only because it seems certain that Alabamians and even some Texans on the advanced skirmish lines distinctly heard the two generals arguing and realized, as a result of the exchange, that a cavalry assault was about to follow. In the lull between the charges of the 1st West Virginia and the 18th Pennsylvania and 5th New York, or any time during the course of the several attacks made by Union cavalry against the Confederate lines that day, the noise of conflict on the field would have been too pronounced for men along the skirmish line to hear two Union generals arguing in the woods, even if Kilpatrick and Farnsworth had been yelling at fever pitch. I have used Parsons's version of the argument as published in *Battle and Leaders* for my source, although several different accounts document the heated words of the two generals. For a slightly different version of Parsons's own recollection, see Parsons, "Farnsworth's Charge," http://www.nps.gov/gett/ getttour/sidebar/farnsworth.htm, July 26, 2001. Other accounts and renditions include John B. Bachelder, "General Farnsworth's Death," *Philadelphia Weekly Times*, Dec. 30, 1882; John H. Bennett, "1st Vermont Cavalry," Farnsworth Charge and Death File, Gettysburg National Military Park (GNMP); Henry Clay Potter, "Personal Experiences of Henry Clay Potter (Capt. 18th Penna. Cavalry) in Battle of Gettysburg," ibid.; S. A. Clark, "Farnsworth's Death," *National Tribune*, Dec. 3, 1891; Benedict, *Vermont in the Civil War*, 2:598–599; Oates, *War*, 235–236; Jeffrey D. Stocker, ed., *From Huntsville to Appomattox: R. T. Coles's History of 4th Regiment, Alabama Volunteer Infantry, C.S.A., Army of Northern Virginia* (Knoxville, 1996), 109–110; Edward Porter Alexander, *Military Memoirs of a Confederate: A Critical Narrative* (New York, 1907), 434; Edwin B. Coddington, *The Gettysburg*

Campaign: A Study in Command (New York, 1968), 524–525; Longacre, *Cavalry at Gettysburg*, 240–244; Gary Kross, "Farnsworth's Charge," *Blue and Gray Magazine* 13 (Feb. 1996): 44–53; Wittenberg, *Gettysburg's Forgotten Cavalry Actions*, 23–27; Jeffry D. Wert, *Gettysburg: Day Three* (New York, 2001), 272–280.

10. On Farnsworth, see Eric J. Wittenberg, "Elon J. Farnsworth: Brigadier General," http://www.civilwarcavalry.com/farnsworthbio.htm, July 26, 2001; J. David Petruzzi, "Biography of Elon J. Farnsworth," http://www.bufordsboys.com/FarnsworthEBiography.htm, July 26, 2001; "The Unsung Hero of Gettysburg: Brig. Gen. Elon J. Farnsworth," http://members.aol.com/Acw6165/farnsworth.html, July 26, 2001.

11. Henry Clay Potter, "Personal Experiences of Henry Clay Potter (Capt. 18th Penna. Cavalry) in Battle of Gettysburg," Farnsworth Charge and Death File, GNMP; Parsons, "Farnsworth's Charge and Death," 394; Longacre, *Cavalry at Gettysburg*, 242–243; Shevchuk, "The 1st Texas Infantry," 85–89; Wittenberg, *Gettysburg's Forgotten Cavalry Actions*, 20–23.

12. Parsons, "Farnsworth's Charge and Death," 394–395; Longacre, *Cavalry at Gettysburg*, 242–243; Wittenberg, *Gettysburg's Forgotten Cavalry Actions*, 27–28.

13. Oates, *War*, 235–236; Seymour H. Wood to H. Nelson Jackson, Nov. 13, 1913, Vermont in the Civil War, http://vermontcivilwar.org/1cav/h/045.shtml, July 26, 2001.

14. Law to Bachelder, June 13, 1876, in Ladd and Ladd, *Bachelder Papers*, 1:496–497; Bachelder, "General Farnsworth's Death," *Philadelphia Weekly Times*, Dec. 30, 1882; Oates, *War*, 236; Stocker, *From Huntsville to Appomattox*, 110–111.

15. Benedict, *Vermont in the Civil War*, 2:600–601; Law, "The Struggle for 'Round Top,'" 329.

16. William C. Oates to Edward Porter Alexander, Aug. 25, 1868, Alexander Papers, Southern Historical Collection, University of North Carolina, Chapel Hill; William C. Oates to John B. Bachelder, March 29, 1876, in Ladd and Ladd, *Bachelder Papers*, 1:466; Oates to Bachelder, Sept. 16, 1888, in ibid., 3:1557; Oates to Bachelder, Sept. 22, 1888, in ibid., 3:1558; Law, "The Struggle for 'Round Top,'" 329; Oates, *War*, 236.

17. Oates, *War*, 236–237; Oates to Alexander, Aug. 25, 1868, Alexander Papers; Oates to Bachelder, March 29, 1876, in Ladd and Ladd, *Bachelder Papers*, 1:466–467; Oates to Bachelder, Sept. 22, 1888, ibid., 3:1559–1560. Adrian later told the same story of Farnsworth's suicide to Robert T. Coles of the 4th Alabama. See Stocker, *From Huntsville to Appomattox*, 112. It is not certain if one or several letters were found on Farnsworth's body, and Oates contradicts himself about whether he personally found the letters in the Union general's coat or if he ordered one of his men to go searching through the dead man's pockets.

18. Oates to Alexander, Aug. 25, 1868, Alexander Papers.

19. Gary W. Gallagher, ed., *Fighting for the Confederacy: The Personal Recollections of General Edward Porter Alexander* (Chapel Hill and London, 1989), xv; Oates to Bachelder, March 29, 1876, in Ladd and Ladd, *Bachelder Papers*, 1:466–467. On Bachelder, see Richard A. Sauers, "John B. Bachelder: Government Historian of the Battle of Gettysburg," *Gettysburg Magazine* 3 (July 1990): 115–127.

20. Oates, "Gettysburg—The Battle on the Right," *Southern Historical Society Papers* 6 (1878): 182; Bachelder, "General Farnsworth's Death," *Philadelphia Weekly Times,* Dec. 30, 1882.

21. Benedict, *Vermont in the Civil War,* 2:602–603; Parsons, "Farnsworth's Charge and Death," 396.

22. Bachelder, "General Farnsworth's Death," *Philadelphia Weekly Times,* Dec. 30, 1882; Oates to Bachelder, Sept. 16, 1888, in Ladd and Ladd, *Bachelder Papers,* 3:1556–1558; Oates to Bachelder, Sept. 22, 1888, in ibid., 3:1558–1560. Bachelder's letters to Oates, dated Sept. 11, 1888 and Sept. 21, 1888, have not survived but are mentioned in Oates's replies.

23. For these various Union protests against the suicide story and Confederate claims to have witnessed Farnsworth in the act of killing himself, see the useful quotations presented in Wittenberg, *Gettysburg's Forgotten Cavalry Actions,* 46–51.

24. Oates to Chamberlain, April 14, 1905, Oates Correspondence, Gettysburg National Military Park.

25. Historian Jeffry Wert dismisses the story of Farnsworth's suicide as "bogus," but in so doing he misses the historical significance of and the complexities surrounding the Union general's death. See Wert, *Gettysburg: Day Three,* 280. "Bogus" means spurious or fraudulent. The Confederates, including Oates, who sincerely thought Farnsworth had committed suicide were not trying to perpetrate a hoax. Nor did they tell the story with the intent of dishonoring the memory of a Union general they knew to have been brave.

26. Oates, *War,* 236–237.

9. Mr. Lincoln's Victory at Gettysburg

This is a revised version of my article published as "Mr. Lincoln and the Lost Opportunity at Gettysburg," *Civil War Times* 54 (Dec. 2005): 26–32, 62–63, and is used with permission.

1. Lincoln to Alexander Reed, Feb. 22, 1863, in Roy P. Basler, ed., *The Collected Works of Abraham Lincoln,* 8 vols. (New Brunswick, N.J., 1953), 6:114.

2. Paine, "Prospects of the Rubicon" (1787), in Philip S. Foner, ed., *The Complete Writings of Thomas Paine,* 2 vols. (New York, 1969), 2:624.

3. Howard K. Beale, ed., *The Diary of Edward Bates, 1859–1866* (Washington, D.C., 1933), 218–220.

4. Speech at Chicago, Illinois, July 10, 1858, in Basler, *Collected Works,* 2:501; James A. Rawley, "The Nationalism of Abraham Lincoln," *Civil War History* 9 (1963): 283–298; Rawley, "The Nationalism of Abraham Lincoln Revisited," *Journal of the Abraham Lincoln Association* 22 (2001): 33–48.

5. Gerhard E. Mulder, "Abraham Lincoln and the Doctrine of Necessity," *Lincoln Herald* 66 (1964): 59–60. Closely related to Lincoln's reliance on "necessity" was his political pragmatism. See David Herbert Donald, "Lincoln and the American Pragmatic Tradition," in *Lincoln Reconsidered: Essays on the Civil War Era* (New York, 1956), 128–143.

6. George B. McClellan to Lincoln, July 7, 1862, in Stephen W. Sears, ed., *The Civil War Papers of George B. McClellan: Selected Correspondence, 1860–1865* (New York, 1989), 344–345.

7. James M. McPherson, "Lincoln and the Strategy of Unconditional Surrender," in *Abraham Lincoln and the Second American Revolution* (New York and Oxford, 1990), 65–91.

8. Weigley, "The Soldier, the Statesman, and the Military Historian," *Journal of Military History* 63 (Oct. 1999): 807–822.

9. Quoted in James M. McPherson, "Tried by War," *Civil War Times Illustrated* 34 (Nov./Dec. 1995): 70.

10. Stephen W. Sears, "In Defense of Fighting Joe," in *Controversies and Commanders: Dispatches from the Army of the Potomac* (Boston and New York, 1999), 181.

11. Lincoln to McClellan, Oct. 13, 1862, in Basler, *Collected Works,* 5:460–461; David Herbert Donald, *Lincoln* (New York, 1995,) 440.

12. Joseph Hooker to Lincoln, June 5, 1863, in U.S. War Department, *The War of the Rebellion: A Compilation of the Official Records of the Union and Confederate Armies,* 128 vols., index, and atlas (Washington, D.C., 1880–1901), Ser. 1, 27, Pt. 1, 30 (hereafter *O.R.,* with all references to Ser. 1); Lincoln to Hooker, June 5, 1863, in Basler, *Collected Works,* 6:249.

13. Hooker to Lincoln, June 10, 1863, in *O.R.,* 27, Pt. 1, 34–35; Lincoln to Hooker, June 10, 1863, in Basler, *Collected Works,* 6:257.

14. Lincoln to Hooker, June 14, 1863, in Basler, *Collected Works,* 6:273.

15. Hooker to Lincoln, June 16, 1863, in *O.R.,* 27, Pt. 1, 45; Lincoln to Hooker, June 16, 1863, in Basler, *Collected Works,* 6:281.

16. Halleck to Meade, June 27, 1863, in *O.R.,* 27, Pt. 1, 61.

17. Announcement of News from Gettysburg, July 4, 1863, in Basler, *Collected Works,* 6:314; Edwin B. Coddington, "Lincoln's Role in the Gettysburg Campaign," *Pennsylvania History* 34 (July 1967): 259.

18. T. Harry Williams, *Lincoln and His Generals* (New York, 1952), 265; McPherson, "Tried by War," 74.

19. Lincoln to Halleck, July 7, 1863, in Basler, *Collected Works,* 6:319.

20. Halleck to George Gordon Meade, July 7, 1863, in *O.R.,* 27, Pt. 1, 83; Halleck to Meade, July 8, 1863, in ibid., Pt. 3, 605.

21. Gabor S. Boritt, " 'Unfinished Work': Lincoln, Meade, and Gettysburg," in Boritt, ed., *Lincoln's Generals* (New York, 1994), 98–102.

22. Tyler Dennett, ed., *Lincoln and the Civil War in the Diaries and Letters of John Hay* (New York, 1939), 66–67; Gideon Welles, *Diary of Gideon Welles,* ed. Howard K. Beale, 3 vols. (New York, 1960), 1:370–371; Noah Brooks, *Washington in Lincoln's Time,* ed. Herbert Mitgang (New York, 1958), 83; Donald, *Lincoln,* 446.

23. Halleck to Meade, July 14, 1863, in *O.R.,* 27, Pt. 1, 92; Meade to Halleck, July 14, 1863, in ibid., 93; Halleck to Meade, July 14, 1863, in ibid., 93–94.

24. Lincoln to Meade, July 14, 1863 [not sent], in Basler, *Collected Works,* 6:327–328.

25. Welles, *Diary,* 1:374; Lincoln to Meade, March 29, 1864, in Basler, *Collected Works,* 7:273.

26. Quoted in Coddington, "Lincoln's Role," 265.

10. Lincoln and the Gettysburg Awakening

This chapter is a slightly revised version of an article with the same title that was published in *Journal of the Abraham Lincoln Association* 16 (Winter 1995): 73–89, and is used with permission.

1. Bruce Catton, "Who Really Won at Gettysburg?" *Saturday Review,* June 15, 1957, 13.

2. Philip B. Kunhardt Jr., *A New Birth of Freedom: Lincoln at Gettysburg* (Boston, 1983), 24. The other standard works on the Gettysburg Address are William E. Barton, *Lincoln at Gettysburg* (Indianapolis, 1930); Allan Nevins, ed., *Lincoln and the Gettysburg Address: Commemorative Papers* (Urbana, Ill., 1964); Louis A. Warren, *Lincoln's Gettysburg Declaration: "A New Birth of Freedom"* (Fort Wayne, Ind., 1964); Garry Wills, *Lincoln at Gettysburg: The Words That Remade America* (New York, 1992); Gabor Boritt, *The Gettysburg Gospel: The Lincoln Speech That Nobody Knows* (New York, 2006).

3. Emory M. Thomas, *Travels to Hallowed Ground: A Historian's Journey to the American Civil War* (Columbia, S.C., 1987), 3.

4. Wills, *Lincoln at Gettysburg,* 78, 89, 185; Kunhardt, *New Birth,* 209; William J. Wolf, *The Almost Chosen People: A Study of the Religion of Abraham Lincoln* (Garden City, N.Y., 1959), 170. Another scholar has pointed out that "the similarities of language and style to the Bible" that are so evident in the Gettysburg Address do not "by themselves" prove anything "about the religious qualities of Lincoln's speech." See Glen E. Thurow, *Abraham Lincoln and American Political Religion* (Albany, 1976), 69.

5. Kunhardt, *New Birth,* 42, 216, 222; Barton, *Lincoln at Gettysburg,* 188.

6. Boritt, *Gettysburg Gospel.*

7. On the controversies and conflicting evidence that have plagued the study of the Gettysburg Address, see, for example, Barton, *Lincoln at Gettysburg,* unpaginated foreword; David C. Mearns and Lloyd A. Dunlap, *Long Remembered: Facsimiles of the Five Versions of the Gettysburg Address in the Handwriting of Abraham Lincoln* (Washington, D. C., 1963), unpaginated "Notes and Comments"; Warren, *Lincoln's Gettysburg Declaration,* 119, 121–123. In 1925, Barton identified some of the stumbling blocks historians inevitably must encounter—and must try to reconcile—in reconstructing the history of the Gettysburg Address: "Lincoln made no preparation for the address, but trusted to the inspiration of the occasion; he made no preparation until he reached Gettysburg, and wrote the address the night before its delivery, or on the morning of its delivery; he wrote it on the train; he wrote it in full in Washington and took it with him; he wrote it in full in Washington and inadvertently left it there; he wrote it partly in Washington, partly on the train, partly the night before delivery, and revised it on the morning of the delivery. He delivered the address without notes; he held his notes in his left hand and read them in part and in part spoke without them; he held the manuscript firmly in both hands, and did not read from it, or read from it in part, or read from it word for word as it was therein written. The address was received without enthusiasm and left the audience cold and disappointed; it was received in a reverent silence too deep for applause; it was received with feeble and perfunctory applause at the

end; it was received with applause in several places and followed by prolonged applause." William E. Barton, *The Life of Abraham Lincoln,* 2 vols. (Indianapolis, 1925), 2:218.

8. Quoted in Frank L. Klement, "Ward H. Lamon and the Dedication of the Soldiers' Cemetery at Gettysburg," *Civil War History* 31 (Dec. 1985): 299.

9. Kunhardt, *New Birth,* 109; Warren, *Lincoln's Gettysburg Declaration,* 66–67.

10. Kunhardt, *New Birth,* 110.

11. Warren, *Lincoln's Gettysburg Declaration,* 66–67; Barton, *Lincoln at Gettysburg,* 60–65.

12. Kunhardt, *New Birth,* 198–199; Klement, "Ward H. Lamon," 300.

13. Quoted in Barton, *Lincoln at Gettysburg,* 180. On the weather conditions that day, see also Warren, *Lincoln's Gettysburg Declaration,* 75–76.

14. Barton, *Lincoln at Gettysburg,* 74–76, 182.

15. Ibid., 76; Carl Sandburg, *Abraham Lincoln: The War Years,* 4 vols. (New York, 1939), 2:467, 470; Warren, *Lincoln's Gettysburg Declaration,* 88–89.

16. Kunhardt, *New Birth,* 198–203; Warren, *Lincoln's Gettysburg Declaration,* 110.

17. Tyler Dennett, ed., *Lincoln and the Civil War in the Diaries and Letters of John Hay* (New York, 1939), 121.

18. Barton, *Lincoln at Gettysburg,* 170, 191; Klement, "Ward H. Lamon," 305; Kunhardt, *New Birth,* 215.

19. Barton, *Lincoln at Gettysburg,* 188, 201. According to Lamon, Lincoln turned to him after finishing the Gettysburg Address and said, "Lamon, that speech won't scour. It is a flat failure and the people are disappointed." Lamon also claimed that Seward and Everett both expressed their opinions on the speakers' platform, but out of earshot of Lincoln, that the president's speech was a failure. Finally, Lamon said that Lincoln brought up the address after they had returned to Washington and remarked, "I tell you Hill, that speech fell on the audience like a wet blanket. I ought to have prepared it with more care." Most historians believe that Lamon fabricated the incidents. Evidence shows, in fact, that Everett marveled at Lincoln's words and later told him so in a note. The other attributions seem to be simply Lamon's prevarications or products of his overly active imagination. On Lamon's lack of credibility, see Frank L. Klement, "Lincoln, the Gettysburg Address, and Two Myths," *Blue and Gray Magazine* (Oct.–Nov. 1984): 7–11.

20. Barton, *Lincoln at Gettysburg,* 183. Trying to recall the audience's reaction to Lincoln's speech, Professor Philip H. Bikle wrote: "I do not remember that there was any applause, but I do remember that there was surprise that his speech was so short" (ibid., 179).

21. Ibid., 167.

22. Ibid., 186.

23. Ibid., 165; Klement, "Lincoln, the Gettysburg Address, and Two Myths," 11.

24. Barton, *Lincoln at Gettysburg,* 118, 121, 167. The emotional appeal was also felt by an editorial writer for the *Philadelphia Evening Bulletin,* who noted: "The President's brief speech of dedication is most happily expressed. It is warm, earnest, unaffected, and touching. Thousands who would not read the long, elaborate oration of Mr. Everett will read the President's few words, and not many will do it without a moistening of the eye and a swelling of the heart" (ibid., 119).

25. Wills, *Lincoln at Gettysburg*, 63–89.

26. Other historians have also been struck by the similarity between the Gettysburg Address and the sermons made at revival meetings. See, for instance, Oscar Handlin and Lilian Handlin, *Abraham Lincoln and the Union* (Boston, 1980), 162.

27. On camp meetings, see Charles A. Johnson, *The Frontier Camp Meeting: Religion's Harvest Time* (Dallas, 1955), 81–98; Timothy L. Smith, *Revivalism and Social Reform: American Protestantism on the Eve of the Civil War* (New York, 1957), 64–68, 123–124, 136–138; Sydney E. Ahlstrom, *A Religious History of the American People* (New Haven, 1972), 429–445; Dickson D. Bruce, Jr., *And They All Sang Hallelujah: Plain-Folk Camp-Meeting Religion, 1800–1845* (Knoxville, 1974), esp. 61–95.

28. Johnson, *Frontier Camp Meeting*, 93.

29. Benjamin P. Thomas, *Abraham Lincoln: A Biography* (New York, 1952), 25; Thomas, *Lincoln's New Salem* (New York, 1954), 50–54; Douglas L. Wilson, "What Jefferson and Lincoln Read," *Atlantic Monthly*, Jan. 1991, 51–62. For camp meetings on the Illinois frontier, see also Helen Van Cleave Blankmeyer, *The Sangamon Country* (Springfield, Ill., 1935), 51–53; John Mack Faragher, *Sugar Creek: Life on the Illinois Prairie* (New Haven, 1986), 156–170.

30. On Lincoln's religious beliefs and practices, see William E. Barton, *The Soul of Abraham Lincoln* (New York, 1920); Albert V. House Jr., "The Genesis of the Lincoln Religious Controversy," *Proceedings of the Middle States Association of History and Social Science Teachers* 36 (1938): 44–54; David Herbert Donald, *Lincoln's Herndon* (New York, 1948), 271–282; Ruth Painter Randall, "Lincoln's Faith Was Born of Anguish," *New York Times Magazine*, Feb. 7, 1954, 11, 26–27; Donald, *Lincoln Reconsidered: Essays on the Civil War*, rev. ed. (New York, 1956), 151–153; Richard N. Current, *The Lincoln Nobody Knows* (New York, 1958), 51–75; Wolf, *Almost Chosen People*; Edmund Wilson, *Patriotic Gore: Studies in the Literature of the American Civil War* (New York, 1962), 99–130; Reinhold Niebuhr, "The Religion of Abraham Lincoln," in Nevins, *Lincoln and the Gettysburg Address*, 72–87; D. Elton Trueblood, *Abraham Lincoln: Theologian of American Anguish* (New York, 1973); Andrew Delbanco, "To the Gettysburg Station," *New Republic*, Nov. 20, 1989, 31–38; Jon Butler, *Awash in a Sea of Faith: Christianizing the American People* (Cambridge, Mass., 1990), 289–295.

31. Cited in Wilson, *Patriotic Gore*, 90. Grierson himself colorfully described an Illinois camp meeting of the late 1850s in his fictionalized memoir, *The Valley of Shadows* (Boston, 1909), 133–152.

32. Barton, *Lincoln at Gettysburg*, 176.

33. Ibid., 165; Warren, *Lincoln's Gettysburg Declaration*, 145. John Dos Passos observes that Lincoln "seemed like a minor prophet come back to life out of the Old Testament"; see Dos Passos, "Lincoln and His Almost Chosen People," in *Lincoln and the Gettysburg Address*, ed. Nevins, 31. In Edmund Wilson's opinion, Lincoln had "his heroic role, in which he was eventually to seem to tower—a role that was political through his leadership of his party; soldierly through his rank as commander-in-chief of the armies of the United States; spiritual . . . as the prophet of the cause of righteousness. And he seems to have known that he was born for this" (*Patriotic Gore*, 115).

34. Wills, *Lincoln at Gettysburg*, 145; Donald, *Lincoln Reconsidered*, 133.

35. As to the importance of the Declaration of Independence, Wills remarks: "The Declaration of Independence [for Lincoln] has replaced the Gospel as an instrument of spiritual rebirth. The spirit, not the blood, is the idea of the Revolution, not its mere temporal battles and chronological outcome. The 'great task remaining' at the end of the Address is not something inferior to the great deeds of the fathers. It is the same work, always being done, and making all its champions the heroes of the nation's permanent ideal" (Wills, *Lincoln at Gettysburg*, 88).

36. William G. McLoughlin, *Revivals, Awakenings, and Reform: An Essay on Religion and Social Change in America, 1607–1977* (Chicago, 1978), esp. 1–23. On great awakenings, see also Anthony F. C. Wallace, "Revitalization Movements," *American Anthropologist* 58 (April 1956): 264–281; Peter Worsley, *The Trumpet Shall Sound* (London, 1968); Kenelm Burridge, *New Heaven, New Earth* (Oxford and New York, 1969).

37. Quoted in Don E. Fehrenbacher, ed., *Abraham Lincoln: Speeches and Writings, 1832–1865*, 2 vols. (New York, 1989), 2:415.

38. The phrase is from Lincoln's "Address to the Young Men's Lyceum of Springfield, Illinois," Jan. 27, 1838, in Fehrenbacher, *Lincoln: Speeches and Writings*, 1:32. See also Glen W. Thurow, "Abraham Lincoln and American Political Religion," in *The Historian's Lincoln: Pseudohistory, Psychohistory, and History*, ed. Gabor S. Boritt and Norman D. Forness (Urbana, Ill., 1988), 125–143.

39. Quoted in Wills, *Lincoln at Gettysburg*, 125. For insights on Lincoln's "religious mysticism," see also Wilson, *Patriotic Gore*, 99–130, and Delbanco, "To the Gettysburg Station," 31–38.

40. On the main ingredients of Lincoln's political philosophy (or "political religion"), see, for example, Allan Nevins, "Introduction," in *Lincoln and the Gettysburg Address*, 1–14; Thurow, *Abraham Lincoln and American Political Religion*, 63–87; Richard N. Current, "Lincoln, the Civil War, and the American Mission," in *The Public and Private Lincoln: Contemporary Perspectives*, ed. Cullom Davis et al. (Carbondale, Ill., 1979), 137–146; Stephen B. Oates, *Abraham Lincoln: The Man behind the Myths* (New York, 1984), 7–17; James M. McPherson, *Abraham Lincoln and the Second American Revolution* (New York, 1990), 113–130.

41. Ezek. 18:31.

11. Memories of Little Round Top

This chapter is a revised version of "Conflicting Memories of Little Round Top," *Columbiad* 3 (Spring 1999): 106–130, and is used with permission.

1. The fight between the 15th Alabama and the 20th Maine on Little Round Top is described in several standard accounts, including William C. Oates, "Gettysburg—The Battle on the Right," *Southern Historical Society Papers* 6 (1878): 172–182; Joshua L. Chamberlain, "Through Blood and Fire at Gettysburg," *Hearst's Magazine* 23 (1913): 894–909; John J. Pullen, *The Twentieth Maine: A Volunteer Regiment in the Civil War* (Philadelphia, 1957), 82–142; Edwin B. Coddington, *The Gettysburg Campaign: A Study in Command* (New York 1968), 389–394; Harry W. Pfanz, *Gettysburg—The Second Day* (Chapel Hill and London, 1897),

232–236; Alice Rains Trulock, *In the Hands of Providence: Joshua L. Chamberlain and the American Civil War* (Chapel Hill and London, 1992), 117–158; Glenn W. LaFantasie, "The Other Man [William C. Oates]," *MHQ: The Quarterly Journal of Military History* 5 (Summer 1993): 69–75; Thomas A. Desjardin, *Stand Firm Ye Boys From Maine: The 20th Maine and the Gettysburg Campaign* (Gettysburg, 1995). Another study, poorly researched and hastily written, is filled with factual errors and fallacious conclusions; see Mark Perry, *Conceived in Liberty: Joshua Chamberlain, William Oates, and the American Civil War* (New York, 1997).

2. Emmor B. Cope, "Account of William C. Oates's Visit to the Gettysburg Battlefield," July 2, 1896, Record of the Positions of Troops on the Battlefield, Volume I, Gettysburg National Military Park, Gettysburg, Pennsylvania (hereafter GNMP); Oates to Cope, Aug. 6, 1904, Oates Correspondence, GNMP; Oates, *The War between the Union and the Confederacy and Its Lost Opportunities* (New York and Washington, D.C., 1905), 221.

3. Joshua L. Chamberlain, "General Chamberlain's Address," in *Dedication of the Twentieth Maine Monument at Gettysburg, Oct. 3, 1889* (Waldoboro, Me., 1891), 27.

4. For some of the discordant memories that led to disagreements among veterans of the Gettysburg battle, see Richard A. Sauers, "Gettysburg Controversies," *Gettysburg Magazine* 4 (Jan. 1991): 113–125. On disagreements between Northern and Southern veterans over what had taken place in the battles they remembered, see Oscar Handlin, "The Civil War as Symbol and Actuality," *Massachusetts Review* 3 (Autumn 1961): 133–143. Several recent studies examine historical memory in the postwar years, but nearly all tend to focus on the role memory played in facilitating reconciliation between North and South rather than any controversies that might have been sparked by conflicting memories. See, for example, Gaines Foster, *Ghosts of the Confederacy: Defeat, the Lost Cause, and the Emergence of the New South* (New York, 1987); Gerald F. Linderman, *Embattled Courage: The Experience of Combat in the American Civil War* (New York, 1987), esp. 266–297; David W. Blight, "'For Something beyond the Battlefield': Frederick Douglas and the Memory of the Civil War," *Journal of American History* 75 (Mar. 1989): 1156–1178; Michael Kammen, *Mystic Chords of Memory: The Transformation of Tradition in American Culture* (New York, 1991), 101–131; Stuart McConnell, *Glorious Contentment: The Grand Army of the Republic, 1865–1900* (Chapel Hill, 1992); Nina Silber, *The Romance of Reunion: Northerners and the South, 1865–1900* (Chapel Hill, 1993); McConnell, "The Civil War and Historical Memory: A Historiographical Survey," *OAH Magazine of History* 8 (Fall 1993): 3–6; Teresa A. Thomas, "For Union, Not for Glory: Memory and the Civil War Volunteers of Lancaster, Massachusetts," *Civil War History* 40 (Mar. 1994): 25–47. On the unreliability of memory, see David Thelen, "Memory and American History," *Journal of American History* 75 (Mar. 1989): 1117–1129; Richard M. Ketchum, "Memory as History," *American Heritage* 42 (Nov. 1991): 142–148.

5. Robert K. Krick, "Introduction," in William C. Oates, *The War between the Union and The Confederacy and Its Lost Opportunities* (1905; Dayton, Ohio, 1985), unpaginated front matter; Glenn W. LaFantasie, "Introduction," in *Gettysburg: Lieutenant Frank A. Haskell and Colonel William C. Oates* (New York, 1992), 1–47; LaFantasie, "The Other Man," 69–75.

6. Oates, unpublished autobiography, ca. 1902, Oates Family Papers, Alabama Department of Archives and History, Montgomery; Oates, *War,* 674.

7. Oates, *War,* 225–227, 674–675.

8. William M. Robbins, Journal, Jan. 11, 1899, Southern Historical Collection, University of North Carolina, Chapel Hill. A copy of Robbins's journal is in the Gettysburg National Military Park library. I am grateful to Thomas A. Desjardin for bringing to my attention this specific reference to Robbins's journal and several others that I have cited below. On the Gettysburg commissioners, see William C. Davis, *Gettysburg: The Story behind the Scenery* (Las Vegas, Nev., 1983), 18–23; Harlan D. Unrau, *Administrative History: Gettysburg National Military Park and National Cemetery, Pennsylvania* (Washington, D.C., 1991), 91–101; Edward Tabor Linenthal, *Sacred Ground: Americans and Their Battlefields,* 2nd ed. (Urbana and Chicago, 1993), 104; Kathleen Georg Harrison, " 'Patriotic and Enduring Effort': An Introduction to the Gettysburg Battlefield Commission," paper presented at the Fourth Annual Gettysburg Seminar, Gettysburg National Military Park, Mar. 4, 1995.

9. Robbins, Journal, June 13, 14, 1899, and June 25, July 5, Sept. 13, 1900; Oates to Robbins, Apr. 1, 1902, Oates Correspondence, GNMP. For a reference to reports in the Southern press about the Gettysburg commissioners' refusal to allow Confederate monuments on the field, see Robbins's journal entries for June 12 and June 14, 1899. The commissioners publicly denied that there was any policy prohibiting Confederate memorials. For brief discussions of the controversy over Confederate monumentation at Gettysburg, see Unrau, *Administrative History,* 93–96; Linenthal, *Sacred Ground,* 106–110.

10. Oates to Robbins, Apr. 1, 1902, Oates Correspondence, GNMP. Oates wanted the following inscribed on the monument: "To the Memory of Lt. John A. Oates and his gallant Comrades who fell here July 2nd, 1863. The 15th Ala. Regt., over 400 strong, reached this spot, but for lack of support had to retire. Lt. Col. Feagin lost a leg[,] Capts. Brainard and Ellison[,] Lts. Oates and Cody and 33 men were killed, 76 wounded[,] and 86 captured. Erected 39th Anniversary of the battle by Gen. Wm. C. Oates[,] who was Colonel of the Regiment."

11. Oates to Robbins, Sept. 24, 1902, Oates Correspondence, GNMP. On Oates's European tour with his wife and son during the summer of 1902, see the privately printed volume, *Letters Written by Gen. Wm. C. Oates While Traveling in Europe* (n.p., 1902).

12. Robbins to Nicholson, Sept. 27, 1902, Oates Correspondence, GNMP. On Robbins's attempts to convince Southern states to erect monuments on the battlefield, see Unrau, *Administrative History,* 94–96; Linenthal, *Sacred Ground,* 106; David G. Martin, *Confederate Monuments at Gettysburg* (Conshohocken, Pa., 1995), 11–12. Later, in 1904 while the squabble over the Oates proposal was continuing, Robbins successfully erected a bronze tablet as a memorial to his own regiment, the 4th Alabama, and placed it on Confederate Avenue near the Alabama State Monument. He paid for the regimental marker out of his own pocket. Davis, *Gettysburg,* 21; Martin, *Confederate Monuments,* 47–48.

13. Robbins to Oates, Oct. 1902, Oates Correspondence, GNMP. On the legal wrangling over the 72nd Pennsylvania's monument, see Richard A. Sauers, "John B.

Bachelder: Government Historian of the Battle of Gettysburg," *Gettysburg Magazine* 3 (July 1990): 124–125.

14. Oates to Robbins, Oct. 2, 1902; Oates to Gettysburg Commissioners, Dec. 9, 1902; Robbins to Oates, Dec. 16, 1902—all Oates Correspondence, GNMP.

15. Oates to Nicholson, Jan. 21, 1903; Nicholson to Oates, Feb. 9, 1903—both Oates Correspondence, GNMP. Nicholson later made the same point to the War Department. See Nicholson to John C. Schofield, Feb. 27, 1903, ibid.

16. Robbins to Nicholson, Feb. 11, 1903, Oates Correspondence, GNMP. For Robbins's fear that he would be held solely responsible for rejecting Oates's proposal, see Robbins to Nicholson, Feb. 26, 1903, ibid.

17. Robbins to Oates, Feb. 11, 1903, Oates Correspondence, GNMP.

18. Oates to Elihu Root, ca. early Feb. 1903, Oates Correspondence, GNMP. The original petition, signed by Oates, is in Cemeterial Files, Gettysburg National Military Park Battlefield Commission, Letters and Reports to the Secretary of War, 1907–1914, Records of the Office of the Quartermaster General, RG92, National Archives, Washington, D.C. (hereafter GNMP Battlefield Commission Records, NA).

19. Oates to Nicholson, Feb. 11, 1903; Oates to Robbins, Feb. 14, 1903—both Oates Correspondence, GNMP.

20. Robbins to Nicholson, Feb. 19, 1903; Robbins to Nicholson, Feb. 26, 1903—both Oates Correspondence, GNMP.

21. Charles A. Richardson to Nicholson, Feb. 3, 1903; Gettysburg Commissioners to Oates (draft), Feb. 3, 1903; Gettysburg Commissioners to Oates, Mar. 5, 1903—all Oates Correspondence, GNMP. Only minor changes were made to Richardson's initial draft, which had been composed even before Oates had submitted his formal application to the Secretary of War.

22. Schofield to Aristo A. Wiley, Mar. 9, 1903, GNMP Battlefield Commission Records, NA; Nicholson to Oates, May 26, 1903, Oates Correspondence, GNMP.

23. Oates to Nicholson, May 14, 1903, Oates Correspondence, GNMP; Root to Oates, May 23, 1903, Oates Family Papers; Nicholson to Oates, May 26, 1903, Oates Correspondence, GNMP.

24. Oates to Root, June 2, 1903; Schofield to Nicholson, June 18, 1903—both Oates Correspondence, GNMP. Copies of Oates's letter to Root may also be found in GNMP Battlefield Commission Records, NA; Oates Family Papers; and Joshua L. Chamberlain Papers, Library of Congress, Washington, D.C.

25. Robbins to Oates, June 20, 1903, Oates Correspondence, GNMP.

26. Robbins to Evander M. Law (draft), June 20, 1903; Oates to Nicholson, Nov. 13, 1903—both Oates Correspondence, GNMP.

27. Nicholson to Schofield, Feb. 26, 1903; Oates to Robbins, July 4, 1903; Nicholson to Joshua L. Chamberlain, Aug. 6, 1903—all Oates Correspondence, GNMP. Oates's book, *The War between the Union and the Confederacy and Its Lost Opportunities,* was published in 1905; its chapters on Gettysburg expanded the treatment he had given the subject in an earlier article (see note 1, above), published in 1878. The book makes no mention of the monument controversy.

28. The most thoroughly researched biography of Chamberlain is Trulock, *In Hands of Providence,* but see also Willard M. Wallace, *Soul of the Lion: A Biography of*

Joshua L. Chamberlain (New York, 1960), and Michael Golay, *To Gettysburg and Beyond: The Parallel Lives of Joshua Lawrence Chamberlain and Edward Alexander Porter* (New York, 1994). A balanced view of Chamberlain as an officer is presented in Desjardin, *Stand Firm Ye Boys From Maine.*

29. Chamberlain to Nicholson, Aug. 14, 1903, Oates Correspondence, GNMP.

30. Nicholson to Chamberlain, Aug. 21, 1903; Nicholson to Chamberlain, Aug. 24, 1903; Nicholson to Root, Aug. 26, 1903; Chamberlain to Nicholson, Sept. 2, 1903—all Oates Correspondence, GNMP.

31. Copy of Senate Joint Resolution, Alabama Legislature, Oct. 9, 1903, GNMP Battlefield Commission Records, NA; William R. Houghton, "Gettysburg in 1903 (Second Paper)," ca. Oct. 1903; Houghton to Nicholson, Nov. 14, 1903; Houghton to Root, Nov. 1903—newspaper clipping and letters in Oates Correspondence, GNMP; Houghton, "Gettysburg in 1903," *Birmingham Age-Herald,* Dec. 13, 1903; Houghton to Robbins, ca. Mar. 1904, Oates Correspondence, GNMP; Houghton to Daniel E. Sickles, Oct. 17, 1904, ibid. For Houghton's memoirs, see W. R. Houghton and M. B. Houghton, *Two Boys in the Civil War and After* (Montgomery, Ala., 1912).

32. An Act to Establish a National Military Park at Gettysburg, Pennsylvania, chap. 80, 28 Stat. 651 (1895); Robbins, "Letters from the People—Monuments at Gettysburg," *Atlanta Constitution,* Oct. 24, 1898; Robbins, "National Park at Gettysburg," *Confederate Veteran* 7 (1899): 23; U.S. War Department, *Annual Reports of the Gettysburg National Military Park Commission to the Secretary of War, 1893–1904* (Washington, D.C., 1905), 23, 30, 39, 45–46, 52–53, 60–61, 70–71, 78–80, 86; Houghton to Robbins, Nov. 2, 1903, Oates Correspondence, GNMP; Houghton, "Gettysburg in 1903"; Robbins to J. F. Means, March 8, 1904, Oates Correspondence, GNMP; Linenthal, *Sacred Ground,* 106–108. On the Maryland monument, see *Southern Historical Society Papers* 14 (1886): 429–446.

33. Robbins, "Gettysburg in 1903" (typescript), Nov. 18, 1903, Oates Correspondence, GNMP; Robbins to Nicholson, Nov. 18, 1903, ibid.; Robbins, "Gettysburg 1903," *Selma Journal,* Nov. 23, 1903; Robbins, "Gettysburg National Park" (printed broadside), Jan. 1904, Oates Correspondence, GNMP.

34. Nicholson to Root, Nov. 25, 1903, GNMP Battlefield Commission Records, NA; Nicholson to Root, Dec. 1, 1903, Oates Correspondence, GNMP; Schofield to Nicholson, Nov. 23, 1903, ibid.; Henry D. Clayton to Root, Dec. 12, 1903, GNMP Battlefield Commission Records, NA.

35. Richardson to Nicholson, Dec. 28, 1903; Richardson to Nicholson, Jan. 2, 1904; Robbins to Nicholson, Jan. 6, 1904; Robbins to Nicholson, Jan. 13, 1904 [misdated 1903]; Gettysburg Commissioners to Root, Jan. 18, 1904—all Oates Correspondence, GNMP.

36. For Oates's submission of a monument design and inscription and his general description of its proposed location, see Oates to Robbins, Apr. 1, 1902; Oates to Nicholson, Feb. 11, 1903; Oates to Root, June 2, 1903; Oates to Robbins, July 4, 1903; Oates to Robbins, July 18, 1904—all Oates Correspondence, GNMP. See note 10, above, for the text of the inscription. Oates demanded that the commission approve the idea of a monument before he would indicate its precise location. See Oates to Nicholson, Nov. 4, 1903; Oates to Nicholson, Nov. 13, 1903—both Oates

Correspondence, GNMP. Robbins warned Nicholson about the existence of Oates's design and inscription in Robbins to Nicholson, Jan. 6, 1904, Oates Correspondence, GNMP.

37. Root to Gettysburg Commissioners, Jan. 22, 1904; Root to Oates, Jan. 22, 1904—both Oates Correspondence, GNMP; Root to Henry D. Clayton, Jan. 22, 1904; Root to Charles W. Thompson, Jan. 22, 1904—both GNMP Battlefield Commission Records, NA.

38. Wiley to Nicholson, Mar. 28, 1904; Nicholson to Wiley, Mar. 31, 1904; Wiley to Nicholson, Apr. 5, 1904—all Oates Correspondence, GNMP.

39. Oates to H. C. Corbin, Mar. 18, 1904; Scaffold to Nicholson, Apr. 1, 1904; Oates to Nicholson, Apr. 2, 1904; Nicholson to Oates, Apr. 6, 1904—all Oates Correspondence, GNMP.

40. Nicholson to Oates, Apr. 6, 1904; Nicholson to Oates, Apr. 13, 1904; Wiley to Nicholson et al. (telegram), July 5, 1904; Wiley to Nicholson (telegram), July 9, 1904—all Oates Correspondence, GNMP.

41. Oates to Robbins, July 18, 1904; Oates to Chamberlain, Apr. 14, 1905—both Oates Correspondence, GNMP.

42. Oates to Chamberlain, Apr. 14, 1905, Oates Correspondence, GNMP. Presumably the letter Nicholson referred to was the one dated Aug. 14, 1903, addressed to Nicholson, in Oates Correspondence, GNMP.

43. Oates to Robbins, July 18, 1904; Oates to Cope, Aug. 6, 1904; Nicholson to Oates, Aug. 12, 1904; Oates to Nicholson, Sept. 30, 1904—all Oates Correspondence, GNMP.

44. Oates to Robbins, Sept. 1, 1904; Robbins to Oates, Sept. 9, 1904; Oates to Nicholson, Dec. 29, 1904—all Oates Correspondence, GNMP.

45. Nicholson to Oates, Jan. 3, 1905, Oates Correspondence, GNMP.

46. Chamberlain to Nicholson, Mar. 16, 1905, Oates Correspondence, GNMP.

47. Oates to Chamberlain, Apr. 14, 1905, Oates Correspondence, GNMP. It was not the first time Oates and Chamberlain had corresponded with one another. In 1897, Chamberlain sent a letter to Oates asking for clarification about the 15th Alabama's route toward Little Round Top, and Oates replied in a long letter that spelled out many of the same details he would later repeat to the commissioners and to Chamberlain during the monument controversy. See Chamberlain to Oates (incomplete draft), Feb. 27, 1897, Chamberlain Collection, Bowdoin College, Brunswick, Maine; Oates to Chamberlain, Mar. 8, 1897, William Clements Library, University of Michigan, Ann Arbor. Interestingly enough, Oates in 1905 did not remember the earlier correspondence; Chamberlain did. See Oates to Chamberlain, Apr. 14, 1905, Oates Correspondence, GNMP.

48. Chamberlain to Oates, May 14, 1905; Nicholson to Chamberlain, May 22, 1905—both Oates Correspondence, GNMP.

49. Nicholson to Oates, Oct. 25, 1905; Oates to Lunsford L. Lomax, Oct. 30, 1905; Lomax to Oates, Nov. 3, 1905; Lomax to J. F. C. Talbot, Apr. 4, 1906—all Oates Correspondence, GNMP.

50. Nicholson to Schofield, Jan. 15, 1910; Monuments, Markers, and Tablets, Gettysburg National Park Commission, Jan. 18, 1910; Eugene Hale to Jacob M. Dickin-

son, Jan. 18, 1910—all GNMP Battlefield Commission Records, NA; Henry S. Burrage to Chamberlain, Mar. 10, 1910, Chamberlain Papers, LC.

12. Ike and Monty Take Gettysburg

A shorter version of this chapter was originally published as "Monty and Ike Take Gettysburg," *MHQ: The Quarterly Journal of Military History* 8 (Autumn 1995): 67–73, and is used with permission. I am very grateful to Bill Achatz—who covered the generals' tour for the Associated Press—for an informative interview that brought some life to the story and helped round out my research in 1994. I also appreciate the help that D. Scott Hartwig, supervisory park historian at Gettysburg National Military Park, gave me in ferreting out the relevant newspaper stories about the tour.

1. For the standard biographies of Eisenhower, see Stephen E. Ambrose, *The Supreme Commander: The War Years of General Dwight D. Eisenhower* (Garden City, N.Y., 1970); Ambrose, *Eisenhower*, 2 vols. (New York, 1983–1984); Peter Lyon, *Eisenhower: Portrait of the Hero* (Boston, 1974); David Eisenhower, *Eisenhower at War, 1943–1945* (New York, 1986); Chester J. Pach Jr. and Elmo Richardson, *The Presidency of Dwight D. Eisenhower*, rev. ed. (Lawrence, Kans., 1991); Tom Wicker, *Dwight D. Eisenhower* (New York, 2002); Carlo D'Este, *Eisenhower: A Soldier's Life* (New York, 2002). See also Alan Brinkley, "A President for Certain Seasons," *Wilson Quarterly* 14 (Spring 1990): 110–119. For Eisenhower's story in his own words, see Dwight D. Eisenhower, *Crusade in Europe* (Garden City, N.Y., 1948); *Mandate for Change: The White House Years, 1953–1956* (Garden City, N.Y., 1963); *Waging Peace: The White House Years—A Personal Account, 1956–1961* (Garden City, N.Y., 1965); *At Ease: Stories I Tell to My Friends* (New York, 1967). For Montgomery, the choices are fewer, but Nigel Hamilton has made up for the lack of biographies by covering the British general's life in three massive volumes. See Hamilton, *Monty: The Making of a General, 1887–1942* (New York, 1981); *Master of the Battlefield: Monty's War Years, 1942–1944* (New York, 1984); *Monty: The Final Years of the Field-Marshal* (New York, 1986). See also Nigel Hamilton, *Montgomery: D-Day Commander* (Dulles, Va., 2006). For Montgomery's autobiography, see Bernard Law Montgomery, *The Memoirs of Field-Marshal, the Viscount Montgomery of Alamein* (London, 1958).
2. *New York Times; Washington Post*—both May 12, 1957.
3. Ellis D. Slater, *The Ike I Knew* (n.p., 1980), 82; Ambrose, *Eisenhower*, 2:228; *Washington Post*, May 12, 1957; "New Battle of Gettysburg," *Time*, May 20, 1957, 28.
4. C. L. Sulzberger, "When Two Old Soldiers Get Together," *New York Times*, May 8, 1957; *Washington Star*, May 11, 1957.
5. Hamilton, *Monty: The Final Years*, 869–870.
6. *New York Times; Washington Star; Gettysburg Times*—all May 11, 1957; "The Battle of the Generals," *U.S. News & World Report*, May 24, 1957, 60.
7. Hamilton, *Monty: Final Years*, 870; *Washington Post*, May 11, 1957.
8. Hamilton, *Monty: Final Years*, 152.

9. Norman Gelb, *Ike and Monty: Generals at War* (New York, 1994), 12.

10. Admiral Sir Andrew Cunningham observed dryly: "I am afraid Montgomery is a bit of a nuisance: he seems to think that all he has to do is to say what is to be done and everyone will dance to the tune of his piping." Quoted in Gelb, *Ike and Monty*, 219.

11. Bruce W. Nelan, "Ike's Invasion," *Time*, June 6, 1994, 41. General Francis De Guingand, Montgomery's own chief of staff, considered Eisenhower a remarkable leader. "There are few cases in history," he said, "where a Supreme Commander was so universally esteemed and honored." Quoted in Gelb, *Ike and Monty*, 11.

12. Quoted in Nelan, "Ike's Invasion," 47.

13. *Gettysburg Times; Washington Star*—both May 11, 1957.

14. *New York Times; Washington Post*—both May 12, 1957. See also President's Appointments Diary, May 11, 1957, Dwight D. Eisenhower Presidential Library, Abilene, Kansas.

15. *New York Times; Washington Post; Washington Star*—all May 12, 1957.

16. *Washington Post*, May 12, 1957; President's Appointment Diary, May 11, 1957, Eisenhower Library.

17. *Gettysburg Times; New York Tribune*—both May 13, 1957; President's Appointments Diary, May 12, 1957, Eisenhower Library.

18. *New York Tribune; Washington Star; Gettysburg Times*—all May 11, 1957. See also "New Battle of Gettysburg," *Time*, May 20, 1957, 28.

19. *New York Tribune; Gettysburg Times; Washington Star*—all May 13, 1957; "New Battle of Gettysburg," *Time*, May 20, 1957, 28.

20. *New York Times; Washington Star; Gettysburg Times*—all May 13, 1957.

21. *Gettysburg Times*, May 13, 1957; author's interview, Bill Achatz, March 30, 1994. See also *New York Times*, May 13, 1957.

22. *New York Times; New York Tribune; Gettysburg Times*—all May 13, 1957.

23. *New York Times; Gettysburg Times; Washington Star; New York Tribune*—all May 13, 1957.

24. *New York Tribune; Gettysburg Times*—both May 13, 1957; author's interview, Bill Achatz, March 30, 1994.

25. Ambrose, *Eisenhower*, 2:393; Hamilton, *Monty: Final Years*, 870; *New York Times; Washington Star; New York Tribune*—all May 13, 1957.

26. Ambrose, *Eisenhower*, 2:392; Hamilton, *Monty: Final Years*, 870.

27. *New York Tribune; New York Times; Gettysburg Times; Washington Star*—all May 13, 1957.

28. *Gettysburg Times*, May 13, 1957; President's Appointments Diary, May 12, 1957, Eisenhower Library.

29. President's Appointments Diary, May 12, 1957, Eisenhower Library. See also *Gettysburg Times; New York Times*—both May 13, 1957.

30. President's Appointments Diary, May 12, 1957, Eisenhower Library.

31. *New York Times; Washington Post; New York Tribune*—all May 13, 1957.

32. *New York Tribune*, May 13, 1957; "Gettysburg Refought," *Time*, May 27, 1957, 74; *Washington Post*, May 14, 1957.

33. *Washington Star,* May 13, 1957; "Gettysburg Refought," *Time,* May 27, 1957, 74; *Washington Post; New York Times*—both May 14, 1957.

34. "Gettysburg Refought," *Time,* May 27, 1957, 74; *Washington Post,* May 14, 1957.

35. "Monty Fit the Battle of Gettysburg," *National Review,* May 25, 1957, 489; "Lee—The Con and Pro," *Newsweek,* May 20, 1957, 35; "The Battle of the Generals," *U.S. News & World Report,* May 24, 1957, 63. See also Walter Millis, "The Generals Take a Stroll," *Saturday Review,* June 1, 1957, 20.

36. *Washington Star,* May 13, 1957; *Washington Post,* May 14, 1957.

37. *Washington Post,* May 14, 1957; Bruce Catton, "Who Really Won at Gettysburg," *Saturday Review,* June 15, 1957.

38. *Washington Post,* May 14, 1957; "Gettysburg Refought," *Time,* May 27, 1957, 74.

39. James M. McPherson, *Battle Cry of Freedom: The Civil War Era* (New York, 1988), 663–667. See also Thomas L. Connelly, *The Marble Man: Robert E. Lee and His Image in American Society* (New York, 1977), 56–57; Richard A. Sauers, *A Caspian Sea of Ink: The Meade-Sickles Controversy* (Baltimore, 1989), 76–89; Edwin B. Coddington, "The Strange Reputation of George G. Meade: A Lesson in Historiography," *Historian* 23 (1962): 145–166. For historiographical appraisals of the battle, see James I. Robertson Jr., "The Continuing Battle of Gettysburg: A Review Essay," *Georgia Historical Quarterly* 68 (1974): 278–282; Richard A. Sauers, "Gettysburg Controversies," *Gettysburg Magazine* 4 (Jan. 1991): 113–125; Glenn W. LaFantasie, "Romance versus Reality at Gettysburg: A Reconnaissance Report of the Books," *New York Times Book Review,* June 12, 1994.

40. *Washington Post,* May 14, 1957; Hamilton, *Monty: Final Years,* 871; *New York Times,* May 14, 1957.

41. Hamilton, *Monty: Final Years,* 871–872; "The Battle of the Generals," *U.S. News & World Report,* May 24, 1957, 63; *New York Times,* May 14, 1957.

42. *Public Papers of the Presidents of the United States: Dwight D. Eisenhower, 1957* (Washington, D.C., 1958), 356; "The Battle of the Generals," *U.S. News & World Report,* May 24, 1957, 63.

43. *Public Papers,* 357.

44. *Public Papers,* 357; *Washington Star,* May 14, 1957.

45. Ambrose, *Eisenhower,* 2:480–481, 487–488.

46. "Gettysburg Refought," *Time,* May 27, 1957, 74.

47. Hamilton, *Monty: Final Years,* 900; Ambrose, *Eisenhower,* 2:499–500.

48. Letter of David Eisenhower to author, Sept. 1, 1994.

49. Hamilton, *Monty: Final Years,* 901; Letter of John S. D. Eisenhower to author, July 30, 1994.

50. Hamilton, *Monty: Final Years,* xxiii.

13. The Many Meanings of Gettysburg

A somewhat different version of this chapter appeared as "Gettysburg in the American Mind," *American History* 38 (Aug. 2003): 58–65, and is used with permission.

1. Quoted in Arthur M. Schlesinger Jr., *The Cycles of American History* (Boston and New York, 1986), 17.
2. Frank L. Byrne and Andrew T. Weaver, eds., *Haskell of Gettysburg: His Life and Civil War Papers* (Kent, Ohio, 1989), 201.
3. Levi W. Baker, *History of the Ninth Massachusetts Battery* (South Framingham, Mass., 1888), 261.
4. "Letter from Major-General Henry Heth," *Southern Historical Society Papers* 4 (1877): 155.
5. Tillie Pierce Alleman, *At Gettysburg, or, What a Girl Saw and Heard of the Battle* (New York, 1889), 76.
6. The most reliable text of Lincoln's Gettysburg Address may be found in Roy P. Basler, ed., *The Collected Works of Abraham Lincoln*, 8 vols. (New Brunswick, N.J., 1953), 7:23. Despite its many interpretive flaws, Garry Wills's *Lincoln at Gettysburg: The Words That Remade America* (New York, 1992) is still considered the best analytical account of the speech.
7. Quoted in William C. Davis, *Gettysburg: The Story behind the Scenery* (Las Vegas, Nev., 1983), 12.
8. *Gettysburg Compiler,* April 14, 1885.
9. Edward Tabor Linenthal, *Sacred Ground: Americans and Their Battlefields,* 2nd ed. (Urbana and Chicago, 1993), 91.
10. Young quoted in Walter H. Blake, *Hand Grips: The Story of the Great Gettysburg Reunion, July 1913* (Vineland, N.J., 1913), 8.
11. Clark quoted in Linenthal, *Sacred Ground,* 95–96.
12. Acel Moore, "U.S. Still a Nation at War with Itself When It Comes to Race," *Knight-Ridder Tribune News Service,* Aug. 24, 1994.
13. Allen B. Ballard, "The Demons of Gettysburg," *New York Times,* May 30, 1999.
14. Gunnar Myrdal, *An American Dilemma* (New York, 1944), 4.

14. Feeling the Past at Gettysburg

1. Bruce Catton, "Where Gallant Spirits Still Tell Their Story," *American Heritage* 9 (Dec. 1957): 49–50.
2. MacKinlay Kantor, *Gettysburg* (New York, 1952), Chapter 1. The rebels, of course, did not eat babies. Kantor's point was that the German-American farmers around Gettysburg, known as Pennsylvania Dutch, demonized the Confederates to such an extent that some of them believed the enemy was truly monstrous.
3. William C. Oates, *The War between the Union and the Confederacy and Its Lost Opportunities* (New York and Washington, D.C., 1905), 212.
4. Ibid., 226.
5. Ibid., 210.
6. Ibid., 211.
7. Ibid.
8. Ibid., 212.
9. Ibid., 213.
10. Ibid., 214.

11. Ibid., 220.
12. Ibid.
13. Joshua Lawrence Chamberlain, "Address," in Samuel Miller, ed., *Dedication of the Twentieth Maine Monuments at Gettysburg, October 3, 1889* (Waldoboro, Me., 1891), 15.
14. William C. Oates, Autobiography, ca. 1902, chapter 1, Oates Family Papers, Alabama Department of Archives and History, Montgomery.

Index

GLENN W. LAFANTASIE, the Richard Frockt Family Professor of Civil War History at Western Kentucky University, is author of *Twilight at Little Round Top* and *Gettysburg Requiem: The Life and Lost Causes of William C. Oates.* He is a regular contributor to *Civil War Times, American History,* and *North & South.* LaFantasie lives with his wife in Bowling Green, Kentucky.